Change Detection and Image Time Series Analysis 1

SCIENCES

*Image*, Field Director – Laure Blanc-Feraud

*Remote Sensing Imagery*, Subject Heads –
Emmanuel Trouvé and Avik Bhattacharya

# Change Detection and Image Time Series Analysis 1

## *Unsupervised Methods*

*Coordinated by*
Abdourrahmane M. Atto
Francesca Bovolo
Lorenzo Bruzzone

WILEY

First published 2021 in Great Britain and the United States by ISTE Ltd and John Wiley & Sons, Inc.

ISTE Ltd
27-37 St George's Road
London SW19 4EU
UK

www.iste.co.uk

John Wiley & Sons, Inc.
111 River Street
Hoboken, NJ 07030
USA

www.wiley.com

Library of Congress Control Number: 2021941648

British Library Cataloguing-in-Publication Data
A CIP record for this book is available from the British Library
ISBN 978-1-78945-056-9

ERC code:
PE1 Mathematics
    *PE1_18 Scientific computing and data processing*
PE10 Earth System Science
    *PE10_3 Climatology and climate change*
    *PE10_4 Terrestrial ecology, land cover change*
    *PE10_14 Earth observations from space/remote sensing*

# Contents

## Chapter 2. Change Detection in Time Series of Polarimetric SAR Images

Knut CONRADSEN, Henning SKRIVER, Morton J. CANTY
and Allan A. NIELSEN

## Chapter 3. An Overview of Covariance-based Change Detection Methodologies in Multivariate SAR Image Time Series

Ammar MIAN, Guillaume GINOLHAC, Jean-Philippe OVARLEZ,
Arnaud BRELOY and Frédéric PASCAL

## Chapter 4. Unsupervised Functional Information Clustering in Extreme Environments from Filter Banks and Relative Entropy

Abdourrahmane M. ATTO, Fatima KARBOU, Sophie GIFFARD-ROISIN
and Lionel BOMBRUN

## Chapter 5. Thresholds and Distances to Better Detect Wet Snow over Mountains with Sentinel-1 Image Time Series

Fatima KARBOU, Guillaume JAMES, Philippe DURAND
and Abdourrahmane M. ATTO

## Chapter 6. Fractional Field Image Time Series Modeling and Application to Cyclone Tracking

Abdourrahmane M. ATTO, Aluísio PINHEIRO, Guillaume GINOLHAC
and Pedro MORETTIN

## Chapter 7. Graph of Characteristic Points for Texture Tracking: Application to Change Detection and Glacier Flow Measurement from SAR Images

Minh-Tan PHAM and Grégoire MERCIER

## Chapter 8. Multitemporal Analysis of Sentinel-1/2 Images for Land Use Monitoring at Regional Scale

Andrea GARZELLI and Claudia ZOPPETTI

## Chapter 9. Statistical Difference Models for Change Detection in Multispectral Images .  . . . . . . . . . . . . . . . . . . . . . . 223

Massimo ZANETTI, Francesca BOVOLO and Lorenzo BRUZZONE

# Preface

Abdourrahmane M. ATTO[1], Francesca BOVOLO[2]
and Lorenzo BRUZZONE[3]

[1] *University Savoie Mont Blanc, Annecy, France*
[2] *Fondazione Bruno Kessler, Trento, Italy*
[3] *University of Trento, Italy*

This book is part of the ISTE-Wiley "*SCIENCES*" Encyclopedia and belongs to the *Image* field of the *Engineering and Systems* department. The *Image* field covers the entire processing chain from acquisition to interpretation by analyzing the data provided by various imaging systems. This field is split into seven subjects, including *Remote Sensing Imagery* (RSI). The heads of this subject are Emmanuel Trouvé and Avik Bhattacharya. In this subject, we propose a series of books that portray diverse and comprehensive topics in advanced remote-sensing images and their application for *Earth Observation* (EO). There has been an increasing demand for monitoring and predicting our planet's evolution on a local, regional and global scale. Hence, over the past few decades, airborne, space-borne and ground-based platforms with active and passive sensors acquire images that measure several features at various spatial and temporal resolutions.

RSI has become a broad multidisciplinary domain attracting scientists across the diverse fields of science and engineering. The aim of the books proposed in this RSI series is to present the state-of-the-art and available scientific knowledge about the primary sources of images acquired by optical and radar sensors. The books cover the processing methods developed by the signal and image processing community to extract useful information for end-users for an extensive range of EO applications in natural resources.

In this project, each RSI book focuses on general topics such as change detection, surface displacement measurement, target detection, model inversion and data assimilation. This first book of the RSI series is dedicated to *Change Detection and Image Time Series Analysis*. It presents methods developed to detect changes and analyze their temporal evolutions using optical and/or synthetic aperture radar (SAR) images in diverse settings (e.g. image pairs, image time series). According to the numerous works and applications in this domain, this book is divided into two volumes, dedicated to *unsupervised* and *supervised* approaches, respectively. Unsupervised methods require little to no expert-based information to resolve a problem, whereas the contrary holds true, especially for methods that are supervised in the sense of providing a wide amount of labeled training data to the method, before testing this method.

## Volume 1: Unsupervised methods

A significant part of this book is dedicated to a wide range of unsupervised methods. The first chapter provides an insight into the motivations of this behavior and introduces two unsupervised approaches to multiple-change detection in bitemporal multispectral images. Chapters 2 and 3 introduce the concept of change detection in time series and postulate it in the context of statistical analysis of covariance matrices. The former chapter focuses on a directional analysis for multiple-change detection and exercises on a time series of SAR polarimetric data. The latter focuses on local analysis for binary change detection and proposes several covariance matrix estimators and their corresponding information-theoretic measures for multivariate SAR data. The last four chapters focus more on applications. Chapter 4 addresses functional representations (wavelets and convolutional neural network filters) for feature extraction in an unsupervised approach. It proposes anomaly detection and functional evolution clustering from this framework by using relative entropy information extracted from SAR data decomposition. Chapter 5 deals with the selection of metrics that are sensitive to snow state variation in the context of the cryosphere, with a focus on mountain areas. Metrics such as cross-correlation ratios and Hausdorff distance are analyzed with respect to optimal reference images to identify optimal thresholding strategies for the detection of wet snow by using Sentinel-1 image time series. Chapter 6 presents time series analysis in the context of spatio-temporal forecasting and monitoring fast-moving meteorological events such as cyclones. The application benefits from the fusion of remote sensing data under the fractional dynamic field assumption on the cyclone behavior. Chapter 7 proposes an analysis based on characteristic points for texture modeling with graph theory. Such an approach overcomes issues arising from large-size dense neighborhoods that affect spatial context-based approaches. The application proposed in this chapter concerns glacier flow measurement in bitemporal images. Chapter 8 focuses on detecting new land-cover types by classification-based change detection or feature/pixel-based change detection. Monitoring the construction of new buildings in urban and suburban scenarios at a large regional scale by means of Sentinel-1 and -2 images is considered as an application. Chapter 9 focuses on the statistical modeling of classes in the difference image and derives from scratch a multiclass model for it in the context of change vector analysis.

## Volume 2: Supervised methods

The second volume of this book is dedicated to supervised methods. Chapter 1 of this volume addresses the fusion of multisensor, multiresolution and multitemporal data. This chapter reviews recent advances in the literature and proposes two supervised Markov random field-based solutions: one relies on a quadtree and the second one is specifically designed to deal with multimission, multifrequency and multiresolution time series. Chapter 2 provides an overview of pixel-based methods for time series classification from the earliest shallow-learning methods to the most recent deep learning-based approaches. This chapter also includes best practices for reference data preparation and management, which are crucial tasks in supervised methods. Chapter 3 focuses on very high spatial resolution data time series and the use of semantic information for modeling spatio-temporal evolution patterns. Chapter 4 focuses on the challenges of dense time series analysis, including pre-processing aspects and a taxonomy of existing methodologies. Finally, since the evaluation of a learning system can be subject to multiple considerations, Chapters 5 and 6 propose extensive evaluations of the methodologies used to produce earthquake-induced change maps, with an emphasis on their strengths and shortcomings (Chapter 5) and the deep learning systems in the context of multiclass multilabel change-of-state classification on glacier observations (Chapter 6).

This book covers both methodological and application topics. From the methodological viewpoint, contributions are provided with respect to feature extraction and a large number of evaluation metrics for change detection, classification and forecasting issues. Analysis has been performed in both bitemporal images and time series, illustrating both unsupervised and supervised methods and considering both binary- and multiclass outputs. Several applications are mentioned in the chapters, including agriculture, urban areas and cryosphere analysis, among others. This book provides a deep insight into the evolution of change detection and time series analysis in the state-of-the-art, as well as an overview of the most recent developments.

July 2021

# List of Notations

| | |
|---|---|
| $\mathcal{I} = (\mathcal{I}_k(p,q))_{k,p,q}$ | Image Time Series: time index $k$ and pixel position $(p,q)$ |
| $\mathcal{I} = (\mathcal{I}_k^c(p,q))_{k,p,q,c}$ | Vector Image Time Series: band/spectral index $c$ |
| $\mathcal{I} = \left(\mathcal{I}_k^{(u,v)}(p,q)\right)_{k,p,q,u,v}$ | Matrix Image Time Series: (polarimetric indices $(u,v)$) |
| $\mathbb{N}, \mathbb{Z}, \mathbb{R}, \mathbb{C}$ | Sets of Natural Numbers, Integers, Real and Complex Numbers |
| $\mu, \boldsymbol{\mu}$ | Means of Random Variables and Random Vectors |
| $\mathbf{C}, \boldsymbol{\Sigma}$ | Physical and Statistical Variance–Covariance Matrices |
| $pdf$ | Probability Density Function |

# 1

# Unsupervised Change Detection in Multitemporal Remote Sensing Images

Sicong LIU[1], Francesca BOVOLO[2], Lorenzo BRUZZONE[3],
Qian DU[4] and Xiaohua TONG[1]

*[1] Tongji University, Shanghai, China*
*[2] Fondazione Bruno Kessler, Trento, Italy*
*[3] University of Trento, Italy*
*[4] Mississippi State University, Starkville, USA*

## 1.1. Introduction

Remote sensing satellites have a great potential to recurrently monitor the dynamic changes of the Earth's surface in a wide geographical area, and contribute substantially to our current understanding of the land-cover and land-use changes (Bruzzone and Bovolo 2013; Song *et al.* 2018; Liu *et al.* 2019c). Scientifically understanding land changes is also essential for analyzing environmental evolution and anthropic phenomena, especially when studying the global change and its impact on human society. Thanks to the satellite revisit property, both long-term (e.g. yearly) and short-term (e.g. daily) satellite observations produce a huge amount of multitemporal images in the data archive (Liu *et al.* 2015). Based on the analysis of multitemporal data, land-cover changes can be automatically discovered and detected, where knowledge of changes can also be acquired. This becomes an important and complementary way of optimizing the traditional *in situ* investigation, which

*Change Detection and Image Time Series Analysis 1,*
coordinated by Abdourrahmane M. ATTO, Francesca BOVOLO and Lorenzo BRUZZONE.
© ISTE Ltd 2021.

is often very costly and labor-intensive. In particular, in some cases such as in a natural disaster scenario, it is very difficult or even impossible to conduct field investigations. Change detection (CD) is the process of identifying change and no-change regions on the Earth's surface by analyzing images acquired from the same geographical area at different times (Singh 1989; Coppin *et al.* 2004; Lu *et al.* 2004; Liu *et al.* 2019c). Therefore, automatic and robust techniques need to be designed to effectively discover, describe and detect changes that occur in multitemporal remote sensing images. In the past decades, CD has become an increasingly active research field and has been widely applied in various remote sensing applications, such as deforestation, disaster evaluation, urban expansion evolution and environment and ecosystem monitoring (Bovolo and Bruzzone 2007a; Bouziani *et al.* 2010; Du *et al.* 2012; Khan *et al.* 2017; Liu *et al.* 2020b).

Basically, CD techniques are developed based on specific remote sensing satellite sensors. In the literature, many excellent articles focused on the discussion of CD problems in different types of satellite sensors: for example, CD in multispectral images (Lu *et al.* 2004; Ban and Yousif 2016), SAR images (Ban and Yousif 2016) and hyperspectral images (Liu *et al.* 2019c), as well as in Lidar data (Okyay *et al.* 2019). Among different sensors mounted on the EO satellites, multispectral scanners can acquire images with both high spatial resolution and wide spatial coverage. In the past decades, due to data availability, multispectral remote sensing images such as Landsat and Sentinel serials contributed the main data source for the Earth's surface monitoring and CD applications (Du *et al.* 2013; Liu *et al.* 2020a). However, with the increasing high quality and spatial resolution in new multispectral sensor images, especially for very high resolution (VHR) images, it is necessary to design advanced CD techniques that can deal with more complex change patterns presented in a more complex CD scenario.

In recent years, many CD methods have been developed for multispectral images, most of which focus on improving the automation, accuracy and applicability of CD (Leichtle *et al.* 2017; Liu *et al.* 2017a, 2019b; Wang *et al.* 2018; Saha *et al.* 2019; Wei *et al.* 2019). In general, according to the automation degree, they can be grouped into three main categories: supervised, semi-supervised and unsupervised methods. Usually, supervised CD approaches have better performance with higher accuracy by taking advantage of certain robust supervised classifiers (Wang *et al.* 2018). However, their implementation relies on the availability of ground reference data, which is often difficult to collect in most practical cases. Semi-supervised CD approaches start from limited training samples or partial prior knowledge learned from the single-time image, where the active learning or transfer learning algorithm can usually be applied to increase the sample representation (Liu *et al.* 2017b, 2019a; Zhang *et al.* 2018; Tong *et al.* 2020). In contrast, unsupervised approaches have higher automation without relying on the availability of ground reference data or prior knowledge (Liu *et al.* 2017a, 2019b; Saha *et al.* 2019). Therefore, the analysis in the unsupervised CD case is mainly data-driven and is actually more challenging than the other two tasks.

However, from a practical application point of view, it is definitely more attractive due to its simplicity and high automation.

In this chapter, we focus on the unsupervised CD problem in multitemporal multispectral images. In particular, we investigate and analyze the spectral–spatial change representation for addressing the important multiclass CD problem. To this end, two approaches are developed, including a multi-scale morphological compressed change vector analysis and a superpixel-level multiclass CD. By taking advantage of the spectral and spatial joint analysis of change information, both approaches show higher performance than the compared state-of-the-art methods. Experimental results obtained from two real multispectral datasets confirmed the effectiveness of the proposed approaches in terms of higher accuracy and efficiency of CD.

The rest of this chapter is organized as follows. Section 1.2 points out the key concepts and challenges in unsupervised CD, and especially reviews the current development of spectral–spatial unsupervised CD techniques. Section 1.3 describes the two proposed unsupervised multiclass CD approaches in detail. Dataset description and experimental setup are provided in section 1.4. Experimental results and discussions are present in section 1.5. Finally, section 1.6 draws the conclusion of this chapter.

## 1.2. Unsupervised change detection in multispectral images

### 1.2.1. *Related concepts*

Depending on the purpose of unsupervised CD tasks, two main categories of methods are defined: *binary change detection* and *multiclass change detection*. The former aims to separate only the change and no-change classes, whereas the latter detects changes and distinguishes different classes within the changed pixels. In this chapter, we consider the latter, which is more attractive but challenging in practical CD applications. Note that in the unsupervised CD case, no ground truth or prior knowledge is available, thus the data-driven CD process is more preferable than the model-driven process. Therefore, the multiclass discrimination represents the inter-change difference associated with specific land-cover class transitions, whereas the detailed "from–to" information is absent, making it essentially different from the supervised case.

In general, the unsupervised CD process includes the following main steps: (1) multitemporal data pre-processing; (2) feature generation and selection; (3) change index construction; (4) CD algorithm design; (5) performance evaluation. The main components of an unsupervised CD are shown in Figure 1.1. Each step is briefly described and discussed as follows.

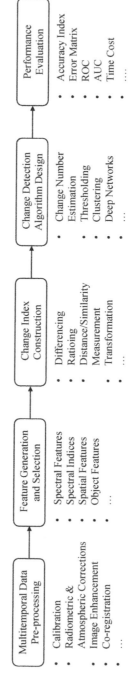

**Figure 1.1.** *The main technical components of an unsupervised CD process*

*Multitemporal data pre-processing*: in this step, different operations such as calibration, band stripe repair (if any), radiometric and atmospheric corrections, image enhancement and image-to-image co-registration are usually conducted in order to generate high-quality pre-processed multitemporal images for CD in the next steps. In particular, a high precision of co-registration is the core operation for a successful CD, which may significantly affect the CD performance due to the presence of remaining residual errors.

*Feature generation and selection*: features extracted from original multitemporal images are the critical carrier for representing different characteristics of objects in the single-time image and their variations in the temporal domain. Features such as original spectral bands, spectral indices (e.g. Normalized Difference Vegetation Index – NDVI, Modified Normalized Difference Water Index – MNDWI, Index-based Built-up Index – IBI) and textures (e.g. mean, contrast, homogeneity) derived from original bands can be considered in CD. In addition, spatial features generated from multispectral bands such as wavelet transformation (Celik and Ma 2011), Gabor filtering (Li *et al*. 2015), morphological filtering (Falco *et al*. 2013), etc., provide important multi-scale geometric information about image objects to improve the change representation. Recently, deep learning-based CD approaches have shown great potential in extracting more high-level deep features, which represents a popular direction in CD research (Mou *et al*. 2019; Saha *et al*. 2019).

*Change index construction*: the change index represents the temporal variations extracted from multitemporal image features. It can be constructed based on different operators and algorithms, such as univariate image differencing (Bruzzone and Prieto 2000a), change vector analysis (CVA) (Bovolo and Bruzzone 2007b), ratioing (Bazi *et al*. 2005), distance or similarity measures (Du *et al*. 2012), etc. Transformation approaches such as iterative reweighted multivariate alteration detection (IR-MAD) (Nielsen 2007), principal components analysis (PCA) and its kernel version (Nielsen and Canty 2008; Celik 2009), independent component analysis (ICA) (Liu *et al*. 2012), are also designed to transform the change information from the original data space into a projected feature space. However, a careful selection of specific components representing user-interested changes is required. This is often very difficult in an unsupervised CD case without prior knowledge about the considered study area and dataset, which may limit the automation degree of the CD application. For a summary of the related methods for constructing different types of change index, readers can refer to the paper by Bovolo and Bruzzone (2015).

*Change detection algorithm design*: unlike the supervised and semi-supervised CD methods that rely on the available reference samples, unsupervised CD algorithms focus more on the automation and accuracy. Thus, basically, most of the unsupervised CD approaches are data-driven by analyzing the multitemporal data itself. Within this context, for binary CD, if we consider a given change index generated in the previous step, for example, the magnitude of differencing image, automatic thresholding such as empirical segmentation (Bruzzone and Prieto 2000b), Kittler–Illingworth (KI) (Bazi *et al.* 2005), Otsu (1979) and Bayesian-based expectation–maximization (EM) (Bruzzone and Prieto 2000a) are all simple but effective algorithms proposed in the literature. However, the successful use of such methods depends on the assumption of a certain data distribution such as Gaussian or Rayleigh–Rice mixture (Bovolo *et al.* 2012; Zanetti *et al.* 2015), where a wrong estimation may lead to many detection errors. On the contrary, clustering algorithms such as k-means, fuzzy c-means and Gustafson–Kessel clustering (GKC) have been used to address the binary CD problem (Celik 2009; Ghosh *et al.* 2011), which are distribution-free but require a specific setting to avoid unstable performance, such as the accuracy decrease due to random initialization.

For a multiclass CD case, the unsupervised task becomes more complex since several sub-problems should be solved simultaneously, including the binary change and no-change separation, the number of multiclass change estimation and the multiclass change discrimination (Liu *et al.* 2019c). In particular, among many solutions, we recall the classical multiple CD technique – change vector analysis (CVA) (Malila 1980). It was designed to analyze possible multiple changes in pairs of bitemporal image bands. A theoretical definition was given to the original CVA approach in the polar domain to provide a more clear mathematical explanation to CVA (Bovolo and Bruzzone 2007b). However, it still has a limitation, i.e. only a part of all possible changes can be detected since only two selected bands are considered in each implementation. If more spectral channels are considered, it becomes very difficult to simultaneously model and visualize multidimensional changes. To break this constraint, a compressed change vector analysis ($C^2VA$) approach was proposed, which successfully extended the original CVA to a two-dimensional (2D) representation of the multi-band problem (Bovolo *et al.* 2012). Other works in the literature developed different variations of CVA. For example, a modified CVA was developed to determine the magnitude threshold and direction by combining single-date image classification results (Chen *et al.* 2003). An improved thresholding approach on change magnitude was designed to optimize the binary separation on each specific change class (Bovolo and Bruzzone 2011). A hierarchical version of $C^2VA$ with an adaptive and sequential projection of spectral change vectors (SCVs) at each level of the hierarchy was proposed to detect multiple changes in bitemporal hyperspectral images (Liu *et al.* 2015). In this chapter, we also explore the potential capability of $C^2VA$ and extend it from the spectral–spatial point of view.

*Performance evaluation*: similar to the supervised CD methods, unsupervised binary and multiclass CD approaches can usually be assessed according to the detection accuracy or error index, such as overall accuracy (*OA*), Kappa coefficient (*Kappa*), omission errors (*OE*) and commission errors (*CE*), receiver operating characteristic (*ROC*) curve and area under the curve (*AUC*) value. In this case, the accuracy evaluation usually relies on the manually interpreted change reference map.

Note that such a reference map is only used for accuracy evaluation, which is not considered as training data as in the supervised case. In addition, the computational time cost is also another important indicator that reflects the automation and efficiency of unsupervised methods.

### 1.2.2. *Open issues and challenges*

The current development of unsupervised CD techniques for multispectral remote sensing images has had great success in many practical applications. However, there are still open issues and challenges that deserve to be further analyzed, which include but are not limited to the following:

1) a high-precision multitemporal pre-processing procedure, for example, co-registration techniques;

2) multitemporal data quality improvement due to bad imaging conditions, such as system noise, cloud contamination and seasonal spectral variations;

3) advanced techniques for correctly estimating the real number of multiclass changes in image scenarios;

4) spectral–spatial modeling of change targets to enhance the original pixel-wise spectral representation;

5) robust and efficient CD approach in an unsupervised fashion, especially for a large complex CD scene;

6) change feature representation by taking advantage of both machine learning and deep learning techniques.

### 1.2.3. *Spectral–spatial unsupervised CD techniques*

Despite the success of aforementioned CD methods, especially the CVA-based methods, they mainly focus on the spectral changes in each individual pixel or a local neighborhood (Bovolo 2009; Bovolo *et al.* 2012; Liu *et al.* 2015). The geometrical characteristics of change targets are not fully modeled and preserved. This may increase the ambiguity due to abnormal spectral variations in isolated pixels and errors (e.g. co-registration errors), leading to the presence of omission and commission errors, especially when dealing with VHR images. In this case, traditional pixel-based CD methods may lose their effectiveness since they were developed under the assumption that pixels are spatially independent. However, for multispectral images in complex urban scenarios, challenging issues may arise due to the limited spectral representation; thus, the same class of objects may have different spectra, or different objects may have the same or very similar spectra. This may significantly increase the detection difficulty, especially when considering the multiclass CD task.

To address the above problems in pixel-based CD (PBCD) techniques, spectral–spatial joint analysis and object-based CD (OBCD) methods are mainstream techniques proposed in the literature. For the former, morphological filters (i.e. self-dual reconstruction filters and alternating sequential filters) were combined with CVA for binary CD in VHR images (Mura et al. 2008). However, a sliding window (i.e. structuring element (SE)) for filtering should be fixed at a given level; thus, it is not robust for multilevel implementation. Morphological attribute profiles (APs) were applied to extract structure-related geometrical features within the scene from each date of panchromatic images (Falco et al. 2013). It includes a multilevel extraction of connected regions in the scene at different scales. Building change information based on the difference in the multitemporal morphological building index (MBI) at the feature and decision level was considered for detecting building changes in VHR images (Huang et al. 2014). A spectral–spatial band expansion approach was developed to enhance the change representation in multispectral images with limited bands, where additional bands were generated from both spectral and spatial viewpoints (Liu et al. 2019b).

For OBCD methods, four main categories exist: image-object, class-object, multitemporal-object and hybrid CD (Chen et al. 2012; Hussain et al. 2013). An object-based CD approach was designed in (Liu and Du 2010), which analyzes different spectral and texture features extracted during the segmentation process from two independent time images. A superpixel segmentation was applied to stacked bitemporal images, and several derived features were used to describe changes in the difference image according to the supervised classification (Wu et al. 2012). An objected-based method was designed to create objects in each single-time image according to segmentation and then generated different representative features (Wang et al. 2018). A weighted Dempster–Shafer theory (wDST) fusion OBCD method was proposed by combining multiple PBCD results, which can automatically calculate and assign a certainty weight for each object of the PBCD result while considering the stability of an object (Han et al. 2020). However, the selection of the optimal segmentation scale is still an open issue and was mainly implemented based on the empirical analysis in OBCD methods (Kaszta et al. 2016). Moreover, most of the above existing work focused on solving a binary CD problem, and very few were designed for dealing with the more challenging unsupervised multiclass CD case (Liu et al. 2019b).

Accordingly, the following problems should be further analyzed: (1) how spatial neighboring pixels have an impact on unsupervised change representation and detection; (2) how to effectively model structural and geometric information of change targets to enhance change representation; (3) how to integrate multiscale and multidimensional change descriptions to increase change separability; (4) how to adaptively find a suitable segmentation scale in the unsupervised OBCD approach. In this chapter, we investigate these issues and develop new spectral–spatial CD approaches in multitemporal multispectral images.

## 1.3. Unsupervised multiclass change detection approaches based on modeling spectral–spatial information

### 1.3.1. *Sequential spectral change vector analysis (S² CVA)*

Here, we first recall a popular state-of-the-art unsupervised multiclass CD method, S²CVA. The two proposed approaches are designed based on it. However, it is important to note that the S²CVA that is pixel-wise only relies on the analysis of spectral information. Originally, from the standard C²VA (Bovolo *et al.* 2012), S²CVA was specially proposed for multiclass CD in bitemporal hyperspectral images according to a hierarchical analysis. It allows the visualization and detection of multiple changes by considering all spectral channels, without neglecting any band. A compressed 2D polar domain is built based on the construction of two change variables (Liu *et al.* 2015), i.e. magnitude $\rho$ and direction $\theta$. More particularly, the magnitude $\rho$ is the Euclidean compression of SCVs. It measures the spectral brightness of changes. The direction $\theta$ is built based on the spectral angle distance (SAD) (Keshava 2004), which points out different changes with respect to the variances in spectral response for a given pixel. However, note that the "from–to" class transition information is not explained due to the unsupervised nature of S²CVA. More specifically, the change variables $\rho$ and $\theta$ are defined as:

$$\rho = \sqrt{\sum_{b=1}^{B} \left(X_D^b\right)^2} = \sqrt{\sum_{b=1}^{B} \left(X_2^b - X_1^b\right)^2} \qquad [1.1]$$

$$\theta = \arccos\left[\left(\sum_{b=1}^{B} \left(X_D^b r^b\right)\right) \Big/ \sqrt{\sum_{b=1}^{B} \left(X_D^b\right)^2 \sum_{b=1}^{B} \left(r^b\right)^2}\right] \qquad [1.2]$$

where $X_D^b$ is the $b$-th ($b=1,...,B$) component of the differencing (SCVs) image $\mathbf{X}_D$, which was calculated on the co-registered images $\mathbf{X}_1$ and $\mathbf{X}_2$, and $B$ is the number of image bands (i.e. the dimensionality of SCVs). $r^b$ is the $b$-th component of an adaptive reference vector $\boldsymbol{r}$. In the standard C²VA, $\boldsymbol{r}$ is defined as a unit constant vector $\boldsymbol{r} = \left[1/\sqrt{B}, ..., 1/\sqrt{B}\right]$ (Bovolo *et al.* 2012). In S²CVA, it is improved as the first eigenvector of the covariance matrix $\mathbf{A}$ of $\mathbf{X}_D$ (Liu *et al.* 2015):

$$\mathbf{A} = cov\left(\mathbf{X}_D\right) = \mathbb{E}\left[\left(\mathbf{X}_D - \mathbb{E}\left[\mathbf{X}_D\right]\right)\left(\mathbf{X}_D - \mathbb{E}\left[\mathbf{X}_D\right]\right)^T\right] \qquad [1.3]$$

where $\mathbb{E}\left[\mathbf{X}_D\right]$ is the expectation of $\mathbf{X}_D$. The eigen-decomposition of $\mathbf{A}$ can be represented as:

$$\mathbf{A} \cdot \mathbf{V} = \mathbf{V} \cdot \mathbf{W} \qquad [1.4]$$

where $\mathbf{W}$ is a diagonal matrix with eigenvalues being sorted in a descending order (i.e. $\lambda^1 > \lambda^2 > ...\lambda^B$) in the diagonal, and $\mathbf{V}$ is the matrix of eigenvectors (i.e.

$\mathbf{V} = [\mathbf{v}^1, \mathbf{v}^2, \mathbf{v}^3, ..., \mathbf{v}^B])$. The reference vector $r$ is defined as the first eigenvector $\mathbf{v}^1$ corresponding to the largest eigenvalue $\lambda^1$, i.e. $\mathbf{r} = \mathbf{v}^1$. Note that this results in an improved change representation by projecting the SCVs into a reference direction that maximizes the variance of the measurement, while preserving the discriminative information of different changes.

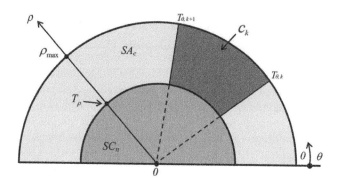

**Figure 1.2.** 2D *polar change representation domain in the* $C^2$ *VA method*

Then a 2D compressed polar domain $\mathbf{D}$ is defined based on $\rho$ and $\theta$:

$$\mathbf{D} = \{\rho \in [0, \rho_{\max}] \text{ and } \theta \in [0, \pi]\} \tag{1.5}$$

where $\rho_{max}$ is the maximum value of $\rho$. A semicircle scattergram (see Figure 1.2) is used for visualizing multiple changes in $\mathbf{D}$. Regions of the semicircle $SC_n$ (which represents the unchanged pixels) and the semiannulus $SA_c$ (which represents the changed pixels) are mathematically defined as:

$$SC_n = (\rho, \theta : 0 \leqslant \rho < T_\rho \text{ and } 0 \leqslant \theta \leqslant \pi) \tag{1.6}$$

$$SA_c = (\rho, \theta : T_\rho \leqslant \rho < \rho_{max} \text{ and } 0 \leqslant \theta \leqslant \pi) \tag{1.7}$$

Under the assumption that $\mathbf{X}_1$ and $\mathbf{X}_2$ are radiometrically and geometrically corrected, in the 2D polar domain, the unchanged SCVs result in low magnitude values close to zero and are thus distributed within $SC_n$, whereas the changed SCVs are represented in $SA_c$ having higher magnitudes. Different spectral behaviors of the SCVs reflected on the direction variable, hence leading to the representation of multiclass changes in each sector of $SA_c$. The considered multiclass CD problem is solved by defining a threshold $T_\rho$ along the magnitude $\rho$ to separate the unchanged and changed SCVs (i.e. associated with $SC_n$ and $SA_c$, respectively), and to separate multiple changes ($C_1,...,C_K$) along the direction $\theta$ by setting multiple thresholds $T_{\theta,k}$ ($k=1,..., K-1$) in $SA_c$. Note that a hierarchical analysis is implemented to discover and detect all possible changes (both strong and subtle changes) in hyperspectral images due to complex change representations in the high dimensionality of hyperspectral images. However, fewer levels may be obtained when only a few spectral bands are considered, as in the multispectral case.

## 1.3.2. *Multiscale morphological compressed change vector analysis*

In this section, we introduce a proposed multiscale morphological compressed change vector analysis ($M^2C^2VA$) method. It aims to investigate a proper way to integrate multiscale spectral–spatial change information, especially to improve multiclass change representation and discrimination in $C^2VA$. The proposed approach consists of three main steps: 1) SCV reconstruction based on multiscale morphological processing; 2) multiscale change information ensemble; 3) multiclass change representation and discrimination. The block scheme of the proposed approach is shown in Figure 1.3.

### 1.3.2.1. *SCV reconstruction based on multiscale morphological processing*

In the standard $C^2VA$, a SCV indicates a pixel that is unchanged or has a possible kind of change according to its specific signature and constructed change variables (i.e. $\rho$ and $\theta$). However, the original SCVs may contain abnormal spectral variations and noises, which may lead to a high number of omission and commission errors. To address this problem, the morphological profile (MP) is applied to better model and preserve the geometrical structure of change targets. It is defined as a sequence of mathematical closing and opening operations on the image with different structural element (SE) sizes. In particular, opening by reconstruction ($O_R$) and closing by reconstruction ($C_R$) (Benediktsson *et al.* 2005) for a gray-level image $f$ are defined as:

$$O_R^i(f) = R_\delta \left[ \varepsilon^i(f) \right] \tag{1.8}$$

$$C_R^i(f) = R_\varepsilon \left[ \delta^i(f) \right] \tag{1.9}$$

where $i$ is the radius of the SE. Here, $\delta^i(\cdot)$ and $\varepsilon^i(\cdot)$ are the dilation and erosion operations, respectively. $R_\delta$ and $R_\varepsilon$ are the geodesic reconstruction by dilation and erosion, respectively. In particular, the components of MP, i.e. $O_R$ and $C_R$, are able to suppress brighter and darker regions, respectively, that are smaller than the moving SE, while preserving the geometrical characteristics of a region larger than the SE (Dalla Mura *et al.* 2010). Small isolated objects are merged into a surrounding local background while the main structure is kept. Due to the fact that different image objects usually have different sizes, multiscale representation allows us to explore different hypothetical spatial domains by using a range of SE sizes, in order to obtain the best response for different structures (Mura *et al.* 2008).

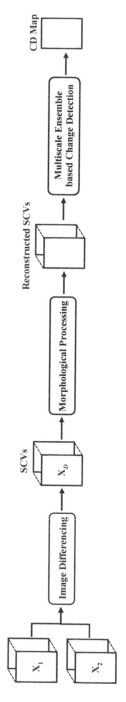

**Figure 1.3.** *Block scheme of the proposed $M^2 C^2 VA$ technique*

For the $B$-dimensional SCVs $\mathbf{X}_D$, at a given scale $i$, its $O_R$ and $C_R$ are also $B$-dimensional:

$$O_R^i(\mathbf{X}_D) = \left\{O_R^i(\mathbf{X}_D^1), \ldots, O_R^i(\mathbf{X}_D^b), \ldots, O_R^i(\mathbf{X}_D^B)\right\} \qquad [1.10]$$

$$C_R^i(\mathbf{X}_D) = \left\{C_R^i(\mathbf{X}_D^1), \ldots, C_R^i(\mathbf{X}_D^b), \ldots, C_R^i(\mathbf{X}_D^B)\right\} \qquad [1.11]$$

$$b \in [1, B], i \in [1, N]$$

Note that either $O_R^i(\mathbf{X}_D)$ or $C_R^i(\mathbf{X}_D)$ can be used as an input for the detector (e.g. S$^2$CVA), but ambiguities may arise due to the selection of a specific operator (i.e. $O_R$ or $C_R$) and its consequential effects (i.e. suppression of brighter or darker objects). The joint use of $O_R$ and $C_R$ is likely to be more reliable. In this work, the four-connected neighborhood was considered, and the marker and mask image represented the dilation result and the original input band (for $O_R$) (or complement image of the original input band for $C_R$), respectively. A disk shape was selected for the SE, which has been demonstrated to be a robust shape in different scenarios (Benediktsson et al. 2005; Mura et al. 2008). The size of the SE $i$ was increased from 1 to 6, in order to implement a multiscale analysis using the reconstructed SCVs.

### 1.3.2.2. Multiscale change information ensemble

By increasing the size of the SE, change objects can be modeled at different scales, while exploring the interaction with the surrounding regions to preserve more geometrical details. Accordingly, a more comprehensive description of change objects is obtained through multiscale analysis. Therefore, a multiscale ensemble is conducted on the reconstructed SCVs. Let $OC_R^i(\mathbf{X}_D)$ be the stacking of the reconstructed SCVs (i.e. $O_R^i(\mathbf{X}_D)$ and $C_R^i(\mathbf{X}_D)$) at a given size $i$, having a dimensionality of $2 \times B$. It is defined as:

$$OC_R^i(\mathbf{X}_D) = \left[O_R^i(\mathbf{X}_D), C_R^i(\mathbf{X}_D)\right] \qquad [1.12]$$

Then, the extended SCV $S[u, v]$ is defined as an integration of sequential $OC_R^i(\mathbf{X}_D)$, with lower and upper bounds equal to $u$ and $v$, respectively:

$$S[u, v] = \left[OC_R^u(\mathbf{X}_D), OC_R^{u+1}(\mathbf{X}_D), \ldots, OC_R^v(\mathbf{X}_D)\right] \qquad [1.13]$$

Consequently, an extended SCV feature set with $2 \times B \times M$ dimensionality is built, where $M$ is the length of components in the sequence, i.e. $M = v - u + 1$. It is worth noting that $S[u, v]$ extends the change representation along the spectral direction, as well as considering the multiscale spatial information in the ensemble process. Then, $S[u, v]$ is used as the input for the detector.

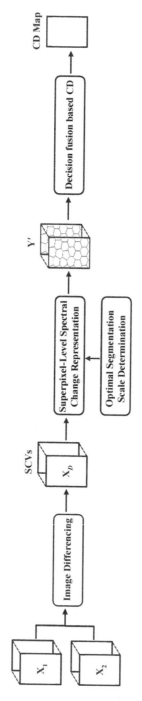

**Figure 1.4.** *Block scheme of the proposed superpixel-level multiclass CD approach*

### 1.3.2.3. *Multiclass change representation and discrimination*

The aim of this step is to visualize and discriminate multiclass changes present in the reconstructed SCVs. To this end, the $S^2$CVA detector introduced in section 1.3.1 is applied on the $S[u, v]$. Note that the detector exploits not only spectral variations, but also spatial variations represented in the reconstructed SCV components. It is also worth noting that the 2D polar scattergram projects multiclass change information from the considered high-dimensional reconstructed SCVs into a low-dimensional (i.e. 2D) feature space, which is lossy and ambiguous on the type of changes. However, the most significant discriminative information of different changes is preserved.

Instead of using thresholding to segment the binary and multiple classes in the variables $\rho$ and $\theta$, the simple but effective clustering, i.e. $k$-means, is used for generating the final CD map, which does not rely on any specific data distribution. This is due to the fact that changed and unchanged pixels in $\rho$ and multiclass changes in $\theta$ do not always follow a Gaussian mixture distribution (Zanetti *et al.* 2015). Thus, for the binary CD step (i.e. separating two classes), the number of clusters $k_\rho$ is equal to 2, and for the multiclass CD step, the number $k_\theta$ is defined as the number of changes observed in the 2D polar scattergram.

## 1.3.3. *Superpixel-level compressed change vector analysis*

In this section, we propose an unsupervised superpixel-level compressed change vector analysis (SPC$^2$VA) approach for multiclass CD. The traditional pixel-level spectral change analysis is converted into the superpixel level. Therefore, the spectral change representation and identification are regularized and enhanced under the superpixel constraints. The block scheme of the proposed approach is shown in Figure 1.4.

### 1.3.3.1. *Superpixel-level spectral change representation*

The original SCVs focus on the spectral variation representation from each individual pixel, thus ignoring spatial correlation with neighboring pixels and the local spectral homogeneity associated with real land-cover objects. This may lead to the commission and omission errors, and a decrease in the overall detection accuracy. Superpixel segmentation can capture image redundancy and generate convenient primitives to compute representative features, while reducing the complexity of the subsequent processing and analysis. In this work, we used the simple linear iterative clustering (SLIC) algorithm (Achanta *et al.* 2012) as the core algorithm for generating superpixel segments. Compared to the other popular segmentation methods, SLIC offers a better performance in boundary adherence and generates superpixels efficiently under the same hardware conditions. Moreover, SLIC is memory efficient, and only requires the storage of the distance from each pixel to its nearest cluster center. Most importantly, it can be smoothly integrated within the proposed method, especially from the pixel to superpixel-level spectral change representation and detection, which drives a proper algorithm utilization.

The general idea of the SLIC algorithm is to find small regional clusters by considering their local homogeneity (Achanta *et al.* 2012). The key step is to calculate the distance $d$ that implements a measurement from the spectral–spatial point of view. Let $d_{color}$ and $d_{xy}$ be the spectral and spatial distances between two given pixels $\alpha$ and $\beta$, respectively, defined as:

$$d_{color} = \sqrt{(L_\alpha - L_\beta)^2 + (A_\alpha - A_\beta)^2 + (B_\alpha - B_\beta)^2} \qquad [1.14]$$

$$d_{xy} = \sqrt{(x_\alpha - x_\beta)^2 + (y_\alpha - y_\beta)^2} \qquad [1.15]$$

Here, $(L, A, B)^T$ denotes the CIELAB color space values, with $L$ being the color lightness and $A$ and $B$ representing color values along red-green and blue-yellow axes, respectively. $(x, y)^T$ denotes the coordinates of a given pixel. A final weighted distance measure $d_{\alpha\beta}$ can be defined as:

$$d_{\alpha,\beta} = \sqrt{d_{color}^2 + m^2 \left(\frac{d_{xy}}{s}\right)^2} \qquad [1.16]$$

where $s$ is the width of grids. It controls the size of created superpixels, i.e. the greater the $s$, the larger the superpixels. A roughly equal-sized grid interval can be defined as $s = \sqrt{(Z/N)}$, where $Z$ is the total number of pixels and $N$ is the desired number of superpixels. In reality, the real number of generated superpixels (defined as $N'$) might be slightly different from $N$. The parameter $m$ controls the relative importance between the color similarity and the spatial proximity. The greater the $m$, the greater the emphasis on spatial proximity and the compactness of a generated superpixel. A regular $m$ value can be defined within the range of [1, 40]. For more details, readers can refer to the paper by Achanta *et al.* (2012).

In order to enhance the spectral variations due to the limited bands in multispectral images, principal component analysis (PCA) is applied to the original SCVs. This strengthens the change representation and extends the feature space. The first three principal components (i.e. PCs) are used in the SLIC algorithm to generate the segments (i.e. superpixels) with the identified boundaries. Then original SCVs are stacked with the PCs to create an enhanced feature set (denoted as SCVs-PC). Note that normalization is conducted on SCVs-PC bands to make data dynamic range consistent. Finally, a mean operation is applied on each segment in the SCVs-PC bands, where the mean vector is used to replace the original SCVs-PC vectors, in order to achieve the enhanced spectral change representation at the superpixel level. Note that, by doing this, the change information is concentrated with spectral–spatial coherence and the computational cost is largely reduced when compared with the original pixel-wise processing.

### 1.3.3.2. *Determination of the optimal segmentation scale*

As mentioned previously, the number of superpixels $N$ and the compactness factor $m$ need to be determined in the SLIC algorithm. Note that in practical implementations, the parameter $m$ impacts less than $N$ on the segmentation results. Therefore, after multiple trials, we fixed $m = 30$ in this work. The only focus is on the determination of the optimal segmentation scale parameter $N$. To this end, an unsupervised strategy is applied based on the analysis of the global entropy. Note that after the mean operation on each superpixel, the texture information in the segments will be relatively suppressed, which may have an influence on the following CD performance. The main idea of the used criterion is to evaluate the information maintained in the superpixel-level segmented image inherited from the original pixel-level image. Thus, the one-dimensional image entropy (Global Entropy, GE) (Han *et al.* 2008) is calculated based on multi-scale segmentation results, where the optimal segmentation scale is determined by analyzing the change of GE values:

$$GE = -\sum_{k=1}^{n} p_k \log p_k \qquad [1.17]$$

where $n$ denotes the gray level and $p = (p_k)_{k=1,2,...,n}$ contains the histogram counts of the first three bands of $\mathbf{Y}'$. It is worth noting that with the increasing $N$, GE values are expected to increase continuously and approach the value of the original image. The logarithmic function is then used to fit the GE results to estimate the threshold for the optimal segmentation scale. A detailed description of this step is provided in Table 1.1.

| |
|---|
| **Step 1**: Initialize $N$, which is approximated as the smaller one in the rows and columns of the input image, and the segmentation scale interval is set approximately equal to (row + column)/20. |
| **Step 2**: Calculate the GE value of each segmented image under different searching scales. |
| **Step 3**: Fit the logarithmic function on the obtained GE results and calculate the gradient. |
| **Step 4**: Estimate the optimal segmentation scale by analyzing the gradient of GE values, where the convergence threshold $T_{GE}$ is defined approximately equal to 100/(row + column) based on the input image. |

**Table 1.1.** *Determination of the optimal segmentation scale based on GE analysis*

### 1.3.3.3. *Decision fusion-based CD*

The multiclass CD is implemented based on the change magnitude and direction variables (i.e. $\rho$ and $\theta$) constructed by $S^2CVA$ at the superpixel level. In paticular, a decision fusion-based CD step is proposed to enhance and optimize the binary CD output (see Figure 1.5), by analyzing the change magnitude of SCVs-PC bands. Three binary CD results are taken into account based on a majority voting process, to determine whether a given superpixel (segment) is changed or not. The first input is made from the pixel-level binary CD result constrained by the segmented boundaries, where a threshold $T_\rho$ is defined on $\rho$ by using the EM algorithm under a Bayesian framework (denoted as Bayesian-EM) (Bruzzone and Prieto 2000a). Change and no-change pixels are counted within each superpixel, respectively, in order to determine the label of that superpixel with respect to the counting majority. The second and third inputs are generated at the superpixel level. The change magnitude of superpixels is calculated on $\mathbf{Y}'$, and binary CD results are obtained using Bayesian-EM thresholding and fuzzy c-means (FCM) clustering, respectively. A three-input majority voting decision is applied by integrating three binary CD results from a pixel-to-superpixel perspective. Note that the final binary CD decision is made on each superpixel, depending on the majority label of three independent inputs, as shown in Figure 1.5. FCM clustering is then applied on the variable $\theta$ but only focuses on the changed superpixels, with the given estimated number of clusters equal to $K$ in the 2D compressed polar domain $D$, as shown in Figure 1.2.

## 1.4. Dataset description and experimental setup

### 1.4.1. *Dataset description*

The first dataset is a pair of QuickBird images acquired over an urban area in Xuzhou city, Jiangsu province (China) in September 2004 ($\mathbf{X}_1$) and May 2005 ($\mathbf{X}_2$), respectively. The Gram–Schmidt (G-S) pan-sharpening algorithm was applied to fuse the multispectral (2.4 m) and panchromatic images (0.6 m), in order to generate the final fused dataset (0.6 m) with four spectral bands (i.e. red, green, blue and near infrared). Images were radiometrically corrected and co-registered (with residual misregistration of about 0.3 pixels), and the final region with a size of $760 \times 370$ pixels was extracted for the CD experiment. A total of six change classes are presented in this scenario. Detailed class transitions are: 1) soil to built-up area (C1); 2) soil to roof (face to the sun) (C2); 3) soil to roof (back to the sun) (C3); 4) built-up area to soil (C4); 5) shadow to soil (C5); 6) trees to soil (C6). The false color composite images $\mathbf{X}_1$ and $\mathbf{X}_2$ are shown in Figure 1.6 (a) and (b), respectively, and Figure 1.6 (c) presents the change reference map made by careful image interpretation.

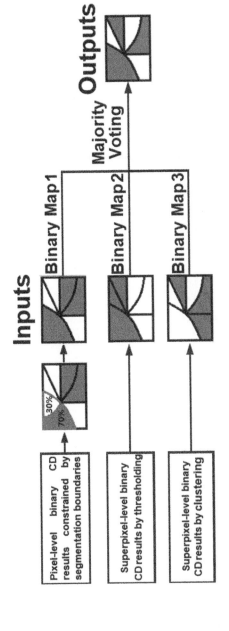

**Figure 1.5.** *Illustration of the decision-level fusion-based binary CD step. For a color version of this figure, see www.iste.co.uk/atto/change1.zip*

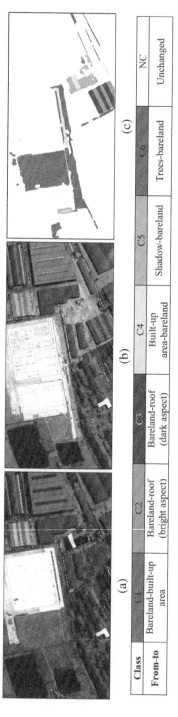

**Figure 1.6.** *Color-infrared composite of bitemporal QuickBird pan-sharpened images (bands 4, 3, 2) over an urban area in Xuzhou city, acquired in (a) 2004 ($X_1$) and (b) 2005 ($X_2$). (c) Change reference map. For a color version of this figure, see www.iste.co.uk/atto/change1.zip*

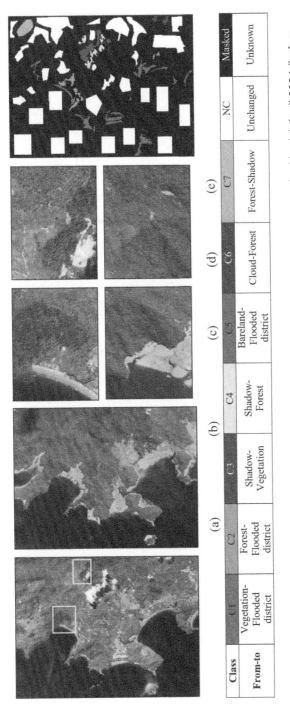

| Class | C1 | C2 | C3 | C4 | C5 | C6 | C7 | NC | Masked |
|-------|-----|-----|-----|-----|-----|-----|-----|-----|--------|
| **From-to** | Vegetation-Flooded district | Forest-Flooded district | Shadow-Vegetation | Shadow-Forest | Bareland-Flooded district | Cloud-Forest | Forest-Shadow | Unchanged | Unknown |

**Figure 1.7.** *False color composite of QuickBird images of the Indonesia tsunami dataset acquired in: (a) April 2004 (before tsunami), (b) January 2005 (after tsunami); (c) and (d) are two subsets selected from the whole scene in the qualitative experimental analysis. (e) Change reference samples. For a color version of this figure, see www.iste.co.uk/atto/change1.zip*

The second dataset is made up of a pair of co-registered QuickBird multispectral images with a spatial resolution of 2.4 m, acquired over a large coastal area in Indonesia in April 2004 and January 2005, respectively (see the two times of the false color composite images shown in Figure 1.7(a) and (b), respectively). The whole study area considered has a size of 3,250×4,350 pixels. Two subsets were selected for detailed qualitative analysis, as shown in Figure 1.7(c) and (d). A change reference sample map was made by careful image interpretation (Figure 1.7(e)). The changes that occurred in this scene were mainly caused by the tsunami in December 2004, which include the following classes: (1) vegetation to flooded district (C1); (2) forest to flooded district (C2); (3) shadow to vegetation (C3); (4) shadow to forest (C4); (5) bareland to flooded district (C5); (6) cloud to forest (C6); (7) forest to shadow (C7).

### 1.4.2. *Experimental setup*

For comparison purposes, CD results obtained by the proposed $M^2C^2VA$ and $SPC^2VA$ approaches were compared with two state-of-the-art unsupervised multiclass CD techniques, including the iteratively reweighted multivariate alteration detection (IR-MAD) (Nielsen 2007), and the sequential spectral change vector analysis ($S^2CVA$) (Liu *et al.* 2015). Note that $M^2C^2VA$ and $SPC^2VA$ considered both spectral and spatial change information, whereas IR-MAD and $S^2CVA$ considered only the spectral change information. Detailed quantitative and qualitative analyses were conducted according to the obtained CD accuracy, i.e. OA and Kappa, and error indices, i.e. omission errors (OE), commission errors (CE), total errors (TE), and the obtained CD maps. In addition, the computational cost was also considered in each method and compared. All of the experiments were conducted using MATLAB R2016b, on an Intel (R) Core (TM) i7-6700 CPU @ 3.40GHz PC with 32 GB of RAM.

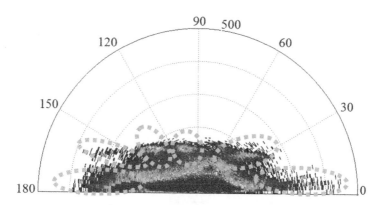

**Figure 1.8.** *2D compressed change representation in the polar domain (Xuzhou dataset). For a color version of this figure, see www.iste.co.uk/atto/change1.zip*

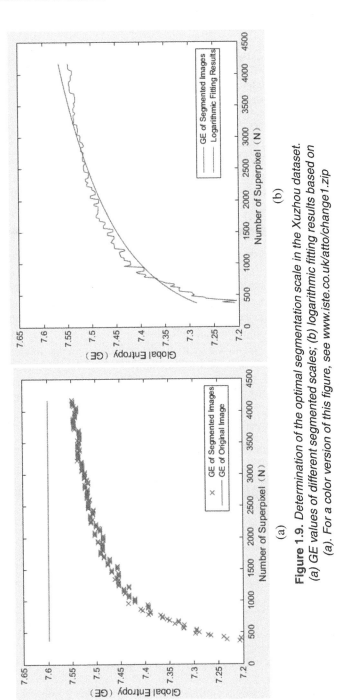

**Figure 1.9.** *Determination of the optimal segmentation scale in the Xuzhou dataset. (a) GE values of different segmented scales; (b) logarithmic fitting results based on (a). For a color version of this figure, see www.iste.co.uk/atto/change1.zip*

## 1.5. Results and discussion

### 1.5.1. *Results on the Xuzhou dataset*

The 2D compressed change representation in the polar domain is shown in Figure 1.8, where six change clusters can be observed, indicating different change directions. Then, $K = 6$ is fixed in the considered CD methods for performing the multiclass CD.

The optimal segmentation scale was estimated by analyzing the GE values (see Figure 1.9(a)) and its logarithmic fitting results (see Figure 1.9(b)). The $T_{GE}$ was calculated and defined as $1 \times 10^{-4}$, then the final segmentation optimal scale was obtained as 1,160.

From the detailed quantitative and qualitative analyses based on the obtained CD accuracy and error indices (see Table 1.2) and the obtained CD maps (see Figure 1.10), it can be observed that the proposed $M^2C^2VA$ and $SPC^2VA$ approaches resulted in higher performance than the reference methods, with respect to the higher OA and Kappa values and smaller detection errors (see Table 1.2). In particular, $SPC^2VA$ achieved the highest accuracy (i.e. OA = 92.74% and Kappa = 0.7464), outperforming the other methods. Improvement can also be observed from the obtained change maps by comparing them with the reference map; the identified change targets are more accurate in the two proposed approaches (i.e. Figure 1.10(c) and (d)) than those in the two reference methods (i.e. Figure 1.10(a) and (b)). In two reference methods, $S^2CVA$ showed better performance than IR-MAD. As for the computational cost, the proposed $SPC^2VA$ approach exhibited efficient performance, which consumed less time than the proposed $M^2C^2VA$ and IR-MAD, and similar or slightly more time than $S^2CVA$ (i.e. 8.91 s vs. 7.12 s), but yielding a significantly higher OA value (i.e. 92.74% vs. 87.74%).

| Processing level (Features) | CD methods | OA % | Kappa | CE (pixels) | OE (pixels) | TE (pixels) | Time cost (s) |
|---|---|---|---|---|---|---|---|
| Pixel-level (Spectral) | IR-MAD | 85.23 | 0.5900 | 41,524 | 17,256 | 58,780 | 9.82 |
| Pixel-level (Spectral) | $S^2CVA$ | 87.74 | 0.6390 | 28,532 | 16,397 | 44,929 | 7.12 |
| Pixel-level (Spectral–spatial) | Proposed $M^2C^2VA$ ($[u, v] = [1, 6]$) | 91.86 | 0.7169 | 11,316 | 17,455 | 28,771 | 18.30 |
| Superpixel-level (Spectral–spatial) | Proposed $SPC^2VA$ ($N = 1160, m = 30$) | 92.74 | 0.7464 | 8,673 | 16,411 | 25,084 | 8.91 |

**Table 1.2.** *Multiclass CD results obtained by the proposed and reference methods (Xuzhou dataset)*

### 1.5.2. *Results on the Indonesia tsunami dataset*

The 2D compressed change representation in the polar domain is shown in Figure 1.11, where seven change clusters (i.e. $K = 7$) can be observed. The optimal segmentation scale was estimated as 35,140 according to Figure 1.12. Note that the CD experiment and the quantitative analysis were carried out on the whole image scene.

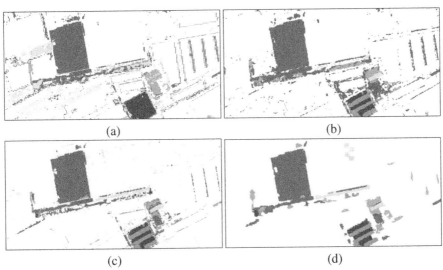

(a)                                        (b)

(c)                                        (d)

**Figure 1.10.** *Comparison of the multiclass CD maps obtained by: (a) IR-MAD; (b) $S^2$CVA; (c) proposed $M^2$ $C^2$VA ([u, v] = [1, 6]); (d) proposed SPC$^2$VA with $N$ = 1,160 and $m$ = 30 (Xuzhou dataset). For a color version of this figure, see www.iste.co.uk/atto/change1.zip*

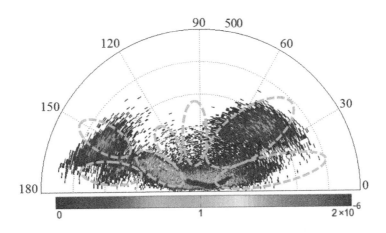

**Figure 1.11.** *2D compressed change representation in the polar domain (Indonesia tsunami dataset). For a color version of this figure, see www.iste.co.uk/atto/change1.zip*

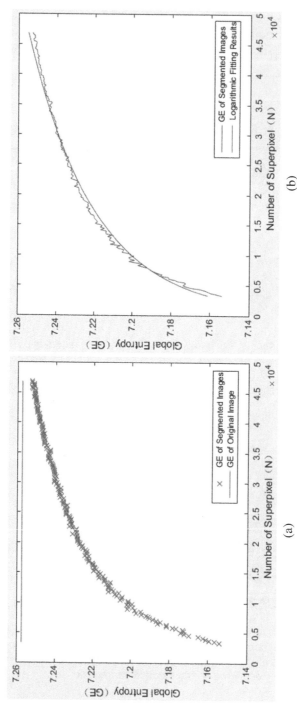

**Figure 1.12.** *Determination of the optimal segmentation scale in the Indonesia tsunami dataset. (a) GE values of different segmented scales; (b) logarithmic fitting results based on (a). For a color version of this figure, see www.iste.co.uk/atto/change1.zip*

| Processing level (Features) | CD methods | OA | Kappa | CE (pixels) | OE (pixels) | TE (pixels) | Time cost (s) |
|---|---|---|---|---|---|---|---|
| Pixel-level (Spectral) | IR-MAD | 81.09 | 0.4578 | 447,773 | 460,876 | 908,649 | 566.58 |
| | $S^2$CVA | 86.04 | 0.6044 | 407,410 | 398,629 | 806,039 | 466.97 |
| Pixel-level (Spectral–spatial) | Proposed $M^2C^2$VA ($[u, v] = [1, 6]$) | 91.15 | 0.7298 | 202,919 | 314,088 | 517,007 | 691.44 |
| Superpixel-level (Spectral–spatial) | Proposed $SPC^2$VA ($N = 35140$, $m = 30$) | 93.69 | 0.8038 | 135,863 | 225,979 | 361,842 | 667.38 |

**Table 1.3.** *Multiclass CD results obtained by the proposed and reference methods (Indonesia tsunami dataset)*

We conducted a careful comparison between the qualitative and quantitative results obtained by two proposed approaches (see the CD maps in Figure 1.13(c) and (d)) and two reference methods (see CD maps in Figure 1.13(a) and (b)) as in the previous dataset. The quantitative evaluation was carried out based on the available change reference samples, as shown in Figure 1.7(e); the numeric results are provided in Table 1.3. Note that the number of multiclass changes was equal to 7 in all of the methods, as estimated in the polar domain (see Figure 1.11).

From the CD maps shown at the global scale (first row) and the local scale (second and third rows) in Figure 1.13 and the CD accuracies in Table 1.3, we can see that the proposed approach $SPC^2$VA obtained the highest accuracy (i.e. OA: 93.69% and Kappa: 0.8244) among all of the considered methods. The proposed $M^2C^2$VA also showed good results and outperformed the two reference methods. Smaller detection errors were found (i.e. 361,842 and 517,007 pixels in the two proposed approaches against 908,649 and 806,039 pixels in the two reference methods), especially the CE values. The detected change targets are more homogeneous and regular with respect to their shapes and spatial distributions (see Figure 1.13(c) and (d)). This demonstrates that the proposed spectral–spatial approaches are able to deal with CD for large-scale data and offer a high detection performance, i.e. enhancing the change targets and suppressing the no-change class. For two pixel-wise reference methods, $S^2$CVA performed better than IR-MAD, as in the IR-MAD results, change and no-change pixels are highly mixed in their spectral representation, leading to a relatively poor detection accuracy. This is due to the complexity of the CD task in the high spatial resolution multispectral images, and the pixel-wise correlation analysis may fail to properly model the change targets solely based on spectral information. From the point of view of the computational cost, the two proposed methods resulted in a higher time cost than the two reference methods, but still at an acceptable level. Therefore, from the careful qualitative analysis on both the global and local scales of the obtained CD maps and the quantitative accuracy analysis, the effectiveness of the proposed approaches in addressing a large complex multi-CD problem is validated.

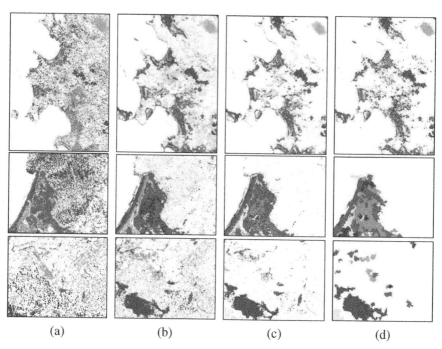

|  (a) |  (b) |  (c) |  (d) |

**Figure 1.13.** *Comparison of the CD maps obtained by: (a) IR-MAD; (b) $S^2CVA$; (c) proposed $M^2C^2VA([u, v] = [1, 6]$; (d) proposed $SPC^2VA$ with $N = 35,140$ and $m = 30$, respectively, where the first row is the whole image scene, and the second and third rows represent two subset results for a detailed visual comparison purpose (Indonesia tsunami dataset). For a color version of this figure, see www.iste.co.uk/ atto/change1.zip*

## 1.6. Conclusion

Owing to the automatic and unsupervised nature, unsupervised CD always represents a very interesting and important CD research and application frontier. However, the absence of ground reference and prior knowledge makes this practical problem more challenging and complex than the supervised ones. In this chapter, we reviewed the current development of unsupervised CD methods in multitemporal multispectral remote sensing images, and analyzed existing open issues and challenges. In particular, we focused on the spectral–spatial perspective to find robust solutions to the important multiclass CD problem. Accordingly, two approaches were proposed, including $M^2C^2VA$ and $SPC^2VA$. By taking advantage of the spectral and spatial joint analysis on the multispectral change representation, the original pixel-level CD performance was enhanced by considering both the spectral variation at the global scale and the spectral homogeneity and spatial connectivity and regularity of change targets at the local scale. Experimental results obtained two real multispectral datasets covering a complex urban scenario, and a large-scale tsunami disaster scenario confirmed the effectiveness of the proposed approaches in terms of higher CD accuracy and computational efficiency when compared with the reference methods. For future works, advanced techniques still need to be designed to deal with more complex real unsupervised CD cases, mainly focusing on, but not limited to the open issues and challenges pointed out in section 1.2.2.

## 1.7. Acknowledgements

This work was supported by the Natural Science Foundation of China under Grant 42071324, 41601354, and by the Shanghai Rising-Star Program (21QA1409100).

## 1.8. References

Achanta, R., Shaji, A., Smith, K., Lucchi, A., Fua, P., Süsstrunk, S. (2012). Slic superpixels compared to state-of-the-art superpixel methods. *IEEE Transactions on Pattern Analysis and Machine Intelligence*, 34(11), 2274–2282.

Ban, Y. and Yousif, O. (2016). *Change Detection Techniques: A Review*. Springer International Publishing, Cham.

Bazi, Y., Bruzzone, L., Melgani, F. (2005). An unsupervised approach based on the generalized Gaussian model to automatic change detection in multitemporal SAR images. *IEEE Transactions on Geoscience and Remote Sensing*, 43(4), 874–887.

Benediktsson, J.A., Palmason, J.A., Sveinsson, J.R. (2005). Classification of hyperspectral data from urban areas based on extended morphological profiles. *IEEE Transactions on Geoscience and Remote Sensing*, 43(3), 480–491.

Bouziani, M., Goïta, K., He, D.-C. (2010). Automatic change detection of buildings in urban environment from very high spatial resolution images using existing geodatabase and prior knowledge. *ISPRS Journal of Photogrammetry and Remote Sensing*, 65(1), 143–153 [Online]. Available at: http://www.sciencedirect.com/science/article/pii/S092427160900121X.

Bovolo, F. (2009). A multilevel parcel-based approach to change detection in very high resolution multitemporal images. *IEEE Geoscience and Remote Sensing Letters*, 6(1), 33–37.

Bovolo, F. and Bruzzone, L. (2007a). A split-based approach to unsupervised change detection in large-size multitemporal images: Application to tsunami-damage assessment. *IEEE Transactions on Geoscience and Remote Sensing*, 45(6), 1658–1670.

Bovolo, F. and Bruzzone, L. (2007b). A theoretical framework for unsupervised change detection based on change vector analysis in the polar domain. *IEEE Transactions on Geoscience and Remote Sensing*, 45(1), 218–236.

Bovolo, F. and Bruzzone, L. (2011). An adaptive thresholding approach to multiple-change detection in multispectral images. *IEEE International Geoscience and Remote Sensing Symposium*, 233–236.

Bovolo, F. and Bruzzone, L. (2015). The time variable in data fusion: A change detection perspective. *IEEE Geoscience and Remote Sensing Magazine*, 3(3), 8–26.

Bovolo, F., Marchesi, S., Bruzzone, L. (2012). A framework for automatic and unsupervised detection of multiple changes in multitemporal images. *IEEE Transactions on Geoscience and Remote Sensing*, 50(6), 2196–2212.

Bruzzone, L. and Bovolo, F. (2013). A novel framework for the design of change-detection systems for very-high-resolution remote sensing images. *Proceedings of the IEEE*, 101(3), 609–630.

Bruzzone, L. and Prieto, D.F. (2000a). Automatic analysis of the difference image for unsupervised change detection. *IEEE Transactions on Geoscience and Remote Sensing*, 38(3), 1171–1182.

Bruzzone, L. and Prieto, D.F. (2000b). A minimum-cost thresholding technique for unsupervised change detection. *International Journal of Remote Sensing*, 21(18), 3539–3544 [Online]. Available at: https://doi.org/10.1080/014311600750037552.

Celik, T. (2009). Unsupervised change detection in satellite images using principal component analysis and $k$-means clustering. *IEEE Geoscience and Remote Sensing Letters*, 6(4), 772–776.

Celik, T. and Ma, K.K. (2011). Multitemporal image change detection using undecimated discrete wavelet transform and active contours. *IEEE Transactions on Geoscience and Remote Sensing*, 49(2), 706–716.

Chen, J., Gong, P., He, C., Pu, R., Shi, P. (2003). Land-use/land-cover change detection using improved change-vector analysis. *Photogrammetric Engineering and Remote Sensing*, 69(4), 369–379.

Chen, G., Hay, G.J., Carvalho, L.M.T., Wulder, M.A. (2012). Object-based change detection. *International Journal of Remote Sensing*, 33(14), 4434–4457 [Online]. Available at: https://doi.org/10.1080/01431161.2011.648285.

Coppin, P., Jonckheere, I., Nackaerts, K., Muys, B., Lambin, E. (2004). Review article digital change detection methods in ecosystem monitoring: A review. *International Journal of Remote Sensing*, 25(9), 1565–1596 [Online]. Available at: https://doi.org/10.1080/0143116031000101675.

Dalla Mura, M., Benediktsson, J.A., Waske, B., Bruzzone, L. (2010). Morphological attribute profiles for the analysis of very high resolution images. *IEEE Transactions on Geoscience and Remote Sensing*, 48(10), 3747–3762.

Du, P., Liu, S., Gamba, P., Tan, K., Xia, J. (2012). Fusion of difference images for change detection over urban areas. *IEEE Journal of Selected Topics in Applied Earth Observations and Remote Sensing*, 5(4), 1076–1086.

Du, P., Liu, S., Xia, J., Zhao, Y. (2013). Information fusion techniques for change detection from multi-temporal remote sensing images. *Information Fusion*, 14(1), 19–27 [Online]. Available at: http://www.sciencedirect.com/science/article/pii/S1566253512000565.

Falco, N., Mura, M.D., Bovolo, F., Benediktsson, J.A., Bruzzone, L. (2013). Change detection in VHR images based on morphological attribute profiles. *IEEE Geoscience and Remote Sensing Letters*, 10(3), 636–640.

Ghosh, A., Mishra, N.S., Ghosh, S. (2011). Fuzzy clustering algorithms for unsupervised change detection in remote sensing images. *Information Sciences*, 181(4), 699–715 [Online]. Available at: http://www.sciencedirect.com/science/article/pii/S0020025510005153.

Han, P., Gong, J., Li, Z. (2008). A new approach for choice of optimal spatial scale in image classification based on entropy. *Wuhan Daxue Xuebao (Xinxi Kexue Ban)/ Geomatics and Information Science of Wuhan University*, 033(7), 676–679.

Han, Y., Javed, A., Jung, S., Liu, S. (2020). Object-based change detection of very high resolution images by fusing pixel-based change detection results using weighted Dempster–Shafer theory. *Remote Sensing*, 12(6) [Online]. Available at: https://www.mdpi.com/2072-4292/12/6/983.

Huang, X., Zhang, L., Zhu, T. (2014). Building change detection from multitemporal high-resolution remotely sensed images based on a morphological building index. *IEEE Journal of Selected Topics in Applied Earth Observations and Remote Sensing*, 7(1), 105–115.

Hussain, M., Chen, D., Cheng, A., Wei, H., Stanley, D. (2013). Change detection from remotely sensed images: From pixel-based to object-based approaches. *ISPRS Journal of Photogrammetry and Remote Sensing*, 80, 91–106 [Online]. Available at: http://www.sciencedirect.com/science/article/pii/S0924271613000804.

Kaszta, A., Van De Kerchove, R., Ramoelo, A., Cho, M.A., Madonsela, S., Mathieu, R., Wolff, E. (2016). Seasonal separation of African savanna components using WorldView-2 imagery: A comparison of pixel- and object-based approaches and selected classification algorithms. *Remote Sensing*, 8(9) [Online]. Available at: https://www.mdpi.com/2072-4292/8/9/763.

Keshava, N. (2004). Distance metrics and band selection in hyperspectral processing with applications to material identification and spectral libraries. *IEEE Transactions on Geoscience and Remote Sensing*, 42(7), 1552–1565.

Khan, S.H., He, X., Porikli, F., Bennamoun, M. (2017). Forest change detection in incomplete satellite images with deep neural networks. *IEEE Transactions on Geoscience and Remote Sensing*, 55(9), 5407–5423.

Leichtle, T., Geiß, C., Wurm, M., Lakes, T., Taubenböck, H. (2017). Unsupervised change detection in VHR remote sensing imagery – An object-based clustering approach in a dynamic urban environment. *International Journal of Applied Earth Observation and Geoinformation*, 54, 15–27 [Online]. Available at: http://www.sciencedirect.com/science/article/pii/S0303243416301490.

Li, H., Celik, T., Longbotham, N., Emery, W.J. (2015). Gabor feature based unsupervised change detection of multitemporal SAR images based on two-level clustering. *IEEE Geoscience and Remote Sensing Letters*, 12(12), 2458–2462.

Liu, S. and Du, P. (2010). Object-oriented change detection from multi-temporal remotely sensed images. *Geographic Object-Based Image Analysis*, number XXXVIII-4/C7.

Liu, S., Bruzzone, L., Bovolo, F., Du, P. (2012). Unsupervised hierarchical spectral analysis for change detection in hyperspectral images. *4th Workshop on Hyperspectral Image and Signal Processing: Evolution in Remote Sensing (WHISPERS)*, pp. 1–4.

Liu, S., Bruzzone, L., Bovolo, F., Zanetti, M., Du, P. (2015). Sequential spectral change vector analysis for iteratively discovering and detecting multiple changes in hyperspectral images. *IEEE Transactions on Geoscience and Remote Sensing*, 53(8), 4363–4378.

Liu, S., Du, Q., Tong, X., Samat, A., Bruzzone, L., Bovolo, F. (2017a). Multiscale morphological compressed change vector analysis for unsupervised multiple change detection. *IEEE Journal of Selected Topics in Applied Earth Observations and Remote Sensing*, 10(9), 4124–4137.

Liu, S., Tong, X., Bruzzone, L., Du, P. (2017b). A novel semisupervised framework for multiple change detection in hyperspectral images. *IEEE International Geoscience and Remote Sensing Symposium (IGARSS)*, 173–176.

Liu, J., Chen, K., Xu, G., Li, H., Yan, M., Diao, W., Sun, X. (2019a). Semi-supervised change detection based on graphs with generative adversarial networks. *IEEE International Geoscience and Remote Sensing Symposium (IGARSS)*, 74–77.

Liu, S., Du, Q., Tong, X., Samat, A., Bruzzone, L. (2019b). Unsupervised change detection in multispectral remote sensing images via spectral-spatial band expansion. *IEEE Journal of Selected Topics in Applied Earth Observations and Remote Sensing*, 12(9), 3578–3587.

Liu, S., Marinelli, D., Bruzzone, L., Bovolo, F. (2019c). A review of change detection in multitemporal hyperspectral images: Current techniques, applications, and challenges. *IEEE Geoscience and Remote Sensing Magazine*, 7(2), 140–158.

Liu, S., Hu, Q., Tong, X., Xia, J., Du, Q., Samat, A., Ma, X. (2020a). A multi-scale superpixel-guided filter feature extraction and selection approach for classification of very-high-resolution remotely sensed imagery. *Remote Sensing*, 12(5) [Online]. Available at: https://www.mdpi.com/2072-4292/12/5/862.

Liu, S., Zheng, Y., Dalponte, M., Tong, X. (2020b). A novel fire index-based burned area change detection approach using Landsat-8 OLI data. *European Journal of Remote Sensing*, 53(1), 104–112 [Online]. Available at: https://doi.org/10.1080/22797254.2020.1738900.

Lu, D., Mausel, P., Brondízio, E., Moran, E. (2004). Change detection techniques. *International Journal of Remote Sensing*, 25(12), 2365–2401 [Online]. Available at: https://doi.org/10.1080/0143116031000139863.

Malila, W. (1980). Change vector analysis: An approach for detecting forest changes with landsat. *LARS Symposia*, Purdue University, West Lafayette, IN.

Mou, L., Bruzzone, L., Zhu, X.X. (2019). Learning spectral-spatial-temporal features via a recurrent convolutional neural network for change detection in multispectral imagery. *IEEE Transactions on Geoscience and Remote Sensing*, 57(2), 924–935.

Mura, M.D., Benediktsson, J.A., Bovolo, F., Bruzzone, L. (2008). An unsupervised technique based on morphological filters for change detection in very high resolution images. *IEEE Geoscience and Remote Sensing Letters*, 5(3), 433–437.

Nielsen, A.A. (2007). The regularized iteratively reweighted mad method for change detection in multi- and hyperspectral data. *IEEE Transactions on Image Processing*, 16(2), 463–478.

Nielsen, A.A. and Canty, M.J. (2008). Kernel principal component analysis for change detection [Online]. Available at: http://www2.compute.dtu.dk/pubdb/pubs/5667-full.html.

Okyay, U., Telling, J., Glennie, C.L., Dietrich, W.E. (2019). Airborne lidar change detection: An overview of earth sciences applications. *Earth-Science Reviews*, 198, 102929 [Online]. Available at: http://www.sciencedirect.com/science/article/pii/S0012825218306470.

Otsu, N. (1979). A threshold selection method from gray-level histograms. *IEEE Transactions on Systems, Man, and Cybernetics*, 9(1), 62–66.

Saha, S., Bovolo, F., Bruzzone, L. (2019). Unsupervised deep change vector analysis for multiple-change detection in VHR images. *IEEE Transactions on Geoscience and Remote Sensing*, 57(6), 3677–3693.

Singh, A. (1989). Review article digital change detection techniques using remotely-sensed data. *International Journal of Remote Sensing*, 10(6), 989–1003 [Online]. Available at: https://doi.org/10.1080/01431168908903939.

Song, X.P., Hansen, M.C., Stehman, S.V., Potapov, S.V., Tyukavina, A., Vermote, E.F., Townshend, J.R. (2018). Global land change from 1982 to 2016. *Nature*, 560, 639–643.

Tong, X., Pan, H., Liu, S., Li, B., Luo, X., Xie, H., Xu, X. (2020). A novel approach for hyperspectral change detection based on uncertain area analysis and improved transfer learning. *IEEE Journal of Selected Topics in Applied Earth Observations and Remote Sensing*, 13, 2056–2069.

Wang, X., Liu, S., Du, P., Liang, H., Xia, J., Li, Y. (2018). Object-based change detection in urban areas from high spatial resolution images based on multiple features and ensemble learning. *Remote Sensing*, 10(2) [Online]. Available at: https://www.mdpi.com/2072-4292/10/2/276.

Wei, C., Zhao, P., Li, X., Wang, Y., Liu, F. (2019). Unsupervised change detection of VHR remote sensing images based on multi-resolution Markov random field in wavelet domain. *International Journal of Remote Sensing*, 40(20), 7750–7766 [Online]. Available at: https://doi.org/10.1080/01431161.2019.1602792.

Wu, Z., Hu, Z., Fan, Q. (2012). Superpixel-based unsupervised change detection using multi-dimensional change vector analysis and SVM-based classification. *ISPRS Annals of Photogrammetry, Remote Sensing and Spatial Information Sciences*, I-7, 257–262 [Online]. Available at: https://www.isprs-ann-photogramm-remote-sens-spatial-inf-sci.net/I-7/257/2012/.

Zanetti, M., Bovolo, F., Bruzzone, L. (2015). Rayleigh–Rice mixture parameter estimation via EM algorithm for change detection in multispectral images. *IEEE Transactions on Image Processing*, 24(12), 5004–5016.

Zhang, W., Lu, X., Li, X. (2018). A coarse-to-fine semi-supervised change detection for multispectral images. *IEEE Transactions on Geoscience and Remote Sensing*, 56(6), 3587–3599.

# 2

# Change Detection in Time Series of Polarimetric SAR Images

Knut CONRADSEN[1], Henning SKRIVER[1],
Morton J. CANTY[2] and Allan A. NIELSEN[1]

[1] Technical University of Denmark, Kongens Lyngby, Denmark
[2] Formerly Jülich Research Center, Germany

## 2.1. Introduction

In this chapter, we will consider the change detection problem in a time series of polarimetric SAR (Synthetic Aperture Radar) images using the covariance representation of multilook polarimetric SAR data. The pixels will then be represented by the complex Wishart distributed Hermitian matrices. The change detection pipeline consists of an omnibus test for testing equality over the whole time span and a subsequent factorization used in assessing individual change time points. The method is easily extended to change detection of "homogeneous" areas, and finally, we will introduce a concept for directional change using the Loewner ordering. The methods are illustrated using airborne as well as satellite data. References to relevant software are provided.

In the first section, we briefly give the background for using an omnibus test instead of pairwise analyses. A more rigorous exposition is given in (Conradsen *et al.* 2016). Furthermore, we introduce some basic concepts from statistical testing theory, and – in the second section – illustrate their usage of in simulation studies in the gamma distribution.

*Change Detection and Image Time Series Analysis 1*,
coordinated by Abdourrahmane M. ATTO, Francesca BOVOLO and Lorenzo BRUZZONE.
© ISTE Ltd 2021.

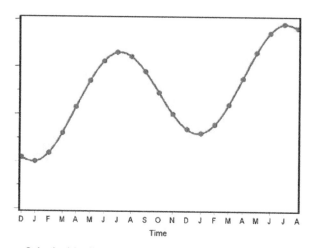

**Figure 2.1.** *An idealized parameter value function showing a linear trend with seasonal (annual) variation for monthly data. For a color version of this figure, see www.iste.co.uk/atto/change1.zip*

### 2.1.1. *The problem*

Synthetic aperture radar (SAR) data are very useful for many applications in remote sensing due to SAR's all-weather capabilities. This enables change detection on a regular basis. Add to this that polarimetric SAR data from satellites are becoming readily available, increasing the need for making efficient algorithms for change detection in time series of both dual-pol and fully polarimetric SAR images. In this chapter, we consider pixels from a series of polarimetric SAR images and use the covariance representation of the data. This entails the pixelwise distributions being gamma distributions in the one-dimensional case and complex Wishart distributions in the multivariate case. Several authors have considered change detection as a statistical task in this connection, see for example, Madsen *et al.* (1991), Christensen *et al.* (1998), Conradsen *et al.* (2003, 2014, 2016), Akbari *et al.* (2016), Muro *et al.* (2016), Canty and Nielsen (2017), Canty (2019), Nascimento *et al.* (2019) and Canty *et al.* (2020).

We will not give a very rigorous presentation of motivation for the methods we are using, but instead will illustrate important concepts through examples. A more rigorous presentation may be found in the original papers and – regarding general concepts – in the literature.

For a single spectral band image taken at time point $t_i$, $i = 1, \cdots, k$, the pixelwise distribution is characterized by a parameter $\beta_i$. In a gamma $G(k, \beta_u)$-distribution, the mean is $k\beta_u$, and the timewise development of monthly data may look as it does in Figure 2.1.

Obviously, we observe changes over the 21 months. The question is how do we address the problem of identifying the changes. Let us be more specific and consider images taken at time points $t_1 < \cdots < t_k$, where the distributions of the pixel values are characterized by parameters

$$\beta_1 = \cdots = \beta_{i-1} \neq \beta_i = \cdots = \beta_{j-1} \neq \beta_j = \cdots = \beta_k$$

It follows that we have changes between $t_{i-1}$ and $t_i$ and between $t_{j-1}$ and $t_j$. A straightforward approach for identifying the intervals where changes occur would be to test the hypothesis $\beta_m = \beta_{m-1}$ of no change against the alternative $\beta_m \neq \beta_{m-1}$, i.e. a change has occurred. This approach may, however, give a large false negative rate, i.e. actual changes may not be detected. This could, for example, be the case in Figure 2.1, which is characterized by small gradual monthly changes. Instead, we propose including the full range of the data variation in one test statistic by using a so-called *omnibus test* of

$$H_0 : \beta_1 = \cdots = \beta_k$$

against all alternatives. If the hypothesis is accepted, we conclude that no changes occurred in the time interval considered. If it is rejected, we conclude that we have at least one change in the interval. The location of the change(s) will then be found by suitable *post hoc* analyses.

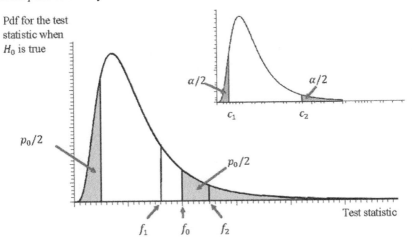

**Figure 2.2.** *Figure showing the connection between the p-value for an outcome of a test and the observed value of the test statistic. The small figure shows the connection between the level of significance $\alpha$ and the critical region $\{f \leqslant c_1\} \cup \{f \geqslant c_2\}$, the values of the test statistic causing rejection of the hypothesis. The p-value is $p_0$ and the observed value of the test statistic is $f_0$. It follows that we reject the hypothesis if and only if the p-value is smaller than the level of significance, i.e. iff $p_0 \leqslant \alpha$. For a color version of this figure, see www.iste.co.uk/atto/change1.zip*

Before developing the general theory, we summarize some important concepts from statistical hypothesis testing and try to clarify the terminology by using, *inter alia* simulated data. As mentioned, the exposition does in no way pretend to be complete, but should be seen as involving illustrations and heuristics.

We consider a statistical test where the decision is based on a test statistic $F$ and the critical region

$$\{F \leqslant c_1\} \cup \{F \geqslant c_2\}$$

DEFINITION 2.1.– *The p-value $P_{value}$ for a test is the probability – given $H_0$ is true – of obtaining an outcome of the test statistic that is more extreme than the actually observed value.*

In Figure 2.2, the observed value of the test statistic is $f_0$ and the $p$-value is $p_0$. If the observed value of the test statistic decreases to, say, $f_1$, the $p$-value increases, and if the test statistic increases to $f_2$, the $p$-value decreases. The $p$-value is a random variable, and from the previous considerations, we readily get – under the null hypothesis – that the distribution of $P_{value}$ is given by

$$P\{P_{value} \leqslant p_0 \mid H_0 \text{ true}\} = 2 \times P\{F > f_0 \mid H_0 \text{ true}\} = p_0,$$

i.e. the $p$-value is uniformly distributed over the interval $[0, 1]$ if the hypothesis is true. The only assumption we must make is that the underlying distribution is continuous. We state this as

THEOREM 2.1.– *If the underlying distribution is continuous, the p-value of a test is uniformly distributed over the unit interval if the hypothesis is true.*

The level of significance is the probability of rejecting the hypothesis when it is true. This is obviously an error. When testing statistical hypotheses, we may actually commit two different types of error as follows:

1) *Type I error: rejecting a true hypothesis*, or stating that a change has occurred although this is not the case. This is also called a *false positive* or a *false alarm*. The *significance level* $\alpha$ of the test or the *false positive rate* is the maximum probability of committing a type I error.

2) *Type II error: accepting a false hypothesis*, or stating that no changes have occurred although there has been a change. This is also called a *false negative*. The probability of committing a type II error is called the *miss rate* or the *false negative rate*. This probability is equal to one minus the *power of the test*.

If a test procedure is based on $n$ independent tests, each with significance level $\alpha_c$, then the significance level of the combined test is $\alpha_{FW} = 1 - (1 - \alpha_c)^n$, the so-called familywise error rate. This error rate increases with the number of tests. For $\alpha_c = 0.1$ and $n = 6, 12, 18$, we get $\alpha_{FW} = 0.4686, 0.7176, 0.8494$. Therefore, if we want to base our analysis on pairwise comparisons, we get quite considerable positive error rates. In order to circumvent this problem in multiple comparisons, we may introduce adjustments like the Bonferroni correction (replace $\alpha_c$ by $\alpha_{FW}/n$). We will not pursue this line of investigation, but refer to Conradsen et al. (2016) for an example and further references.

### 2.1.2. Important concepts illustrated by means of the gamma distribution

The main purpose of this section is to provide illustrations that may mimic images taken at two time points, one pair where the similarity is greater than we have in the case with independent, random replications, and one pair where the similarity is smaller. We will then compare the histograms of the $p$-values based on all pixel values with the histograms of the test statistics. The advantage of looking at the $p$-value is that the target distribution under the null hypothesis is a uniform distribution (with a constant pdf); therefore, we must compare the $p$-value histogram with a constant instead of comparing the test-statistic histogram with a curved pdf (here, an $F(12, 12)$-distribution).

First, we summarize some useful facts about tests in the gamma distribution. We consider the independent gamma distributed random variables $U \sim G(k, \beta_u)$ and $V \sim G(\ell, \beta_v)$. Furthermore, we consider the statistical hypothesis $H_0 : \beta_u = \beta_v$ against the alternative $H_1 : \beta_u \neq \beta_v$. The likelihood ratio test statistic becomes

$$Q = \frac{(k + \ell)^{k+\ell}}{k^k \ell^\ell} \frac{U^k V^\ell}{(U + V)^{k+\ell}}.$$

The critical region is given by $Q \leqslant q_\alpha$ which is equivalent to

$$\frac{U/k}{V/\ell} \leqslant c_1 \text{ or } \frac{U/k}{V/\ell} \geqslant c_2.$$

Under the null hypothesis, the test statistic

$$F = \frac{U/k}{V/\ell} \sim F(2k, 2\ell)$$

follows Fisher's $F$-distribution. Therefore, the critical values may be determined by means of quantiles in the $F$-distribution, i.e. for significance level $\alpha$, we get

$$c_1 = F(2k, 2\ell)_{\alpha/2} \text{ and } c_2 = F(2k, 2\ell)_{1-\alpha/2}.$$

The power of the test is

$$\rho\left(\beta_u, \beta_v\right) = P\left\{F(2k, 2\ell) \leqslant \frac{\beta_v}{\beta_u}c_1\right\} + P\left\{F(2k, 2\ell) \geqslant \frac{\beta_v}{\beta_u}c_2\right\}.$$

The power function is depicted in Figure 2.3. We see that even when one parameter value is three times as large as the other, the power is only around 60%, giving a false negative rate around 40%.

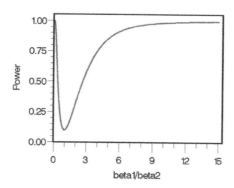

**Figure 2.3.** *The power function for testing whether two $G(6, \beta_t)$-distributions, $t = 1, 2$, have the same scale parameters. The power function only depends on the ratio between the scale parameters. For a given ratio, the power is the probability that the test for equal scale parameters will be rejected. The value at 1 corresponding to $H_0 : \beta_1 = \beta_2$ is the level of significance, here $\alpha = 10\%$. For a color version of this figure, see www.iste.co.uk/atto/change1.zip*

Sometimes, the interval between image acquisitions is much shorter than the time constants involved in creating changes. This may be the case for satellite-based observations near either pole or for airborne observations. In order to illustrate the effect of this, we introduce a (non physical) **signal + noise model**. For $\ell = 1, \cdots, 6$ we consider random variables representing the generation of **noise parts**

$$X_i^{(n,\ell)} \sim G(\ell, \beta), \quad i = t, t + 1$$

and a random variable representing the generation of a **signal part**

$$X^{(s,\ell)} \sim G(6 - \ell, \beta).$$

For $\ell = 6$, we assume that $X^{(s,\ell)}$ is equal to zero. All random variables are assumed to be independent. For time points $t$ and $t + 1$, we observe

$$Y_t^{(\ell)} = X^{(s,\ell)} + X_t^{(n,\ell)} \sim G(6, \beta)$$

$$Y_{t+1}^{(\ell)} = X^{(s,\ell)} + X_{t+1}^{(n,\ell)} \sim G(6, \beta),$$

i.e. they follow the same gamma distribution. However, they are not independent because of the common signal term. More specifically, we have that the variables $Y_t^{(\ell)}$ and $Y_{t+1}^{(\ell)}$ are correlated with correlation coefficient equal to

$$\rho_{t,t+1}^{(\ell)} = \rho^{(\ell)} = \frac{\text{Cov}(Y_t^{(\ell)}, Y_{t+1}^{(\ell)})}{\sqrt{\text{V}(Y_t^{(\ell)})\text{V}(Y_{t+1}^{(\ell)})}} = \frac{6-\ell}{6}.$$

For $\ell = 6$, the ratio

$$\frac{Y_t^{(\ell)}/12}{Y_{t+1}^{(\ell)}/12} = \frac{X^{(s,\ell)} + X_t^{(n,\ell)}}{X^{(s,\ell)} + X_{t+1}^{(n,\ell)}} \sim F(12,12)$$

follows Fisher's $F$-distribution with $(12,12)$ degrees of freedom. For $\ell = 5, 4, 3, 2, 1$, this is not the case due to the positive correlation between numerator and denominator.

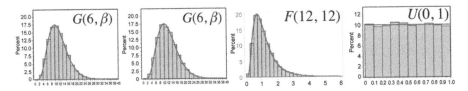

**Figure 2.4.** *Simulating 128 × 128 pixel values at two time points with independent measurements. The first two histograms show the distributions of the pixel values at the two time points. The theoretical $G(6,\beta)$-pdfs are shown in red. The third histogram shows the empirical distribution of the $F$-statistics, in the case of an $F(12,12)$-distribution. Finally, we show the histogram for the $p$-values together with the uniform distribution. For a color version of this figure, see www.iste.co.uk/atto/change1.zip*

We have simulated 128 × 128 pixel values according to this signal + noise model. The results for $\ell = 1$ are shown in Figure 2.5. In row one, we see the two noise distributions – both $\sim G(1,\beta)$ – and the common signal distribution – $\sim G(5,\beta)$. In the second row, we see the observed signal + noise distributions – both $\sim G(6,\beta)$ – and the distribution of the $F$-test statistic. The red curve is the pdf of the $F(12,12)$-distribution, the theoretical distribution if the observations at the two time points are independent. This is not the case since the correlation between pixel values at the two time points is 5/6. Therefore, values measured at two time points at a pixel will be more similar compared to what the random variation would give. This is in accordance with the shape of the histogram. This has a mode close to 1 whereas the $F(12,12)$-distribution has mode 5/7. Furthermore, the empirical standard deviation is 0.28, the "theoretical" is 0.81. Thus, we see that the probabilities of observing very large or very small values of the test statistic are considerably smaller than expected under the independence assumption.

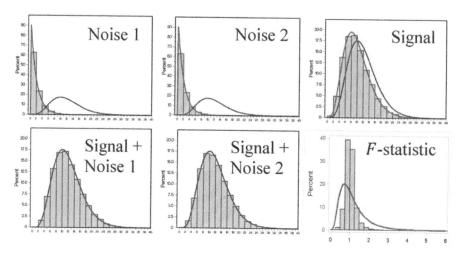

**Figure 2.5.** *Simulating 128 × 128 pixel values according to the signal + noise model described in the text. The histograms for the $G(1, \beta)$-distributed noise component (theoretical pdf: red) at the two time points are the first two histograms in row one, and the histogram of the common $G(5, \beta)$-distributed signal part (theoretical pdf: red) is shown in the third histogram. The first two histograms in the second row show the distributions of the observed values, i.e. the distributions of the sums of the noise and the signal components. The blue probability density functions in the five histograms are in all cases the $G(6, \beta)$-pdf, and it readily follows that the observations at the two time points in both cases closely follow the $G(6, \beta)$-distribution. The histogram of the $F$-statistic, i.e. the ratio between pixel values at the two time points is given in the third column, and the red pdf corresponds to the $F(12, 12)$-distribution, the theoretical pdf, had the observations been independent. For a color version of this figure, see www.iste.co.uk/atto/change1.zip*

Therefore, we get much fewer rejects than we would expect under the independence assumption. For each pixel, we have computed the $p$-value assuming the independence – or, equivalently – assuming that the distribution of the test statistic is the $F(12, 12)$-distribution. The histogram of those $p$-values is shown in the first column in the last row of Figure 2.6. The first two rows show the histograms and pdfs for the signal part and the $F$-statistic. We see that – compared to the uniform distribution presented in Figure 2.4 – there is a strong overrepresentation of pixels with very large $p$-values, i.e. of pixels that are very far from being characterized as pixels with a change.

The following four columns show the same statistics for the signal + noise models with correlations $\rho^{(\ell)} = 2/3, 1/2, 1/3, 1/6$. We see that the $p$-value distributions are becoming increasingly similar to the uniform distribution with decreasing correlations between the two timepoints.

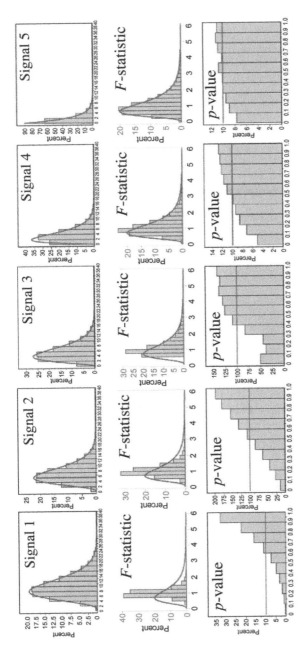

**Figure 2.6.** *Each column represents a simulation study on the distribution of $128 \times 128$ pixel values from the same scene at two time points using the signal + noise model described in the text and illustrated in Figure 2.5. The first column corresponds to the situation depicted in Figure 2.5. The first row shows the histograms and pdfs for the signal part corresponding to shape parameters 5, 4, 3, 2 and 1. The noise parts are not shown, but their corresponding shape parameters are 1, 2, 3, 4 and 5. The correlations between pixel measurements at the two time points are $\rho^{(\ell)} = 5/6, 2/3, 1/2, 1/3$ and $1/6$. The second row shows the histogram for the $F$-statistic and the independent case theoretical $F(12, 12)$-pdf. The last row shows the histogram of the observed $p$-values and the pdf of the uniform distribution. For a color version of this figure, see www.iste.co.uk/atto/change1.zip*

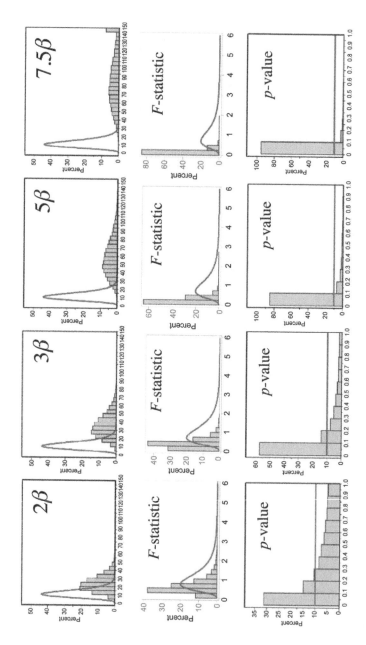

**Figure 2.7.** *Simulating $128 \times 128$ pixel values at two time points with independent measurements. The pixelwise distribution at the first time point is a $G(6, \beta)$-distribution, at the second time point, a $G(6, k\beta)$-distribution, $k = 2, 3, 5, 7.5$. The first row shows the histograms and fitted $G'(6, k\beta)$-distributions. The second row shows the null-hypothesis distribution of the ratio (= the test statistic), and the fourth row shows the distribution of the observed p-values. The proportion in the first class $[0, \alpha] = [0, 0.1]$ corresponds to the power of the test for the ratio considered. In the last column, the histogram is truncated at 150. For a color version of this figure, see www.iste.co.uk/atto/change1.zip*

In Figure 2.4, the numerator and denominator are independent, and the test statistic therefore follows the $F(12, 12)$-distribution, and we see that this results in a perfect uniform distribution of the $p$-values.

In Figure 2.7, we show the results of simulating $128 \times 128$ pixel values at two time points with independent measurements. The pixelwise distribution at the first time point is a $G(6, \beta)$-distribution, at the second time point, it is a $G(6, k\beta)$-distribution, $k = 2, 3, 5, 7.5$. The first row shows the distributions at the second time point, the second row shows the histogram of the $F$-statistic and its null hypothesis distribution, i.e. an $F(12, 12)$-distribution. The last row shows the distributions of the $p$-values overlaid with the uniform distribution, the null hypothesis distribution. We see a development towards distributions concentrated on the smaller values. Getting smaller and smaller $p$-values corresponds to getting more and more rejects (as we should have). The significance level chosen is $0.1$; therefore, we can directly read the power of the test for the given ratio as the proportion of $p$-values in the interval $[0, \alpha] = [0, 0.1]$.

To sum up: the differences between the $F$-statistic histograms in, for example, column one in Figure 2.6 and column one in Figure 2.7 may look subtler than the differences between the accompanying $p$-value histograms. In the first situation, we have fewer rejects and, in the second, more rejects than the null hypothesis would give. Or, putting it differently: in the first case, the data are more similar, and in the second case, less similar than pure randomness would give, an important issue to underline if we want to characterize the dynamic behavior of change statistics.

## 2.2. Test theory and matrix ordering

In this section, we summarize the theoretical results on tests in the complex Wishart distribution developed in (Conradsen *et al.* 2003, 2016, 2021) and introduce the Loewner ordering of matrices.

### 2.2.1. *Test for equality of two complex Wishart distributions*

Let the independent $p \times p$ Hermitian, positive definite matrices $\boldsymbol{X}$ and $\boldsymbol{Y}$ be complex Wishart distributed, i.e. $\boldsymbol{X} \sim W_{\mathbb{C}}(p, n, \boldsymbol{\Sigma}_x)$ and $\boldsymbol{Y} \sim W_{\mathbb{C}}(p, m, \boldsymbol{\Sigma}_y)$. The maximum likelihood estimators for the parameters are $\widehat{\boldsymbol{\Sigma}}_x = \boldsymbol{X}/n$ and $\widehat{\boldsymbol{\Sigma}}_y = \boldsymbol{Y}/m$. We now want to test the hypothesis that the two parameters are equal against all alternatives, i.e. testing

$$H_0 : \boldsymbol{\Sigma}_x = \boldsymbol{\Sigma}_y \text{ against } H_1 : \boldsymbol{\Sigma}_x \neq \boldsymbol{\Sigma}_y.$$

Under the null hypothesis $\boldsymbol{\Sigma}_x$ and $\boldsymbol{\Sigma}_y$ assume a common value $\boldsymbol{\Sigma} = \boldsymbol{\Sigma}_x = \boldsymbol{\Sigma}_y$ and the maximum likelihood estimator for the common value is $\widehat{\boldsymbol{\Sigma}} = (\boldsymbol{X}+\boldsymbol{Y})/(n+m)$ and $(\boldsymbol{X} + \boldsymbol{Y}) \sim W_{\mathbb{C}}(p, n + m, \boldsymbol{\Sigma})$. With this set-up, we are now able to state

THEOREM 2.2.– *Let the situation be as above. The likelihood ratio test statistic for testing $H_0$ against $H_1$ is then*

$$Q = \frac{(n+m)^{p(n+m)}}{n^{pn}m^{pm}} \frac{(\det X)^n (\det Y)^m}{(\det (X+Y))^{n+m}}.$$

*The distribution of $Q$ under $H_0$ is independent of the common value $\Sigma$. The hypothesis is rejected for small values of $Q$, i.e. the critical region is of the form $\{Q < q_\alpha\}$, where*

$$P\{Q < q_\alpha \mid H_0 \text{ true}\} = \alpha.$$

PROOF.– See Conradsen *et al.* (2003).

In determining the distribution of $Q$, we may use the general result that $-2 \log Q$ is asymptotically $\chi^2$- distributed with the decrease in numbers of parameters from $H_0 \vee H_1$ to $H_0$ (i.e. $p^2$) as degrees of freedom. The number of free parameters in, for example, $\Sigma_x$, is $2(p^2-p)/2+p$, where the reason for the factor 2 is that the covariance terms consist of two parameters (real and imaginary parts), the $-p$ term corresponds to the subtraction of variance terms (the diagonal elements), the divisor 2 is caused by the Hermitian symmetry, and the last term is the $p$ real variances (diagonal elements). Therefore, the reduction in number of free parameters is $2p^2 - p^2 = p^2$.

A better approximation to the distribution of $Q$ under the null hypothesis is given in

THEOREM 2.3.– *Let the situation be as above, and define*

$$\rho = 1 - \frac{2p^2 - 1}{6p} \left( \frac{1}{n} + \frac{1}{m} - \frac{1}{n+m} \right)$$

*and*

$$\omega_2 = -\frac{p^2}{4}\left(1 - \frac{1}{\rho}\right)^2 + \frac{p^2(p^2-1)}{24} \left( \frac{1}{n^2} + \frac{1}{m^2} - \frac{1}{(n+m)^2} \right) \frac{1}{\rho^2}.$$

*Then, if $H_0$ is true,*

$$P\{-2\rho \log Q \leqslant z\} \cong P\{\chi^2\left(p^2\right) \leqslant z\} +$$
$$\omega_2 \left[ P\{\chi^2\left(p^2 + 4\right) \leqslant z\} - P\{\chi^2\left(p^2\right) \leqslant z\} \right].$$

PROOF.– Omitted. See Conradsen *et al.* (2003).

## 2.2.2. *Test for equality of k-complex Wishart distributions*

THEOREM 2.4.– *We consider independent random variables (i.e. $p \times p$ random matrices)*

$$X_i \sim W_{\mathbb{C}}\left(p, n_i, \Sigma_i\right), \quad i = 1, \cdots, k$$

*and want to test the hypotheses*

$$H_0 : \Sigma_1 = \cdots = \Sigma_k \text{ against } H_1 : \exists\, i, j : \Sigma_i \neq \Sigma_j.$$

*Then, the likelihood ratio test statistic is*

$$Q = \frac{(n_1 + \cdots + n_k)^{p(n_1 + \cdots + n_k)}}{n_1^{pn_1} \cdots n_k^{pn_k}} \frac{(\det X_1)^{n_1} \cdots (\det X_k)^{n_k}}{(\det(X_1 + \cdots + X_k))^{n_1 + \cdots + n_k}}$$

$$= \frac{N^{pN}}{n_1^{pn_1} \cdots n_k^{pn_k}} \frac{(\det X_1)^{n_1} \cdots (\det X_k)^{n_k}}{(\det X)^N},$$

*where*

$$N = n_1 + \cdots + n_k$$

*and*

$$X = X_1 + \cdots + X_k.$$

PROOF.– Omitted. See Conradsen *et al.* (2016).

THEOREM 2.5.– *The asymptotic chi-square distribution for* $-2 \log Q$ *under the null hypothesis has* $(k-1)p^2$ *degrees of freedom, i.e.*

PROOF.– The number of free parameters is, without $H_0$,

$$\sum_i \left\{ 2(p^2 - p)/2 + p \right\} = kp^2.$$

Under $H_0$, it is $p^2$, and the result follows.

COROLLARY 2.1.– *If the degrees of freedom are equal, i.e.* $n_1 = \cdots = n_k = n$, *the likelihood ratio test statistic becomes*

$$Q = k^{pkn} \frac{\prod_{i=1}^{k} (\det X_i)^n}{(\det X)^{nk}} = \left\{ k^{pk} \frac{\prod_{i=1}^{k} \det X_i}{(\det X)^k} \right\}^n$$

PROOF.– Straightforward.

In this case, a better approximation of the distribution of $Q$ under the null hypothesis is given in the following theorem.

THEOREM 2.6.– *Let the situation be as in the corollary above and define*

$$f = (k - 1) p^2,$$

$$\rho = 1 - \frac{1}{6 (k - 1) p} (2p^2 - 1) \left( \frac{k}{n} - \frac{1}{nk} \right),$$

$$\omega_2 = - (k - 1) \frac{p^2}{4} \left( 1 - \frac{1}{\rho} \right)^2 + \frac{1}{24} \left( \frac{k}{n^2} - \frac{1}{(nk)^2} \right) \frac{1}{\rho^2}.$$

*We then have the following approximation to the distribution of the likelihood ratio statistic under the null hypothesis:*

$$P \{-2\rho \log Q \leqslant z \} \cong P \{\chi^2 (f) \leqslant z \}$$
$$+ \omega_2 \left[ P \{\chi^2 (f + 4) \leqslant z \} - P \{\chi^2 (f) \leqslant z \} \right].$$

PROOF.– See (Conradsen *et al.* 2016).

Next, we consider partial hypotheses in the following two theorems.

THEOREM 2.7.– *Given that – for $j = 2, \cdots, k$ –*

$$\Sigma_1 = \cdots = \Sigma_{j-1},$$

*then, the likelihood ratio test statistic for testing*

$$H_{0,j} : \Sigma_j = \Sigma_{j-1} \text{ against } H_{1,j} : \Sigma_j \neq \Sigma_{j-1}$$

*is*

$$R_j = \frac{j^{jpn}}{(j - 1)^{(j-1)pn}} \frac{(\det (X_1 + \cdots + X_{j-1}))^{(j-1)n} (\det X_j)^n}{(\det (X_1 + \cdots + X_j))^{jn}}$$

*Furthermore*

$$Q = \prod_{j=2}^{k} R_j$$

*and if $H_0$ is true, i.e. $\Sigma_1 = \cdots = \Sigma_k$, then the random variables $R_2, \cdots, R_k$ are independent.*

PROOF.– See Conradsen *et al.* (2016).

Furthermore, we have

THEOREM 2.8.– *For*

$$f = p^2$$

$$\rho_j = 1 - \frac{2p^2 - 1}{6pn}\left(1 + \frac{1}{j(j-1)}\right)$$

$$\omega_{2,j} = -\frac{p^2}{4}\left(1 - \frac{1}{\rho_j}\right)^2 + \frac{p^2(p^2 - 1)}{24n^2}\left(1 + \frac{2j-1}{j^2(j-1)^2}\right)\frac{1}{\rho_j^2}$$

*we finally have*

$$P\{-2\rho_j\log R_j \leqslant z\} \cong P\{\chi^2(f) \leqslant z\} + $$
$$\omega_{2,j}\left[P\{\chi^2(f+4) \leqslant z\} - P\{\chi^2(f) \leqslant z\}\right]$$

PROOF.– See Conradsen *et al.* (2016).

## 2.2.3. *The block diagonal case*

We consider independent random variables $X_1, \cdots, X_k$, each similarly partitioned into $t$ independent components $X_{i\tau}, \tau = 1, \cdots, t$. $X_{i\tau}$ is a $p_\tau \times p_\tau$ matrix, $p = p_1 + \cdots + p_t$ so that

$$X_i = \begin{bmatrix} X_{i1} & \cdots & 0_{p_1 p_t} \\ \vdots & \ddots & \vdots \\ 0_{p_t p_1} & \cdots & X_{it} \end{bmatrix}$$

with

$$X_{i\tau} \sim W_{\mathbb{C}}(p_\tau, n_i, \Sigma_{i\tau}), \quad \tau = 1, \cdots, t, \ i = 1, \cdots, k.$$

We put

$$\Sigma_i = \begin{bmatrix} \Sigma_{i1} & \cdots & 0 \\ \vdots & \ddots & \vdots \\ 0 & \cdots & \Sigma_{it} \end{bmatrix}$$

and want to test the hypothesis

$$H_0 : \; \Sigma_1 = \cdots = \Sigma_k \;\; \text{or} \;\; \Sigma_{1\tau} = \cdots = \Sigma_{k\tau}, \; \tau = 1, \cdots, t$$

against all alternatives.

THEOREM 2.9.– *The criterion for testing $H_0$ against all alternatives is the product of the marginal criteria*

$$Q = \prod_{\tau=1}^{t} \frac{N^{p_\tau N}}{n_1^{p_\tau n_1} \cdots n_k^{p_\tau n_k}} \frac{(\det X_{1\tau})^{n_1} \cdots (\det X_{k\tau})^{n_k}}{(\det X_{.\tau})}$$

$$= \frac{N^{pN}}{n_1^{pn_1} \cdots n_k^{pn_k}} \frac{(\det X_1)^{n_1} \cdots (\det X_k)^{n_k}}{(\det(X_1 + \cdots + X_k))^N}.$$

*The asymptotic chi-square distribution of $-2 \log Q$ under the null hypothesis is given by*

$$P\{-2 \log Q \leqslant z\} \cong P\left\{ \chi^2 \left( (k-1) \sum_{\tau=1}^{t} p_\tau^2 \right) \leqslant z \right\}.$$

PROOF.– The first part follows from results on the determinant of a block diagonal matrix, for example,

$$\det X_i = \det \begin{bmatrix} X_{i1} & \cdots & 0_{p_1 p_t} \\ \vdots & \ddots & \vdots \\ 0_{p_t p_1} & \cdots & X_{it} \end{bmatrix} = (\det X_{i1}) \cdots (\det X_{it}).$$

Without the null hypothesis, the number of free parameters is

$$\sum_i \sum_\tau p_\tau^2 = k \sum_\tau p_\tau^2,$$

and, under the hypothesis,

$$\sum_\tau p_\tau^2.$$

Thus, the reduction is

$$(k-1) \sum_{\tau=1}^{t} p_\tau^2$$

and the theorem follows. ∎

We again consider the case where the degrees of freedom are equal, i.e. $n_1 = \cdots = n_k = n$ and get

THEOREM 2.10.– *Let the situation be as described above. The test criterion then becomes*

$$Q = \left\{ k^{pk} \frac{\det X_1 \cdots \det X_k}{(\det(X_1 + \cdots + X_k))^k} \right\}^n$$

*For*

$$f = (k-1) \sum_{\tau=1}^{t} p_\tau^2$$

$$\rho = 1 - \frac{1}{6f} \left( \frac{k}{n} - \frac{1}{nk} \right) \sum_{\tau=1}^{t} p_\tau (2p_\tau^2 - 1)$$

$$\omega_2 = -\frac{f}{4} \left( 1 - \frac{1}{\rho} \right)^2 + \frac{1}{24\rho^2} \left( \frac{k}{n^2} - \frac{1}{(nk)^2} \right) \sum_{\tau=1}^{t} p_\tau^2 (p_\tau^2 - 1),$$

*we have*

$$P\{-2\rho \log Q \leqslant z\} \cong P\{\chi^2(f) \leqslant z\} +$$
$$\omega_2 \left[ P\{\chi^2(f+4) \leqslant z\} - P\{\chi^2(f) \leqslant z\} \right].$$

PROOF.– See Conradsen *et al.* (2021).

We now turn to the distribution of the $R_j$ quantities in the block diagonal case. For $\tau = 1, \cdots, t$, we assume that

$$\Sigma_{1\tau} = \cdots = \Sigma_{(j-1)\tau}, \quad \tau = 1, \cdots, t$$

and that the degrees of freedom are equal, i.e. we have

$$X_{i\tau} \sim W_{\mathbb{C}}(p_\tau, n, \Sigma_{1\tau}), \quad i = 1, \cdots, j-1$$

$$X_{j\tau} \sim W_{\mathbb{C}}(p_\tau, n, \Sigma_{j\tau}).$$

Then, the likelihood ratio test statistic for testing

$$H_{0,j} : \Sigma_{j\tau} = \Sigma_{(j-1)\tau} \text{ against } H_{1,j} : \Sigma_{j\tau} \neq \Sigma_{(j-1)\tau}$$

is

$$R_{j\tau} = \frac{j^{jp_\tau n}}{(j-1)^{(j-1)p_\tau n}} \frac{\left( \det \left( X_{1\tau} + \cdots + X_{(j-1)\tau} \right) \right)^{(j-1)n} (\det X_{j\tau})^n}{(\det (X_{1\tau} + \cdots + X_{j\tau}))^{jn}}.$$

Since $p = p_1 + \cdots + p_t$, we get

$$\prod_{\tau=1}^{t} \frac{j^{jp_\tau n}}{(j-1)^{(j-1)p_\tau n}} = \frac{j^{jpn}}{(j-1)^{(j-1)pn}}.$$

With this, we can now state

THEOREM 2.11.– *We consider the criterion*

$$R_j = \prod_{\tau=1}^{t} R_{j\tau}$$

$$= \frac{j^{jpn}}{(j-1)^{(j-1)pn}} \prod_{\tau=1}^{t} \frac{\left(\det\left(\mathbf{X}_{1\tau} + \cdots + \mathbf{X}_{(j-1)\tau}\right)\right)^{(j-1)n}(\det\mathbf{X}_{j\tau})^n}{(\det\left(\mathbf{X}_{1\tau} + \cdots + \mathbf{X}_{j\tau}\right))^{jn}}$$

$$= \left\{ \frac{j^{jp}}{(j-1)^{(j-1)p}} \frac{\left(\det\left(\mathbf{X}_1 + \cdots + \mathbf{X}_{j-1}\right)\right)^{j-1}\det\mathbf{X}_j}{(\det\left(\mathbf{X}_1 + \cdots + \mathbf{X}_j\right))^j} \right\}^n$$

*and define*

$$g = \sum_{\tau=1}^{t} p_\tau^2$$

$$\rho_j = 1 - \frac{1}{6gn}(1 + \frac{1}{j(j-1)}) \sum_{\tau=1}^{t} p_\tau(2p_\tau^2 - 1)$$

$$\omega_{2,j} = -\frac{g}{4}\left(1 - \frac{1}{\rho_j}\right)^2 + \frac{1}{24n^2\rho_j^2}\left(1 + \frac{2j-1}{j^2(j-1)^2}\right) \sum_{\tau=1}^{t} p_\tau^2(p_\tau^2 - 1).$$

*Then*

$$P\{-2\rho_j\log R_j \leqslant z\} \cong P\{\chi^2(g) \leqslant z\}$$
$$+ \omega_{2,j}\left[P\{\chi^2(g+4) \leqslant z\} - P\{\chi^2(g) \leqslant z\}\right].$$

PROOF.– See Conradsen *et al.* (2021).

## 2.2.4. *The Loewner order*

Let $C_p$ denote the set of all $p \times p$ complex matrices, $H_p$ denote the subset of Hermitian matrices, and let $H_p^{\geqslant}$ and $H_p^{>}$ denote the subsets of positive semidefinite and positive definite Hermitian matrices, respectively. For matrices $X$, $Y \in C_p$, we define the Loewner ordering by

$$Y \leqslant_L X \Leftrightarrow X - Y \in H_p^{\geqslant}$$

i.e. $Y$ is below $X$ in the Loewner ordering if and only if $X - Y$ is positive semidefinite. This implies that

$$\lambda_i(Y) \leqslant \lambda_i(X), \; i = 1, \cdots, p,$$

where $\lambda_1(Z) \geqslant \cdots \geqslant \lambda_p(Z)$ are the ordered (real) eigenvalues of the matrix $Z$. We say that $Y$ is strictly below $X$ ($Y <_L X \Leftrightarrow X - Y \in H_p^{>}$) if $X - Y$ is positive definite. The relation $\leqslant_L$ is a *partial ordering*, i.e.

1) *reflexive* ($X \leqslant_L X$ for all $X$);

2) *antisymmetric* ($X \leqslant_L Y$ and $Y \leqslant_L X$ implies $X = Y$); and

3) *transitive* ($X \leqslant_L Y$ and $Y \leqslant_L Z$ implies $X \leqslant_L Z$).

It is, however, not a *total ordering*, i.e. there exist matrices $X$, $Y \in H_p^{\geqslant}$ for which neither $X \leqslant_L Y$ nor $Y \leqslant_L X$ is true. In this case, $X - Y$ will be indefinite.

An important property is that for any $X$, $Y \in H_p^{>}$, we have

$$Y \leqslant_L X \Leftrightarrow X^{-1} \leqslant_L Y^{-1},$$

i.e. the Loewner order is *antitonic* with respect to matrix inversion.

## 2.3. The basic change detection algorithm

We now assume that we have observations taken at time points $t_1 < \cdots < t_k$ corresponding to distributions characterized by the parameters $\Sigma_1, \cdots, \Sigma_k$. The basic idea in our change detection algorithm is that we start by testing whether all $\Sigma_j$ parameters may be assumed to be equal. If this hypothesis is accepted, we conclude that no changes have taken place in the time interval $[t_1, \cdots, t_k]$. If the hypothesis is rejected, we conclude that a change has taken place. We identify the interval with the first change by successively testing equality with all the previous parameters until the first reject at, say, test number $g - 1$, i.e. we successively conclude

$$\Sigma_2 = \Sigma_1,$$

$$\Sigma_3 = \Sigma_2 (= \Sigma_1),$$

$$\vdots$$

$$\Sigma_{g-1} = \Sigma_{g-2} (= \Sigma_{g-3} = \cdots = \Sigma_1),$$

$$\Sigma_g \neq \Sigma_{g-1}.$$

Assuming that the last hypothesis is the first reject, we conclude that the first change occurs in the interval $[t_{g-1}, t_g]$. If the first $g - 1$ parameters $\Sigma_1, \cdots, \Sigma_{g-1}$ are equal, the statistics for testing the equalities will be independent (according to Theorem 2.8) and their product will be the test statistic for testing equality of the first $g - 1$ parameters. A possible first change in the interval $[t_g, t_k]$ is now identified similarly by considering similar tests between the parameters $\Sigma_g, \cdots, \Sigma_k$ and so on.

In order to formalize this, we introduce the global hypothesis that the last $k - \ell + 1$ parameters are equal, i.e. the parameters from time point no $\ell$ (which is $t_\ell$) are equal:

$$H_0^{(\ell)} : \Sigma_\ell = \cdots = \Sigma_k, \ \ell = 1, \cdots, k - 1$$

and the pairwise hypothesis

$$H_{0,j}^{(\ell)} : \Sigma_{\ell+j-1} = \Sigma_{\ell+j-2} \left(= \Sigma_{\ell+j-3} = \cdots = \Sigma_\ell\right), \ j = 2, \cdots, k - \ell + 1$$

where, in setting up each test statistic, we use the fact that the previous tests have been accepted.

COROLLARY 2.2.– *The likelihood ratio criterion for testing* $H_0^{(\ell)}$ *against all alternatives is*

$$Q^{(\ell)} = \left\{ (k - \ell + 1)^{p(k-\ell+1)} \frac{(\det X_\ell) \cdots (\det X_k)}{(\det(X_\ell + \cdots + X_k))^{k-\ell+1}} \right\}^n.$$

*For*

$$f^{(\ell)} = (k - \ell) \sum_{\tau=1}^{t} p_\tau^2$$

$$\rho^{(\ell)} = 1 - \frac{1}{6f} \left( \frac{k - \ell + 1}{n} - \frac{1}{n(k - \ell + 1)} \right) \sum_{\tau=1}^{t} p_\tau (2p_\tau^2 - 1)$$

$$\omega_2^{(\ell)} = -\frac{f}{4} \left( 1 - \frac{1}{\rho} \right)^2$$

$$+ \frac{1}{24\rho^2} \left( \frac{k - \ell + 1}{n^2} - \frac{1}{(n(k - \ell + 1))^2} \right) \sum_{\tau=1}^{t} p_\tau^2 (p_\tau^2 - 1)$$

*we have*

$$P\left\{-2\rho^{(\ell)}\log Q^{(\ell)} \leqslant z\right\} \cong P\left\{\chi^2(f^{(\ell)}) \leqslant z\right\}$$
$$+ \omega_2 \left[P\left\{\chi^2(f^{(\ell)} + 4) \leqslant z\right\} - P\left\{\chi^2(f^{(\ell)}) \leqslant z\right\}\right].$$

COROLLARY 2.3.– *For $j = 2, \cdots, k - \ell + 1$, we consider the criterion for testing* $H_{0,j}^{(\ell)}$

$$R_j^{(\ell)} = \left\{\frac{j^{jp}}{(j-1)^{(j-1)p}} \frac{(\det{(X_\ell + \cdots + X_{\ell+j-2})})^{(j-1)}\det X_{\ell+j-1}}{(\det{(X_\ell + \cdots + X_{\ell+j-1})})^j}\right\}^n$$

*and define*

$$g = \sum_{\tau=1}^{t} p_\tau^2$$

$$\rho_j = 1 - \frac{1}{6gn}\left(1 + \frac{1}{j(j-1)}\right)\sum_{\tau=1}^{t} p_\tau(2p_\tau^2 - 1)$$

$$\omega_{2,j} = -\frac{g}{4}\left(1 - \frac{1}{\rho_j}\right)^2 + \frac{1}{24n^2\rho_j^2}\left(1 + \frac{2j-1}{j^2(j-1)^2}\right)\sum_{\tau=1}^{t} p_\tau^2(p_\tau^2 - 1).$$

*Then*

$$P\left\{-2\rho_j \log R_j^{(\ell)} \leqslant z\right\} \cong P\left\{\chi^2(g) \leqslant z\right\}$$
$$+ \omega_{2,j}\left[P\left\{\chi^2(g+4) \leqslant z\right\} - P\left\{\chi^2(g) \leqslant z\right\}\right].$$

*Let $q_{obs}^{(\ell)}$ and $r_{j,obs}^{(\ell)}$ be the observed values of $Q^{(\ell)}$ and $R_j^{(\ell)}$. Then, the p-values for the hypotheses are $P\left\{Q^{(\ell)} < q_{obs}^{(\ell)}\right\}$ and $P\left\{R_j^{(\ell)} < r_{j,obs}^{(\ell)}\right\}$.*

## 2.4. Applications

Applications of the methods described here may be found for example in references Conradsen *et al.* (2003, 2014, 2016), Schou *et al.* (2003), Muro *et al.* (2016), Canty and Nielsen (2017), Canty *et al.* (2020), Nielsen *et al.* (2015, 2017a, 2017b, 2017c, 2019, 2020) and Nielsen (2019). We have categorized applications under three major headings: visualization of changes, fieldwise changes and directional changes, which will be illustrated in the following three sections.

| $H_{0,j}^{(\ell)}$ | $\ell$ | $1$ | $\vdots$ | $g$ | $\vdots$ | $i$ | $\vdots$ | $m$ |
|---|---|---|---|---|---|---|---|---|
| | $H_0^{(\ell)}$ | $\Sigma_1 = \cdots = \Sigma_k$ | $\vdots$ | $\Sigma_g = \cdots = \Sigma_k$ | $\vdots$ | $\Sigma_i = \cdots = \Sigma_k$ | $\vdots$ | $\Sigma_m = \cdots = \Sigma_k$ |
| | $P\left\{Q^{(\ell)} < q_{obs}^{(\ell)}\right\}$ | $p_{obs} < \alpha$ | $\vdots$ | $p_{obs} < \alpha$ | $\vdots$ | $p_{obs} < \alpha$ | $\vdots$ | $p_{obs} < \alpha$ |
| | $j$ | $P\left\{R_j^{(1)} < r_{j,obs}\right\}$ | $\vdots$ | $P\left\{R_j^{(g)} < r_{j,obs}\right\}$ | $\vdots$ | $P\left\{R_j^{(i)} < r_{j,obs}\right\}$ | $\vdots$ | $P\left\{R_j^{(m)} < r_{j,obs}^{(m)}\right\}$ |
| $\Sigma_2 = \Sigma_1$ | $2$ | $p_{obs} \geq \alpha$ | | | | | | |
| $\Sigma_3 = \Sigma_2$ | $3$ | $p_{obs} \geq \alpha$ | | | | | | |
| $\cdots$ | $\cdots$ | $\cdots$ | | | | | | |
| $\Sigma_g = \Sigma_{g-1}$ | $g$ | $p_{obs} < \alpha$ | | | | | | |
| $\Sigma_{g+1} = \Sigma_g$ | $2$ | | | $p_{obs} \geq \alpha$ | | | | |
| $\Sigma_{g+2} = \Sigma_{g+1}$ | $3$ | | | $p_{obs} \geq \alpha$ | | | | |
| $\cdots$ | $\cdots$ | | $\vdots$ | $\cdots$ | | | | |
| $\Sigma_i = \Sigma_{i-1}$ | $i - g + 1$ | | $\vdots$ | $p_{obs} < \alpha$ | $\vdots$ | | | |
| $\Sigma_{i+1} = \Sigma_i$ | $2$ | | | | $\vdots$ | $p_{obs} \geq \alpha$ | | |
| $\Sigma_{i+2} = \Sigma_{i+1}$ | $3$ | | | | | $p_{obs} \geq \alpha$ | | |
| $\cdots$ | $\cdots$ | | | | $\vdots$ | $\cdots$ | $\vdots$ | |
| $\Sigma_m = \Sigma_{m-1}$ | $m - i + 1$ | | | | | $p_{obs} < \alpha$ | $\vdots$ | |
| $\Sigma_{m+1} = \Sigma_m$ | $2$ | | | | | | $\vdots$ | $p_{obs} \geq \alpha$ |
| $\Sigma_{m+2} = \Sigma_{m+1}$ | $3$ | | | | | | $\vdots$ | $p_{obs} \geq \alpha$ |
| $\cdots$ | $\cdots$ | | | | | | | $\cdots$ |

**Table 2.1.** *Table summarizing the p-values obtained, i.e. the probabilities of getting more extreme values of the test statistics than the observed outcome, given that the hypothesis is true. Here $p_{obs} \geq \alpha$, respectively, $p_{obs} < \alpha$ indicates that the observed p-values $P\left\{Q^{(\ell)} < q_{obs}^{(\ell)}\right\}$ or $P\left\{R_j^{(\ell)} < r_{j,obs}^{(\ell)}\right\}$ are, respectively, bigger than or smaller than the level of significance $\alpha$. We have it that $p_{obs} \geq \alpha$ corresponds to acceptance and $p_{obs} \geq \alpha$ to rejection of the hypothesis. Only the values in red boxes need to be computed. The values are obtained sequentially: first, we compute the p-value $P\left\{Q^{(1)} < q_{obs}^{(1)}\right\}$ corresponding to the first global hypothesis $H_0^{(1)}$. Assuming that this is rejected, we sequentially find the p-values $P\left\{R_j^{(1)} < r_{j,obs}^{(1)}\right\}, j = 1, \cdots, g-1$, corresponding to the pairwise hypothesis $H_{0,j}^{(1)}$, where g is defined by the fact that we have the first reject $(\Sigma_g \neq \Sigma_{g-1})$. With terms from the block diagram, this identifies the new $\ell$ as $\ell_{new} = \ell_{old} + r = 1 + (g - 1) = g$. If a global hypothesis is accepted, the search for new change points ends. For a color version of this table, see www.iste.co.uk/atto/change1.zip*

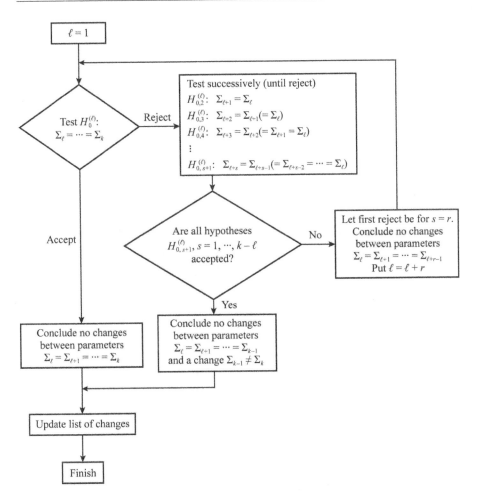

**Figure 2.8.** *Flowchart for the change detection algorithm. In the left part, we are investigating whether there are changes in the interval $[t_\ell, t_k]$ using the test statistic $Q^{(\ell)}$. If the answer is no, the analysis is finished. If the answer is yes, we have at least one change in $[t_\ell, t_k]$, and we go to the middle part of the diagram. Based on observations at $t_\ell, \cdots, t_{\ell+s}$ (i.e. $X_\ell, \cdots, X_{\ell+s}$), for $s = 1, \cdots, k - \ell$ we successively (until first reject at, say, $s = r$) investigate whether there are changes between time points $t_{\ell+s-1}$ and $t_{\ell+s}$. This is done by the test statistics $R_j^{(\ell)}$. As mentioned, we assume that the first reject we identify in $[t_\ell, t_k]$ corresponds to $s = r$. We conclude that there are no changes in $[t_\ell, t_{\ell+r-1}]$, and that there is a change in $[t_{\ell+r-1}, t_{\ell+r}]$ or – expressed in parameters – $\Sigma_\ell = \cdots = \Sigma_{\ell+r-1}$ and $\Sigma_{\ell+r-1} \neq \Sigma_{\ell+r}$. We update $\ell$ to $\ell + r$ and start again in the leftmost part. If we do not identify any changes before time point $t_{k-1}$, we conclude that the change in $[t_\ell, t_k]$ falls in the interval $[t_{k-1}, t_k]$*

### 2.4.1. *Visualizing changes*

The SAR data used in this and the next section were acquired by the fully polarimetric Danish airborne SAR system EMISAR, which operates at C-band (5.3 GHz/5.7 cm wavelength) and L-band (1.25 GHz/24 cm wavelength). The nominal one-look spatial resolution is 2 m × 2 m, the ground range swath is approximately 12 km, and typical incidence angles range from 35° to 60°, see (Madsen *et al.* 1991; Christensen *et al.* 1998). Figure 2.9 shows RGB images of diagonal elements of the L-band SAR data acquired in 1998 over a Danish agricultural test site on March 21, April 17, May 20, June 16, July 15 and August 16. In Conradsen *et al.* (2003, 2016), we show many detailed analyses on bitemporal and multitemporal change detection using these data.

**Figure 2.9.** *RGB images of diagonal elements of L-band SAR data acquired in 1998 over a Danish agricultural test site on March 21, April 17, May 20, June 16, July 15 and August 16. (Top row, from left to right: March, April and May. Bottom row, from left to right: June, July and August). For a color version of this figure, see www.iste.co.uk/ atto/change1.zip*

A straightforward visualization of the change detection analyses is shown in Figure 2.10. Here, we present the values of $-2\rho \log q_{obs}$ to the left and $1 - P\{Q > q_{obs} \mid H_0\}$, i.e. one minus the *p*-value to the right. However, this plot is not very useful if we are interested in the temporal dynamics: When are changes occurring, how many changes do we have, etc. Some solutions to this are presented in Nielsen *et al.* (2017c), and some of the possibilities are given in Figure 2.11. From left to right, we show an illustration of when the first change is detected, when the last (most recent) change is detected, and the frequency of changes detected. The last image is a false color composite showing changes in the 1., 3. and the 5. time intervals as red, green and blue, respectively.

**Figure 2.10.** *Left: the values of the likelihood ratio test statistic for the omnibus hypothesis "Mar=Apr=May=Jun=Jul=Aug". Right: (one minus the p-value) for the omnibus test. A dark area corresponds to a high p-value, i.e. acceptance of the hypothesis of no change. The "connected" black areas are mainly forest or (to the northwest) a lake*

### 2.4.2. *Fieldwise change detection*

Often one will know the geographical extent of individual fields, either *a priori* or after a clustering/segmentation. In such cases, the change index for a field may be defined by first considering the empirical distributions of the $P\left\{Q^{(l)} < q^{(l)}\right\}$-values and $P\left\{R_j^{(l)} < r_j^{(l)}\right\}$-values and then applying the one-pixel definition on suitable measures of location for those distributions such as, for example, mean or median. We show the histograms of the $p$-values $P\{Q^{(1)} < q_{obs}^{(1)}\}$ and $P\{R_j^{(1)} < r_{j,obs}^{(1)}\}$ for a forested area (top) and for a rye field (bottom) in Figure 2.12.

The global test for forest concludes that there are no changes in the sequence of data. This is confirmed by looking at the intermediate hypotheses (which we normally would not compute since the omnibus test of no change is accepted). We see that the distributions of the $p$-values are not uniform. They all have larger probabilities for values below 0.5, i.e. there is a preponderance of small ($\sim$ extreme) values of the test statistic, meaning that we see more rejects or near rejects than we would under the assumption of no changes. This is in accordance with Figure 2.10, where the black area is not homogeneously black, but filled with scattered white pixels.

**Figure 2.11.** *The first image shows when the first detected change occurred. In this and the subsequent images black (0) means no change over the time span. Here, 1 means the first change occurred between $t_1$ and $t_2$, and so on. No change occurred in wooded regions and most of the lake to the north-west. The second image shows when the last/most recently detected change occurred. 1 means the last change occurred between $t_1$ and $t_2$, and so on. The third image shows the number of changes/change frequency. The fourth image shows changes from $t_1$ to $t_2$ as red, from $t_3$ to $t_4$ as green and from $t_5$ to $t_6$ as blue. From (Nielsen et al. 2017c). For a color version of this figure, see www.iste.co.uk/atto/change1.zip*

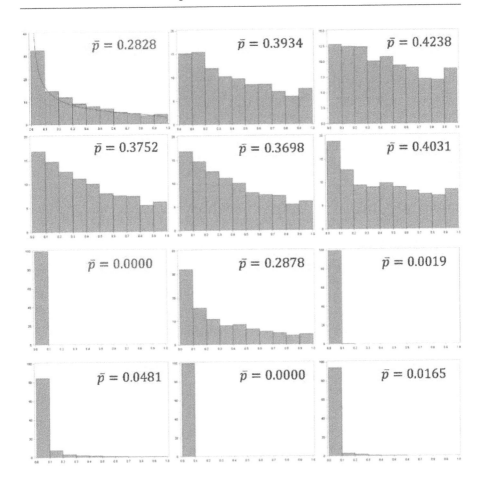

$\bar{p} = 0.2828$

$\bar{p} = 0.3934$

$\bar{p} = 0.4238$

$\bar{p} = 0.3752$

$\bar{p} = 0.3698$

$\bar{p} = 0.4031$

$\bar{p} = 0.0000$

$\bar{p} = 0.2878$

$\bar{p} = 0.0019$

$\bar{p} = 0.0481$

$\bar{p} = 0.0000$

$\bar{p} = 0.0165$

**Figure 2.12.** *Histograms for intermediate p-values for areas covered with forest (top) and with rye (bottom). The p-values depicted are $P\{Q^{(1)} < q_{obs}^{(1)}\}$ and $P\{R_j^{(1)} < r_{j,obs}^{(1)}\}$ for $j = 1, 2, 3, 4, 5$ corresponding to testing the global hypothesis "Mar=Apr=May= Jun=Jul=Aug" and the marginal hypotheses "Apr=Mar", "May=Apr(=Mar)", "Jun= May(=Apr=Mar)", "Jul=Jun(=May=Apr=Mar)" and "Aug=Jul(=Jun=May=Apr=Mar)". The average p-value is inserted in the upper right corner of each histogram. For a color version of this figure, see www.iste.co.uk/atto/change1.zip*

For rye, the global hypothesis is strongly rejected since the average $p$-value is 0.0000. The first intermediate hypothesis "Apr=Mar" is accepted; however, the second intermediate hypothesis "May=Apr(=Mar)" is rejected, since the average $p$-value is 0.0019. Normally, the last three histograms would not be computed. Instead, we would conclude that we have a change between May and April, and we would continue with the next iteration testing the second global hypothesis "May=Jun=Jul=Aug". The tests we must make in order to assess the change structure are given in Table 2.2. The column under $\ell = 1$ corresponds to the six rye-histograms shown in Figure 2.12, the remaining are calculated similarly. We conclude that there are three changes: between May and April, between June and July, and between July and August. This corresponds well with the growing stages of rye. Tillering starts in April, and until then the height is negligible. With the booting in May, the height increases to around 60 cm and the growth increases to around 110 cm in the flowering stage in June. With the ripening in July, the height decreases to around 90 cm, and after harvesting in August the height is of course negligible.

| $\ell$ | | 1 | 3 | 5 |
|---|---|---|---|---|
| $H_0^{(\ell)}$ | | "Mar=Apr=May= Jun=Jul=Aug" | "May=Jun= Jul=Aug" | "Jul=Aug" |
| $P\left\{Q^{(\ell)} < q_{obs}^{(\ell)}\right\}$ | | 0.000000 | 0.000277 | 0.0003457 |
| $H_{0,j}^{(\ell)}$ | $j$ | $P\left\{R_j^{(1)} < r_{j,obs}^{(1)}\right\}$ | $P\left\{R_j^{(3)} < r_{j,obs}^{(3)}\right\}$ | $P\left\{R_j^{(5)} < r_{j,obs}^{(5)}\right\}$ |
| "Apr=Mar" | 2 | 0.287795 | | |
| "May=Apr(=Mar)" | 3 | 0.001938 | | |
| "Jun=May" | 2 | | 0.355445 | |
| "Jul=Jun(=May)" | 3 | | 0.004676 | |
| "Aug=Jul" | 2 | | | 0.003457 |

**Table 2.2.** *The average p-values used in determining points of change for a rye field. The table is constructed like Table 2.1, but using average p-values instead of pixelwise p-values. The values in the column corresponding to $\ell = 1$ correspond to the histogram averages in Figure 2.11. For a color version of this table, see www.iste. co.uk/atto/change1.zip*

### 2.4.3. *Directional changes using the Loewner ordering*

When monitoring changes in a one-dimensional signal, the most natural question to raise when a change has been detected is: has the signal value increased or decreased? This question has no immediate, simple answer when the signal is a complex valued Hermitian matrix following a complex Wishart distribution. However, we are, of course, interested in looking into whether the radar response increases, decreases or changes structure from one time point to the other. Nielsen *et al.* (2020) present a solution to this problem, namely, replacing the usual ordering of real numbers with the Loewner ordering between the matrix valued signal values. In practice, we compute the difference between observations where a change has been detected, and determine whether the difference is positive definite, negative definite or indefinite. If the difference is definite, it is meaningful to consider a "direction" of change, if it is indefinite, we conclude that the change has a nature that is not detectable with the Loewner order.

In the following, we present cases from Canty *et al.* (2020) and Nielsen *et al.* (2020) in order to illustrate the potential of the concepts. For a more thorough description of the cases, we will refer to the original papers.

In the first case from Nielsen *et al.* (2020), we consider a zoomed-in view from two 12-look polarimetric Radarsat-2 images over Bonn, Germany. The scenes were acquired on August 29 and October 16, 2009 and have 500 rows by 650 columns of 20.5 m pixels. In Figure 2.13, top, the data are shown in the Pauli presentation (red is $|S_{hh} - S_{vv}|^2$, green is $|S_{hv} + S_{vh}|^2$, and blue is $|S_{hh} + S_{vv}|^2$). The middle row shows the test statistic and the thresholded $p$-value. The final row shows the definiteness of the matrix difference. The structures in the middle are two moving dredging arms in the lake at Quarzwerke Witterschlick. We clearly see that where we have red pixels "something" (e.g. a dredging arm) is present at time point one and not at time point two, and where we have green pixels "something" is present at time point two and not at time point one. The few yellow pixels correspond to changes with indefinite matrix differences.

The second case stems from Canty *et al.* (2020). In part due to the refugee crisis in the Mediterranean and also because of political instability, ports along the coast of Libya have been the subject of recent attention, many of them having been closed periodically to international traffic. Arrivals and departures of large sea vessels are easily recorded with the algorithm, as can be seen, for example, in Figure 2.14 for the port of Tripoli. Positive definite significant differences (arrivals) are in red, and negative definite differences (departures) in green. The port of Benghazi, for example, was closed in the first part of 2017, reopening on October 5, 2017. This is confirmed in the chart of Figure 2.15.

As another illustration of harbor activities, effects of the 2020 Covid-19 lockdown, starting in early March, are illustrated in Figure 2.16 by the changes at the main shipping docks in Venice, Italy.

Cyclone Idai, recorded as the worst weather-based event to ever occur in the Southern Hemisphere, made landfall near the city of Beira, Mozambique on March 15, 2019, causing widespread inundation in Mozambique and Tanzania and a death toll of more than 1,300. Figure 2.17 shows a sequence of six change maps generated with a GEE time series of Sentinel-1a and Sentinel-1b images. The reduction of backscatter from the flooded areas in both the VV and VH bands corresponds to a negative definite covariance matrix difference (green pixels, center left), the rapid receding of flood waters and hence increased backscatter due to the appearance of the original terrain to a positive definite change (red pixels, center right).

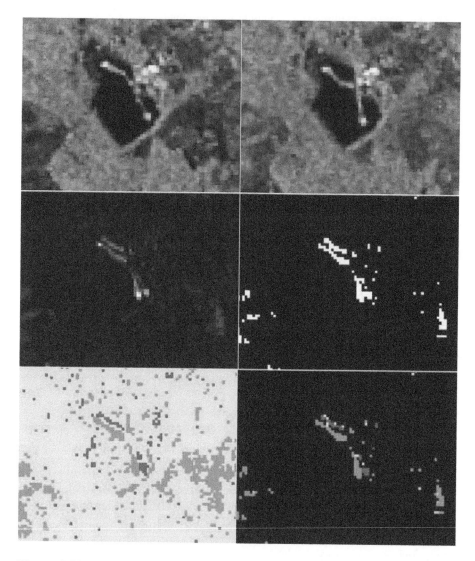

**Figure 2.13.** *(Top) Zoomed-in views of Radarsat-2 images showing two moving dredging arms. (Middle left) Test statistic ($-2 \log Q$) for change detected between the two time points. High values, i.e. bright pixels, indicate change. (Middle right) Associated $p$-value thresholded at 99.9999%. (Bottom left) In this example, positive definite matrix differences (present at time point one) in red, negative definite matrix differences (present at time point two) in green and indefinite matrix differences in yellow. (Bottom right) Same combination where the $p$-values in the test are larger than 99.9999%. From (Nielsen et al. 2020). For a color version of this figure, see www.iste.co.uk/atto/change1.zip*

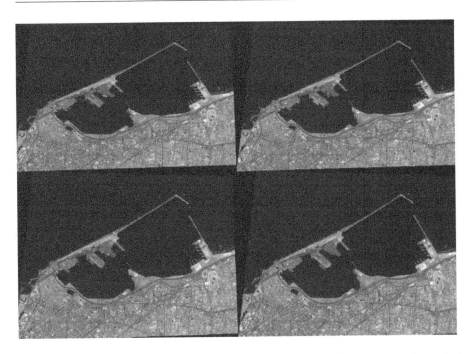

**Figure 2.14.** *Port of Tripoli: First four change maps of a total of 68 covering the period May 7, 2018 through June 7, 2019 at six-day intervals. The background is a Sentinel-2 image acquired within the time interval. Changes are shown for a multi-polygon region of interest chosen to exclude noise from water surfaces. The color indicates the Loewner order, in this example, red means positive definite (present at time point two) and green means negative definite (present at time point one). For a color version of this figure, see www.iste.co.uk/atto/change1.zip*

In a similar vein, the Don river in South Yorkshire, England, overflowed its banks in November 2019, causing widespread flooding. The newly inundated areas are clearly seen in the change image on the left hand side of Figure 2.18. Receding floodwaters then cause the positive definite changes in the right hand image.

Finally, Figure 2.19 shows change fractions over a growing season for canola in Manitoba, Canada. The peaks correspond to spring and early summer growth and late summer harvesting.

### 2.4.4. *Software availability*

Software for sequential SAR change detection is available in MATLAB and on GitHub in Python.

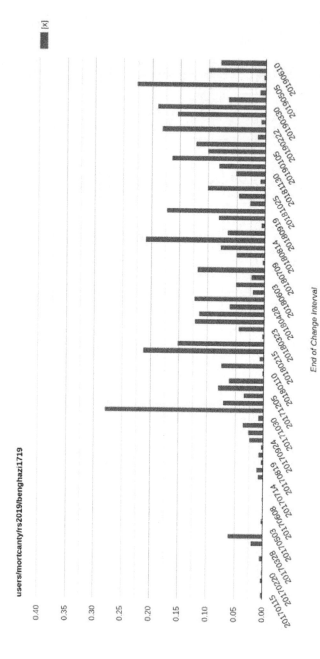

**Figure 2.15.** *Fraction of positive definite changes (vessel arrivals) at the main docks of the port of Benghazi, January 2017 through June 2019. For a color version of this figure, see www.iste.co.uk/atto/change1.zip*

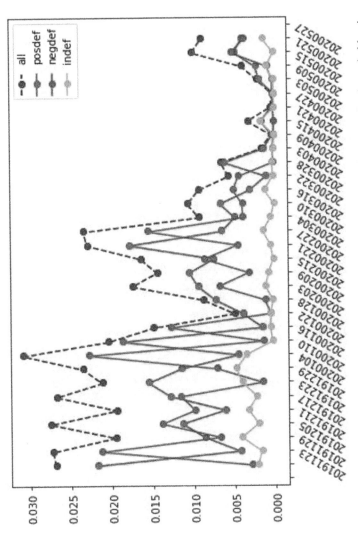

**Figure 2.16.** *Change fractions showing effects of the 2020 Covid-19 lockdown starting in early March, main shipping docks in Venice, Italy. For a color version of this figure, see www.iste.co.uk/atto/change1.zip*

**Figure 2.17.** *Buzi district, Mozambique: Six change maps of a total of 15 for 16 images covering the period January 1, 2019 through June 7, 2019. Each image has an area of approximately 3,000 km². The gray scale background is the temporal average of the VV band of all 16 images. The maps, read top to bottom, left to right, are for the intervals April 18 to March 2, March 2–14, March 14–20, March 20–26, March 26 to April 1 and April 1–7. Positive definite changes are red, negative definite changes are green, and indefinite changes are yellow. For a color version of this figure, see www.iste.co.uk/atto/change1.zip*

**Figure 2.18.** *Change images for the region around Fishlake, South Yorkshire. Left: November 5–11, 2019. Right: November 17–23. Positive definite changes are red, negative definite changes are green and indefinite changes are yellow. For a color version of this figure, see www.iste.co.uk/atto/change1.zip*

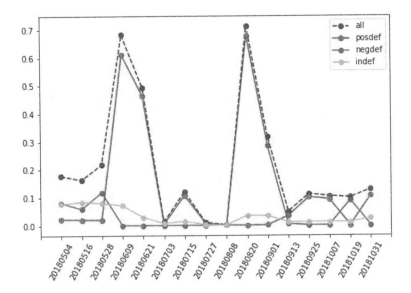

**Figure 2.19.** *Change fractions over the 2018 growing season for agricultural fields (canola) near Winnipeg, Manitoba. For a color version of this figure, see www.iste.co.uk/atto/change1.zip*

MATLAB code for datasets where input and results are stored in memory is available at https://people.compute.dtu.dk/alan/software.html.

The Python implementation (https://mortcanty.github.io/EESARDocker/) is written specifically against the Google Earth Engine (GEE) Python API and is intended to be run as a Docker container serving Jupyter notebooks to the user's local browser. The pre-built Docker image can be pulled and run directly from Dockerhub and is platform-independent. Since the algorithm runs on the Google servers, the client-side requirements are slight and a Raspberry Pi image is also available. Installation instructions are included in the Github ReadMe file. The Jupyter notebook included with the software displays a simple and convenient graphical interface allowing easy data exploration of the entire GEE Sentinel-1 archive, together with the previewing of change results. Provision is also made for processing the user's own image collections, for example, Radarsat-2 quad pol or Sentinel-1 full dual pol data. Change maps can be exported to the user's assets on the GEE code editor or to their Google Drive.

## 2.5. References

Akbari, V., Anfinsen, S.N., Doulgeris, A.P., Eltoft, T., Moser, G., Serpico, S.B. (2016). Polarimetric SAR change detection with the complex Hotelling–Lawley trace statistic. *IEEE Transactions on Geoscience and Remote Sensing*, 54(7), 3953–3966.

Canty, M.J. (2019). *Image Analysis, Classification and Change Detection in Remote Sensing, with Algorithms for Python*, 4th revised edition. Taylor & Francis, CRC Press, Boca Raton.

Canty, M.J. and Nielsen, A.A. (2017). Spatio-temporal analysis of change with Sentinel imagery on the Google Earth Engine. *ESA Conference on Big Data from Space (BiDS)*, 126–129.

Canty, M.J., Nielsen, A.A., Conradsen, K., Skriver, H. (2020). Statistical analysis of changes in Sentinel-1 time series on the Google Earth Engine. *Remote Sensing*, 12(46), 1–16.

Christensen, E.L., Skou, N., Dall, J., Woelders, K., Jørgensen, J.H., Granholm, J., Madsen, S.N. (1998). EMISAR: An absolutely calibrated polarimetric L- and C-band SAR. *IEEE Transactions on Geoscience and Remote Sensing*, 36, 1852–1865.

Conradsen, K., Nielsen, A.A., Schou, J., Skriver, H. (2003). A test statistic in the complex Wishart distribution and its application to change detection in polarimetric SAR data. *IEEE Transactions on Geoscience and Remote Sensing*, 41(1), 4–19.

Conradsen, K., Nielsen, A.A., Skriver, H. (2014). Change detection in polarimetric SAR data over several time points. *IEEE International Geoscience and Remote Sensing Symposium (IGARSS)*, 4540–4543, Quebec City, Canada, 13–18 July.

Conradsen, K., Nielsen, A.A., Skriver, H. (2016). Determining the points of change in time series of polarimetric SAR data. *IEEE Transactions on Geoscience and Remote Sensing*, 54(5), 3007–3024.

Conradsen, K., Nielsen, A.A., Skriver, H. (2021). Omnibus change detection in block diagonal covariance matrix polSAR data from Sentinel-1 and Radarsat-2. Research Report. Submitted.

Madsen, S.N., Christensen, E.L., Skou, N., Dall, J. (1991). The Danish SAR system: Design and initial tests. *IEEE Transactions on Geoscience and Remote Sensing*, 29, 417–426.

Muro, J.M., Canty, M.J., Conradsen., K., Hüttich, C., Nielsen, A.A., Skriver, H., Remy, F., Strauch, A., Thonfeld, F., Menz, G. (2016). Short-term change detection in wetlands using Sentinel-1 time series. *Remote Sensing*, 8(10), 795.

Nascimento, A.D.C., Frery, A.C., Cintra, R.J. (2019). Detecting changes in fully polarimetric SAR imagery with statistical information theory. *IEEE Transactions on Geoscience and Remote Sensing*, 57(3), 1380–1392.

Nielsen, A.A. (2019). Fast matrix based computation of eigenvalues and the Loewner order in PolSAR data. *IEEE Geoscience and Remote Sensing Letters (Early Access)*, 1–5.

Nielsen, A.A., Conradsen, K., Skriver, H. (2015). Change detection in full and dual polarization, single- and multi-frequency SAR data. *IEEE Journal of Selected Topics in Applied Earth Observations and Remote Sensing*, 8(8), 4041–4048.

Nielsen, A.A., Canty, M.J., Skriver, H., Conradsen, K. (2017a). Change detection in multi-temporal dual polarization Sentinel-1 data. *IEEE International Geoscience and Remote Sensing Symposium (IGARSS)*, Fort Worth, USA, 23–28 July.

Nielsen, A.A., Conradsen, K., Skriver, H. (2017b). Corrections to "Change detection in full and dual polarization, single- and multi-frequency SAR data". *IEEE Journal of Selected Topics in Applied Earth Observations and Remote Sensing*, 10(11), 5143–5144.

Nielsen, A.A., Conradsen, K., Skriver, H., Canty, M.J. (2017c). Visualization of and software for omnibus test based change detected in a time series of polarimetric SAR data. *Canadian Journal of Remote Sensing*, 43(6), 582–592.

Nielsen, A.A., Canty, M.J., Skriver, H., Conradsen, K. (2019). Cloud based spatio-temporal analysis of change in sequences of Sentinel images. *ESA Conference on Big Data from Space (BiDS)*, 105–108, Munich, Germany, 19–21 February.

Nielsen, A.A., Skriver, H., Conradsen, K. (2020). The Loewner order and direction of detected change in Sentinel-1 and Radarsat-2 data. *IEEE Geoscience and Remote Sensing Letters*, 17(2), 242–246.

Schou, J., Skriver, H., Nielsen, A.A., Conradsen, K. (2003). CFAR edge detector for polarimetric SAR images. *IEEE Transactions on Geoscience and Remote Sensing*, 41(1), 20–32.

# 3

# An Overview of Covariance-based Change Detection Methodologies in Multivariate SAR Image Time Series

Ammar MIAN[1,2], Guillaume GINOLHAC[2], Jean-Philippe OVARLEZ[3], Arnaud BRELOY[4] and Frédéric PASCAL[1]

[1] CentraleSupélec, Paris-Saclay University, Gif-sur-Yvette, France
[2] University Savoie Mont Blanc, Annecy, France
[3] ONERA, Palaiseau, France
[4] Paris Nanterre University, France

## 3.1. Introduction

Change detection (CD) for remotely sensed images of the Earth has been a popular subject of study in the past decades. It has indeed attracted a plethora of scholars due to the various applications, in both military (activity monitoring) and civil (geophysics, disaster assessment, etc.) contexts. With the increase in the number of spatial missions with embedded synthetic aperture radar (SAR) sensors, the amount of readily available observations has now reached the "big data" era. To efficiently process and analyze this data, automatic algorithms therefore have to be developed. Notably, CD algorithms have been thoroughly investigated: the literature on the subject is dense, and a variety of methodologies can be envisioned[1].

---

1. See Hussain *et al.* (2013) or Hecheltjen *et al.* (2014, pp. 145–178) for overviews.

*Change Detection and Image Time Series Analysis 1*,
coordinated by Abdourrahmane M. ATTO, Francesca BOVOLO and Lorenzo BRUZZONE.
© ISTE Ltd 2021.

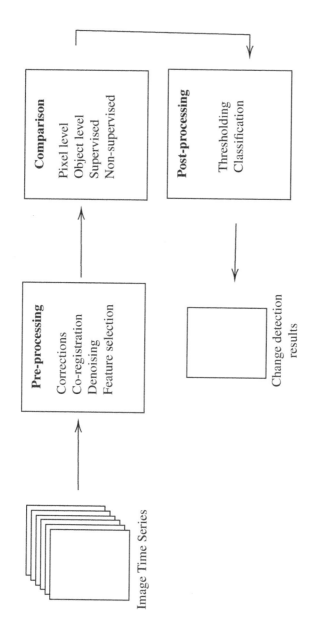

**Figure 3.1.** *General procedure for a change detection methodology*

Broadly speaking, a change detection algorithm can be synthesized as in Figure 3.1, and it relies on three main separate elements:

– a pre-processing phase, in which the time series of images have to be co-registered, meaning that a geometric transformation is applied so that each pixel of every image corresponds to the same physical localization. Various methodologies also considered a denoising step in which the speckle noise is reduced thanks to filtering techniques (Achim *et al.* 2003; Foucher and Lopez-Martinez 2014). Finally, local features can be selected to obtain a more concise (or descriptive) representation of the data. Among others, some possibilities include wavelet decompositions (Mian *et al.* 2017, 2019b), Markov fields (Wang *et al.* 2013) or principal component analysis (Yousif and Ban 2013);

– a comparison step, in which the selected features from each date are compared among themselves. This step consists of building a relevant distance to measure the dissimilarities of the features. Depending on the feature space, many principles (geometry, statistics, etc.) generally exist to choose/build this distance;

– a post-processing step, which varies depending on the methodology used for the comparison step. It can either correspond to a thresholding (Bruzzone and Prieto 2000; Kervrann and Boulanger 2006) or involve machine learning classification algorithms (Gong *et al.* 2016).

In this large context, this chapter proposes an overview of the comparison step methodologies based on the local covariance matrices of the multivariate pixels. The scope of this overview can thus be specified by the following remarks:

– the focus is put on unsupervised CD methodologies. The CD problem is indeed challenging due to the lack of available ground truths, which does not allow applying supervised methods from the image processing literature. Moreover, it is well known that SAR images are subjected to speckle noise, which makes traditional optical approaches prone to high false alarm rates. In this case, unsupervised methodologies, often based on statistical tools, have yielded interesting approaches;

– we consider multivariate pixels, where the channels can correspond to a polarimetric diversity, or another kind of diversity depending on the pre-processing. The main example will be the spectro-angular diversity, obtained through wavelet transforms (Mian *et al.* 2019b);

– the presented methodologies are *pixel-level*, as opposed to *object-level* methodologies (Hussain *et al.* 2013). In this paradigm, the comparison is done on a local spatial neighborhood (patches) through the principle of the sliding windows: for each pixel, a spatial neighborhood is defined and a distance function is computed to compare the similarities of this neighborhood between the images at different times;

– we consider statistical parametric methodologies, as opposed to non-parametric methodologies (Aiazzi *et al.* 2013; Prendes *et al.* 2015). Hence, the CD process will rely on a probability model and its associated parameters. Within this methodology, the covariance matrix of the local patches will be considered as a main feature to infer the changes in the time series.

The covariance-based approach has been a popular subject of study thanks to seminal work Conradsen *et al.* (2001), which demonstrated its use for CD in multivariate SAR image time series (ITS). One of its main interests is notably the possibility to leverage well-established results from the statistical literature, which is why numerous works consequently followed such an approach. Our aim is therefore to present a general overview of this topic, as well as recent developments considering the choice of statistical models, the dissimilarity measure and the use of structured covariance matrices.

The rest of this chapter is organized as follows. Section 3.2 describes the dataset and the different scenes used to illustrate the performance of the change detectors[2]. Section 3.3 introduces several families of elliptical distributions (and associated parameters) that can be used to model multivariate SAR images. Section 3.4 details several dissimilarity functions based on covariance matrices, which are then compared for CD on the considered datasets. Section 3.5 presents an extension of a statistical detection methodology that allows us to account for low-rank structures in the covariance matrix, whose interest is also illustrated on the real dataset. Finally, section 3.6 draws the conclusions and perspectives of this study.

## 3.2. Dataset description

We consider three SAR ITS datasets from UAVSAR (courtesy of NASA/JPL-Caltech). The two first scenes are displayed, respectively, in Figures 3.2 (four images) and 3.3 (two images). The CD ground truths for these scenes are collected from Ratha *et al.* (2017) and Nascimento *et al.* (2019) and are shown in Figures 3.5. The third scene, displayed in Figure 3.4, is referenced under label Snjoaq_14511 and corresponds to a series of $T = 17$ images. The ground truth has been realized by the present authors. The SAR images correspond to full-polarization data with a resolution of 1.67 m in range and 0.6 m in azimuth. Since the scatterers present in the scenes exhibit an interesting spectro-angular behavior, each polarization of these images can be subject to the wavelet transform from Mian *et al.* (2019b), yielding pixels of dimension $p = 12$ (only used in the last section). Table 3.1 gives an overall perspective of the scenes used in the study.

---

2. The codes (in Python 3.7) for all the change detectors are available at: https://github.com/AmmarMian/WCCM-2019 for section 3.4, and at: https://github.com/AmmarMian/Robust-Low-Rank-CD for section 3.4. The datasets can be obtained from the UAVSAR website (https://uavsar.jpl.nasa.gov) using the labels given, and the ground truth may be obtained from the author's website: https://ammarmian.github.io/.

| Dataset | Url | Resolution | Scene | $p$ | $T$ | Size | Coordinates (top-left px) |
|---|---|---|---|---|---|---|---|
| UAVSAR SanAnd_26524_03 Segment 4 April 23, 2009 - May 15, 2011 | https://uavsar.jpl.nasa.gov | Rg: 1.67m Az: 0.6m | Scene 1 | 3 or 12 | 2 or 4 | 2360 × 600 px | [Rg, Az] = [2891, 28891] |
| | | | Scene 2 | 3 or 12 | 2 | 2300 × 600 px | [Rg, Az] = [3236,25601] |
| Snjoaq_14511 | | | Scene 3 | 3 | 17 | 2300 × 600 px | [Rg, Az] = [3236,25601] |

**Table 3.1.** *Description of SAR data*

## 3.3. Statistical modeling of SAR images

### 3.3.1. *The data*

Denote by $\mathbb{W} = \{\mathbf{X}_1, \ldots, \mathbf{X}_T\}$ a collection of $T$ mutually independent groups of $p$-dimensional i.i.d complex vectors: $\mathbf{X}_t = [\mathbf{x}_1^t, \ldots, \mathbf{x}_N^t] \in \mathbb{C}^{p \times N}$. With regard to the single look complex (SLC) SAR images, these sets correspond to the local observations in spatially sliding windows, as illustrated in Figure 3.6. The subscript $k$ corresponds to a spatial index, while the superscript $t$ corresponds to a time index.

### 3.3.2. *Gaussian model*

The centered complex Gaussian distribution is the most encountered one in the SAR literature, notably for modeling polarimetric images. Indeed, since each pixel consists of the coherent sum of the contribution of many scatterers, it is expected that, thanks to the central limit theorem, the Gaussian model is not too far from the actual empirical distribution. A random vector $\mathbf{x} \in \mathbb{C}^p$ is said to be distributed along the complex Gaussian distribution (which we denote $x \sim \mathbb{C}\mathcal{N}$) if its probability density function (p.d.f) is:

$$p_{\mathbf{x}}^{\mathbb{C}\mathcal{N}}(\mathbf{x}; \boldsymbol{\Sigma}) = \frac{1}{\pi^p |\boldsymbol{\Sigma}|} \exp(-\mathbf{x}^H \boldsymbol{\Sigma}^{-1} \mathbf{x}) \qquad [3.1]$$

When we have a dataset $\{\mathbf{x}_k\}_{k \in [1,N]}$ of i.i.d. data, the maximum likelihood estimator (MLE) of the covariance matrix is the well-known sample covariance matrix estimator (SCM):

$$\hat{\boldsymbol{\Sigma}} = \frac{1}{N} \sum_{k=1}^{N} \mathbf{x}_k \mathbf{x}_k^H \qquad [3.2]$$

This estimate matrix obtained through data averaging is assumed to be Wishart distributed as a consequence. In our time series configuration, the statistical model for the pixels on a sliding window is:

$$\mathbf{x}_k^t \sim \mathcal{CN}(\mathbf{0}_p, \boldsymbol{\Sigma}_t) \qquad [3.3]$$

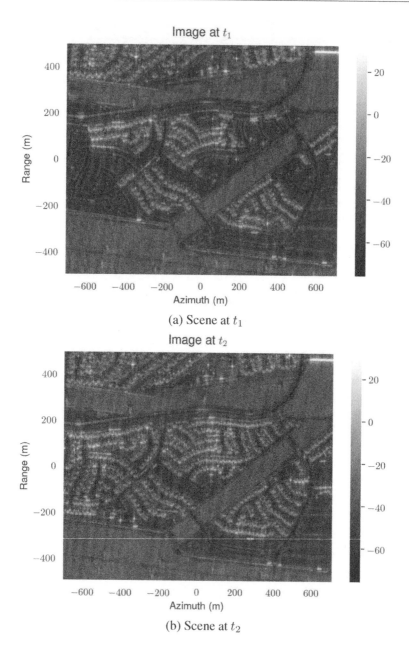

(a) Scene at $t_1$

(b) Scene at $t_2$

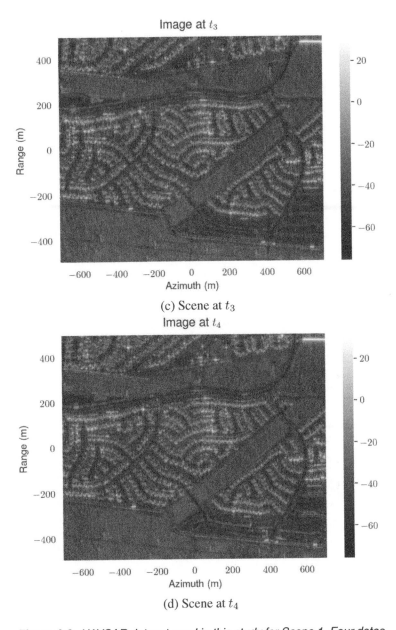

(c) Scene at $t_3$

(d) Scene at $t_4$

**Figure 3.2.** *UAVSAR dataset used in this study for Scene 1. Four dates are available between April 23, 2009, and May 15, 2011. For a color version of this figure, see www.iste.co.uk/atto/change1.zip*

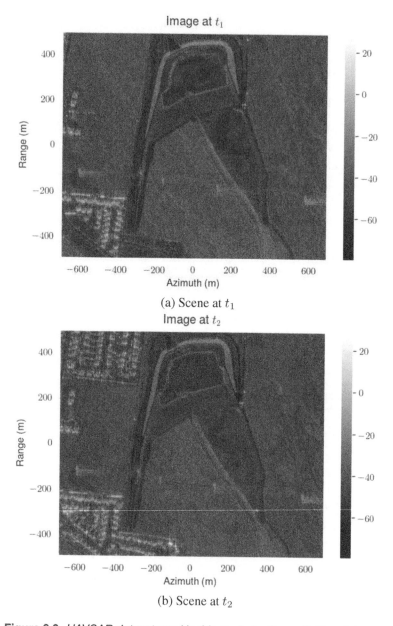

(a) Scene at $t_1$

(b) Scene at $t_2$

**Figure 3.3.** *UAVSAR dataset used in this study for Scene 2. Two dates are available between April 23, 2009, and May 15, 2011. For a color version of this figure, see www.iste.co.uk/atto/change1.zip*

**Figure 3.4.** *UAVSAR dataset used in this study for Scene 3*

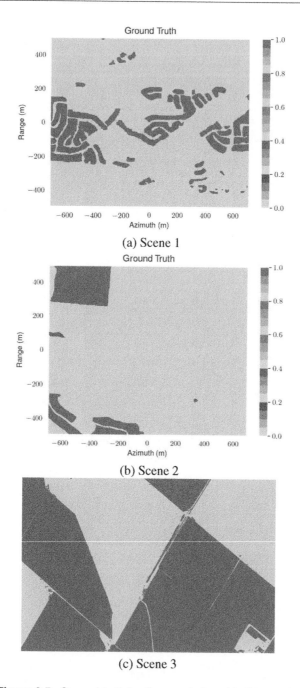

(a) Scene 1

(b) Scene 2

(c) Scene 3

**Figure 3.5.** *Ground truth for Scenes 1, 2 and 3. For a color version of this figure, see www.iste.co.uk/atto/change1.zip*

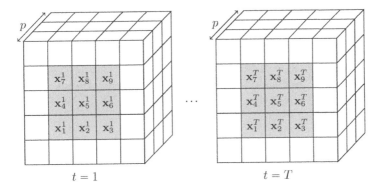

**Figure 3.6.** *Illustration of the sliding windows (in gray) approach*
$(p = 3, N = 9)$. *The central pixel* $(x_5^t)$ *corresponds to the test pixel*

### 3.3.3. *Non-Gaussian modeling*

While the Gaussian distribution is popular, it fails to accurately describe the heterogeneity observed in very high-resolution images, as described in Greco and Gini (2007), Gao (2010) and Ollila *et al.* (2012b). Indeed, in those images, the amount of scatterers in each pixel has been greatly reduced with regard to low-resolution images.

To better describe the observed distribution of data, other models have been considered. For example, the K-distribution has been considered in Yueh *et al.* (1989) and Muller (1994), the Weibull distribution in Bucciarelli *et al.* (1995) or inverse generalized Gaussian distribution in Freitas *et al.* (2005). These various models belong to the family of complex elliptical symmetric (CES) distributions, which generalize them, as discussed in Ollila *et al.* (2012a), which is a model depending on a density generator function $g : \mathbb{R}^+ \to \mathbb{R}^+$ that satisfies the condition $\mathfrak{m}_{p,g} = \int_{\mathbb{R}^+} t^{p-1} g(t)\, dt < \infty$ and a positive definite matrix $\Xi \in \mathbb{S}_H^p$: a random vector $\mathbf{x} \in \mathbb{C}^p$ follows a complex elliptical distribution (denoted $\mathbf{x} \sim \mathbb{C}\mathcal{E}[\mathbf{0}_p][g][\Xi]$) if its p.d.f is the following:

$$p_{\mathbf{x}}^{\mathbb{C}\mathcal{E}}(\mathbf{x}; \Xi, g) = \mathfrak{C}_{p,g} \, |\Xi|^{-1} \, g\left(\mathbf{x}^H \, \Xi^{-1} \, \mathbf{x}\right), \qquad [3.4]$$

where $\mathfrak{C}_{p,g}$ is a normalization constraint ensuring that $\int_{\mathbb{C}^p} p_{\mathbf{x}}^{\mathbb{C}\mathcal{E}}(\mathbf{x}; \Xi, g) d\mathbf{x} = 1$. The MLE depends on the function $g$. For example, the $t$-distribution is also a particular case of the CES family, and in this case, $g$ is equal to:

$$g(t) = \left(1 + \frac{2\,t}{d}\right)^{-(2p+d)/2}, \qquad [3.5]$$

where $d$ is the degree of freedom of the distribution. For this distribution and when we have a dataset $\{\mathbf{x}_k\}_{k \in [1,N]}$ of i.i.d. data, the MLE of the covariance matrix is the result of the following fixed-point equation:

$$\hat{\Sigma}_{student} = \frac{d+p}{N} \sum_{k=1}^{N} \frac{\mathbf{x}_k \, \mathbf{x}_k^H}{d + \mathbf{x}_k^H \, \hat{\Sigma}_{student}^{-1} \, \mathbf{x}_k} \qquad [3.6]$$

Another representation of those distributions can be found through the compound Gaussian model, sometimes referred as the product model. In this case, a random vector $\mathbf{x}$ follows a complex compound Gaussian (CCG) distribution if:

$$\mathbf{x} = \sqrt{\tau} \, \mathbf{z}, \qquad [3.7]$$

where $\mathbf{z} \sim \mathbb{CN}(\mathbf{0}_p, \Sigma)$, called the speckle, and $\tau$, called the texture, follow a distribution probability on $\mathbb{R}^+$. This quantity is often assumed to be deterministic in order to generalize the Gaussian distribution, without having to consider a model on the texture. For this distribution and when we have a dataset $\{\mathbf{x}_k\}_{k \in [1,N]}$ of i.i.d. data, the MLE of the covariance matrix is the result of the following fixed-point equation:

$$\hat{\Sigma}_{tyl} = \frac{p}{N} \sum_{k=1}^{N} \frac{\mathbf{x}_k \, \mathbf{x}_k^H}{\mathbf{x}_k^H \, \hat{\Sigma}_{tyl}^{-1} \, \mathbf{x}_k} \qquad [3.8]$$

In our time series configuration, the statistical model for the pixels in a sliding window is written as:

$$\mathbf{x}_k^t \sim \sqrt{\tau_k^t} \, \mathbf{z}_k^t, \qquad [3.9]$$

where $\tau_k^t \in \mathbb{R}^+$ is deterministic and $\mathbf{z}_k^t \sim \mathbb{CN}(\mathbf{0}_p, \Sigma_t)$.

The elliptical and CCG distributions are probability models in the scope of the robust statistical literature initiated by works such as Yohai (1974), Maronna (1976) and Martin and Pierre (2000). More details can be found in the works by Maronna *et al.* (2006) and Zoubir *et al.* (2018). Following their definition, a method is said to be robust, in this chapter's context, when its statistical properties are independent of the density generator function in the elliptical case or independent of the set of texture parameters for the deterministic CCG case.

Using these various models, we will describe, hereafter, various dissimilarity measures for those models, which can be used for change detection.

## 3.4. Dissimilarity measures

### 3.4.1. *Problem formulation*

Under a parametric approach, CD can be achieved by deciding between the two following alternative hypotheses:

$$\begin{cases} \mathrm{H}_0 : \boldsymbol{\theta}_1 = \ldots = \boldsymbol{\theta}_T = \boldsymbol{\theta}_0 \ (\text{no change}) \\ \mathrm{H}_1 : \exists (t, t'), \, \boldsymbol{\theta}_t \neq \boldsymbol{\theta}_{t'} \quad (\text{change}) \end{cases}, \qquad [3.10]$$

where $\theta$ corresponds to the parameters of the distribution used as a model.

In order to decide, a dissimilarity measure between the data over time is needed. It can be seen as a function, also called statistic:

$$\hat{\Lambda} : \begin{matrix} \mathbb{C}^{p \times N \times T} \longrightarrow \mathbb{R} \\ \mathbb{W} \qquad \longrightarrow \hat{\Lambda}(\mathbb{W}), \end{matrix}$$

such that $\hat{\Lambda}(\mathbb{W})$ is high when $H_1$ is true and low otherwise.

An interesting property of such a function is the constant false alarm rate (CFAR) property. This property is valid when the distribution of the statistic under the $H_0$ hypothesis is not a function of the parameters of the problem. This allows the selection of a threshold value for the detection which is directly linked to the probability of false alarm. The threshold is often obtained by deriving the distribution of the statistic, or can be obtained by Monte-Carlo simulations when it is not available.

### 3.4.2. *Hypothesis testing statistics*

The first kind of dissimilarity measures comes from the statistical literature on hypothesis testing. These functions, also known as test statistics, are obtained by adapting semi-closed formulas to the problem of detection undertaken. Many of such formulas have been designed and studied in statistical literature, giving an insight into the expected distribution of the resulting statistic under null hypothesis. In some cases, the resulting statistic from different techniques can yield statistically equivalent tests, as shown in Ciuonzo *et al.* (2017).

Among those possibles techniques, we recall here, under the problem formulation from [3.10], the most well-known ones:

- **Generalized likelihood ratio test (GLRT):**

$$\hat{\Lambda} = \frac{\displaystyle\max_{[\boldsymbol{\theta}_1,\dots,\boldsymbol{\theta}_T]} p_{\mathbb{W}_{1,T}}\left(\mathbb{W}_{1,T} / H_1; \boldsymbol{\theta}_1,\dots,\boldsymbol{\theta}_T\right)}{\displaystyle\max_{\boldsymbol{\theta}_0} p_{\mathbb{W}_{1,T}}\left(\mathbb{W}_{1,T} / H_0; \boldsymbol{\theta}_0\right)} \underset{H_0}{\overset{H_1}{\gtrless}} \lambda. \qquad [3.11]$$

- **Terell gradient statistic:**

$$\lambda_{\text{grad}} = \left. \frac{\partial \log p_{\mathbb{W}_{1,T}}\left(\mathbb{W}_{1,T}/H_1; \boldsymbol{\theta}_1,\dots,\boldsymbol{\theta}_T\right)}{\partial \boldsymbol{\theta}^T} \right|_{\boldsymbol{\theta}=\hat{\boldsymbol{\theta}}_0} (\hat{\boldsymbol{\theta}}_1 - \hat{\boldsymbol{\theta}}_0) \underset{H_0}{\overset{H_1}{\gtrless}} \lambda. \qquad [3.12]$$

- **Wald statistic:**

$$\lambda_{\text{Wald}} = (\hat{\boldsymbol{\theta}}_1 - \boldsymbol{\theta}_0)^T \left( \left[ \mathbf{I}^{-1}(\hat{\boldsymbol{\theta}}_1) \right]_{\boldsymbol{\theta}} \right)^{-1} (\hat{\boldsymbol{\theta}}_1 - \boldsymbol{\theta}_0) \underset{H_0}{\overset{H_1}{\gtrless}} \lambda, \qquad [3.13]$$

where $\mathbf{I}(\boldsymbol{\theta})$ is the Fisher information matrix of the problem of estimation under the $H_1$ hypothesis.

### 3.4.2.1. *Gaussian assumption*

Under Gaussian assumption, the derivation of the GLRT has the following expression:

$$
\hat{\Lambda}_{G} = \frac{\left|\hat{\Sigma}_{0}^{SCM}\right|^{TN}}{\prod_{t=1}^{T}\left|\hat{\Sigma}_{t}^{SCM}\right|^{N}},
\tag{3.14}
$$

where:

$$
\forall t, \hat{\Sigma}_{t}^{SCM} = \frac{1}{N}\sum_{k=1}^{N} \mathbf{x}_{k}^{t}\mathbf{x}_{k}^{t\,H} \text{ and } \hat{\Sigma}_{0}^{SCM} = \frac{1}{T}\sum_{t=1}^{T}\hat{\Sigma}_{t}^{SCM}.
\tag{3.15}
$$

This statistic is well known in the literature, and its properties have been well studied. Anderson (2003) has derived the distribution under the null hypothesis and proposed an approximation as a function of $\chi^2$ distributions, only depending on the parameters $p$, $T$ and $N$. Therefore, this statistic has the CFAR property.

Concerning the Terell gradient statistic, it has been shown in Ciuonzo *et al.* (2017) that its form is statistically equivalent to the following reduced expression:

$$
\hat{\Lambda}_{t_1} = \frac{1}{T}\sum_{t=1}^{T} \text{Tr}\left[\left(\left(\hat{\Sigma}_{0}^{SCM}\right)^{-1}\hat{\Sigma}_{t}^{SCM}\right)^{2}\right].
\tag{3.16}
$$

This statistic has the CFAR property and has a $\chi^2$ asymptotic distribution (when $N \to \infty$).

Finally, the Wald statistic yields the following result:

$$
\hat{\Lambda}_{Wald} = N\sum_{t=2}^{T} \text{Tr}\left[\left(\mathbf{I}_{p} - \hat{\Sigma}_{1}^{SCM}\left(\hat{\Sigma}_{t}^{SCM}\right)^{-1}\right)^{2}\right]
$$
$$
- q\left(N\sum_{t=1}^{T}\left(\hat{\Sigma}_{t}^{SCM}\right)^{-\dagger} \otimes (\hat{\Sigma}_{t}^{SCM})^{-1}, \text{vec}\left(\sum_{t=2}^{T}\Upsilon_{t}\right)\right),
\tag{3.17}
$$

where † is the transpose operator,

$$
q(\mathbf{x}, \Sigma) = \mathbf{x}^{H}\Sigma^{-1}\mathbf{x},
\tag{3.18}
$$

and where

$$
\Upsilon_{t} = N\left((\hat{\Sigma}_{t}^{SCM})^{-1} - (\hat{\Sigma}_{t}^{SCM})^{-1}\hat{\Sigma}_{1}^{SCM}(\hat{\Sigma}_{t}^{SCM})^{-1}\right).
\tag{3.19}
$$

This statistic has the CFAR property and has a $\chi^2$ asymptotic distribution (when $N \to \infty$). It is, however, computationally more complex than the previous ones due to the Kroenecker product.

### 3.4.2.2. *Non-Gaussian assumption*

Concerning non-Gaussian models, Mian *et al.* (2019a) have considered the derivation of the GLRT using the compound Gaussian model with deterministic texture parameters:

$$
\hat{\Lambda}_{\mathrm{MT}} = \frac{\left|\hat{\Sigma}_0^{\mathrm{MT}}\right|^{TN}}{\prod\limits_{t=1}^{T}\left|\hat{\Sigma}_{\mathbb{W}_t}^{\mathrm{TE}}\right|^{N}} \prod_{k=1}^{N} \frac{\left(\sum\limits_{t=1}^{T} q\left(\hat{\Sigma}_0^{\mathrm{MT}}, \mathbf{x}_k^t\right)\right)^{Tp}}{T^{Tp}\prod\limits_{t=1}^{T}\left(q\left(\hat{\Sigma}_{\mathbb{W}_t}^{\mathrm{TE}}, \mathbf{x}_k^t\right)\right)^{p}}, \qquad [3.20]
$$

where $\mathbb{W}_t = \{\mathbf{x}_k^t : 1 \leqslant k \leqslant N\}$ and $\hat{\Sigma}_{\mathbb{W}_t}^{\mathrm{TE}}$ is defined in [3.8] and

$$
\hat{\Sigma}_0^{\mathrm{MT}} = \frac{p}{N} \sum_{k=1}^{N} \frac{\sum\limits_{t=1}^{T} \mathbf{x}_k^t \left(\mathbf{x}_k^t\right)^{H}}{\sum\limits_{t=1}^{T} q\left(\hat{\Sigma}_0^{\mathrm{MT}}, \mathbf{x}_k^t\right)}, \qquad [3.21]
$$

where $q(\Sigma, \mathbf{x})$ is defined in [3.18].

This statistic has been shown to have better robustness to very heterogeneous data for which the Gaussian model is very far. This comes, however, at a cost of complexity. Indeed, there is a need to compute the solution of two fixed-point equations, which is computationally expensive. The statistic has the CFAR property, but the distribution under null hypothesis has not yet been derived.

The derivation of the Terell gradient and Wald statistics under this non-Gaussian model has not been considered yet and remains an open problem.

### 3.4.3. *Information-theoretic measures*

Information theory tools are based on another approach, which consists of measuring quantities related to the information at disposition on the data. In order to compare two distributions, distances can be computed. When a parametric model is used, the distance is often dependent on the parameters of the two distributions compared. Since the parameters are not known in many applications, estimates are plugged into the distance function.

The Kullback–Leibler (KL) divergence is a popular measure between probability density functions, encountered notably in SAR change detection problems (Inglada and Mercier 2007). It is defined as:

$$
d\left(p_{\mathbf{X}}, p_{\mathbf{Y}}\right) = E\left[\log\left\{\frac{p_{\mathbf{X}}(\mathbf{x})}{p_{\mathbf{Y}}(\mathbf{x})}\right\}\right] = \int_{\mathbb{C}^p} p_{\mathbf{X}}(\mathbf{x}) \log\left\{\frac{p_{\mathbf{X}}(\mathbf{x})}{p_{\mathbf{Y}}(\mathbf{x})}\right\} d\mathbf{x} \qquad [3.22]
$$

For two zero-mean multivariate Gaussian distributions, it leads to:

$$d_{\text{KL}}\left(\boldsymbol{\Sigma}_1, \boldsymbol{\Sigma}_2\right) = d\left(p_{\mathbf{X}}, p_{\mathbf{Y}}\right) = \frac{1}{2}\left(\text{Tr}\left(\boldsymbol{\Sigma}_1^{-1}\boldsymbol{\Sigma}_2\right) + \log\left(\frac{|\boldsymbol{\Sigma}_1|}{|\boldsymbol{\Sigma}_2|}\right)\right) \qquad [3.23]$$

For the Gaussian case, a statistical test can be defined through the symmetrized version of the divergence (J-Divergence) between the two covariance matrix estimates:

$$\hat{\Lambda}_{\text{KL}} = \frac{1}{2}\left(d_{\text{KL}}\left(\hat{\boldsymbol{\Sigma}}_0^{\text{SCM}}, \hat{\boldsymbol{\Sigma}}_1^{\text{SCM}}\right) + d_{\text{KL}}\left(\hat{\boldsymbol{\Sigma}}_1^{\text{SCM}}, \hat{\boldsymbol{\Sigma}}_0^{\text{SCM}}\right)\right), \qquad [3.24]$$

Frery *et al.* (2014) have shown that this statistic is asymptotically distributed as a $\chi^2$ distribution.

Other measures include Renyi entropy or Bhattacharya distance, which have been shown to behave similarly in Frery *et al.* (2014). They will thus be omitted in this chapter. An alternative complex Hotelling–Lawley statistic has been proposed by Akbari *et al.* (2016) for the case $T = 2$. The distance used is given by:

$$\hat{\Lambda}_{\text{HTL}} = \text{Tr}\left((\hat{\boldsymbol{\Sigma}}_0^{\text{SCM}})^{-1} \hat{\boldsymbol{\Sigma}}_1^{\text{SCM}}\right). \qquad [3.25]$$

The authors also derived the distribution under null hypothesis and showed that it can be approximated by a Fisher–Snedecor distribution. The study showed a potential improvement of detection rate compared to the GLRT statistic.

For a non-Gaussian model, Liu *et al.* (2014) proposed a measure for $T = 2$, based on the principle of mutual information. The proposed approach assumes a scenario where the pixels have been averaged on a small window of size $L$ to reduce the speckle noise, before performing the change detection (multi-look scenario). The distance, based on a gamma model on the texture parameters, is a generalization of the one proposed in Beaulieu and Touzi (2004):

$$\hat{\Lambda}_{\text{MLL}} = \text{MLL}(\mathbb{W}_1) + \text{MLL}(\mathbb{W}_2) - \text{MLL}(\mathbb{W}_{12}), \qquad [3.26]$$

with $\mathbb{W}_{12} = \mathbb{W}_1 \cup \mathbb{W}_2$ and where

$$\text{MLL}(\mathbb{W}) = N\frac{\nu + pL}{2}\left(\log(L\nu) - \log(\mu)\right) - NL\log\left|\boldsymbol{\Sigma}_{\mathbb{W}}^{\text{TE}}\right|$$

$$+ \frac{\nu - pL}{2}\sum_{\mathbf{x}_k^t \in \mathbb{W}} \log\left[\text{Tr}\left((\boldsymbol{\Sigma}_{\mathbb{W}}^{\text{TE}})^{-1}\mathbf{x}_k^t\,\mathbf{x}_k^{t\,H}\right)\right] - N\log|\Gamma(\nu)|$$

$$+ \sum_{\mathbf{x}_k^t \in \mathbb{W}} \log\left[K_{\nu - pL}\left(2\sqrt{\text{Tr}\left((\boldsymbol{\Sigma}_{\mathbb{W}}^{\text{TE}})^{-1}\mathbf{x}_k^t\,\mathbf{x}_k^{t\,H}\right)L\nu/\mu}\right)\right], \qquad [3.27]$$

where $\Gamma(.)$ is the Gamma function, $\boldsymbol{\Sigma}_{\mathbb{W}}^{\mathrm{TE}}$ is defined in equation [3.8], $K_\nu(z)$ is the modified Bessel function of the second kind and $(\mu, \nu)$ are the parameters of a Gamma distribution found by fitting the distribution of the texture parameters set

$$\mathcal{T} = \left\{ \hat{\tau}_k^t = q\left(\boldsymbol{\Sigma}_{\mathbb{W}}^{\mathrm{TE}}, \mathbf{x}_k^t\right) / p : \mathbf{x}_k^t \in \mathbb{W} \right\}. \tag{3.28}$$

The method used has a high computational cost, since the test statistic relies on a Bessel function, as well as a fitting of a Gamma distribution.

### 3.4.4. *Riemannian geometry distances*

Riemannian geometry is an alternative concept that allows us to compare distributions. Indeed, when the parameters of a distribution lie in a Riemannian manifold (e.g. covariance matrices lie in Riemannian manifold of positive definite matrices $\mathbb{S}_{\mathbb{H}}^p$ (Skovgaard 1984)), it is possible to define a metric, which can be related to the Kullback–Leibler divergence. Consequently, distances between two probability distributions, which take into account the geometry properties of the parameter space, have been considered in the literature. Notably, for a Gaussian model, we have the following distance (Smith 2005):

$$\hat{\Lambda}_{\mathcal{RE}} = \left\| \log\left( \left(\hat{\boldsymbol{\Sigma}}_1^{\mathrm{SCM}}\right)^{-\frac{1}{2}} \hat{\boldsymbol{\Sigma}}_2^{\mathrm{SCM}} \left(\hat{\boldsymbol{\Sigma}}_1^{\mathrm{SCM}}\right)^{-\frac{1}{2}} \right) \right\|_F^2, \tag{3.29}$$

where log is the logarithm of matrices, which for $\boldsymbol{\Sigma} \in \mathbb{S}_{\mathbb{H}}^p$, having the eigenvalue decomposition $\boldsymbol{\Sigma} = \mathbf{U} \boldsymbol{\Lambda} \mathbf{U}^{\mathrm{H}}$, is defined as follows:

$$\log(\boldsymbol{\Sigma}) = \mathbf{U} \log_{\odot}(\boldsymbol{\Lambda}) \mathbf{U}^{\mathrm{H}}, \tag{3.30}$$

where $\log_{\odot}$ is the pointwise logarithm.

For the elliptical case, a Riemannian CES distance can be obtained as well (Breloy *et al.* 2019):

$$\hat{\Lambda}_{\mathcal{RE}} = \alpha \sum_{i=1}^p \log^2 \lambda_i + \beta \left( \sum_{i=1}^p \log \lambda_i \right)^2, \tag{3.31}$$

where $\lambda_i$ is the $i$-th eigenvalue of $\left(\hat{\boldsymbol{\Sigma}}_1^{\mathrm{MLE}}\right)^{-1} \hat{\boldsymbol{\Sigma}}_2^{\mathrm{MLE}}$, $\hat{\boldsymbol{\Sigma}}_{\epsilon \in \{0,1\}}^{\mathrm{MLE}}$ is the MLE of the scatter matrix in CES case and $\alpha, \beta$ depend on the density generator function. For a Student's t distribution, we have:

$$\alpha = \frac{d+p}{d+p+1}, \beta = \alpha - 1, \tag{3.32}$$

and $\hat{\boldsymbol{\Sigma}}_\epsilon^{\mathrm{MLE}}$ is defined in equation [3.6].

The concept of Riemannian geometry has also been considered in Ratha *et al.* (2017), where a methodology has been proposed for polarimetric SAR images based on the Kennaugh matrix decomposition. This distance, however, is not based on a probability model and will thus be omitted in this chapter.

### 3.4.5. *Optimal transport*

Finally, a distance can be obtained through the concept of optimal transport, which defines a distance $d_W(.,.)$ depending on a cost to *displace* parts of a reference distribution into a target distribution. Let $p_{\mathbf{X}}(.)$ and $p_{\mathbf{Y}}(.)$ be two multivatiate distributions. Assuming a quadratic cost, the optimal transport problem can be stated as finding the joint distributions $p_{\mathbf{X},\mathbf{Y}}(.,.)$ to minimize:

$$d(p_{\mathbf{X}}, p_{\mathbf{Y}}) := \inf_{p_{\mathbf{X},\mathbf{Y}}(.,.) \geqslant 0} \left\{ E\left(\|\mathbf{X} - \mathbf{Y}\|^2\right) \mid \int_{\mathbf{x}} p_{\mathbf{X},\mathbf{Y}}(\mathbf{x}, \mathbf{y})\, d\mathbf{x} = p_{\mathbf{Y}}(\mathbf{y}), \right.$$

$$\left. \int_{\mathbf{y}} p_{\mathbf{X},\mathbf{Y}}(\mathbf{x}, \mathbf{y})\, d\mathbf{y} = p_{\mathbf{X}}(\mathbf{x}) \right\}. \tag{3.33}$$

It has been shown in Gelbrich (1990) that this distance has a closed form for Gaussian distributions, $\mathbf{X} \sim \mathcal{CN}(0, \boldsymbol{\Sigma}_1)$, $\mathbf{Y} \sim \mathcal{CN}(0, \boldsymbol{\Sigma}_2)$ and $E\left[\mathbf{X}\,\mathbf{Y}^H\right] = \mathbf{C}$. In that case, $E\left(\|\mathbf{X} - \mathbf{Y}\|^2\right) = \mathrm{Tr}\left(\boldsymbol{\Sigma}_1 + \boldsymbol{\Sigma}_2 - 2\,\mathbf{C}\right)$ and the problem remains to solve:

$$d(p_{\mathbf{X}}, p_{\mathbf{Y}}) = \min_{\mathbf{C}} \left\{ \mathrm{Tr}\left(\boldsymbol{\Sigma}_1 + \boldsymbol{\Sigma}_2 - 2\,\mathbf{C}\right) \mid \begin{bmatrix} \boldsymbol{\Sigma}_1 & \mathbf{C} \\ \mathbf{C}^H & \boldsymbol{\Sigma}_2 \end{bmatrix} \geqslant 0 \right\}, \tag{3.34}$$

which leads to $\mathbf{C} = \boldsymbol{\Sigma}_2^{-1/2}\left(\boldsymbol{\Sigma}_2^{1/2}\,\boldsymbol{\Sigma}_1\,\boldsymbol{\Sigma}_2^{1/2}\right)^{1/2}\boldsymbol{\Sigma}_2^{1/2}$. The final result leads to:

$$d_{\mathrm{W}}(\boldsymbol{\Sigma}_1, \boldsymbol{\Sigma}_2) = d(p_{\mathbf{X}}, p_{\mathbf{Y}}),$$

$$= \mathrm{Tr}\left(\boldsymbol{\Sigma}_1 + \boldsymbol{\Sigma}_2 - 2\left(\boldsymbol{\Sigma}_2^{1/2}\,\boldsymbol{\Sigma}_1\,\boldsymbol{\Sigma}_2^{1/2}\right)^{1/2}\right). \tag{3.35}$$

The corresponding optimal transport problem for two Gaussian distributions can be derived through a distance between two covariance matrices. Plugging estimates of the two covariance matrices leads to defining the associated Wasserstein statistic for Gaussian hypothesis:

$$\hat{\Lambda}_{\mathcal{WG}} = d_{\mathrm{W}}\left(\hat{\boldsymbol{\Sigma}}_1^{\mathrm{SCM}}, \hat{\boldsymbol{\Sigma}}_2^{\mathrm{SCM}}\right). \tag{3.36}$$

Thanks to this result, we can define a statistic elliptical case by plugging estimates of the covariance matrices. A Wasserstein statistic in the elliptical can be obtained by taking:

$$\hat{\Lambda}_{\mathcal{WE}} = d_{\mathrm{W}}\left(\hat{\tau}_1\,\hat{\boldsymbol{\Sigma}}_1^{\mathrm{TE}}, \hat{\tau}_2\,\hat{\boldsymbol{\Sigma}}_2^{\mathrm{TE}}\right), \tag{3.37}$$

where $\hat{\boldsymbol{\Sigma}}_{\epsilon\in\{0,1\}}^{TE}$ is defined in equation [3.21] and $\hat{\tau}_{\epsilon\in\{0,1\}} = \dfrac{p}{N} \displaystyle\sum_{k=1}^{N} q\left(\hat{\boldsymbol{\Sigma}}_\epsilon^{\mathrm{TE}}, \mathbf{x}_k^\epsilon\right)$.

| Statistic | Reference | Model | Equation | $T > 2$ | CFAR | Asymptotic null distribution |
|---|---|---|---|---|---|---|
| $\hat{\Lambda}_G$ | (Conradsen et al. 2001) | Gaussian | [3.14] | ✓ | ✓ | $\chi^2$ (asymptotic) |
| $\hat{\Lambda}_{t_1}$ | (Ciuonzo et al. 2017) | Gaussian | [3.16] | ✓ | ✓ | $\chi^2$ (asymptotic) |
| $\hat{\Lambda}_{\text{Wald}}$ | (Ciuonzo et al. 2017) | Gaussian | [3.17] | ✓ | ✓ | $\chi^2$ (asymptotic) |
| $\hat{\Lambda}_{\text{HTL}}$ | (Akbari et al. 2016) | Gaussian | [3.25] | × | ✓ | Fisher–Snedecor (approximation) |
| $\hat{\Lambda}_{\text{MT}}$ | (Mian et al. 2019a) | Deterministic CCG | [3.20] | ✓ | ✓ | × |
| $\hat{\Lambda}_{\text{KL}}$ | (Frery et al. 2014) | Gaussian | [3.24] | × | ✓ | $\chi^2$ (asymptotic) |
| $\hat{\Lambda}_{\text{MLL}}$ | (Liu et al. 2014) | Compound Gaussian | [3.26] | × | × | × |
| $\hat{\Lambda}_{\mathcal{RG}}$ | (Smith 2005) | Gaussian | [3.29] | × | × | × |
| $\hat{\Lambda}_{\mathcal{RE}}$ | (Breloy et al. 2019) | Student's t | [3.31] | × | × | × |
| $\hat{\Lambda}_{W\mathcal{G}}$ | (Ghaffari and Walker 2018) | Gaussian | [3.36] | × | × | × |
| $\hat{\Lambda}_{W\mathcal{E}}$ | (Ghaffari and Walker 2018) | Elliptical | [3.37] | × | × | × |

**Table 3.2.** *Summary of statistics with their respective properties*

### 3.4.6. Summary

A summary of the different statistics with their respective properties can be found in Table 3.2.

### 3.4.7. Results of change detectors on the UAVSAR dataset

We recall that the dataset and the scenes used are described in section 3.2. For Scene 1, we only use two dates (the first and fourth images) like for Scene 2. All of the dates of Scene 3 are considered in the tests.

The ROC (Receiver Operating Characteristic) for all statistics and the three scenes is presented in Figure 3.7. A transcription of the detection performance at $P_{\text{FA}} = 0.01$ is also given in Table 3.3.

The first observation that can be made is that $\hat{\Lambda}_{\text{MLL}}$ generally have poorer performance of detection than the other statistics. This is mostly explained by the fact that it has been developed for a scenario where the data is denoised through an averaging before change detection, which was not the case here. Thus, the statistic yields poorer detection performance than most of the other statistics.

The statistics obtained through the Wasserstein distance, $\hat{\Lambda}_{W\mathcal{G}}$ and $\hat{\Lambda}_{W\mathcal{E}}$, do not appear to work well for this CD problem, since the performance of detection compared to others distance is lower, especially for Scene 2.

For the case $T = 2$, considering the Gaussian-derived statistics $\hat{\Lambda}_G$, $\hat{\Lambda}_{t_1}$, $\hat{\Lambda}_{\text{KL}}$, $\hat{\Lambda}_{\text{HTL}}$ and $\hat{\Lambda}_{\mathcal{RG}}$, it is difficult to discern a best statistics since depending on the scene, their relative performance varies. When the number of images is high, $\hat{\Lambda}_{\text{Wald}}$ appears to be lower in all cases, but the performance of detection is not far. For $T > 2$, $\hat{\Lambda}_G$ seems to have better performance than its counterpart, but no conclusion can be made since only one set of data with $T > 2$ was available.

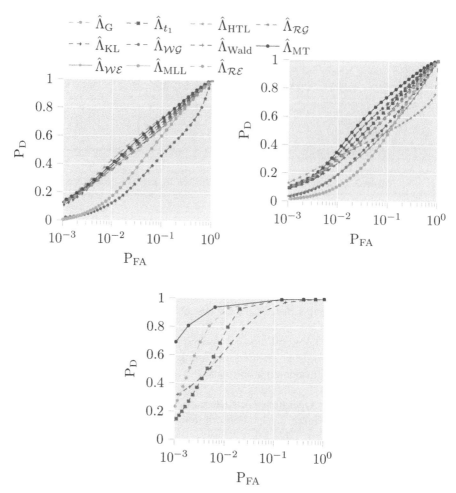

**Figure 3.7.** *ROC plots for a window size of* $5 \times 5$ *for the three scenes. Top: Scene 1; middle: Scene 2; bottom: Scene 3. For a color version of this figure, see www.iste.co.uk/atto/change1.zip*

| Statistic | $\hat{\Lambda}_G$ | $\hat{\Lambda}_{t_1}$ | $\hat{\Lambda}_{Wald}$ | $\hat{\Lambda}_{HTL}$ | $\hat{\Lambda}_{MT}$ | $\hat{\Lambda}_{KL}$ | $\hat{\Lambda}_{MLL}$ | $\hat{\Lambda}_{\mathcal{RG}}$ | $\hat{\Lambda}_{\mathcal{RE}}$ | $\hat{\Lambda}_{\mathcal{WG}}$ | $\hat{\Lambda}_{\mathcal{WE}}$ |
|---|---|---|---|---|---|---|---|---|---|---|---|
| Scene 1 | 0.41 | 0.41 | 0.35 | **0.43** | 0.41 | 0.40 | 0.18 | 0.41 | 0.39 | 0.12 | 0.36 |
| Scene 2 | 0.33 | 0.30 | 0.27 | 0.32 | **0.39** | 0.32 | 0.11 | 0.33 | 0.29 | 0.19 | 0.19 |
| Scene 3 | 0.90 | 0.75 | 0.62 | | **0.95** | | | | | | |

**Table 3.3.** *Probability of detection at a false alarm rate of 1%*

Finally, concerning robust statistics $\hat{\Lambda}_{MT}$ has the overall best performance for all scenes. In Scene 1, it has slightly lower performance than $\hat{\Lambda}_{HTL}$, but in the other scenes (especially Scene 3), the performance of detection is greatly improved. The gain of this statistic compared to the Gaussian one is explained by the heterogeneity of the images at the transition between objects. As an example, the outputs of both $\hat{\Lambda}_G$ and $\hat{\Lambda}_{MT}$ are presented in Figure 3.8. For this data, the Gaussian-derived statistic, which does not take into account the heterogeneity, yields a high value of the statistic at the transition between the fields while the CCG statistic does not, which constitutes a big improvement concerning false alarms. The natural Student's t statistic $\hat{\Lambda}_{W\mathcal{E}}$ does not have good performance of detection, which is explained by a mismatch in the degrees of freedom chosen to model the distribution of the data. Moreover, the Student's t model can be inaccurate when modeling the actual data. In those regards, $\hat{\Lambda}_{MT}$ is able to achieve better performance without relying on a specific elliptical model and thus has a better robustness to mismatch scenarios.

To compare the attractiveness of the different statistics described in this section with regard to computational complexity, we consider an experimental Monte-Carlo analysis on synthetic Gaussian data.

A set of data $\mathbb{W}$ is generated with parameter values $p = 10$, $N = 25$ and $T = 2$. The Gaussian data is generated with a covariance matrix $(\Sigma)_{ij} = 0.5^{|i-j|}$ and $4,000$ Monte-Carlo trials have been considered. For statistics involving fixed-point equations, we fixed the number of iterations to $15$ and we choose $L = 1$ (Single Look data). Finally, the simulation has been done on a $2.50$ GHz processor in Python 3.7. The mean execution times are provided in Table 3.4.

Several observations can be made:

– most of the Gaussian-derived statistics have similar time consumption since the statistic are based on the computation of the SCM, which is less expensive than a fixed-point estimation. The Wald statistic is more expensive than the Gaussian GLRT and $t1$ statistics due to the inverse of a Kronecker product, which is more expensive than a simple inverse. $\hat{\Lambda}_{\mathcal{RG}}$ has the highest time consumption, even compared to non-Gaussian methodologies, due to the fact that it requires the computation of the square root of matrices, which can take a lot of time depending on the implementation (the one used corresponds to the Scipy implementation, which can be improved with regard to complexity);

– concerning non-Gaussian statistics, the time consumption is generally higher than Gaussian methodologies due to the fixed-point estimation. The best methodology with regard to time consumption is $\hat{\Lambda}_{MT}$ since it requires fewer operations than the others. Moreover, some solutions based on the stochastic Riemannian gradient (Zhou and Said 2019) should allow us to reduce the computational cost of the covariance estimator used in $\hat{\Lambda}_{MT}$.

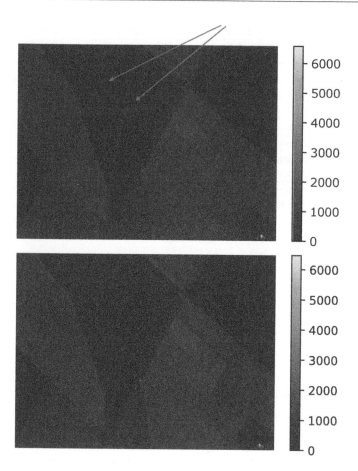

**Figure 3.8.** *Output of $\hat{\Lambda}_{\mathrm{G}}$ (top) and $\hat{\Lambda}_{\mathrm{MT}}$ (bottom) on Scene 3. The major difference between the two statistics is highlighted by red arrows. For a color version of this figure, see www.iste.co.uk/atto/change1.zip*

| $\hat{\Lambda}_{\mathrm{G}}$ | $\hat{\Lambda}_{t_1}$ | $\hat{\Lambda}_{\mathrm{Wald}}$ | $\hat{\Lambda}_{\mathrm{HTL}}$ | $\hat{\Lambda}_{\mathrm{MT}}$ | $\hat{\Lambda}_{\mathrm{KL}}$ | $\hat{\Lambda}_{\mathrm{MLL}}$ | $\hat{\Lambda}_{\mathcal{RG}}$ | $\hat{\Lambda}_{\mathcal{RE}}$ | $\hat{\Lambda}_{\mathcal{WG}}$ | $\hat{\Lambda}_{\mathcal{WE}}$ |
|------|------|------|------|------|------|------|------|------|------|------|
| 0.001 | 0.001 | 0.003 | 0.001 | 0.004 | 0.001 | 0.006 | 0.011 | 0.007 | 0.002 | 0.007 |

**Table 3.4.** *Time consumption in seconds*

## 3.5. Change detection based on structured covariances

In Mian *et al.* (2017), we have shown that the performance of the detectors (Gaussian and non-Gaussian) improves with the increase of the diversity (here the spectro-angular diversity obtained with the method proposed in Mian *et al.* (2019b)) and so on $p$. When $p$ is increased, the number of data to estimate the covariance matrix has to be increased too. The relation $N = 2p$ (obtained in array processing (Reed *et al.* 1974)) is often used to choose this number. But in our configuration, it can be difficult to handle with large $N$. First, the hypothesis of i.i.d. data to estimate the covariance is not fulfilled if $N$ is too large, and second, we loose resolution when $N$ increases (because of the method used in Mian *et al.* (2019b) to highlight the spectro-angular diversity). Therefore, if we want to choose a large $p$ to obtain good performance, we have to find a method to keep a value of $N$ reasonable.

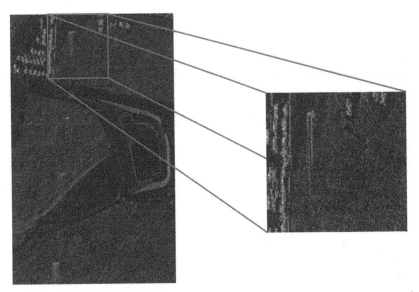

(a) UAVSAR data (Courtesy NASA/JPL-Caltech). Selection of the area on scene 2.

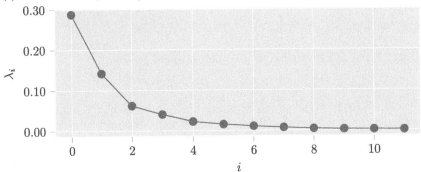

(b) Spectrum of UAVSAR data (wavelets + polarimetry). $p = 12$.

**Figure 3.9.** *Low-rank properties of UAVSAR data with polarimetric and spectro-angular diversity. For a color version of this figure, see www.iste.co.uk/atto/change1.zip*

Two kinds of approaches exist to reduce the number of $N$ needed to determine the estimation of the covariance matrix: the first one is to shrink the covariance towards to the identity matrix (Ledoit and Wolf 2004; Ollila and Tyler 2014; Pascal *et al.* 2014), and the second one is to resort on the inherent structure of data. A common structure for RADAR data is that they lie in a low-dimensional subspace. In this case, the covariance matrix has a low-rank (LR) structure, i.e. it can be written as the sum of an LR matrix and a diagonal matrix (where we will assume that all eigenvalues are equal).

We illustrate this property on the UAVSAR data already tested in the previous sections. In Figure 3.9, we have computed and plotted the mean of the eigenvalues of the selected area of Scene 2. In this simulation, the data size is equal to $p = 12$, with four spectro-angular diversities and three polarimetric channels. We note that the eigenvalues decrease significantly, and we conclude that the data lie in a low-dimensional subspace. In the following, the rank $R$ is assumed to be known or pre-estimated (either globally or locally) by using rank estimation methods from the literature, such as information theory-based methods (Stoica and Selen 2004).

The detectors derived in the previous sections assume unstructured covariance matrices. In this section, we propose to derive Gaussian and non-Gaussian detectors when the covariance matrix of the data has an LR structure. We only focus on the GLRT approach, even it is of course possible to extend the other approaches presented in section 3.4.

### 3.5.1. *Low-rank Gaussian change detector*

We recall that the dataset $\{\mathbf{x}_k\}$, where $\mathbf{x}_k \sim \mathcal{CN}(\mathbf{0}_p, \boldsymbol{\Sigma})$, has the following likelihood function

$$\mathcal{L}_{\mathcal{G}}\left(\{\mathbf{x}_k\}_{k=1}^N \mid \boldsymbol{\Sigma}\right) \propto \prod_{k=1}^K |\boldsymbol{\Sigma}|^{-1} \exp(-\mathbf{x}_k^H \boldsymbol{\Sigma}^{-1} \mathbf{x}_k) \qquad [3.38]$$

Since $\boldsymbol{\Sigma}$ has an LR structure, it is written as follows:

$$\boldsymbol{\Sigma} = \boldsymbol{\Sigma}_R + \sigma^2 \mathbf{I} \qquad [3.39]$$

where $\boldsymbol{\Sigma}_R$ belongs to the set of Hermitian positive semi-definite matrices of rank $R$, denoted $\mathcal{H}_{p,R}^+$. A Gaussian GLRT that accounts for this prior knowledge denoted $\hat{\Lambda}_{\text{LRG}}$ (LRG: low-rank Gaussian) can be formulated according to [3.10] with the following distribution parameters:

$$
\begin{aligned}
&\text{Model: } \mathbf{x}_k^t \sim \mathcal{CN}\left(\mathbf{0}, \boldsymbol{\Sigma}_R^t + \sigma_t^2 \mathbf{I}\right)\\
&\qquad\quad \text{Likelihood in [3.38]}\\
&\text{Param.: } \mathrm{H}_0 : \boldsymbol{\theta}_0 = \left\{\boldsymbol{\Sigma}_R^0, \sigma_t^2\right\}\\
&\qquad\quad\; \mathrm{H}_1 : \{\boldsymbol{\theta}_t\}_{t=1}^T = \left\{\boldsymbol{\Sigma}_R^t, \sigma_t^2\right\}_{t=1}^T
\end{aligned} \qquad [3.40]
$$

The corresponding detector, when we assume that the white Gaussian noise level is known, has been derived in Abdallah *et al.* (2019). To derive the corresponding GLRT, we have $\theta_t = \left\{ \Sigma_R^t, \sigma_t^2 \right\}$ & $\Phi_t = \varnothing$. Finally, for the expression of $\hat{\Lambda}_{\mathrm{LRG}}$ we obtain:

$$\hat{\Lambda}_{\mathrm{LRG}} = \frac{\mathcal{L}\left( \left\{ \{\mathbf{x}_k^t\}_{k=1}^N \right\}_{t=1}^T / \mathrm{H}_1; \mathcal{T}_R\left\{\hat{\Sigma}_1\right\}, \ldots, \mathcal{T}_R\left\{\hat{\Sigma}_T\right\} \right)}{\mathcal{L}\left( \left\{ \{\mathbf{x}_k^t\}_{k=1}^N \right\}_{t=1}^T / \mathrm{H}_0; \mathcal{T}_R\left\{\hat{\Sigma}_0\right\} \right)} \underset{\mathrm{H}_0}{\overset{\mathrm{H}_1}{\gtrless}} \lambda. \quad [3.41]$$

where $\hat{\Sigma}_t = \frac{1}{N} \sum_{k=1}^N \mathbf{x}_k^t \left(\mathbf{x}_k^t\right)^H$. From $\Sigma \overset{\mathrm{EVD}}{=} \mathbf{U} \operatorname{diag}(\mathbf{d}) \mathbf{U}^H$, we obtain $\mathcal{T}_R\{\Sigma\}$:

$$\mathcal{T}_R\{\Sigma\} = \mathbf{U}\operatorname{diag}\left(\tilde{\mathbf{d}}\right)\mathbf{U}^H$$

where $\tilde{\mathbf{d}} = \left[ d_1, \ldots, d_R, \hat{\sigma}_t^2, \ldots, \hat{\sigma}_t^2 \right]$ and $\hat{\sigma}_t^2 = \sum_{r=R+1}^p \frac{d_r}{p-R}$.

In the next section, we make the same derivation when the data follow the compound Gaussian model.

### 3.5.2. *Low-rank compound Gaussian change detector*

We recall that the dataset $\{\mathbf{x}_k\}$, where $\mathbf{x}_k \mid \tau_k \sim \mathcal{CN}(\mathbf{0}_p, \tau_k \Sigma)$, has the following likelihood function

$$\mathcal{L}_{\mathcal{CG}}\left( \{\mathbf{x}_k\}_{k=1}^N \mid \tau_k \Sigma \right) \propto \prod_{k=1}^K |\tau_k \Sigma|^{-1} \exp(-\mathbf{x}_k^H \left(\tau_k \Sigma\right)^{-1} \mathbf{x}_k) \qquad [3.42]$$

where like for the Gaussian version, $\Sigma = \Sigma_R + \sigma^2 \mathbf{I}$.

The corresponding GLRT for CD, denoted $\hat{\Lambda}_{\mathrm{LRCG}}$ (LRCG: low-rank compound Gaussian), corresponds to equation [3.10] with the following distribution/parameters:

Model: $\mathbf{x}_k^t \sim \mathcal{CN}\left( \mathbf{0}_p, \tau_k^t \left( \Sigma_R^t + \sigma_t^2 \mathbf{I} \right) \right)$
Likelihood in [3.42]

Param.: $\mathrm{H}_0 : \theta_0 = \left\{ \Sigma_R^0, \sigma_0^2, \{\tau_k^0\}_{k=1}^N \right\}$    [3.43]

$\mathrm{H}_1 : \{\theta_t\}_{t=1}^T = \left\{ \Sigma_R^t, \sigma_t^2, \{\tau_k^t\}_{k=1}^N \right\}_{t=1}^T$

Here, the test accounts for a possible change of both the covariance matrix and the textures between acquisitions, as it was shown to be the most relevant approach for SAR-ITS in section 3.4 and in Mian *et al.* (2019a).

Evaluating $\Lambda_{\mathrm{LRCG}}$ according to the generic equation [3.11] requires us to compute:

$$\hat{\Lambda}_{\mathrm{LRCG}} = \frac{\mathcal{L}_{LRCG}^{\hat{H}_1}\left(\left\{\{\mathbf{x}_k^t\}_{k=1}^N\right\}_{t=1}^T \mid \hat{\boldsymbol{\theta}}_{\mathrm{LRCG}}^{H_1}\right)}{\mathcal{L}_{LRCG}^{H_0}\left(\left\{\{\mathbf{x}_k^t\}_{k=1}^N\right\}_{t=1}^T \mid \hat{\boldsymbol{\theta}}_{\mathrm{LRCG}}^{H_0}\right)}, \qquad [3.44]$$

where $\mathcal{L}_{LRCG}^{H_0}$ and $\mathcal{L}_{LRCG}^{H_1}$ are the likelihood (derived from equation [3.42]) under $H_0$ and $H_1$, respectively, and where

$$\begin{aligned}
\hat{\boldsymbol{\theta}}_{\mathrm{LRCG}}^{H_0} &= \left\{ \hat{\boldsymbol{\Sigma}}_R^0, \hat{\sigma}_0^2, \{\hat{\tau}_k^0\}_{k=1}^N \right\}, \\
\hat{\boldsymbol{\theta}}_{\mathrm{LRCG}}^{H_1} &= \left\{ \hat{\boldsymbol{\Sigma}}_R^t, \hat{\sigma}_t^2, \{\hat{\tau}_k^t\}_{k=1}^N \right\}_{t=1}^T
\end{aligned} \qquad [3.45]$$

are the maximum likelihood estimators under $H_0$ and $H_1$, respectively. As for the Gaussian version, we do not have any closed form for this CD.

In the following, we present the method to obtain $\hat{\boldsymbol{\theta}}_{\mathrm{LRCG}}^{H_1}$. The approach to have $\hat{\boldsymbol{\theta}}_{\mathrm{LRCG}}^{H_0}$ is very close and only the differences will be given.

### 3.5.2.1. *Maximum likelihood under* $H_1$

Under $H_1$, the likelihood is separable in $t$. For a fixed $t$, the maximum likelihood estimation of the unknown parameters $\left\{ \hat{\boldsymbol{\Sigma}}_R^t, \hat{\sigma}_t^2, \{\hat{\tau}_k^t\}_{k=1}^N \right\}$ consists of solving the problem

$$\begin{aligned}
\underset{\{\tau_k^t, \boldsymbol{\Sigma}_k^t\}_{k=1}^N, \boldsymbol{\Sigma}_R^t, \sigma_t^2}{\text{maximize}} \quad & \sum_{k=1}^N \log\left(\mathcal{L}_{H_1}^t\left(\mathbf{x}_k^t \mid \boldsymbol{\Sigma}_k^t\right)\right) \\
\text{subject to} \quad & \boldsymbol{\Sigma}_k^t = \tau_k^t\left(\boldsymbol{\Sigma}_R^t + \sigma_t^2\,\mathbf{I}\right) \\
& \boldsymbol{\Sigma}_R^t \succcurlyeq \mathbf{0}, \text{ and } \mathrm{rank}(\boldsymbol{\Sigma}_R^t) = R \\
& \sigma_t^2 > 0, \text{ and } \tau_k^t > 0, \forall k
\end{aligned} \qquad [3.46]$$

where $\mathcal{L}_{H_1}^t\left(\mathbf{x}_k^t \mid \boldsymbol{\Sigma}_k\right)$ reads directly from equation [3.42]. The solution to this problem cannot be obtained in closed form, but the following sections derive the practical block-coordinate descent algorithm in order to evaluate it. The algorithm is summed up in Algorithm 3.1.

– Update of the textures ($H_1$): Assuming a fixed covariance matrix $\boldsymbol{\Sigma}_R^t + \sigma_t^2\,\mathbf{I}$, the maximum likelihood estimator of the texture parameters is obtained in closed form (Pascal *et al.* 2008), with

$$\hat{\tau}_k^t = \frac{1}{p}\left(\mathbf{x}_k^t\right)^H\left(\boldsymbol{\Sigma}_R^t + \sigma_t^2\,\mathbf{I}\right)^{-1}\mathbf{x}_k^t \qquad [3.47]$$

---

**Algorithm 3.1.–** MLE under $H_1$ and fixed $t$

---

**Input:** $R, t, \{\mathbf{x}_k^t\}_{k=1}^N$

**while** *(convergence criterion not met)* **do**

$\quad|\quad$ Update textures with equation [3.47] Update covariance matrix parameters with equations

$\quad|\quad$ [3.49]–[3.50]

**return** $\hat{\boldsymbol{\Sigma}}_R^t, \hat{\sigma}_t^2, \{\hat{\tau}_k^t\}_{k=1}^N$

---

– Update of the covariance matrix parameters ($H_1$): Assuming fixed textures $\{\tau_k^t\}_{k=1}^N$, equation [3.46] can be re-expressed as:

$$\underset{\boldsymbol{\Sigma}_t, \boldsymbol{\Sigma}_R^t, \sigma_t^2}{\text{minimize}} \quad \log|\boldsymbol{\Sigma}_t| + \text{Tr}\left\{\tilde{\mathbf{S}}_t\,\boldsymbol{\Sigma}_t^{-1}\right\}$$

$$\text{subject to} \quad \boldsymbol{\Sigma}_t = \boldsymbol{\Sigma}_R^t + \sigma_t^2\,\mathbf{I} \qquad\qquad\qquad [3.48]$$

$$\boldsymbol{\Sigma}_R^t \succcurlyeq \mathbf{0}, \text{ and rank}\left(\boldsymbol{\Sigma}_R^t\right) = R$$

$$\sigma_t^2 > 0$$

with $\tilde{\mathbf{S}}_t = \dfrac{1}{N}\displaystyle\sum_{k=1}^N \dfrac{\mathbf{x}_k^t\,(\mathbf{x}_k^t)^H}{\tau_k^t}$. The solution is given in Tipping and Bishop (1999) and leads to the update

$$\boldsymbol{\Sigma}_t = \mathbf{U}\,\text{diag}\left(\tilde{\mathbf{d}}\right)\mathbf{U}^H \triangleq \mathcal{T}_R\left(\tilde{\mathbf{S}}_t\right) \qquad\qquad [3.49]$$

defined through the operator $\mathcal{T}_R$, with

$$\tilde{\mathbf{S}}_t \overset{\text{EVD}}{=} \mathbf{U}\,\text{diag}\,(\mathbf{d})\,\mathbf{U}^H$$

$$\mathbf{d} = [d_1, \ldots, d_R, d_{R+1}, \ldots, d_p]$$

$$\tilde{\mathbf{d}} = [d_1, \ldots, d_R, \hat{\sigma}_t^2, \ldots, \hat{\sigma}_t^2] \qquad\qquad [3.50]$$

$$\hat{\sigma}_t^2 = \dfrac{1}{p-R}\displaystyle\sum_{r=R+1}^p d_r.$$

### 3.5.2.2. *Maximum likelihood under* $H_0$

$$\underset{\{\tau_k^0, \boldsymbol{\Sigma}_k^0\}_{k=1}^N, \boldsymbol{\Sigma}_R^0, \sigma_0^2}{\text{maximize}} \quad \displaystyle\sum_{t=1}^T \sum_{k=1}^N \log\left(\mathcal{L}_{H_0}^t\left(\mathbf{x}_k^t \mid \boldsymbol{\Sigma}_k^0\right)\right)$$

$$\text{subject to} \quad \boldsymbol{\Sigma}_k^0 = \tau_k^0\left(\boldsymbol{\Sigma}_R^0 + \sigma_0^2\,\mathbf{I}\right) \qquad\qquad [3.51]$$

$$\boldsymbol{\Sigma}_R^0 \succcurlyeq \mathbf{0}, \text{ and rank}\left(\boldsymbol{\Sigma}_R^0\right) = R$$

$$\sigma_0^2 > 0, \text{ and } \tau_k^0 > 0, \forall k$$

This problem can be solved as the one in equation [3.46], with some modifications due to the likelihood function. The differences are detailed below and summed up in Algorithm 3.2.

---

**Algorithm 3.2.–** MLE under $H_0$

**Input:** $R, \left\{\{\mathbf{x}_k^t\}_{k=1}^N\right\}_{t=1}^T$

**while** *(convergence criterion not met)* **do**

　　│　Update textures with equation [3.52] Update covariance matrix parameters with equations
　　│　[3.49]–[3.50] applied to equation [3.53]

**return** $\hat{\boldsymbol{\Sigma}}_R^0, \hat{\sigma}_0^2, \{\hat{\tau}_k^0\}_{k=1}^N$

---

– Update of the textures ($H_0$): Assuming a fixed covariance matrix $\boldsymbol{\Sigma}^0 = \boldsymbol{\Sigma}_R^0 + \sigma_0^2\, \mathbf{I}$, the maximum likelihood estimator of the texture parameters is obtained in closed form (Mian *et al.* 2019a), with

$$\hat{\tau}_k^0 = \frac{1}{Tp} \sum_{t=1}^T \left(\mathbf{x}_k^t\right)^H \left(\boldsymbol{\Sigma}_R^0 + \sigma_0^2\, \mathbf{I}\right)^{-1} \mathbf{x}_k^t \qquad [3.52]$$

– Update of the covariance matrix parameters ($H_0$): Assuming fixed textures, the update problem can be reformulated as in [3.48], using

$$\tilde{\mathbf{S}}_0 = \frac{1}{NT} \sum_{t=1}^T \sum_{k=1}^N \frac{\mathbf{x}_k^t\, \left(\mathbf{x}_k^t\right)^H}{\tau_k^0} \qquad [3.53]$$

instead of $\tilde{\mathbf{S}}_t$. The solution is then obtained as in equations [3.49] and [3.50], and yields $\boldsymbol{\Sigma}_0 \triangleq \mathcal{T}_R(\tilde{\mathbf{S}}_0)$.

### 3.5.3. *Results of low-rank change detectors on the UAVSAR dataset*

We recall that the dataset and the used scenes are described in section 3.2. In this experimentation, Scene 1 with four dates and Scene 2 are tested.

The performance of the change detectors $\Lambda_{\mathrm{LRG}}$ and $\Lambda_{\mathrm{LRCG}}$ are tested on a SAR ITS dataset and assessed with ROC curves (displaying the probability of detection versus the false alarm rate). As a mean to assess the effectiveness of using the LR structure, they are compared to the following detectors: *i)* the classic Gaussian detector proposed in Conradsen *et al.* (2003) and Ciuonzo *et al.* (2017) and given in [3.14], denoted $\hat{\Lambda}_G$; *ii)* the compound Gaussian detector proposed in Mian *et al.* (2019a) and given in [3.20], denoted $\hat{\Lambda}_{CG}$.

The rank $R$ is chosen according to Figure 3.9, which has displayed the eigenvalues of the total sample covariance matrix. For this dataset, $R = 3$ appears to be an interesting value to separate signal from noise components. Notably, this rank gathers 81% of the total variance.

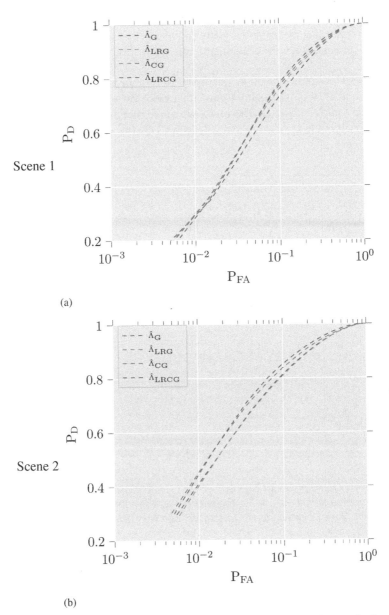

(a)

(b)

**Figure 3.10.** *Comparison between four methods: Gaussian, low-rank Gaussian, compound Gaussian (CG) and low-rank compound Gaussian (LRCG). $p = 12$, rank is fixed as 3, the window size is $7 \times 7$ and $\sigma^2$ is assumed unknown for both low-rank models. For a color version of this figure, see www.iste.co.uk/atto/change1.zip*

Figure 3.10 displays the ROC curves for the four detectors applied to Scenes 1 and 2. It assesses that the proposed method achieves the best performance in terms of probability of detection versus false alarm rate.

Figure 3.11 displays the ROC curves of $\Lambda_{\text{LRCG}}$ on Scene 1 for three different values of rank $R$. It is interesting to note that these curves do not vary significantly with respect to this parameter. Therefore, we can expect that a slight error in the rank estimation will not lead to a significant drop in CD performance.

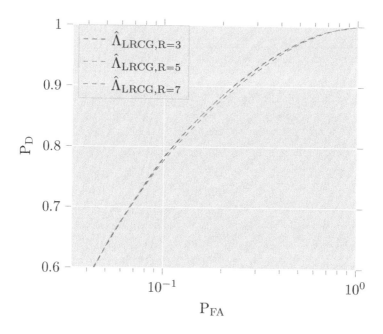

**Figure 3.11.** *Comparison for Scene 1 of the LRCG (low-rank compound Gaussian) for different rank values. $p = 12$, the window size fixed at $7 \times 7$ and $\sigma^2$ assumed unknown. For a color version of this figure, see www.iste.co.uk/atto/change1.zip*

## 3.6. Conclusion

The local covariance matrix of pixel patches appears to be relevant feature to analyze multivariate image time series (especially when dealing with SAR images). In this scope, this chapter presented an overview of covariance-based change detection algorithms.

Most of the standard methods were initially driven from the Gaussian distribution assumption and can be divided into two groups. The first one consists of two-step approaches, where plug-in estimates of the local covariance matrices are used to evaluate a distance, assessing for the dissimilarity (i.e. change) between the patches. Multiple theoretical frameworks motivated the use of various matrix distances (each with their own merits), notably information theory, Riemannian geometry and optimal transport. The second approach consists of one-step procedures, based on the derivation of a test statistic suited to the binary hypothesis test ("change" or "no change" in the local covariance matrix). The most common statistic for this problem is the GLRT, but many others exist, such as the $t_1$ and Wald statistics.

When dealing with high-resolution SAR images, it is well known that the Gaussian assumption is no longer valid. Conversely, the compound Gaussian modeling was shown to be more suited to reflect the empirical distribution of the data. This family of distributions notably drove robust covariance estimation methods, leading to various matrix estimates (notably, $M$-estimators) that can be used in plug-in approaches. Moreover, compound Gaussian distributions can serve as a basis to derive robust test statistics, such as the GLRT. Empirical experiments were conducted on various UAVSAR datasets, which illustrated the practical interest of compound Gaussian modeling. However, it is to be noted that the gain in detection performance is obtained at the cost of a slight increase in computational complexity.

In some cases, this spectro-angular diversity of the scatterers (obtained through wavelet-transform of the polarimetric data) can be useful in enhancing the change detection performance. This transformation generally increases the size of the data ($p > 3$), which implies a need for larger patches in order to correctly estimate the local covariance matrix. This dimensionality issue can be mitigated by exploiting some structures exhibited by the data, such as the low-rank one observed in the covariance matrix. This chapter concluded by presenting a generalization of the GLRT approaches accounting for this structure and by illustrating the interest of the approach.

## 3.7. References

Abdallah, R.B., Mian, A., Breloy, A., Korso, M.N.E., Lautru, D. (2019). Detection methods based on structured covariance matrices for multivariate SAR images processing. *IEEE Geoscience and Remote Sensing Letters*, 16(7), 1160–1164.

Achim, A., Tsakalides, P., Bezerianos, A. (2003). SAR image denoising via Bayesian wavelet shrinkage based on heavy-tailed modeling. *IEEE Transactions on Geoscience and Remote Sensing*, 41(8), 1773–1784.

Aiazzi, B., Alparone, L., Baronti, S., Garzelli, A., Zoppetti, C. (2013). Nonparametric change detection in multitemporal SAR images based on mean-shift clustering. *IEEE Transactions on Geoscience and Remote Sensing*, 51(4), 2022–2031.

Akbari, V., Anfinsen, S.N., Doulgeris, A.P., Eltoft, T., Moser, G., Serpico, S.B. (2016). Polarimetric SAR change detection with the complex Hotelling–Lawley trace statistic. *IEEE Transactions on Geoscience and Remote Sensing*, 54(7), 3953–3966.

Anderson, T. (2003). *An Introduction to Multivariate Statistical Analysis*. New Jersey [Online]. Available at: https://books.google.es/books?id=Cmm9QgAACAAJ.

Beaulieu, J. and Touzi, R. (2004). Segmentation of textured polarimetric SAR scenes by likelihood approximation. *IEEE Transactions on Geoscience and Remote Sensing*, 42(10), 2063–2072.

Breloy, A., Ginolhac, G., Renaux, A., Bouchard, F. (2019). Intrinsic Cramér–Rao bounds for scatter and shape matrices estimation in CES distributions. *IEEE Signal Processing Letters*, 26(2), 262–266.

Bruzzone, L. and Prieto, D.F. (2000). Automatic analysis of the difference image for unsupervised change detection. *IEEE Transactions on Geoscience and Remote Sensing*, 38(3), 1171–1182.

Bucciarelli, T., Lombardo, P., Oliver, C.J., Perrotta, M. (1995). A compound Weibull model for SAR texture analysis. *IEEE International Geoscience and Remote Sensing Symposium, IGARSS '95*. Quantitative Remote Sensing for Science and Applications, 1, 181–183.

Ciuonzo, D., Carotenuto, V., Maio, A.D. (2017). On multiple covariance equality testing with application to SAR change detection. *IEEE Transactions on Signal Processing*, 65(19), 5078–5091.

Conradsen, K., Nielsen, A.A., Schou, J., Skriver, H. (2001). Change detection in polarimetric SAR data and the complex Wishart distribution. *Scanning the Present and Resolving the Future. IEEE International Geoscience and Remote Sensing Symposium, IGARSS 2001*, 6, 2628–2630.

Conradsen, K., Nielsen, A.A., Schou, J., Skriver, H. (2003). A test statistic in the complex Wishart distribution and its application to change detection in polarimetric SAR data. *IEEE Transactions on Geoscience and Remote Sensing*, 41(1), 4–19.

Foucher, S. and Lopez-Martinez, C. (2014). Analysis, evaluation, and comparison of polarimetric SAR speckle filtering techniques. *IEEE Transactions on Image Processing*, 23(4), 1751–1764.

Freitas, C.C., Frery, A.C., Correia, A.H. (2005). The polarimetric G distribution for SAR data analysis. *Environmetrics*, 16(1), 13–31 [Online]. Available at: https://onlinelibrary.wiley.com/doi/abs/10.1002/env.658.

Frery, A.C., Nascimento, A.D.C., Cintra, R.J. (2014). Analytic expressions for stochastic distances between relaxed complex Wishart distributions. *IEEE Transactions on Geoscience and Remote Sensing*, 52, 1213–1226.

Gao, G. (2010). Statistical modeling of SAR images: A survey. *Sensors*, 10(1), 775–795.

Gelbrich, M. (1990). On a formula for the L2 Wasserstein metric between measures on Euclidean and Hilbert spaces. *Mathematische Nachrichten*, 147(1), 185–203.

Ghaffari, N. and Walker, S. (2018). On multivariate optimal transportation. arXiv preprint arXiv:1801.03516.

Gong, M., Zhao, J., Liu, J., Miao, Q., Jiao, L. (2016). Change detection in synthetic aperture radar images based on deep neural networks. *IEEE Transactions on Neural Networks and Learning Systems*, 27(1), 125–138.

Greco, M.S. and Gini, F. (2007). Statistical analysis of high-resolution SAR ground clutter data. *IEEE Transactions on Geoscience and Remote Sensing*, 45(3), 566–575.

Hecheltjen, A., Thonfeld, F., Menz, G. (2014). *Recent Advances in Remote Sensing Change Detection – A Review*. Springer Netherlands, Dordrecht.

Hussain, M., Chen, D., Cheng, A., Wei, H., Stanley, D. (2013). Change detection from remotely sensed images: From pixel-based to object-based approaches. *{ISPRS} Journal of Photogrammetry and Remote Sensing*, 80, 91–106 [Online]. Available at: http://www.sciencedirect.com/science/article/pii/S0924271613000804.

Inglada, J. and Mercier, G. (2007). A new statistical similarity measure for change detection in multitemporal SAR images and its extension to multiscale change analysis. *IEEE Transactions on Geoscience and Remote Sensing*, 45(5), 1432–1445.

Kervrann, C. and Boulanger, J. (2006). Optimal spatial adaptation for patch-based image denoising. *IEEE Transactions on Image Processing*, 15(10), 2866–2878.

Ledoit, O. and Wolf, M. (2004). A well-conditioned estimator for large-dimensional covariance matrices. *Journal of Multivariate Analysis*, 88, 365–411.

Liu, M., Zhang, H., Wang, C., Wu, F. (2014). Change detection of multilook polarimetric SAR images using heterogeneous clutter models. *IEEE Transactions on Geoscience and Remote Sensing*, 52(12), 7483–7494.

Maronna, R.A. (1976). Robust *M*-estimators of multivariate location and scatter. *Annals of Statistics*, 4(1), 51–67.

Maronna, R.A., Martin, D.R., Yohai, V.J. (2006). *Robust Statistics: Theory and Methods*, 1st edition, Wiley, New Jersey.

Martin, B. and Pierre, D. (2000). Robust estimation of the SUR model. *Canadian Journal of Statistics*, 28(2), 277–288 [Online]. Available at: https://onlinelibrary.wiley.com/doi/abs/10.2307/3315978.

Mian, A., Ovarlez, J.-P., Ginolhac, G., Atto, A.M. (2017). Multivariate change detection on high resolution monovariate SAR image using linear time-frequency analysis. *25th European Signal Processing Conference (EUSIPCO)*, 1942–1946.

Mian, A., Ginolhac, G., Ovarlez, J.-P., Atto, A.M. (2019a). New robust statistics for change detection in time series of multivariate SAR images. *IEEE Transactions on Signal Processing*, 67(2), 520–534.

Mian, A., Ovarlez, J.-P., Atto, A.M., Ginolhac, G. (2019b). Design of new wavelet packets adapted to high-resolution SAR images with an application to target detection. *IEEE Transactions on Geoscience and Remote Sensing*, 57(6), 3919–3932.

Muller, H. (1994). K statistics of terrain clutter in high resolution SAR images. *IEEE International Geoscience and Remote Sensing Symposium, IGARSS '94*, vol. 4, 2146–2148.

Nascimento, A.D.C., Frery, A.C., Cintra, R.J. (2019). Detecting changes in fully polarimetric SAR imagery with statistical information theory. *IEEE Transactions on Geoscience and Remote Sensing*, 57(3), 1380–1392.

Ollila, E. and Tyler, D. (2014). Regularized m-estimators of scatter matrix. *IEEE Transactions on Signal Processing*, 62(22), 6059–6070.

Ollila, E., Tyler, D.E., Koivunen, V., Poor, H.V. (2012a). Complex elliptically symmetric distributions: Survey, new results and applications. *IEEE Transactions on Signal Processing*, 60(11), 5597–5625.

Ollila, E., Tyler, D.E., Koivunen, V., Poor, H.V. (2012b). Compound-Gaussian clutter modeling with an inverse Gaussian texture distribution. *IEEE Signal Processing Letters*, 19(12), 876–879.

Pascal, F., Chitour, Y., Ovarlez, J.-P., Forster, P., Larzabal, P. (2008). Covariance structure maximum-likelihood estimates in compound Gaussian noise: Existence and algorithm analysis. *IEEE Transactions on Signal Processing*, 56(1), 34–48.

Pascal, F., Chitour, Y., Quek, Y. (2014). Generalized robust shrinkage estimator and its application to STAP detection problem. *IEEE Transactions on Signal Processing*, 62(21), 5640–5651.

Prendes, J., Chabert, M., Pascal, F., Giros, A., Tourneret, J. (2015). Change detection for optical and radar images using a Bayesian nonparametric model coupled with a Markov random field. *IEEE International Conference on Acoustics, Speech and Signal Processing (ICASSP)*, 1513–1517.

Ratha, D., De, S., Celik, T., Bhattacharya, A. (2017). Change detection in polarimetric SAR images using a geodesic distance between scattering mechanisms. *IEEE Geoscience and Remote Sensing Letters*, 14(7), 1066–1070.

Reed, I., Mallett, J., Brennan, L. (1974). Rapid convergence rate in adaptive arrays. *IEEE Transactions on Aerospace and Electronic Systems*, 10(6), 853–863.

Skovgaard, L.T. (1984). A Riemannian geometry of the multivariate normal model. *Scandinavian Journal of Statistics*, 11, 211–223.

Smith, S.T. (2005). Covariance, subspace, and intrinsic Cramér–Rao bounds. *IEEE Transactions on Signal Processing*, 53(5), 1610–1630.

Stoica, P. and Selen, Y. (2004). Model-order selection: A review of information criterion rules. *IEEE Signal Processing Magazine*, 21(4), 36–47.

Tipping, M. and Bishop, C. (1999). Probabilistic principal component analysis. *Journal of the Royal Statistical Society: Series B (Statistical Methodology)*, 61(3), 611–622.

Wang, F., Wu, Y., Zhang, Q., Zhang, P., Li, M., Lu, Y. (2013). Unsupervised change detection on SAR images using triplet Markov field model. *IEEE Geoscience and Remote Sensing Letters*, 10(4), 697–701.

Yohai, V.J. (1974). Robust estimation in the linear model. *Annals of Statististics*, 2(3), 562–567 [Online]. Available at: https://doi.org/10.1214/aos/1176342717.

Yousif, O. and Ban, Y. (2013). Improving urban change detection from multitemporal SAR images using PCA-NLM. *IEEE Transactions on Geoscience and Remote Sensing*, 51(4), 2032–2041.

Yueh, S., Kong, J., Jao, J., Shin, R., Novak, L. (1989). K-distribution and polarimetric terrain radar clutter. *Journal of Electromagnetic Waves and Applications*, 3(8), 747–768 [Online]. Available at: https://doi.org/10.1163/156939389X00412.

Zhou, J. and Said, S. (2019). Fast, asymptotically efficient, recursive estimation in a Riemannian manifold. *Entropy*, 21(10), 1–21.

Zoubir, A.M., Koivunen, V., Ollila, E., Muma, M. (2018). *Robust Statistics for Signal Processing*. Cambridge University Press, Cambridge.

# 4

# Unsupervised Functional Information Clustering in Extreme Environments from Filter Banks and Relative Entropy

Abdourrahmane M. ATTO[1], Fatima KARBOU[2],
Sophie GIFFARD-ROISIN[3] and Lionel BOMBRUN[4]

[1] University Savoie Mont Blanc, Annecy, France
[2] Université Grenoble Alpes, University of Toulouse, CNRM, CNRS,
Centre d'Études de la Neige at Météo-France, Grenoble, France
[3] Université Grenoble Alpes, France
[4] University of Bordeaux, France

This chapter addresses feature extraction from wavelets and convnet (Convolutional Neural Network) filters for unsupervised image time series analysis. We exploit the ability of wavelets and neuro-convolutional filters to capture non-trivial invariance properties, as well as the new centroid solutions proposed in this chapter, for high-level relative entropy-based feature analysis. Anomaly detection and functional evolution clustering are developed from this framework.

## 4.1. Introduction

Convolutional neural networks (CNNs, convnets) provide new filters for feature extraction in images. In supervised learning approaches, labeled examples of

*Change Detection and Image Time Series Analysis 1*,
coordinated by Abdourrahmane M. ATTO, Francesca BOVOLO and Lorenzo BRUZZONE.
© ISTE Ltd 2021.

object/texture classes are available in quantity and quality. The main challenges are the design of convnets, the selection of convnet operators and the optimization of convnet parameters. In this context, several scenarios associated with a large class of training databases have made it possible to discover suitable network configurations (Krizhevsky *et al.* 2012, pp. 1097–1105; Jia *et al.* 2014; Simonyan and Zisserman 2014; Chollet *et al.* 2015; Szegedy *et al.* 2015; Yoon *et al.* 2015; He *et al.* 2016; Seide and Agarwal 2016; Carreira and Zisserman 2017; Chollet 2017) that have led to insightful filters with good statistical properties (Atto *et al.* 2020). We will use convnets as filter banks without their corresponding standard learning paradigms. When training databases are less consequent, semi-supervised approaches in terms of transfer learning capitalize on the above configurations and consider up to and more than 90% of the learned parameters, the few remaining ones being used for the sake of adapting to the problem/database under analysis.

In this chapter, we consider unsupervised approaches without any requirement of the availability of training labels. Indeed, remote sensing imagery is a large source of images acquired in extreme geographical areas where collecting ground truths is usually very difficult. In order to take advantage of the available convnet architectures, this chapter considers their generic decomposition spaces and builds a decision framework by proposing several statistics for unsupervised spatio-temporal analysis.

This chapter begins with a model selection framework summarizing the feature extraction addressed (section 4.2). This framework is then spread out with respect to anomaly detection (section 4.3) and functional evolution clustering (section 4.4) in image time series. Anomaly detection from remote sensing imagery includes the monitoring of natural hazards such as deforestation and avalanches. Functional evolution clustering is of interest for analyzing moving objects (e.g. identifying acceleration and deceleration zones over a glacier) or dynamic textures (e.g. comparing snow states or vegetation growth). Experimental results will be provided with respect to synthetic aperture radar (SAR) imagery.

## 4.2. Parametric modeling of convnet features

This section considers multi-date divergence matrices (MDDM) developed in (Atto *et al.* 2013) (wavelet framework) in a context of convnet-based feature analysis. The sequence $\mathcal{I} = \{\mathcal{I}_m, m = 1, 2, \ldots, M\}$ of analyzed images or textures is assumed to follow from similar remote sensing sensors. The main steps involved in the feature extraction procedure proposed are described in the block diagram presented in Figure 4.1.

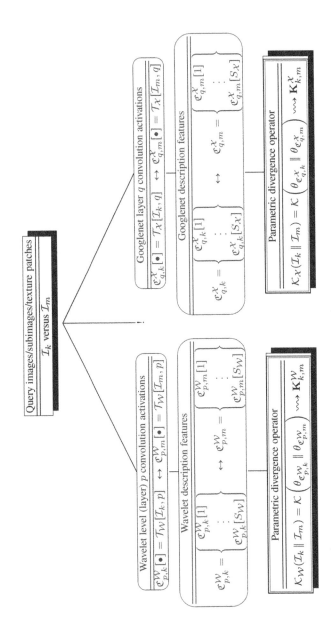

**Figure 4.1.** *Flowchart providing the steps involved in MDDM computation from wavelets and convnets. In this flowchart, the symbol $\theta$ denotes the set of description parameters (either multivariate mean and covariance matrix or the double indexed sequence of scale and shape parameters, for example). For a color version of this figure, see www.iste.co.uk/atto/change1.zip*

Given a convnet $\mathcal{T}$, the unsupervised feature extraction proposed in this chapter first identifies a generic layer $j$ that will be used to compute features (activations). Activations of $\mathcal{T}$ at a layer $j$ for image $\mathcal{I}_k$ yield the sequence of outputs (images): $\mathfrak{C}_{j,k} = (\mathfrak{C}_{j,k}[s])_{s=1,2,\ldots,S}$, where $S$ denotes the number of maps returned by the layer $j$. We will focus on convolution layers later in this chapter.

For statistical consistency in the multivariate case, a good candidate layer should be such that the total number of spatial data in any given convolution output is at least two times the number $S$ of convolution filters in this layer. Such layers correspond, for example, to $2 \leqslant j \leqslant 32$ for Xception convnet (Chollet 2017) denoted by $\mathcal{X}$ and $2 \leqslant j \leqslant 6$ for Alexnet convnet (Yoon *et al.* 2015), etc. An alternative is to directly extract only the desired convolution filter sequence from the convnet and use this convolution sequence to compute image features, as in Atto *et al.* (2020).

We consider two categories of model for $\mathfrak{C}_{j,k}[s]$: either a dependent multivariate Gaussian random vector model $\mathcal{N}\big(\mu_{\mathfrak{C}_{j,k}}, \Sigma_{\mathfrak{C}_{j,k}}\big)$ or an independent multivariate Weibull distributed random vector model $\mathcal{W}\big(\alpha_{|\mathfrak{C}_{j,k}|}, \beta_{|\mathfrak{C}_{j,k}|}\big)$, where $\alpha_{|\mathfrak{C}_{j,k}|}, \beta_{|\mathfrak{C}_{j,k}|}$ are sequences of *scale* and *shape* parameters associated with magnitudes of layer $j$ convolution outputs. The Kullback–Leibler divergence (relative entropy) is used to evaluate dissimilarity between $\mathcal{I}_k$ and $\mathcal{I}_m$ features in terms of:

$$\mathcal{K}(\mathcal{I}_k \parallel \mathcal{I}_m) = \frac{1}{2}\Big( (\mu_{\mathfrak{C}j,m} - \mu_{\mathfrak{C}j,k})\,{}^{\prime}\Sigma_{\mathfrak{C}j,m}{-1}\,(\mu_{\mathfrak{C}j,m} - \mu_{\mathfrak{C}j,k})$$

$$+ \operatorname{trace}\Big(\Sigma_{\mathfrak{C}j,m}{-1}\Sigma_{\mathfrak{C}j,k}\Big) + \log\frac{|\Sigma_{\mathfrak{C}j,m}|}{|\Sigma_{\mathfrak{C}j,k}|} - S\Big) \qquad [4.1]$$

when using the $\mathcal{N}\big(\mu_{\mathfrak{C}_{j,\bullet}}, \Sigma_{\mathfrak{C}_{j,\bullet}}\big)$ model and

$$\mathcal{K}(\mathcal{I}_k \parallel \mathcal{I}_m) = \sum_{s=1}^{S}\Big( -\mathcal{H}\big([\alpha_{|\mathfrak{C}_{j,k}[s]|}, \beta_{|\mathfrak{C}_{j,k}[s]|}]\big) \qquad [4.2]$$

$$+\mathcal{H}\big([\alpha_{|\mathfrak{C}_{j,k}[s]|}, \beta_{|\mathfrak{C}_{j,k}[s]|}] \parallel [\alpha_{|\mathfrak{C}_{j,m}[s]|}, \beta_{|\mathfrak{C}_{j,m}[s]|}]\big)\Big)$$

when using the $\mathcal{W}\big(\alpha_{|\mathfrak{C}_{j,\bullet}|}, \beta_{|\mathfrak{C}_{j,\bullet}|}\big)$ model, where

$$\mathcal{H}\big([\alpha, \beta]\big) = \mathfrak{e}\Big(1 - \frac{1}{\beta}\Big) + \log\Big(\frac{\alpha}{\beta}\Big) + 1 \qquad [4.3]$$

is the entropy of a Weibull distributed random variable with a couple of [scale, shape] parameters $[\alpha, \beta]$ and

$$\mathcal{H}\big([\alpha_k, \beta_k] \parallel [\alpha_m, \beta_m]\big) = \beta_m \log\frac{\alpha_m}{\alpha_k} + \log\frac{\alpha_k}{\alpha_m}$$

$$+\mathfrak{e}\Big(\frac{\beta_m - 1}{\beta_k}\Big) + \Big(\frac{\alpha_k}{\alpha_m}\Big)^{\beta_m}\Gamma\Big(1 + \frac{\beta_m}{\beta_k}\Big) \qquad [4.4]$$

is the cross-entropy between two Weibull distributed random variables with [scale, shape] parameters $[\alpha_k, \beta_k]$ and $[\alpha_m, \beta_m]$, respectively, with $\mathfrak{e}$ being the *Euler–Mascheroni* constant. The calculus steps for deriving these closed-form relative Gaussian entropy, Weibull entropy and Weibull cross-entropy can be found in Duchi (2007), Kwitt and Uhl (2008) and Atto *et al.* (2013).

The divergence measurements (from either equations [4.1] or [4.2]) yield symmetric MDDM:

$$\mathbf{K} = (\mathcal{K}(\mathcal{I}_k \parallel \mathcal{I}_m) + \mathcal{K}(\mathcal{I}_m \parallel \mathcal{I}_k))_{1 \leqslant k \leqslant M, 1 \leqslant m \leqslant M} \qquad [4.5]$$

In the following, we will integrate these analytic convnet divergence measures to solve two issues: the first concerns multiple anomaly detection in image time series and the second is dedicated to evolution clustering in image time series. For the experimental results, we will specifically focus on:

– Haar wavelet filters associated with a six-level stationary wavelet decomposition;

– Xception-L2 (layer number 2) convnet filters: this layer provides $3 \times 32 = 96$ spatial filters that are used to convolve any SAR image channel for feature extraction.

## 4.3. Anomaly detection in image time series

The method proposed below for anomaly detection in image time series involves two analysis stages that are highlighted in Figure 4.2. Given that an anomaly can occur due to changes in the mean/scale/power or in the texture/shape parameters, we consider testing parameters independently, instead of the joint approach where the aggregated dissimilarities can blur the origin of the anomaly. Since changes in mean/scale are easier to detect and because of page limitation, we will only focus on texture/shape changes in the rest of this chapter.

The texture analysis is performed over small image patches that are normalized to have zero-mean in the multivariate Gaussian case and unitary scale parameter in the Weibull-based modeling. Given a series of normalized local textures $\mathcal{I} = \{\mathcal{I}_m, m = 1, 2, \ldots, M\}$ that are likely to contain several abrupt changes, the first-stage analysis consists of computing MDDM as defined in equation [4.5] from divergences defined by equations [4.1] and [4.2]. Because only Bi-Date Features (BDF), i.e. a couple $(\mathfrak{C}_{\bullet,k}, \mathfrak{C}_{\bullet,m})$, are considered for computing any element of this matrix, we will use the terminology of BDF-MDDM (Bi-Date Features – Multi-Date Divergence Matrices).

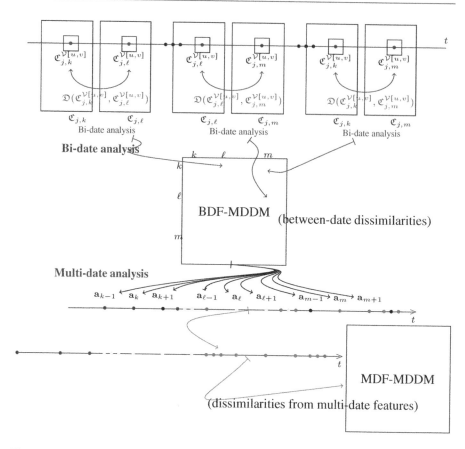

**Figure 4.2.** *Block diagram representing the framework for the detection and analysis of natural hazards at the texture level. In this diagram, $\mathcal{V}[u,v]$ represents the spatial neighborhood associated with coordinates $\mathcal{V}[u,v]$ and $\mathbf{a}_k$ represents the textural information given in $\mathcal{I}_k^{\mathcal{V}[u,v]}$. For a color version of this figure, see www.iste.co.uk/atto/change1.zip*

This BDF-MDDM may contain several disturbances, such as the presence of outlier-textures. An outlier is a texture $\mathcal{I}_m$ that is significantly different from its preceding and succeeding observations. It can be recognized by a higher row/column in the BDF-MDDM. The second stage considers refining the BDF-MDDM by iteratively removing outliers. Retrieval of outliers is performed by analyzing the empirical distribution of series

$$\lambda[m] = \sum_{k=1}^{M} \mathbf{K}_{m,k} \qquad\qquad [4.6]$$

where $\mathbf{K}$ is a matrix defined as in equation [4.5]. An outlier index $m$ is such that there exist sufficiently small natural numbers $\epsilon_0$ and $\epsilon_1$ such that for all $k \in \{m - \epsilon_0, m - \epsilon_0 + 1, \ldots, m - 1, m + 1, m + 2, \ldots, m + \epsilon_1\}$, we have $\lambda[k_i] \ll \lambda[m]$. The procedure for the removal of outlier is such that: if $\mathcal{I}_m \triangleq \{\mathfrak{C}_{j,m}[s] : 1 \leqslant s \leqslant S\}$ is an outlier, then replace its description parameters $\{\theta_{\mathfrak{C}_{j,m}[s]} : 1 \leqslant s \leqslant S\}$ by the more similar parameters observed in the closed neighborhood of $\mathcal{I}_m$. Let $\mathbb{O}_m = \{\theta_{\mathfrak{C}_{j,m-\epsilon_0}[s]}, \ldots, \theta_{\mathfrak{C}_{j,m+\epsilon_1}[s]}\} \backslash \{\theta_{\mathfrak{C}_{j,m}[s]}\}$ denote the neighborhood of outlier texture $\mathcal{I}_m$ activation series. The parameter replacement is performed by the assignment:

$$\theta_{\mathfrak{C}_{j,m}[s]} \leftarrow \theta^*_{\mathfrak{C}_{j,m}[s]} = \arg\min_{\theta \in \mathbb{O}_m} F_{\theta_{\mathfrak{C}_{j,k}[s]}}(\theta) \tag{4.7}$$

where $\theta^*_{\mathfrak{C}_{j,m}[s]}$ is the local centroid computed with respect to objective dissimilarities:

$$F_{\theta_{\mathfrak{C}_{j,k}[s]}}(\theta) = \sum_{k=m-\epsilon_0}^{m+\epsilon_1} \mathcal{K}(\theta_{\mathfrak{C}_{j,k}[s]} \| \theta) + \mathcal{K}(\theta \| \theta_{\mathfrak{C}_{j,k}[s]}) \tag{4.8}$$

Note that the final descriptor $\{\theta^*_{\mathfrak{C}_{j,m}[s]} : 1 \leqslant s \leqslant S\}$ of $\mathcal{I}_m$ will generally involve parameters coming from different $(\mathcal{I}_k)_k$ for $k \in \{m - \epsilon_0, m - \epsilon_0 + 1, \ldots, m - 1, m + 1, m + 2, \ldots, m + \epsilon_1\}$.

In practice, the complexity for solving equation [4.7] depends on the model. For the multivariate Gaussian model and under zero-mean concerns (texture outliers), equation [4.8] equals:

$$F_{\boldsymbol{\Sigma}_{\mathfrak{C}_{j,m}[s]}}(\boldsymbol{\Sigma}) = -S(\epsilon_0 + \epsilon_1 + 1)$$
$$+ \sum_{k=m-\epsilon_0}^{m+\epsilon_1} \frac{\text{trace}\left(\boldsymbol{\Sigma}^{-1}\boldsymbol{\Sigma}_{\mathfrak{C}_{j,k}}\right) + \text{trace}\left(\boldsymbol{\Sigma}_{\mathfrak{C}_{j,k}}^{-1}\boldsymbol{\Sigma}\right)}{2} \tag{4.9}$$

Solving the minimization problem, equation [4.7] under zero-mean Gaussian objective of equation [4.9] amounts to computing $\epsilon_0 + \epsilon_1$ values $\{F_{\boldsymbol{\Sigma}_{\mathfrak{C}_{j,m}[s]}}(\boldsymbol{\Sigma}_k) : k \in \{m - \epsilon_0, m - \epsilon_0 + 1, \ldots, m - 1, m + 1, m + 2, \ldots, m + \epsilon_1\}$, sorting these values and considering the argument of the smallest one. The corresponding centroid solution has no analytical closed form; it is neither a standard Euclidean mean nor a medoid.

For the Weibull magnitude model with normalized unitary scales, equation [4.8] simplifies in:

$$F_{\beta_{\mathfrak{C}_{j,m}[s]}}(\beta) = -2(\epsilon_0 + \epsilon_1 + 1) + \sum_{k=m-\epsilon_0}^{m+\epsilon_1} \left[ \Gamma\left(1 + \frac{\beta_{\mathfrak{C}_{j,k}[s]}}{\beta}\right) \right.$$
$$\left. + \Gamma\left(1 + \frac{\beta}{\beta_{\mathfrak{C}_{j,k}[s]}}\right) + \mathfrak{e}\left(\frac{\beta_{\mathfrak{C}_{j,k}[s]}}{\beta} + \frac{\beta}{\beta_{\mathfrak{C}_{j,k}[s]}} - 2\right) \right] \tag{4.10}$$

which is a strictly convex objective. Furthermore, since the shape constraint set $\mathbb{R}^+$ is also strictly convex, we deduce that the minimization problem equation [4.7] under the Weibull objective given by equation [4.10] has the following centroid solution:

$$\beta^*_{\mathfrak{C}_{j,m}[s]} = \left\{ \beta \in \mathbb{R}_+ \middle/ \sum_{k=m-\epsilon_0}^{m+\epsilon_1} \Gamma\left(1 + \frac{\beta_{\mathfrak{C}_{j,k}[s]}}{\beta}\right) \psi\left(1 + \frac{\beta_{\mathfrak{C}_{j,k}[s]}}{\beta}\right) \right.$$

$$- \frac{\beta^3_{\mathfrak{C}_{j,k}[s]}}{\beta^3} \Gamma\left(\frac{\beta}{\beta_{\mathfrak{C}_{j,k}[s]}}\right) \psi\left(1 + \frac{\beta}{\beta_{\mathfrak{C}_{j,k}[s]}}\right)$$

$$\left. + \mathfrak{e}\left(1 - \frac{\beta^2}{\beta^2_{\mathfrak{C}_{j,k}[s]}}\right) = 0 \right\} \qquad [4.11]$$

where $\psi$ is the *digamma* function.

The MDDM computed by using Multi-Date Features (MDF) from $\{\mathcal{I}_{m-\epsilon_0}, \mathcal{I}_{m-\epsilon_0+1}, \ldots, \mathcal{I}_{m+\epsilon_1}\}$ and the outlier removal stage is called MDF-MDDM. Figure 4.3 shows an example associated with two abrupt changes in a cyclostationary BDF-MDDM and MDF-MDDM. In practice, we update equation [4.6] and iterate outlier removals for the sake of obtaining a very clean matrix. Figure 4.4 provides the anomalies detected from MDF-MDDM of Figure 4.3.

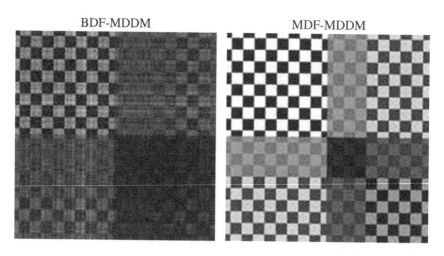

BDF-MDDM                          MDF-MDDM

**Figure 4.3.** *Illustration of a BDF-MDDM and its clean version (MDF-MDDM) when two abrupt changes occur in data associated with seasonal variations (quasi-cyclostationary process); see Figure 4.2 for information on the calculus steps. For a color version of this figure, see www.iste.co.uk/atto/change1.zip*

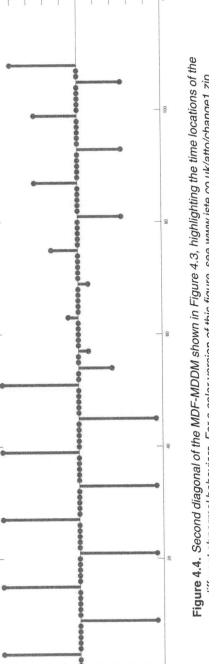

**Figure 4.4.** *Second diagonal of the MDF-MDDM shown in Figure 4.3, highlighting the time locations of the different abnormal behaviors. For a color version of this figure, see www.iste.co.uk/atto/change1.zip*

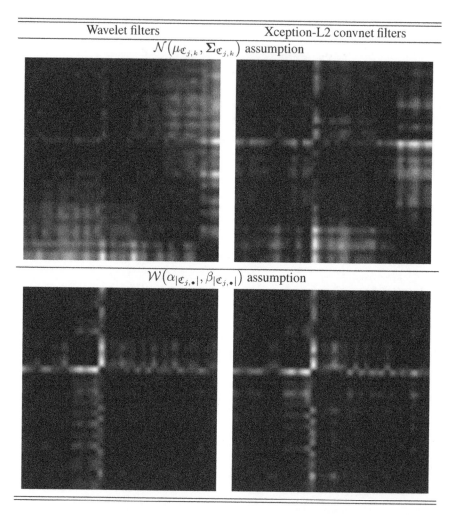

**Figure 4.5.** *MDF-MDDM computed at a large scale, approximately 200 square kilometers around latitude: 44° 38′ 51-North and longitude: 6° 49′ 28-East (French Alps, altitudes vary between 1,200 m and 3,100 m). We have used Sentinel-1 level 1 ground range detected products in descending direction orbits. Acquisition dates vary between August 2017 and March 2018. For a color version of this figure, see www.iste.co.uk/atto/change1.zip*

We deployed such a framework for analyzing the spatio-temporal evolution at large over a French Alps area located near Grenoble, around latitude 44°38′51-N and longitude 6°49′28-E. Polarimetric SAR (PolSAR) image time series are available for this area from the Copernicus Sentinel-1 program in VV and VH transmitter-versus-receiver wave polarization. The analysis is performed at a large scale to detect main seasonal changes (impacts on vegetation or snow state variation) and/or one-off changes (in case of snow fall events, for example). Figure 4.5 shows the corresponding wavelet- and convnet-based MDF-MDDMs. We can note different sensitivity levels depending on the decomposition space and the model used. But from a global analysis of shared detection, we found a very stable state in a period including [October 11, 2017, October 29, 2017], followed by a sharp anomaly visible from the November 10, 2017 Sentinel-1 acquisition.

## 4.4. Functional image time series clustering

The method proposed for functional image time series clustering (FITSC) relates to finding similarities between pixel evolution paths. It assumes a (pre-processing) stage associated with clustering MDDDs computed as in section 4.3 in order to determine the similar pixel evolutions. This yields a *spatial clustering of spatio-temporal data* that will be performed with respect to the flowchart of Figure 4.7. The analysis stages of FITSC are detailed below.

The first stage considers a sub-selection of seasonal representative images from the series. For this analysis, we propose the framework developed in section 4.3 but at the image scale. The main difference with respect to section 4.3 is that outlier images are definitely removed from the series: the output series from stage 1 therefore have length $N$ with $N \ll M$. For example, when the reason for the analysis is glacier displacement evaluation then images impacted by the responses of fresh snow or melted snow due to intense rain events are discarded from the representative series because these images can lead to highly disturbed estimations.

These representatives are expected to be invariant with respect to intra-seasonal disparities. The second-stage analysis computes MDDMs for any pixel subsequence from the seasonal representative image time series.

The second-stage analysis computes the MDF-MDDM evolution map at the pixel level between the output sequences issued from the first stage (see Figure 4.2). A seasonal representative pixel subsequence is denoted $\mathbb{P}^u_{m_i}$, where $u = [u_1, u_2]$ denotes the spatial pixel location. $\mathbb{P}^u_{m_i}$ is considered as a multi-date vector of spatial random variables, and dissimilarities with respect to such paths are the sequence $\left( \mathcal{K}(\mathbb{P}^u_{m_i} \parallel \mathbb{P}^v_{m_i}) \right)_i$. The variable $i$ represents a color channel in the graph of Figure 4.7. Indeed, dissimilarities are restricted to intra-season variability in this analysis.

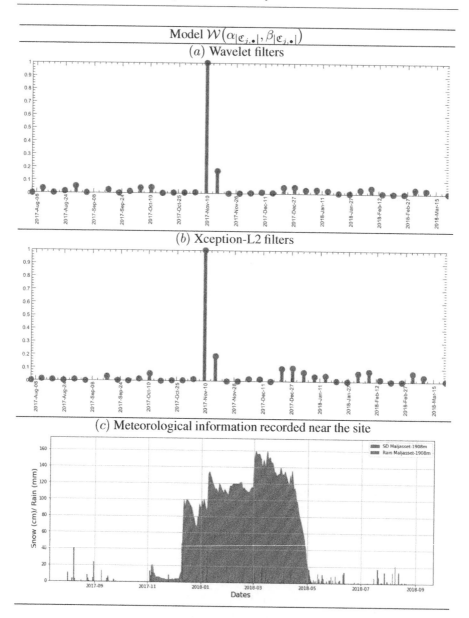

**Figure 4.6.** *Second diagonals of the MDF-MDDMs shown in Figure 4.5 when restricted to the Weibull model and for (a) the wavelet and (b) the xception-L2 convnet features. Daily snow heights and rainfall rates measured at the Maljasset station, located near the test site, are given in (c). Note that the high peak observed in (a) and (b) (November 10, 2017) corresponds to a conjunction of rain/snow episodes at high altitude after several weeks of drought. For a color version of this figure, see www.iste.co.uk/atto/change1.zip*

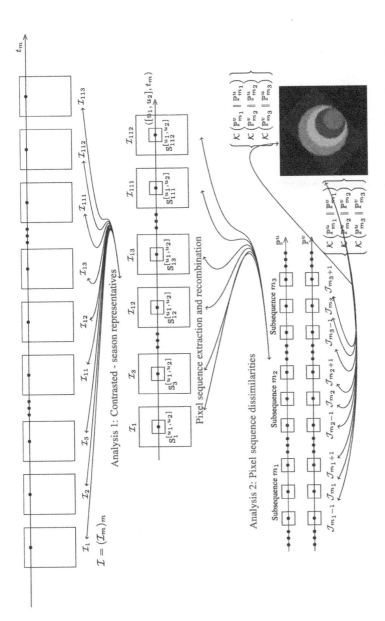

**Figure 4.7.** *Framework for evolution clustering. Analysis 1 involves dissimilarities at large spatial scales for the sake of invariance to seasonal disturbances. The sub-series passing analysis 1 is then processed at the pixel level for highlighting similar evolutions (analysis 2). For a color version of this figure, see www.iste.co.uk/atto/change1.zip*

**Figure 4.8.** *Clusters of dynamics for the Chamonix-Mont Blanc site. Cyan square: example of dynamic and known anomaly. Valley "Les Houches → Chamonix → Argentière": high and sparse dynamic near the touristic glacier sites and their car parking. For a color version of this figure, see www.iste.co.uk/atto/change1.zip*

In contrast with the texture approach, in practice, pixel observation $\mathbb{S}^u_{m_{i_k}}$ has small spatial sizes. Thus, we do not consider a convnet for its decomposition before feature extraction. Instead, divergences are directly computed with respect to a gamma model on the samples because the small sample concern makes the assumption of homogeneity more valid, in contrast with the texture context. For the sake of an illustration given with respect to the notation of Figure 4.7, in the independent Weibull model case, the divergence equation is:

$$\mathcal{M}\left(\mathbb{P}^u_{m_i}\right) = \sum_{v \in \mathcal{N}(u)} \sum_{k,\ell} \left(\mathcal{K}\left(\mathbb{S}^u_{m_{i_k}} \| \mathbb{S}^v_{m_{i_\ell}}\right) + \mathcal{K}\left(\mathbb{S}^v_{m_{i_\ell}} \| \mathbb{S}^u_{m_{i_k}}\right)\right)$$

where $\mathcal{N}(u)$ is the spatial set of pixels sharing similar MDDM as $u$ (see section 4.3).

The test site used for experiments is now Chamonix-Mont Blanc in France, and we consider PolSAR image time series issued from the Copernicus Sentinel-1. After pre-processing of 1059 acquisitions covering the site, 160 couples (each consisting of a ascending and descending image) of seasonal representative images are detected in the period from 2016 to 2019. These pairs of seasonal representative images correspond to numbers 21, 45, 47 and 47 of Sentinel-1 couple acquisitions, respectively, for years 2016, 2017, 2018 and 2019.

Functional image time series clustering results are provided for the Chamonix-Mont Blanc site in Figure 4.8. This figure shows some colored clusters where the color composition is associated with the intensity of local variations. It is worth mentioning that the analysis is intended for large-sized regional areas that are $(i)$ associated with extreme weather conditions and $(ii)$ difficult to access in practice: obtaining ground truths is not straightforward in such areas, but the analysis of Figure 4.8 shows several outstanding clusters. For example, the Argentière glacier seems to have a higher dynamic than the *Mer de glace* glacier, especially at its lower terminal tongue.

## 4.5. Conclusion

This chapter has proposed a new framework for anomaly detection and functional evolution clustering in image time series. This framework involves new centroid objectives and analytical forms upon convnet parameters for capturing non-trivial invariance. Detailed experimental tests will be presented at the conference for highlighting the relevance of this fully unsupervised method in the analysis of remote sensing image time series.

## 4.6. References

Atto, A.M., Trouvé, E., Berthoumieu, Y., Mercier, G. (2013). Multidate divergence matrices for the analysis of SAR image time series. *IEEE Transactions on Geoscience and Remote Sensing*, 51(4), 1922–1938.

Atto, A.M., Bisset, R.R., Trouvé, E. (2020). Frames learned by prime convolution layers in a deep learning framework. *IEEE Transactions on Neural Networks and Learning Systems*, 1–9.

Carreira, J. and Zisserman, A. (2017). Quo vadis, action recognition? A new model and the kinetics dataset. *2017 IEEE Conference on Computer Vision and Pattern Recognition (CVPR)*, 4724–4733, Honolulu, 21–26 July.

Chollet, F. (2017). Xception: Deep learning with depthwise separable convolutions. *2017 IEEE Conference on Computer Vision and Pattern Recognition (CVPR)*, 1800–1807, Honolulu, 21–26 July.

Chollet, F., Eldeeb, A., Bursztein, E., Jin, H., Scott Zhu, Q. (2015). Keras [Online]. Available at: https://github.com/fchollet/keras.

Duchi, J. (2007). Derivations for linear algebra and optimization. Research Report, Stanford University, CA [Online]. Available at: https://web.stanford.edu/~jduchi/projects/general_notes.pdf.

He, K., Zhang, X., Ren, S., Sun, J. (2016). Deep residual learning for image recognition. *2016 IEEE Conference on Computer Vision and Pattern Recognition (CVPR)*, 770–778, Las Vegas, NV, 27–30 June.

Jia, Y., Shelhamer, E., Donahue, J., Karayev, S., Long, J., Girshick, R., Guadarrama, S., Darrell, T. (2014). Caffe: Convolutional architecture for fast feature embedding. *Proceedings of the 22nd ACM International Conference on Multimedia, MM '14, ACM*, 675–678, New York, 10–16 October [Online]. Available at: http://doi.acm.org/10.1145/2647868.2654889.

Krizhevsky, A., Sutskever, I., Hinton, G.E. (2012). Imagenet classification with deep convolutional neural networks. In *Advances in Neural Information Processing Systems 25*, Pereira, F., Burges, C.J.C., Bottou, L., Weinberger, K.Q. (eds). Curran Associates, Inc., Red Hook, NY.

Kwitt, R. and Uhl, A. (2008). Image similarity measurement by Kullback–Leibler divergences between complex wavelet subband statistics for texture retrieval. *IEEE International Conference on Image Processing*, 933–936, San Diego, CA, 12–15 October.

Seide, F. and Agarwal, A. (2016). CNTK: Microsoft's open-source deep-learning toolkit. *Proceedings of the 22nd ACM SIGKDD International Conference on Knowledge Discovery and Data Mining, KDD '16, ACM*, 2135–2135, San Francisco, CA, 13–17 August [Online]. Available at: http://doi.acm.org/10.1145/2939672.2945397.

Simonyan, K. and Zisserman, A. (2014). Very deep convolutional networks for large-scale image recognition. *CoRR* [Online]. Available at: https://arxiv.org/abs/1409.1556

Szegedy, C., Sermanet, P., Reed, S., Anguelov, D., Erhan, D., Vanhoucke, V., Rabinovich, A. (2015). Going deeper with convolutions. *2015 IEEE Conference on Computer Vision and Pattern Recognition (CVPR)*, 1–9, Boston, MA, 7–12 June.

Yoon, Y.-G., Dai, P., Wohlwend, J., Chang, J.-B., Marblestone, A.H., Boyden, E.S. (2015). BVLC AlexNet model [Online]. Available at: https://github.com/BVLC/caffe/tree/master/models/bvlc_alexnet.

# 5

# Thresholds and Distances to Better Detect Wet Snow over Mountains with Sentinel-1 Image Time Series

**Fatima Karbou[1], Guillaume James[2,3], Philippe Durand[3] and Abdourrahmane M. Atto[4]**

[1] *Université Grenoble Alpes, University of Toulouse, CNRM, CNRS, Centre d'Études de la Neige at Météo-France, Grenoble, France*
[2] *Inria Grenoble – Rhône-Alpes Research Center, France*
[3] *CNES, Toulouse, France*
[4] *University Savoie Mont Blanc, Annecy, France*

## 5.1. Introduction

In mountain regions, seasonal snow monitoring is very important for many applications such as hydrology, mountain ecosystems, meteorology and avalanche forecasting. For example, a good knowledge of snow extent, of its evolution over time and in particular the starting date of snow-melt is of prime importance for hydro power production and for anticipating flood risks. A good knowledge of starting date of snow-melt is also of great importance for mountain ecosystem studies. Space-based remote sensing allows monitoring of seasonal snow at scales of time and space that are not comparable to ground-based measuring stations. The Sentinel-1 satellites provide cloud insensitive C-band Synthetic Aperture Radar (SAR) data and allow snow cover to be observed day and night at unprecedented temporal and spatial resolutions. The sensitivity of the measurements to snow liquid water content has enabled the development and evaluation of algorithms for detecting wet snow (Baghdadi *et al.* 1998; Magagi and Bernier 2003; Nagler *et al.* 2016; Karbou *et al.* 2020). SAR observations, however, require heavy pre-processing steps and are complex to use in areas of high relief. Most wet snow detection algorithms are based on the use of thresholds to distinguish wet snow from dry snow or soil by comparing a winter image with a reference image without snow. This approach gives satisfactory results during melting periods but has important limitations. In the literature, there are several studies on this topic. Nagler and Rott (2000) used a fixed threshold to map wet snow using a reference image taken under either dry snow or frozen ground conditions. However, the use of a threshold of 2–3 dB does not always guarantee good results because detection errors may occur in situations linked to some specific surface types, snow surface roughness values and moisture content (Baghdadi *et al.* 2000). The use of a fixed threshold is particularly problematic in forest areas where the variation of the SAR signal is relatively small (sometimes below the 2–3 dB range). The interaction of the SAR signal and the forest depends on the density and structure of the vegetation. The seasonal phenology of trees with pre-winter leaf fall can also have a significant impact on radar signals. To date, a few studies have focused on the detection of wet snow in forested areas. Koskinen *et al.* (1997) suggested using two reference images instead of one, taken before and after the melting season to better estimate the relative fraction of snow-free soil. This does not solve all problems as false detection of wet snow occurs if the soil in the second reference image was already drying (Luojus *et al.* 2007). Marin *et al.* (2020) have recently shown that the melting phases (moistening, ripening and runoff) can be identified using multi-temporal SAR backscatter. Other studies have used threshold functions instead of a fixed threshold to better account for signal variability with land cover (e.g. sigmoid functions have been used by Malnes and Guneriussen (2002), Longépé *et al.* (2009) and Rondeau-Genesse *et al.* (2016)). Optical satellite measurements have also been used to correct possible inconsistencies in wet snow estimates, particularly in forests or waterlogged soils (Rondeau-Genesse *et al.* (2016)). In this chapter, we discuss wet snow extent estimation using Nagler's backscatter thresholding method (noted reference method hereafter). We also examine some other interesting options to improve wet snow detection by exploring the use of similarity metrics (such as the normalized cross correlation ratio, the Hausdorff distance and some other more refined image distance functions). Several distances are calculated and tested on a database of Sentinel-1 SAR image time series of different sizes over the French Alps. The resulting metrics are discussed and compared with the reference method, as well as with independent data.

## 5.2. Test area and data

As observations, we used the C-band backscatter coefficients from the SAR instrument aboard the European Space Agency (ESA) Sentinel-1 satellites as part of the Copernicus program. The Sentinel-1 missions were launched in April 2014 and April 2016, respectively. On our test areas, the revisit period was six days. We used level 1 products from the Ground Range Detected (GRD, with a spatial resolution of 20 m in VV and VH polarizations) available on the CNES and ESA websites[1]. For each orbit direction (ascending and descending), we used one image every six days between August 1, 2017 and August 31, 2018, resulting in a continuous time series of more than 130 images. The time period of this study included highly disturbed meteorological and winter snow conditions (Goetz 2018; Stoffel and Corona 2018). We relied on CNES facilities to perform pre-processing of SAR images using the Orfeo ToolBox software. Thermal noise removal, speckle filtering, radiometric calibration and terrain correction were carried out using the SRTM Digital Elevation Model (DEM) at 30 m. The DEM was also used to link each pixel of the satellite images with an altitude, slope and orientation. For evaluation and comparison purposes, we made use of *in situ* snow measurements from the Météo-France station network and also used Theia snow products derived from cloud free optical Sentinel-2 satellite data (Gascoin *et al.* 2019). Our test zones were heterogeneous steep mountain areas located in the French Alps with complex topography and a wide range of surface types; we chose three embedded zones of different areas as shown in Figure 5.1: area 1 with 10,900 × 10,900 pixels, area 2 with 1,759 × 1,381 pixels and area 3 with 24 × 28 pixels.

## 5.3. Wet snow detection using Sentinel-1

Change detection is a feature of interest for snow monitoring in the mountains because it allows us to identify and analyze changes in a scene from images acquired at different dates. Radar imagery has the ability to observe at any time of the day or night, and is therefore very useful in complex situations with poor weather conditions. The challenge is to isolate the changes occurring over a time series of images and to accurately assign these changes in the image to some changes in the environment (related to the state of snow, vegetation, soil, etc.). Unsurprisingly, change detection is widely used for wet snow detection from SAR images (Baghdadi *et al.* 1998; Magagi and Bernier 2003; Nagler *et al.* 2016). A review of methods for wet snow detection using SAR data is given in Tsai *et al.* (2019). C-band measurements are sensitive to wet snow due to the high dielectric contrast with non-wet snow covered surfaces, as dry snow generally lacks C-band backscatter in co- or cross-polarisation. An image ratio (with and without snow) is calculated and a threshold is applied to obtain a wet snow mask.

---

1. https://scihub.copernicus.eu/dhus/; https://peps.cnes.fr

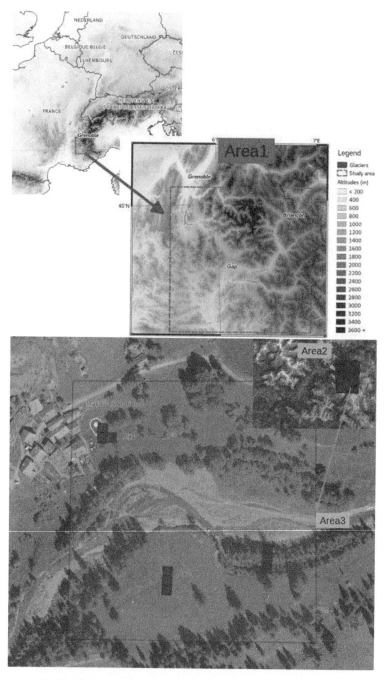

**Figure 5.1.** *Location of the study areas. For a color version*
*of this figure, see www.iste.co.uk/atto/change1.zip*

**Figure 5.2.** *Altitude–time diagrams of VH SAR backscatters from the ascending orbit A161 (early morning) computed for test area 2 and for southern orientations. For a color version of this figure, see www.iste.co.uk/atto/change1.zip*

Figure 5.2 shows altitude–time diagrams of VH SAR backscatters from the Sentinel-1 ascending orbit A161 (early morning) computed for test area 2 and for southern orientations. Altitudes vary between 1,200 m and 3,100 m and mean backscatters range from -20 dB to -8 dB. We observed signal variations throughout the season that may be partly due to rain-on-snow effects and snowmelt (from the end of March 2018). This is characterized by a significant drop in the backscatter for some individual dates associated with rain-on-snow events such as early January 2018, 22 January 2018, and mid-February and mid-March 2018. We also observed a continuous decrease of the backscatter starting at the end of March, coinciding with the beginning of the snowpack melting.

In order to look more specifically at the variation of the SAR signal during the 2017–2018 season, we selected a small alpine area at about 1,900 m close to the *in situ* station (called Maljasset), of the Météo-France station network, from which daily measurements of snow depth, rain rate and temperature (min, max) were made. Within test area 3 (shown in Figure 5.1), three small sites are selected in the vicinity of the Maljasset station: an open area very close to the station (called Pix1-NearStation), a wooded zone (called Pix2-Forest) and another open area (called Pix3-Grassland). For each of these selected areas, three Sentinel-1 observation pixels were monitored over one year: August 2017 to July 2018 (pixels shown in blue squares in Figure 5.1).

Figure 5.3 shows Sentinel-1 VH time series observations from the ascending orbit for our three selected sites in area 3 (see location in Figure 5.1). Results are shown for Pix1-NearStation (black curves), Pix2-Forest (green curves) and for Pix3-Grassland (magenta curves). Daily snow height and rain rate measured at the Maljasset station are displayed as shaded blue areas and green bars, respectively. We noted that, overall, wooded areas have higher backscatter coefficients than open or mixed areas. We also noted fluctuations in the SAR signal, which varies depending on the type of surface, some of these fluctuations can be explained by the effects of snow accumulation or rain on snow. Furthermore, there was an overall gradual increase of backscatters with snow accumulation until the beginning of the melting process. The increase in backscattering may be due to snow volume scattering; this effect is more pronounced for morning passes and open areas (the increase of backscatters with snow accumulation is also observed for VV polarization (not shown)). Regarding the evolution of temperatures (not shown), we noted roughly three main periods of variation: August to October 2017 with summer conditions, November to mid-April with much lower temperatures (the minimum reaching -23°C at the end of February) and a third period until August 2018, again with more moderate temperatures. Marin *et al.* (2020) proposed simple rules for identifying snow melting phases through analysis of SAR time series. A decrease in the afternoon backscatters (i.e. with the ascending orbit) of at least 2 dB or more from the winter trend would indicate the beginning of the melting process. The ripening phase is identified as soon as this phenomenon is also observed in the morning time series (descending orbit). This phase, characterized by several oscillations, ends when the morning and afternoon backscatters reach local minimums. The authors suggest taking the mean date among the local minima as the beginning of the runoff phase, which is characterized by a monotonous increase in the backscatter coefficient. It is particularly difficult to apply these rules over our study period, as the winter of 2017–2018 was exceptionally eventful with successive weather events bringing a lot of snow and rain on snow (rain on snow events mid-December, early January, etc.). The snow depth and rainfall rate curves measured at Maljasset station indicate the extent of these events. Following (Marin *et al.* 2020) rules and apart from rain-on-snow events, we could note a strong decrease of afternoon backscatters on March 22–23, 2018. This decrease is much more pronounced for mixed and open areas than for areas with trees (over which less than 2 dB of change was noted). Prior to this, several signal oscillations were observed and there was a continuous decrease in backscatter (evening) until April 16 for mixed areas and later for unvegetated areas (April 28) before backscatters began to increase. Signals over forested areas are more complex to interpret despite some variations due to snow or rain-on-snow events.

Another example at larger scale is given in Figure 5.4 (over test area 1). The figure compares (a) wet snow detection derived from Sentinel-1 images of April 27–28, 2018 from descending and ascending orbits using a 2-dB threshold method (late August 2017 being used as reference) with (b) snow extent obtained from Sentinel-2 optical image of April 25, 2018. The Sentinel-2 scene was almost cloud-free and the agreement between Sentinel-1 and Sentinel-2 snow products is rather good for this period. It should be noted that Sentinel-2 measurements detect the extent of total snow, whether dry or wet, while Sentinel-1 detects only wet snow; therefore, the comparison is not between two identical products. In addition, observations from the two satellites were not acquired on the same day or at the same time of day.

## 5.4. Metrics to detect wet snow

As discussed in the introduction, there are several possible limitations to the use of threshold methods. For instance, there is the need to optimize the selection of one or two reference images as this is a key factor in wet snow detection results. There is also the need to adjust the threshold values to better account for the variability of the SAR signal by surface type. To discuss these issues in further detail, we propose to explore the potential of different mathematical metrics that would (1) allow for better detection of snow cover induced changes in SAR image time series by maximizing the sensitivity to wet snow and/or (2) make a better selection of reference images. In this chapter, we discuss the usefulness of robust image comparison metrics to isolate wet snow pixels (see Zamperoni and Starovoitov (1996); Starovoitov and Samal (1998); Di Gesu and Starovoitov (1999) and references therein for reviews on distance-based image comparison in a more general context). We test different similarity measures based on the *normalized cross correlation ratio*, different matrix norms and the *Hausdorff distance*.

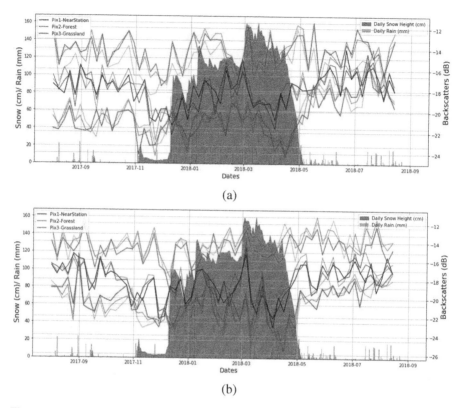

**Figure 5.3.** (a) Time series of Sentinel-1 VH observations from the ascending orbit for 3 selected sites in the vicinity of the measuring station Maljasset (see its location in Figure 5.1). Results are shown for a mixed zone very close to the station (called Pix1-NearStation, curves in black), a wooded zone (called Pix1-Forest, curves in green) and an open area (grassland) zone (called Pix1-Grassland, curves in magenta). For each of these selected areas three observation pixels were monitored over time (shown in blue in Figure 5.1). For each of these areas three observation pixels were monitored over time. Daily snow heights measured at the Maljasset station are displayed as shaded blue areas and green bars indicate measured daily rainfall rates (in mm). (b) Same as (a) but for descending orbit. For a color version of this figure, see www.iste.co.uk/atto/change1.zip

In order to define different distances, we start by introducing some matrix norms. Given a real $m \times n$ matrix $A$ and $p \in [1, \infty]$, we define the norms

$$\text{for } p \in [1, \infty), \ \| A \|_p = \left( \sum_{1 \leqslant i \leqslant m, 1 \leqslant j \leqslant n} |a_{ij}|^p \right)^{1/p},$$

$$\| A \|_\infty = \max_{1 \leqslant i \leqslant m, 1 \leqslant j \leqslant n} |a_{ij}|.$$

[5.1]

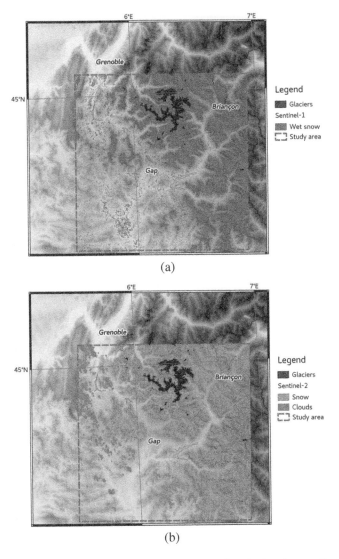

**Figure 5.4.** *(a) Wet snow cover extent derived from Sentinel-1 descending/ascending images of April 27/28, 2018 and (b) snow extent mask derived from Sentinel-2 optical image of April 25, 2018. Background: SRTM Digital elevations. For a color version of this figure, see www.iste.co.uk/atto/change1.zip*

Classical values correspond to $p = 1$ (mean error), $p = 2$ (root-mean-square or rms error) and $p = \infty$ (maximal error or supremum norm), the latter being more sensitive to the perturbation of a small number of matrix coefficients for large matrices.

The norms [5.1] apply in particular to vectors (case $m = 1$ or $n = 1$). We also consider the operator norms (or induced norms) defined by

$$\|A\|_p = \sup_{x \in \mathbb{R}^n, x \neq 0} \frac{\|Ax\|_p}{\|x\|_p}, \tag{5.2}$$

our main focus being $p = 2$ (spectral norm). It is a classical result that $\|A\|_2$ is the largest singular value of $A$, i.e. the square root of the largest eigenvalue of $A^T A$, where $(\cdot)^T$ denotes the transpose. Each of the above matrix norms $\| \|$ induces a distance $D(A, B) = \|A - B\|$.

Another similarity measure between two $m \times n$ non-zero matrices $A$, $B$ is given by the normalized cross correlation ratio (CO)

$$CO(A, B) = 1 - \frac{1}{\|A\|_2 \|B\|_2} \sum_{1 \leqslant i \leqslant m, 1 \leqslant j \leqslant n} a_{ij} b_{ij}, \tag{5.3}$$

which vanishes if and only if $B = \lambda A$ for some positive constant $\lambda$.

The Hausdorff distance provides another similarity measure which can be interesting to capture small interface motions within images, while being more sensitive than $\| \|_1$ and $\| \|_2$ to localized perturbations. The Hausdorff distance H between two real $m \times n$ matrices $A$, $B$ is defined as follows. Each matrix is identified with a function defined on a grid of size $m \times n$, and we consider the Hausdorff distance between the two corresponding graphs

$$G_A = \left\{ A_{ij} = \left( \frac{i}{m}, \frac{j}{n}, a_{ij} \right), 1 \leqslant i \leqslant m, 1 \leqslant j \leqslant n \right\},$$

$$G_B = \left\{ B_{kl} = \left( \frac{k}{m}, \frac{l}{n}, b_{kl} \right), 1 \leqslant k \leqslant m, 1 \leqslant l \leqslant n \right\}.$$

In this work, we measure the distance between points with the city block distance $\| \|_1$, leading to $\|A_{ij} - B_{kl}\|_1 = \frac{|i-k|}{m} + \frac{|j-l|}{n} + |a_{ij} - b_{kl}|$. We then have

$$H(A, B) = \max_{1 \leqslant i \leqslant m, 1 \leqslant j \leqslant n} \{ d(A_{ij}, G_B), d(B_{ij}, G_A) \}, \tag{5.4}$$

where $d(A_{ij}, G_B) = \min_{B_{kl}} \|A_{ij} - B_{kl}\|_1$ and $d(B_{ij}, G_A)$ is defined similarly.

It should be noted that the above distances lead to different computational costs. If $m \approx n$, the computation of the entrywise norms [5.1] and correlation [5.3] require $O(n^2)$ floating-point operations. Evaluating the spectral norm takes $O(n^3)$ operations and a naive algorithm for computing the Hausdorff distance requires $O(n^4)$ operations.

We use the following logarithmic similarity measures between non-negative $m \times n$ matrices, which are based on the previous ones [5.1], [5.2], [5.3] and [5.4] :

$$d_p(A, B) = \| \ln A - \ln B \|_p, \qquad p = 1, 2, \infty, \qquad\qquad [5.5]$$

$$\tilde{d}_2(A, B) = \| | \ln A - \ln B | \|_2, \qquad\qquad [5.6]$$

$$H_{\log}(A, B) = H(\ln A, \ln B), \qquad\qquad [5.7]$$

$$CO_{\log}(A, B) = CO(\ln A, \ln B), \qquad\qquad [5.8]$$

with the natural logarithm applied component-wise, conditionally with respect to $B$, to the positive entry pairs:

$$(\ln A)_{ij} = \begin{cases} \ln a_{ij} & \text{if } a_{ij} > 0 \text{ and } b_{ij} > 0, \\ 0 & \text{otherwise,} \end{cases}$$

$$(\ln B)_{ij} = \begin{cases} \ln b_{ij} & \text{if } a_{ij} > 0 \text{ and } b_{ij} > 0, \\ 0 & \text{otherwise.} \end{cases}$$

The sign condition allows us to neglect non-meaningful zero entries in the comparison of matrices arising from SAR images.

Moreover, when $B$ corresponds to a reference state with higher values of the matrix coefficients (absence of wet snow), the sensitivity to the decrease of coefficients in $A$ (presence of wet snow) can be enhanced by modifying the above distances in a suitable way. More precisely, we consider solely the entry pairs with $a_{ij} \leqslant b_{ij}$, which leads to the modified similarity measures:

$$d_p^+(A, B) = \| \ln A_+ - \ln B_+ \|_p, \qquad p = 1, 2, \infty, \qquad\qquad [5.9]$$

$$\tilde{d}_2^+(A, B) = \| | \ln A_+ - \ln B_+ | \|_2, \qquad\qquad [5.10]$$

$$H_{\log}^+(A, B) = H(\ln A_+, \ln B_+), \qquad\qquad [5.11]$$

$$CO_{\log}^+(A, B) = CO(\ln A_+, \ln B_+), \qquad\qquad [5.12]$$

where

$$(\ln A_+)_{ij} = \begin{cases} \ln a_{ij} & \text{if } b_{ij} \geqslant a_{ij} > 0, \\ 0 & \text{otherwise,} \end{cases} \quad (\ln B_+)_{ij} = \begin{cases} \ln b_{ij} & \text{if } b_{ij} \geqslant a_{ij} > 0, \\ 0 & \text{otherwise.} \end{cases}$$

It should be noted that these similarity measures are not symmetric with respect to the arguments $A$ (current image) and $B$ (reference image).

We will also consider modified distances restricted to a certain subset of indices $(i, j)$, corresponding, for example, to a given range of altitudes. Let us consider a grid subset $\Gamma \subset \{1, 2, \dots, m\} \times \{1, 2, \dots, n\}$ (corresponding to a subset of pixels), an $m \times n$ matrix $A$, and define the $m \times n$ matrix $A_{|\Gamma}$ through

$$(A_{|\Gamma})_{ij} = \begin{cases} a_{ij} & \text{if } (i, j) \in \Gamma, \\ 0 & \text{otherwise.} \end{cases} \quad\quad [5.13]$$

For all similarity measures $D$ defined above in equations [5.5]–[5.12], we denote

$$D_{|\Gamma}(A, B) = D(A_{|\Gamma}, B_{|\Gamma}). \quad\quad [5.14]$$

Hereafter, we denote by "norme1", "rms" and "normeinf" the distances [5.5] or [5.9] with $p = 1$, $p = 2$ and $p = \infty$, respectively. In the same way, "normeop2" refers to [5.6] and [5.10], "haus" to [5.7] and [5.11], and "correl" to [5.8] and [5.12].

## 5.5. Discussion

Let us first look at the correlation between images. Here, we consider the descending orbit SAR images on area 2. Figure 5.5 shows "1 minus correlation" matrix computed using SAR time series. As expected, correlations between images decrease during the snowmelt period (roughly between March 22, 2018 and June 20, 2018). Outside the melting period, we find situations where the correlation decreases; this may be related to rain-on-snow events that significantly impacted the observations. It is worth noting that the correlation matrix allows a global view of the entire time series and potentially better selection of one or more reference dates, without running the risk of selecting a date already subject to significant fluctuations in the SAR signal. For instance, it would appear relevant to consider the image of October 17 as a reference rather than that of the end of August 2017.

Figure 5.6 shows the similarity curves obtained using area 3 SAR images (descending orbit) according to the following metrics defined in section 5.4: correlation $CO_{\log}$, mean error $d_1$, maximal error $d_\infty$, spectral norm $\tilde{d}_2$ and Hausdorff distance $H_{\log}$; the reference image is October 17, 2017. The distances are calculated on area 3 (see Figure 5.1) which includes the Maljasset station, whose measurements of snow depth and daily rain rate are also shown for comparison. The distance curves have been smoothed using the Legendre polynomial method for better readability (dotted symbols represent true estimates and solid lines are filtered distances). When using October 17 as reference, the maximal error $d_\infty$ and Hausdorff distance $H_{\log}$ (blue and green curves) vary similarly, but the computation of the maximal error is much faster. We also observe similar variations between the mean error $d_1$ and spectral norm $\tilde{d}_2$ (red and magenta curves). Almost all distances display a peak for the melting period indicating a strong dissimilarity with the chosen reference (slightly earlier using the Hausdorff distance). A secondary distance peak is detected (mainly using $d_1$ and $\tilde{d}_2$); this peak would correspond to the presence of wet snow following the first snowfall in early November on still-warm soil. Fluctuations in the distances are observed for some events often related to rain on snow.

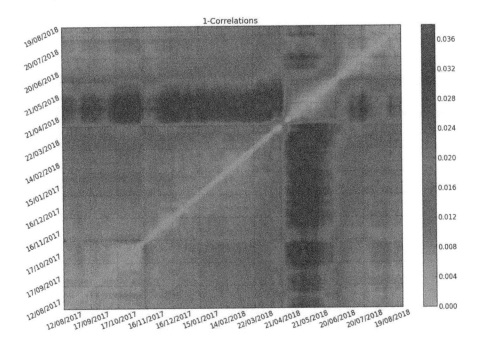

**Figure 5.5.** *Correlation matrix of observation time series computed from formula [5.8]. For a color version of this figure, see www.iste.co.uk/atto/change1.zip*

Figure 5.7 provides a complement to these statistics by showing the distance results using test area 2 and by selecting two other reference dates: June 8, 2017 (Figure 5.7(b)) and July 2, 2018 (Figure 5.7(c)) in addition to October 17, 2017. The main peak is detected generally later on with the maximal error $d_\infty$. Note that the date of the maximum amount of snow, and therefore the beginning of the melting, is not the same between area 2 and area 3. Globally, the distribution of the distances according to the selected reference are quite similar, overall with a less flat distribution for the spectral norm $\tilde{d}_2$. For the larger area 2, $\tilde{d}_2$ and $d_1$ display significantly different time series, unlike for the small area 3. The Hausdorff distance is omitted because of its time-consuming computation in this larger area.

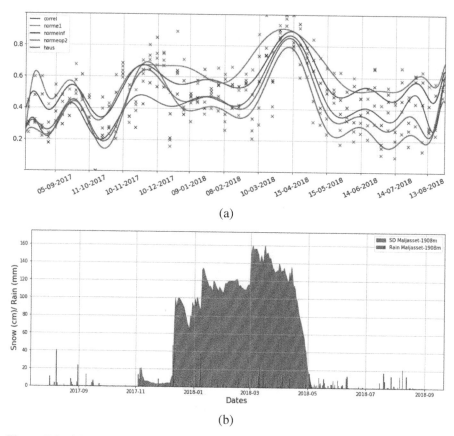

(a)

(b)

**Figure 5.6.** (a) Metrics computed over test area 3 near Maljasset station using October 17, 2017 image as reference. The black points correspond to the correlation [5.8] between the current image $A$ and the reference image $B$ corresponding to October 17, 2017. The red and blue points correspond to the distances [5.5] with $p = 1$ (mean error) and $p = \infty$ (maximal error), respectively, and the magenta points to the distance [5.6] derived from the spectral norm. The green points correspond to the Hausdorff distance [5.7]. Each distance is rescaled by its maximal value over the time series. The curves correspond to least square fits using Legendre polynomials. (b) Snow depth and daily rain rates observed at Maljasset station. For a color version of this figure, see www.iste.co.uk/atto/change1.zip

In Figure 5.8, we restrict the computation of Figure 5.7(a) to pixels for which the logarithm of the ratio between the current image A and the reference B (October 17, 2017) is negative. This is done by replacing the similarity measures [5.5]–[5.8] by the modified ones [5.9]–[5.12]. With this pixel selection, the mean error $d_1$ and spectral norm $\tilde{d}_2$ (red and magenta curves) display very similar variations, while the computation of $d_1$ is numerically less expensive.

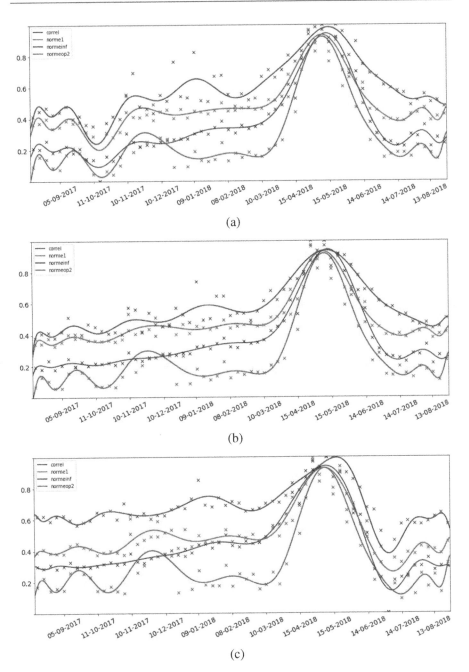

(a)

(b)

(c)

**Figure 5.7.** *(a) Same as Figure 5.6(a) but for test area 2 using October 17, 2017 as reference, (b) same as (a) but using August 6, 2017 as reference image (c) same as (a) but using February 7, 2018 as reference image. For a color version of this figure, see www.iste.co.uk/atto/change1.zip*

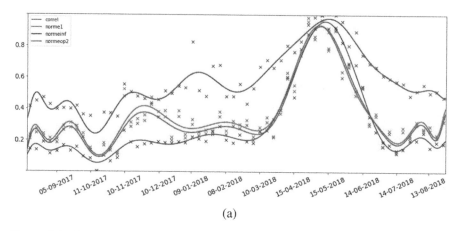

(a)

**Figure 5.8.** *Same as Figure 5.7(a) but using pixels for which the logarithm of the ratio between the current image A and the reference B (October 17, 2017) is negative. Black points: correlation [5.12]. Red and blue: distances [5.9] with $p = 1$ (mean error) and $p = \infty$ (maximal error). Magenta: distance [5.10] derived from the spectral norm. Each distance is rescaled by its maximal value over the time series and the curves correspond to least square fits with Legendre polynomials. For a color version of this figure, see www.iste.co.uk/atto/change1.zip*

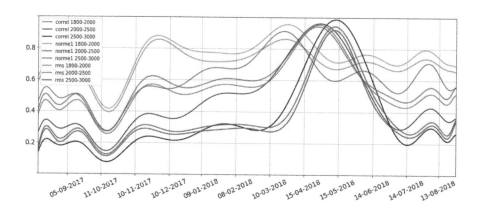

**Figure 5.9.** *Selection of metrics computed over test area 2 for ranges of altitudes: 1,800–2,000m, 2,000–2,500m and 2,500–3,000m; the reference image is October 17, 2017. We consider the correlation [5.8] (black curves), the mean error [5.5] with $p = 1$ (red curves) and the rms error [5.5] with $p = 2$ (green curves). The distances are modified according to formula [5.13] and [5.14], where $\Gamma$ denotes the subset of pixels whose altitudes belong to the given range. Each distance is rescaled by its maximal value over the time series and the curves correspond to least square fits with Legendre polynomials. For a color version of this figure, see www.iste.co.uk/atto/change1.zip*

The timing of the peak of the maximum distance is variable depending on the altitude. Figure 5.9 shows the distances by altitude intervals (1,800–2,000 m, 2,000–2,500 m, 2,500–3,000 m) and highlights that this peak is delayed for high altitudes. The distribution of distances is also less flat for high altitudes, with the exception of the distance increase in early November at 1,800–2,000 m, which is detected mainly using mean error $d_1$ and rms error $\tilde{d}_2$. We can note that these two distances display similar variations, but the numerical evaluation of the rms error is more expensive.

## 5.6. Conclusion

In this chapter, we reported on results from a first evaluation of the potential of different mathematical metrics that would help to better detect wet snow pixels in SAR image time series. Particular emphasis was placed on methods that would allow optimal selection of the reference images that are required to apply change detection methods. The correlation values of the images over the whole time series offer some very promising possibilities for the selection of reference images. The criteria for such a selection still remain to be studied in depth. The different metrics studied show variations that can be linked to significant changes in the SAR signal (related to rain-on-snow episodes, snow humidification, etc.) which is promising for implementing inversion methods integrating the time series of images as a whole. The distances introduced in this work could be improved in several ways:

– filtering effects (Starovoitov and Samal 1998) could be introduced in a nontrivial way, taking into account the terrain characteristics such as altitude, orientation and slope;

– given the relatively large size of full images (test area 1 of the order of $11,000 \times 11,000$ pixels), it will be necessary to achieve a good balance between the computational cost of the distance functions and their efficiency for wet snow detection.

## 5.7. Acknowledgements

The authors would like to acknowledge the support from the Centre National d'Etudes Spatiales (CNES) through access to the computing and storage facilities of the PEPS platform and through the funding of the APR SHARE project.

## 5.8. References

Baghdadi, N., Livingstone, C., Bernier, M. (1998). Airborne C-band SAR measurements of wet snow-covered areas. *IEEE Transactions on Geoscience and Remote Sensing*, 36(6), 1977–1981.

Baghdadi, N., Gauthier, Y., Bernier, M., Fortin, J.-P. (2000). Potential and limitations of RADARSAT SAR data for wet snow monitoring. *IEEE Transactions on Geoscience and Remote Sensing*, 38(1), 316–320.

Di Gesu, V. and Starovoitov, V. (1999). Distance-based functions for image comparison. *Pattern Recognition Letters*, 20, 207–214.

Gascoin, S., Grizonnet, M., Bouchet, M., Salgues, G., Hagolle, O. (2019). Theia snow collection: High-resolution operational snow cover maps from Sentinel-2 and Landsat-8 data. *Earth System Science Data*, 11, 492–514.

Goetz, D. (2018). Bilan nivo-météorologique de l'hiver 2017–2018. *Revue de l'ANENA* [Online]. Available at: https://www.anena.org/5042-la-revue-n-a.htm.

Karbou, F., Veyssière, G., Coléou, C., Dufour, A., Gouttevin, I., Durand, P., Gascoin, S., Grizonnet, M. (2020). Monitoring wet snow over an alpine region using Sentinel-1 observations. *IEEE Transactions on Geoscience and Remote Sensing*, 13(3), 381.

Koskinen, J., Pulliainen, J., Hallikainen, M. (1997). The use of ERS-1 SAR data in snow melt monitoring. *IEEE Transactions on Geoscience and Remote Sensing*, 35(3), 601–610.

Luojus, K., Pulliainen, J., Metsamaki, S., Hallikainen, M. (2007). Snow-covered area estimation using satellite radar wide-swath images. *IEEE Transactions on Geoscience and Remote Sensing*, 45, 978–989.

Magagi, R. and Bernier, M. (2003). Optimal conditions for wet snow detection using radarsat SAR data. *Remote Sensing of Environment*, 84, 221–233.

Marin, C., Bertoldi, G., Premier, V., Callegari, M., Brida, C., Hürkamp, K., Tschiersch, J., Zebisch, M., Notarnicola, C. (2020). Use of Sentinel-1 radar observations to evaluate snowmelt dynamics in alpine regions. *The Cryosphere*, 14, 935–956.

Nagler, T. and Rott, H. (2000). Retrieval of wet snow by means of multitemporal SAR data. *IEEE Transactions on Geoscience and Remote Sensing*, 38, 754–765.

Nagler, T., Rott, H., Ripper, E., Bippus, G., Hetzenecker, M. (2016). Advancements for snowmelt monitoring by means of sentinel-1 SAR. *Remote Sensing*, 8(4) [Online]. Available at: http://www.mdpi.com/2072-4292/8/4/348.

Starovoitov, V. and Samal, D. (1998). Experimental study of color image similarity. *Machine Graphics and Vision*, 11, 455–462.

Stoffel, M. and Corona, C. (2018). Future winters glimpsed in the Alps. *Nature Geoscience*, 11, 458–460.

Tsai, Y.L., Dietz, S., Oppelt, A., Kuenzer, N. (2019). Wet and dry snow detection using Sentinel-1 SAR data for mountainous areas with a machine learning technique. *Remote Sensing*, 11(8), 895.

Zamperoni, P. and Starovoitov, V. (1996). On measures of dissimilarity between arbitrary gray-scale images. *International Journal of Shape Modeling*, 2(2&3), 189–213.

# 6

# Fractional Field Image Time Series Modeling and Application to Cyclone Tracking

**Abdourrahmane M. ATTO[1], Aluísio PINHEIRO[2],
Guillaume GINOLHAC[1] and Pedro MORETTIN[3]**

[1]*University Savoie Mont Blanc, Annecy, France*
[2]*University of Campinas, Brazil*
[3]*University of São Paulo, Brazil*

## 6.1. Introduction

Cyclonic fields are violent atmospheric disturbances associated with swirling winds. These quasi-stochastic fields are the cause of many natural disasters, which motivate early detection methods as well as time monitoring of changing conditions (see, for instance, Chen *et al.* (2016)). Here, we discuss some methods for time monitoring and prediction of cyclonic fields. Time monitoring will be done by analyzing the cyclonic field's dynamics and local intensity variations over space and time. Predicting the cyclone's future state from its present and past dynamics will be made possible through model selection and validation steps.

Satellite imagery is one of the most important sensing tools for regular observations, amongst all the meteorological sources of information available for cyclone monitoring. This is especially true for hurricanes, because of the difficulties in the coverage of large marine areas (Goto *et al.* 2015; Nastos *et al.* 2015; Mas *et al.* 2016). We propose the characterization of cyclonic fields based on satellite image time series.

*Change Detection and Image Time Series Analysis 1*,
coordinated by Abdourrahmane M. ATTO, Francesca BOVOLO and Lorenzo BRUZZONE.
© ISTE Ltd 2021.

The analysis of cyclonic fields requires the detection and localization of the *cyclone eye* and *cyclone eyewall*, as well as estimating cyclone intensity variations. The detection and estimation procedures must be performed subject to a highly disturbed and dynamic environment. We consider hereafter in the same framework both:

– analysis and prediction of intensity variations;

– tracking of the cyclone eye on spatio-temporal variables.

This framework requires cyclone intensity model identification and parameter estimation. It also requires identifying the cyclone eye from its geometrical and/or statistical characteristics (Terry and Kim 2015; Rozoff *et al.* 2016; Xu and Liu 2016; Zheng *et al.* 2016).

Figure 6.1 provides an overview of cyclone characteristics. The eyewall is thicker and more compact than the remaining outflow clouds, whereas the cyclone eye is blurred by the eyewall upstairs outflow when the imaging system operates an upstairs-sensing with near-optical image modality.

**Figure 6.1.** *Cyclonic field model. The eyewall has a usual diameter of 30–60 km. The eyewall diameter may go up to 150 kilometers. For a color version of this figure, see www.iste.co.uk/atto/change1.zip*

There are several approaches in the literature to cyclone analysis and tracking based on geometric eye detection, such as:

– non-parametric segmentation (based on boundaries' identification of cloud clusters in Gamba (1999) and Doraiswamy *et al.* (2013), or by the characterization of cloud's in Caban *et al.* (2007));

Isaac hurricane image time series

**Figure 6.2.** *Isaac hurricane images. Courtesy:  @Nasa-Images, Geostationary Operational Environmental Satellite (GOES)-13, August 27, 2012. The hurricane is a vortex field with very low central pressure (eye: no rain, low wind) and highest winds that are approximately 130 kilometers per hour around the eyewall. For a color version of this figure, see www.iste.co.uk/atto/change1.zip*

– parametric shape-based segmentation (geometric shape; for instance, we may determine the eye from a spiral center of mass concern (Jaiswal and Kishtawal 2011) or from watershed transform (Lakshmanan *et al.* 2003, 2009));

– expert-aided mixed analysis and visualization as in Joshi *et al.* (2009).

We should note that eye detection based on geometric approaches is biased when using satellite optical images (see Kodama and Yamada 2005; Chang *et al.* 2009) because of

– the outflow cloud disturbances on top of the eye blur the eye position and make a direct shape-based eyewall inference that is too intricate (the eyewall has variable geometry, see Figure 6.2) to be useful in real-time detection and prediction problems;

– several shape asymmetries, which make the use of a fixed rule for the center of mass computation untenable in real applications.

In practice, satellite imagery-based eye detection remains a challenge, even when the eyewall has been correctly detected and localized.

The contributions involved in the chapter are as follows. First, we propose a statistical model associated with a fractional pink random field in order to characterize the cyclone eyewall and eye roughness (texture modeling). Second, we propose a method for estimating the parameter of this pink fractional field model and detecting cyclone eye spatial position. Eye detection is performed per image frame, by seeking the region with the smallest fractal parameter under the constraint that this region is surrounded by regions associated with maximal fractal intensity parameters (eyewall). Eye tracking is proposed based on the eye detection method as well, by focusing on a tighter window search and detecting the future eye position. We build a time sequence of parameters associated with every geo-referenced spatial position and describe this sequence as an Autoregressive Fractionally Integrated Moving Average (ARFIMA) process. The ARFIMA model captures both long-term and short-term statistical variations of the cyclone random fractal intensity process. The Isaac hurricane is used as a case study.

The remainder of the chapter is organized as follows. Section 6.2 provides (from wavelet-based spectral analysis) the fractional random field model whose parameter can be seen as a cyclone field *fractal intensity* feature (indicator of local or global cyclone strength). Section 6.3 addresses cyclone eye detection and tracking. Section 6.4 addresses the intensity dynamics of the fractal cyclone parameter over time and presents the ARFIMA modeling and prediction of time evolution of the cyclone intensities. Section 6.5 concludes the chapter, and presents some prospects to the proposed methodology.

## 6.2. Random field model of a cyclone texture

One of the requirements of real-time detection of cyclone formation and evolution should be a simple, albeit correct, low-dimension characterization based on an image time series of a cyclone field, which retains the significant information from these phenomena. At the end of this section, we arrive at a single parameter description of a cyclone filed. This description is derived by analyzing wavelet-based spectral features and removing the non-informative variables.

The test dataset analyzed in this chapter is a spatio-temporal field (Isaac hurricane), whose dynamic is studied through an Image Time Series (ITS) $\mathcal{I}$:

$$\mathcal{I} = \{\mathcal{I}_m : m = 1, 2, \ldots, M\} \qquad [6.1]$$

with $M = 288$. Four sample images of this ITS are given in Figure 6.2. We see Isaac moving from the Gulf of Mexico (images $\approx \mathcal{I}_1$) to Louisiana (images $\approx \mathcal{I}_{288}$). Rotation parameters are well-known and depend on the hemisphere: thus, rotational analysis is not considered here. This chapter focuses on capturing cyclonic intensity variations through texture analysis and descriptors.

### 6.2.1. *Cyclone texture feature*

A cyclone field can be characterized by color and texture (Kandaswamy *et al.* 2005). Color information is used to discriminate between the image background and the cyclone pixels. Due to saturation, which occurs in the cyclone's cloudy environment and the outflow clouds that enfold the cyclone eye, except for a few cases, the information conveyed by color cannot be used directly to compute cyclone intensity or detect the cyclone center. Texture is thus the most informative feature for characterizing a cyclone. We propose the extraction of cyclone textural information by the wavelet details of the cyclone field as follows.

Consider a wavelet-based framework so that the input sample field $\mathcal{I}_m$ is projected on subspaces

$$\{\mathbf{W}_{\theta_k}, k = 0, 1, \ldots, N - 1\}$$

where $\mathbf{W}_{\theta_0}$ is the *scaling/approximation subspace*, and all other subspaces represent *shifted wavelet subspaces*. Standard wavelet transforms are: DWT (Discrete Wavelet Transform)/DWPT (Discrete Wavelet Packet Transform) and their stationary versions (redundant, non-decimated) known as SWT (Stationary Wavelet Transform) and SWPT (Stationary Wavelet Packet Transform), see Daubechies (1992), Coifman and Donoho (1995) and Mallat (1998) for general literature.

Let $\mathcal{W}_\theta$ be the wavelet projector on subspace $\mathbf{W}_\theta$ and $\mathcal{W}_\theta^{-1}$ be its *inverse* (or reverse, in the wide sense), when restricting on $\mathbf{W}_\theta$. The instantaneous field observation $\mathcal{I}_m$ (image, subimage, boxcar neighborhood or region-of-interest in a mono-channel image) has subspace $\mathbf{W}_\theta$ coefficients denoted by:

$$\mathbf{C}_\theta\{\mathcal{I}_m\} = \mathcal{W}_\theta\left[\mathcal{I}_m\right] = \left(\mathbf{C}_\theta\{\mathcal{I}_m\}[k_1, k_2]\right)_{k_1, k_2 \in \mathbb{Z}}; \qquad [6.2]$$

and this image is represented as:

$$\mathcal{I}_m = \sum_{k=0}^{N-1} \mathcal{W}_{\theta_k}^{-1}\left[\mathbf{C}_{\theta_k}\{\mathcal{I}_m\}\right]. \qquad [6.3]$$

At high wavelet decomposition levels, the corresponding approximation or scaling coefficients $\theta = \theta_0$ are smooth trends and as such, not texture-representatives. Texture can thus be retrieved by using a sufficiently high decomposition level and then focusing on wavelet details, i.e. the coefficients associated with $\theta \neq \theta_0$. The textural field $\mathcal{T}_m$ is thus derived hereafter by forcing to zero high-level approximation/scaling coefficients:

$$\mathcal{T}_m = \sum_{k=1}^{N-1} \mathcal{W}_{\theta_k}^{-1}\left[\mathbf{C}_{\theta_k}\{\mathcal{I}_m\}\right]. \qquad [6.4]$$

SWT details of Isaac hurricane images

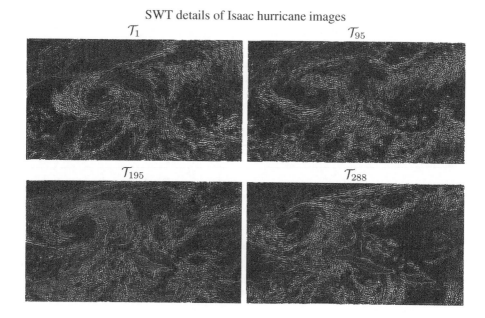

*Figure 6.3. Sample $\mathcal{T}$ textures reconstructed by forcing to zero SWT approximation of $\mathcal{I}$, while keeping all SWT wavelet coefficients (details). Compare with the corresponding image $\mathcal{T}$ samples given in Figure 6.2*

Figure 6.3 highlights the rich textural information captured by using SWT and equation [6.4]. This textural information is such that the cyclone eye and eyewall appear as dark. This texture-based approach thus enables us to capture the intensity of the cyclone outflow.

Given the aim of a parsimonious dynamic texture model, we focus on the analysis of the spectral wavelet features of Isaac sample images. We assume that $\mathbf{C}_\theta\{\mathcal{T}_m\}$ has zero mean wavelet details due to the very low mean values observed in practice[1].

## 6.2.2. *Wavelet-based power spectral densities and cyclone fields*

We can distinguish two types of wavelet correlation structures:

– intra-correlations that are intrinsic to a given wavelet node $\theta$ (correlations involved in set $\mathbf{C}_\theta\{\mathcal{I}_m\}$, for instance);

---

1. A straightforward zero-mean testing on the detail wavelet coefficients of the time series considered in this chapter confirms the negligible mean assumption. In general, it suffices to remove the non-representative mean by differencing.

– inter-correlations that are relative to two arbitrary nodes $\theta_k$ and $\theta_\ell$ (dependencies between $\mathbf{C}_{\theta_k}\{\mathcal{I}_m\}$ and $\mathbf{C}_{\theta_\ell}\{\mathcal{I}_m\}$).

When using high order wavelets (for instance, Daubechies wavelets with orders $r \geqslant 7$), the sequence

$$\{\mathbf{C}_{\theta_k}\{\mathcal{I}_m\}, k = 0, 1, \ldots, N-1\}$$

has weak intra- and inter- correlation structures, and we can focus on the diagonal elements of the wavelet correlation matrix. These diagonal elements are the set of variances:

$$\{\mathrm{Var}\left[\mathbf{C}_{\theta_k}\{\mathcal{I}_m\}\right], k = 0, 1, \ldots, N-1\}.$$

These variances are the key elements for defining the wavelet-based Power Spectral Density (PSD) of $\mathcal{I}_m$. The following presents DWT/SWT and DWPT/SWPT-based PSD derivation.

When DPWT/SWPT are considered and a high-order wavelet is used for the decomposition, then the PSD sampling operated by wavelets is regular and defined by (see Atto *et al.* (2013)):

$$\widehat{\gamma} = \sum_{\substack{n_1 \in \{0, \ldots, 2^J-1\} \\ n_2 \in \{0, \ldots, 2^J-1\}}} \mathrm{var}[c_{J,[F(n_1), F(n_2)]}] \times \delta_{\frac{n_1\pi}{2^J}, \frac{n_2\pi}{2^J}} \qquad [6.5]$$

where $F(p)$ denotes the Gray code permutation of $p$ defined by

$$F(p) = \sum_{\ell=1}^{j} \left(\epsilon_\ell \oplus \epsilon_{\ell-1}\right) 2^{j-\ell} \qquad [6.6]$$

if $p$ admits the base-2 numeral form $p = \sum_{\ell=1}^{j} \epsilon_\ell 2^{j-\ell}$, with $\epsilon_\ell \in \{0, 1\}$ and $\oplus$ denoting the *bitwise exclusive "or"*.

Some DWPT-based PSD samples of cyclone fields are given in Figure 6.4 where, for a given texture $\mathcal{I}_m$, the variance terms $\mathrm{var}[c_{j,[n_1, n_2]}]$ involved in equation [6.5] become $\mathrm{var}[c_{j,[n_1, n_2]}\{\mathcal{I}_m\}]$. We observe from Figure 6.4 that the PSD of cyclone fields satisfy the following properties:

– [*p1*] spectral information is concentrated in low frequencies;

– [*p2*] almost isotropy property holds true from the corresponding spectral information;

– [*p3*] all PSD can be seen as functions with exponential power decay.

The first property [*p1*] makes the restriction to DWT/SWT non-regular PSD sampling convenient for cyclone field analysis: these transforms avoid a fine analysis of higher frequencies and save computational time, without significant loss of performance. When DWT/SWT are considered and a wavelet with high order is used for the decomposition, the PSD sampling is irregular and corresponds to the block diagram given by Table 6.1. In this case, the 2D DWT/SWT PSD $\hat{\gamma}$ is defined as follows:

$$\hat{\gamma} = \mathrm{var}[c_{J,[0,0]}] \times \delta_{0,0}$$

$$+ \sum_{\substack{j=1,2,...,J \\ n_1,n_2 \in \{0,1\} \\ (n_1,n_2) \neq (0,0)}} \mathrm{var}[c_{j,[n_1,n_2]}] \times \delta_{\frac{n_1\pi}{2^j},\frac{n_2\pi}{2^j}} \qquad [6.7]$$

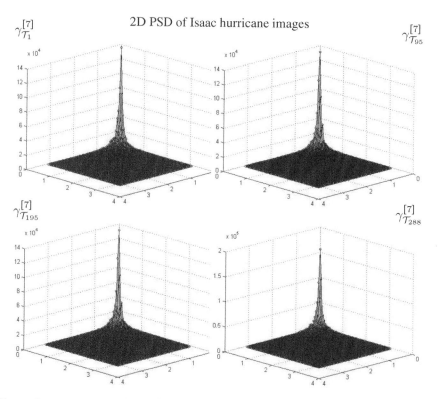

**Figure 6.4.** *2D DWPT PSD of for the sample images* $\mathcal{I}_m$ *given by Figure 6.2. The PSD have been computed with six decomposition levels and a Daubechies wavelet of order 7. Spectra for the corresponding textures* $\mathcal{T}_m$ *(see Figure 6.3) are deduced by removing the high peaks at frequency* $(0,0)$ *in the displayed PSD. Spectra for SWPT are visually similar to DWPT spectra and are thus omitted. Spectra for DWT and SWT are averaged versions of these spectra and are also omitted. For a color version of this figure, see www.iste.co.uk/atto/change1.zip*

with the following standard index correspondences

$$(n_1, n_2) = \begin{cases} (0,1) \rightsquigarrow \text{Horizontal SWT subspace,} \\ (1,0) \rightsquigarrow \text{Vertical SWT subspace,} \\ (1,1) \rightsquigarrow \text{Diagonal SWT subspace.} \end{cases}$$    [6.8]

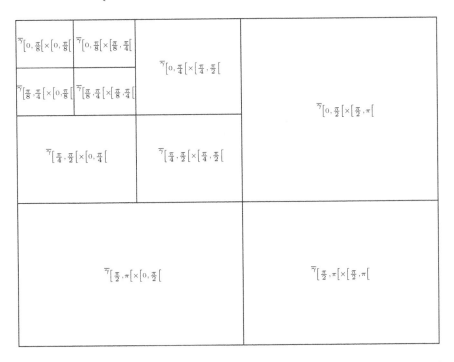

**Table 6.1.** *2D SWT non-uniform PSD estimate $\gamma$ for $J = 3$. The spectrum can be seen as a coarse approximation involving constant shapes over intervals with larger sizes at higher frequencies and smaller sizes at lower frequencies. This PSD estimate (see equation [6.7]) is only reasonable for random fields with flat spectral information in highest frequencies*

### 6.2.3. *Fractional spectral power decay model*

The second property [p2], obtained in section 6.2.2, allows the simplification of the overall cyclone field analysis by restricting the computations to diagonal spectral elements. By taking property [p2] and the last property [p3] into account (see also Figure 6.4), the cyclone spectral information can be characterized as

$$\gamma(\omega_1, \omega_2) \propto \frac{1}{||(\omega_1, \omega_2)||^{\alpha}}$$    [6.9]

computed on the basis of the diagonal DWT, DWPT, SWT or SWPT PSD samples.

The parameter $\alpha$ involved in equation [6.9] will be used as a descriptor of the cyclonic texture intensity and will be called the fractal intensity parameter. Small values of $\alpha$ correspond to a nearly white Gaussian noise, whereas large values of $\alpha$ will be associated with more regular (dense/compact cloud) fields. Equation [6.9] thus presents:

– a concise and parsimonious field model pertaining to the class of fractal fields ($\alpha$ is not an integer in general, as seen in Figure 6.5);

– a simple model in the sense that its parameter estimation is straightforward.

Concerning parameter estimation, we propose a regression on the set of diagonal wavelet spectra. Formally, when considering the standard notation $\theta = (j, [n_1, n_2])$ in terms of decomposition level $j$ and 2D shift parameter $[n_1, n_2]$, then, in the DWPT/SWPT domains (regular PSD sampling), we have:

$$\alpha = - \sum_{\substack{n,p \in \{1,2,\ldots,2^J-1\} \\ n>p}} \frac{\log \dfrac{\mathrm{var}\left[\mathbf{C}_{J,[n,n]}\right]}{\mathrm{var}\left[\mathbf{C}_{J,[p,p]}\right]}}{\log \dfrac{n}{p}} \qquad [6.10]$$

whereas in the DWT/SWT domains (non-regular PSD sampling), we derive that the estimation of the shape parameter $\alpha$ reduces to

$$\alpha = - \sum_{\substack{j,k \in \{1,2,\ldots,J\} \\ j>k}} \frac{\log \dfrac{\mathrm{var}\left[\mathbf{C}_{J-j+1,[1,1]}\{\mathcal{T}_m\}\right]}{\mathrm{var}\left[\mathbf{C}_{J-k+1,[1,1]}\{\mathcal{T}_m\}\right]}}{\log \dfrac{2^j + 2^{j-1} - 1}{2^k + 2^{k-1} - 1}} \qquad [6.11]$$

where $[n_1, n_2] = [1, 1]$ stands for the diagonal DWT/SWT subspace. Note that in both equations [6.10] and [6.11], the approximation subspace associated with zero PSD frequency is not considered: as $J$ tends to infinity, $\gamma(0)$ tends to infinity for $\alpha > 0$. Hence, approximation coefficients have not been taken into account in equation [6.4].

Figure 6.5 provides diagonal DWPT and SWT spectral information, as well as the fit by using the model from equation [6.9], when parameters $\alpha[\mathcal{T}_m]$ have been estimated from equations [6.10] and [6.11]. It further illustrates that a single parameter relating exponential power decay of the PSD is sufficient for modeling cyclone textural information.

The results summarized in Figure 6.5 confirm the fact that there is no need to perform a full wavelet packet splitting (DWPT or SWPT). For the sake of compromise between computational complexity and redundancy of information, SWT is the wavelet framework used in the rest of the chapter. In comparison with DWT, SWT has the advantage of a more concise variance estimate due to non-decimation. This advantage is negligible for highly resolved data.

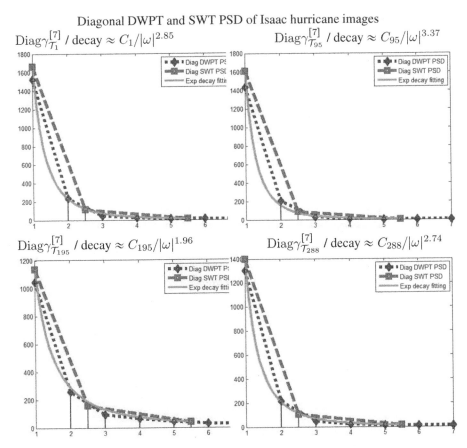

**Figure 6.5.** *Comparison of diagonal elements (isotropy concern) of 2D DWPT and SWT PSD for the sample images given by Figure 6.2. The PSD have been computed by using three decomposition levels and a Daubechies wavelet of order 7. The diagonal spectral curves have been fitted by the exponential decay model from equation [6.9]. For a color version of this figure, see www.iste.co.uk/atto/change1.zip*

Figure 6.6 presents a map of the fractal intensity parameters computed on the eyewall of an Isaac image. The map is associated with $\alpha$-values computed from sliding and overlapping $16 \times 16$ windows on the whole image. The detected eye is indicated in Figure 6.6 and is shown to be coherent with the visual perception of the eye in the original image (given at the top of Figure 6.6). A geometric centroid approach based on a variant of the watershed transform for eyewall segmentation (see Lakshmanan *et al.* (2009)) is also shown. As can be seen in Figure 6.6, the geometric centroid fails to detect the eye, as long as the eye is not located near the center (which is usually the case, see Figure 6.2 for cyclone eye instances).

Eyewall (red)

Watershed centroid

Fractal intensities

**Figure 6.6.** *[Top]: an Isaac image and the corresponding eyewall; [Middle]: watershed segmentation and geometric centroid of the eyewall in blue star; [Bottom]: fractal intensity parameters computed on $16 \times 16$ pixel neighborhoods (eye location is with low fractal intensity and is indicated by an orange arrow). The eye is generally not located at the center of the eyewall and this causes large imprecisions for eye location in the geometric centroid approach, in contrast to measuring fractal intensities. For a color version of this figure, see www.iste.co.uk/atto/change1.zip*

## 6.3. Cyclone field eye detection and tracking

### 6.3.1. *Cyclone eye detection*

Eye detection is performed for each image on the time series $\mathcal{I}$. The method proposed for eye detection relies on the fractal parameter $\alpha$. Assuming that image background is composed of smooth or piecewise regular objects, then only white Gaussian noise can be observed locally, and this corresponds to $\alpha \approx 0$ (white Gaussian noise has a constant PSD and corresponds to $\alpha = 0$).

The increase of $\alpha$ (assumed to be a positive real number) leads to the increase of stochastic regularity, i.e. to the increase of roughness and thickness in practice. Thus, the spatial neighborhood with a higher fractal intensity parameter is supposed to be more regular than a neighborhood with a smaller fractal intensity parameter. *The eye is stable when there is very low wind and no rain/clouds. On the contrary, the eyewall is unstable where outflow clouds occur. Then, the eyeball is the most regular stochastic area and should have a higher fractal intensity parameter, in comparison to both the background and the eye...*

On the basis of the assumption that cyclone eye is the minimally regular cyclone area pertaining to the interior of the eyewall field, the following procedure is proposed for cyclone eye detection:

– [S1] removal of image background[2] and retrieval of a "pure cyclone" Region-Of-Interest (ROI) denoted $R$;

– [S2] doing, while patch size is larger than a pre-specified size $d$:

- [S2.1] splitting $R$ into overlapping boxcar patches denoted $\mathcal{P} = \{P_1, P_2, \ldots, P_Q\}$,

- [S2.2] computing, from equation [6.11], the fractal intensity parameter associated with every patch, say $\alpha [P_k]$,

- [S2.3] retrieval of the patch(es) with lowest fractal intensity parameter and affecting this patch(es) to the temporary ROI item $R$:

$$R \leftarrow \arg\min_{P \in \mathcal{P}} \alpha [P]$$

- [S2.4] divide the patch size by 2 (and return to step S2.1);

– [S3] set: "eye" $\leftarrow R$.

From Step [S1], the ROI $R$ obtained is a coarse segmentation of the eyewall. Step 2 then recursively splits this ROI in order to derive smaller and smaller patches containing the cyclone eye: at the end of the recursions, $R$ is a small ROI with minimal stochastic regularity over its surroundings regions.

---

2. The straightforward *intraclass and interclass variance-based thresholding* given in Sezgin and Sankur (2004) is considered for the removal of image background.

Note that all surroundings patches of the eye are expected to have larger fractal parameters than the eye. Otherwise, the pre-specified patch size $d$ is not appropriate and we should re-run the procedure by modifying this size variable.

The ideal pre-specified size is the one adjusted to the cyclone eye: in practice, this depends on the satellite image resolution and the cyclone temporal evolution. We consider here a fixed, sufficiently small size that is assumed to suit all of the image frames ($d = 16 \times 16$ pixels).

### 6.3.2. *Dynamic fractal field eye tracking*

The eye tracking is performed on the assumption that the cyclone eye statistical properties do not change significantly over time. Tracking is then a straightforward frame-to-frame eye detection from the algorithm described in section 6.3.1. In order to reduce the overall tracking complexity, we use the *a priori* that eye displacement speed is low, so that given the eye position in the current image frame $\mathcal{I}_0$, the initial ROI $R$ of the next frame is chosen to be tight and centered on the eye position.

Isaac trajectory from minimum fractal parameter

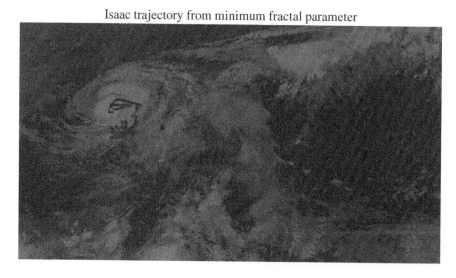

**Figure 6.7.** *Color composition showing the initial and final states of Isaac cyclone (see images $\mathcal{I}_1$ and $\mathcal{I}_{288}$ given in Figure 6.2). Blue color: initial state $\mathcal{I}_1$, Red color: final state $\mathcal{I}_{288}$, Black line delimited by squares: Isaac trajectory computed from minimum fractal parameters on $16 \times 16$ pixels. For a color version of this figure, see www.iste.co.uk/atto/change1.zip*

Figure 6.7 provides a tracking of the eye using this procedure. We can observe:

– the initial state (Gulf of Mexico);

– the west-north, north-west, west-north trajectory;

– the final state (Louisiana, west of Port Fourchon).

This trajectory is coherent with the NOAA report description: *Isaac entered the southeastern Gulf of Mexico early on 27 August, moving more slowly towards the west-northwest and northwest as it reached the southwestern periphery of the subtropical ridge. Isaac made its first landfall along the coast of Louisiana at Southwest Pass on the mouth of the Mississippi River around 0000 UTC 29 August. The center then wobbled westward back over water and made a second landfall just west of Port Fourchon, Louisiana, around 0800 UTC 29 August*[3].

Note that the geometric shape-based centroid fails to detect the eye position with high precision (see Figure 6.6), and as a result, tracking the geometric centroid will suffer from the same imprecision. One additional contribution of the stochastic approach proposed in this chapter is that it makes prediction possible.

## 6.4. Cyclone field intensity evolution prediction

As seen in section 6.2, a cyclone texture can be efficiently described by the diagonal SWT PSD on an isotropic field framework with fractional $1/||\omega||^{\alpha}$ wavelet power spectral decay.

Since the eyewall contains the most intensive cyclone features, the cyclone global intensity analysis of the time series $\mathcal{I}$, given by equation [6.1], will thus be performed by considering the sequence of the eyewall fractal intensity parameters:

$$\underline{\alpha} = \{\alpha_m = \alpha[\mathcal{T}_m] : m = 1, 2, \dots, M\}, \tag{6.12}$$

where $\alpha_m$ are the spectral fractal parameters of texture $\mathcal{T}_m$ (see equation [6.4]).

Figure 6.8 provides the sequence $\underline{\alpha}$ for the Isaac dataset considered as the case study. This sequence exhibits four main episodes, two among them with high fractal intensity parameters. From the NOAA (National Oceanic and Atmospheric Administration), we have the following validated observations: *several measurements from cyclone hunters have led to classifying Isaac as a hurricane 1200 UTC 28 August* (index $m = 161$ of the time series corresponds to August 28, 2012 1145 UTC), *after reporting a gradual strengthening while moving across the Gulf of Mexico* ($m = 50$, corresponds to August 27, 2012 1740 UTC) *and more organized deep convection in*

---

3. See www.nhc.noaa.gov/archive/2012/ISAAC.html.

*a ring around the center.* This validates the fractal estimations of Figure 6.8 (gradual strengthening from $m = 50$ to $m = 148$), in particular the classification as a hurricane on August 28[4].

Fractal $\alpha$ time series for the cyclonic field Isaac

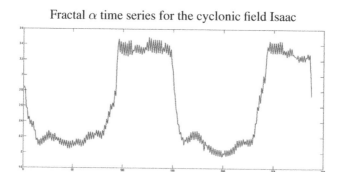

**Figure 6.8.** *Time series of fractal intensities* $(\alpha_m)_{m=1,2,\ldots,288}$ *computed from equation [6.11] on the cyclonic field of Isaac (illustrative samples of Isaac are given in Figure 6.2 and the corresponding texture information is given in Figure 6.3). For a color version of this figure, see www.iste.co.uk/atto/change1.zip*

Since, in general, we have no *prioris* on the variations/properties of $\underline{\alpha}$, we need to consider a wide range of possible statistical behaviors. One such class of statistical models, which allows for several types of dependencies, is the $K$-factor Generalized AutoRegressive Moving Average model ($K$-factor GARMA) (Gray *et al.* (1989); Woodward *et al.* (1998); Ramachandran and Beaumont (2001)), given by

$$\Phi(B) \prod_{k=1}^{K} \left(1 - 2\psi_k B + B^2\right)^{\delta_k} X(t) = \Theta(B)Z(t), \qquad [6.13]$$

where $\Phi$, $\Theta$ represent the AutoRegressive (AR) and Moving Average (MA) contributions:

$$\Phi(B) = I - \sum_{q=1}^{Q} \phi_q B^q$$

and

$$\Theta(B) = I - \sum_{p=1}^{P} \theta_p B^p;$$

---

4. See www.nhc.noaa.gov/archive/2012/ISAAC.html.

$Z$ is a white Gaussian noise; $B$ is the differential operator defined by: $BX(t) = X(t-1)$, and $I$ is the identity operator.

The $K$-factors involved in equation [6.13] are descriptors of quasi-periodic phenomena in the image time series. Note that the sequence $\underline{\alpha} \equiv X$ obtained for the Isaac fractal intensities does not show several quasi-periodic dependencies (Figure 6.8). Hence, we may restrict to $K = 1$, and the model becomes

$$\Phi(B) \left(1 - 2\psi B + B^2\right)^\delta X(t) = \Theta(B)Z(t). \qquad [6.14]$$

For the specific case of the Isaac hurricane, preliminary tests highlight that we have $\psi \approx 1$ and $\delta \approx 0.4725$: we are finally restricted to the subclass of the GARMA known as ARFIMA

$$\Phi(B) \left(1 - B\right)^d X(t) = \Theta(B)Z(t) \qquad [6.15]$$

with $d = 2\delta = 0.945$.

We finally test several orders for the AR and MA (ARMA) components and the results in terms of prediction are given by Figure 6.9. We may conclude that

– ARMA(1,1) prediction without considering the FI (Fractionally Integrated) contribution varies too slowly in comparison to the true $\underline{\alpha}$ sequence;

– ARMA(1,1) and FI(0.945), thus ARFIMA(1,0.945,1) yield very good forecasting performance;

– using an AR-FI(0.945)-MA with higher-order AR/MA contributions is very sensitive to the high increase of $\underline{\alpha}$ and leads to less relevant forecasting performance than ARFIMA(1,0.945,1).

The relevant model for Isaac hurricane texture intensity is thus an ARFIMA(1,0.945,1).

## 6.5. Discussion

In this chapter, we have proposed statistical fractional random field modeling for a cyclone eyewall texture analysis and the retrieval of the cyclone eye position. The model derived is associated with cyclonic field strength due to a fractal intensity parameter of an isotropic observation model.

The procedure proposed for eye detection is based on identifying the patch with lowest fractal intensity (the eye) among surroundings patches with high fractal intensities (eyewall). This method is used to build a cyclone eye tracking algorithm. The results obtained for the tracking of the Isaac hurricane have shown coherency with the available official source of information.

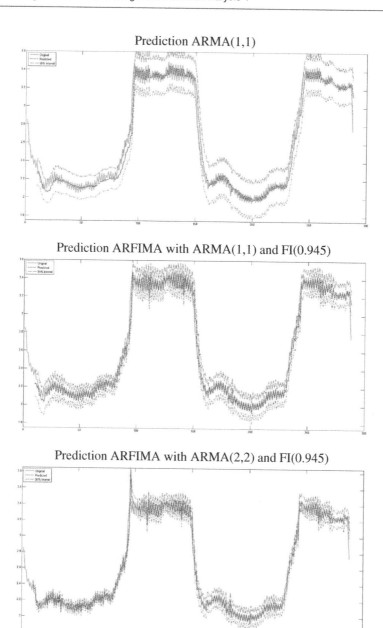

**Figure 6.9.** *ARFIMA* $(p, d, q)$*-based prediction on the fractal intensity time series* $(\alpha_m)_{m=1,2,\ldots,288}$ *of the Isaac field. Prediction starts at sample 10 and is one length ahead (shortest prediction horizon). For a color version of this figure, see www.iste.co.uk/atto/change1.zip*

In addition, the chapter has shown that ARFIMA modeling is relevant for predicting values of this fractal intensity parameter. The intensity prediction on the Isaac cyclone has been shown to be relevant with respect to the Isaac episodes, which led to the classification of Isaac into the category of "hurricanes" on August 28, 2012.

Prospects to the works concern both analysis, prediction and tracking: the analysis needs to be invariant with respect to both image saturation and outflow clouds. This has been obtained by using wavelet-based texture information. An investigation on the derivation of the best cyclone texture extractor, especially when considering third generation wavelets discovered by deep machine learning (for instance, *distortlets*, see Atto *et al.* (2020)), can lead to more robust and more invariant methods with respect to these disturbances.

Concerning prediction, the proposed approach applies to the eyewall: a distributed prediction on georeferenced localizations may lead to some improvement on the ARFIMA prediction (distributed ARFIMA models).

Tracking precision can be addressed by using a joint approach involving the statistical framework proposed in this chapter and the geometric spiral center-based approach. This requires a fusion rule for deciding the position of the center, depending on the strengths/limitations of each approach.

Finally, combining several ground-based measurements with the image time series framework can certainly be beneficial to the whole cyclone characterization. In particular, taking into account sea-level measurements can provide additional information about the eye height above normal tide levels.

## 6.6. Acknowledgements

The authors would like to acknowledge the support from the Centre National d'Etudes Spatiales (CNES) through the access to the computing and storage facilities of the PEPS platform and through the funding of the APR SHARE project.

## 6.7. References

Atto, A.M., Berthoumieu, Y., Bolon, P. (2013). 2-D wavelet packet spectrum for texture analysis. *IEEE Transactions on Image Processing*, 22(6), 2495–2500 [Online]. Available at: http://dx.doi.org/10.1109/TIP.2013.2246524.

Atto, A.M., Bisset, R.R., Trouvé, E. (2020). Frames learned by prime convolution layers in a deep learning framework. *IEEE Transactions on Neural Networks and Learning Systems*, 1–9.

Caban, J., Joshi, A., Rheingans, P. (2007). Texture-based feature tracking for effective time-varying data visualization. *IEEE Transactions on Visualization and Computer Graphics*, 13(6), 1472–1479.

Chang, P.-L., Jou, B., Zhang, J. (2009). An algorithm for tracking the eyes of tropical cyclones. *Weather and Forecast*, 24, 245–261.

Chen, J., Abbady, S., Duggimpudi, M.-B. (2016). Spatiotemporal outlier detection: Did buoys tell where the hurricanes where? *Papers in Applied Geography*, 2(3), 289–314.

Coifman, R.R. and Donoho, D.L. (1995). *Translation Invariant De-Noising*. Lecture Notes in Statistics, 103, 125–150.

Daubechies, I. (1992). *Ten Lectures on Wavelets*. SIAM, Philadelphia, PA.

Doraiswamy, H., Natarajan, V., Nanjundiah, R. (2013). An exploration framework to identify and track movement of cloud systems. *IEEE Transactions on Visualization and Computer Graphics*, 19(12), 2896–2905.

Gamba, P. (1999). Meteorological structures shape description and tracking by means of BI-RME matching. *IEEE Transactions on Geoscience and Remote Sensing*, 37(2), 1151–1161.

Goto, K., Goto, T., Nmor, J., Minematsu, K., Gotoh, K. (2015). Evaluating salinity damage to crops through satellite data analysis: Application to typhoon affected areas of Southern Japan. *Natural Hazards*, 75(3), 2815–2828.

Gray, H.L., Zhang, N.-F., Woodward, W.A. (1989). On generalized fractional processes. *Journal of Time Series Analysis*, 10(3), 233–257.

Jaiswal, N. and Kishtawal, C. (2011). Automatic determination of center of tropical cyclone in satellite-generated IR images. *IEEE Geoscience and Remote Sensing Letters*, 8(3), 460–463.

Joshi, A., Caban, J., Rheingans, P., Sparling, L. (2009). Case study on visualizing hurricanes using illustration-inspired techniques. *IEEE Transactions on Visualization and Computer Graphics*, 15(5), 709–718.

Kandaswamy, U., Adjeroh, D., Lee, M.-C. (2005). Efficient texture analysis of SAR imagery. *IEEE Transactions of Geoscience and Remote Sensing*, 43(9), 2075–2083.

Kodama, Y.-M. and Yamada, T. (2005). Detectability and configuration of tropical cyclone eyes over the Western North Pacific in TRMM PR and IR observations. *Monthly Weather Review*, 133(8), 2213–2226.

Lakshmanan, V., Rabin, R., DeBrunner, V. (2003). Multiscale storm identification and forecast. *Atmospheric Research*, European Conference on Severe Storms 2002, 67–68, 367–380.

Lakshmanan, V., Hondl, K., Rabin, R. (2009). An efficient, general-purpose technique for identifying storm cells in geospatial images. *Journal of Atmospheric and Oceanic Technology*, 26(3), 523–537.

Mallat, S. (1998). *A Wavelet Tour of Signal Processing*. Academic Press, Cambridge, MA.

Mas, E., Bricker, J., Kure, S., Adriano, B., Yi, C., Suppasri, A., Koshimura, S. (2016). Field survey report and satellite image interpretation of the 2013 super typhoon Hayan in the Philippines. *Natural Hazards and Earth System Sciences*, 15, 805–816.

Nastos, P.-T., Karavana-Papamidou, K., Matsangouras, I.-T. (2015). Tropical-like cyclones in the Mediterranean: Impacts and composite daily means and anomalies of synoptic conditions. *Proceedings of the 14th International Conference on Envionmental Science and Technology*, Rhodes, Greece, 3–5 September.

Ramachandran, R. and Beaumont, P. (2001). Robust estimation of GARMA model parameters with an application to cointegration among interest rates of industrialized countries. *Computational Economics*, 17(2–3), 179–201.

Rozoff, C., Velden, C., Kaplan, J., Kossin, J., Wimmers, A.-J. (2016). Improvements in the probability prediction of tropical cyclone rapid intensification with passive microwave observations. *Weather and Forecasting*, 31(5), 1016–1038.

Sezgin, M. and Sankur, B. (2004). Survey over image thresholding techniques and quantitative performance evaluation. *Journal of Electronic Imaging*, 13(1), 146–168.

Terry, J.-P. and Kim, I.-H. (2015). Morphometric analysis of tropical storm and hurricane tracks in the North Atlantic basin using a sinuosity-based approach. *International Journal of Climatology*, 35(6), 923–934.

Woodward, W.A., Cheng, Q.C., Gray, H.L. (1998). A k-factor GARMA long-memory model. *Journal of Time Series Analysis*, 19(4), 485–504.

Xu, X. and Liu, C. (2016). A novel algorithm for the objective detection of tropical cyclone centers using infrared satellite images. *Remote Sensing Letters*, 7(6), 541–550.

Zheng, G., Yang, J., Liu, A., Li, X., Pichel, W.-G., He, S. (2016). Comparison of typhoon centers from SAR and IR images and those from best track data sets. *IEEE Transactions of Geoscience and Remote Sensing*, 54(2), 1000–1012.

# 7

# Graph of Characteristic Points for Texture Tracking: Application to Change Detection and Glacier Flow Measurement from SAR Images

Minh-Tan PHAM[1] and Grégoire MERCIER[2]

[1] *IRISA Laboratory, Université Bretagne Sud, Lorient, France*
[2] *eXo maKina, Digital Technologies, Paris, France*

## 7.1. Introduction

Thanks to the capacity of data acquisition under any atmospheric or weather conditions, one of the most significant applications of synthetic aperture radar (SAR) imagery is to exploit multitemporal data for change detection, which serves for understanding and evaluating land-cover changes occurring after a natural or anthropic disaster, or for identifying and monitoring land-use development over time within certain agricultural, forestry and urban areas (Bovolo and Bruzzone 2007; Del Frate *et al.* 2008; Mercier *et al.* 2010; Ban and Yousif 2012). This chapter is dedicated to the context of unsupervised change detection using bitemporal SAR images. To tackle this task, we propose to perform texture tracking based on the characteristic points extracted from the images and modeled by a graph structure. Then, another application using bitemporal SAR data to detect and measure the glacier flows is also

*Change Detection and Image Time Series Analysis 1,*
coordinated by Abdourrahmane M. ATTO, Francesca BOVOLO and Lorenzo BRUZZONE.
© ISTE Ltd 2021.

investigated based on the proposed texture tracking approach. We first review some related works in unsupervised SAR image change detection in the literature.

Many methods have been proposed to tackle the problem of image change detection. Two systematic surveys on change detection techniques in remote sensing can be found in Radke *et al.* (2005) and Asokan and Anitha (2019). However, change detection using SAR images is still considered to be a challenging task due to the image perturbation caused by speckle noise. This intrinsic multiplicative noise often increases the miss-detection (MD) and false alarm (FA) rates, hence considerably reducing the detection performance. Consequently, unlike in optical remote sensing, any change detection technique dealing with SAR image data should take into account the existence of speckle (Mercier *et al.* 2010).

In the scope of unsupervised SAR image change detection, one of the most classical approaches is the mean-ratio detector (MRD) which is based on the ratio of local intensity means of pixel patches (Rignot and van Zyl 1993). To reduce the effect of multiplicative speckle noise, many authors proposed the use of the log-ratio detector (LRD) by performing logarithm operator on the ratio of local means (Bazi *et al.* 2005; Bovolo and Bruzzone 2005). Some studies proposed the combining of these two ratio operators to exploit their complementary information. In Gong *et al.* (2012) and Ma *et al.* (2012), the authors performed the wavelet-based fusion technique on both the mean-ratio and log-ratio images, in order to generate the final difference image (DI). In Hou *et al.* (2014), the Gauss-log ratio DI was proposed by applying a Gaussian low-pass filter on pixel patches before performing the log-ratio operator. This DI was then fused with the log-ratio DI using wavelet transform to produce the final fused DI. In fact, these ratio operators are robust to speckle but they are limited to the comparison of first-order statistics since only the mean intensity of pixel patches is considered. Therefore, in cases where the mean values of pixel patches stay the same, they are not able to detect changes, which probably increases the MD rate.

Taking into account this drawback, other methods have proposed consideration of higher-order statistics of pixel patches by using the similarity measure of their local probability density functions (PDFs). In Inglada (2003) and Inglada and Mercier (2007), the authors investigated several approaches for PDF estimation and exploited the Kullback–Leibler divergence (KLD) as a distance measure for PDF comparison. As a result, they proposed some local statistical measures for DI production, including the Pearson-based KLD (PKLD) and the cumulant-based KLD (CKLD). These detectors can be generated based on the first four-order statistics of pixel local patches (Inglada and Mercier 2007). The Pearson-based PDF estimation is characterized by two parameters and can hold eight different types of distribution (e.g. Gaussian, Gamma, etc.). Being more robust, the CKLD is derived from the Edgeworth series expansion and can deal with non-parametric PDFs. However, the CKLD is still dependent on the accuracy of Edgeworth approximation from which the estimated

PDFs are not too far from Gaussian models. In Zheng and You (2013), by using a modified KLD called Jeffrey divergence, the authors proposed the projection-based Jeffrey detector (PJD) which preliminarily performs better than the CKLD in certain conditions. Nevertheless, all of these local statistics-based approaches are still constrained to the evaluation of dense neighborhoods around image pixels. Hence, in order to achieve good detection (GD) performance, large-size windows should be generally considered.

Taking into account the aforementioned issues, our motivation is to avoid using a large-size dense neighborhood around each pixel to measure its change level, which is usually considered by the aforementioned methods. We propose to exploit the interaction between characteristic points to develop a novel texture tracking method to address the change detection task by embedding the keypoint-based approach into a weighted graph model. Within this chapter, we show that the local extrema keypoints are capable of capturing the image's important radiometric and contextual information. Their interaction can be encoded by a graph model based on their similarity measures for which only small pixel patches around keypoints are required. More importantly, the constructed graph is able to characterize both intensity and geometry information from the image content, hence relevant for texture tracking. To this end, if a graph is constructed from one of the two SAR images, the change level between them can be measured from how much the information of the other image still conforms to that graph's structure. This remark leads to our proposed texture tracking strategy for unsupervised change detection within this chapter.

In section 7.2, we present our motivation and approach to exploit local extrema keypoints to represent textures in remote sensing images, and the adaptation to SAR data. Next, in the main section of this chapter (section 7.3), the proposed keypoint graph-based texture tracking approach applied to change detection is described followed by an experimental study conducted on two SAR data sets in section 7.4. In section 7.5, another direct application of the proposed texture tracking technique is performed, using bitemporal SAR images to detect and measure the glacier flows. Section 7.6 concludes the chapter.

## 7.2. Texture representation and characterization using local extrema

### 7.2.1. *Motivation and approach*

Our study is inspired from the concept of the empirical mode decomposition (EMD) (Huang *et al.* 1998; Nunes *et al.* 2003; Flandrin *et al.* 2004) which is a decomposition method for non-stationary signals. In contrast to the Fourier transform and the wavelet transform, which break down a signal into several components based on spectral analysis, the EMD decomposes the signal directly from the time domain. It works by producing smooth envelopes defined by local maxima and minima of a signal. Then, the so-called intrinsic mode functions (IMFs) are obtained by subtracting the mean of these envelopes from the initial signal (after a number of iterations). An illustration can be found in Figure 7.1. Here, we display only the first iteration to show how the local maxima envelope $E_{max}$ and local minima envelope $E_{min}$ are produced, and how the residue is computed by subtracting the mean envelope $E_M$ from the signal. The process continues on the residue to obtain the first IMF (with a stopping criterion) of the decomposition. For more details about the EMD strategy, readers are invited to consult the related papers (Huang *et al.* 1998; Nunes *et al.* 2003; Flandrin *et al.* 2004). In short, the EMD generates a set of IMFs and a final residue which allow us to analyze the smooth approximation and multiscale details of the signal. This principle of EMD reveals that a non-stationary signal may be decomposed and characterized using the local maxima and minima extracted from the signal. These local extrema are capable of capturing significant information on the signal content. Hence, they may be sufficient for a non-dense approach to represent and analyze non-stationary signals.

In this work, we propose to perform a texture analysis approach based on the local extrema (i.e. local maximum and local minimum pixels in terms of intensity) extracted from the image. According to this point of view, an image texture is formed by a spatial arrangement of pixels (on the image plane) which hold some variations of intensity. Hence, different textures are reflected by different types of pixel spatial arrangement and intensity variation. These meaningful arrangements and variations can be approximately represented and discriminated by the local maximum and local minimum pixels. To clarify, let us illustrate and analyze Figure 7.2. The figure provides an example of different texture zones from a grayscale image crop (i.e. optical panchromatic in remote sensing). Let us consider two distinctive textures localized by the red and green circles. The 3-D surface model on top is built by using the image intensity as surface height. The 1-D signal in blue at the bottom is obtained by tracing the yellow line across the image plane. From this 1-D model, we compare the first texture signal with high variation of amplitude to the second one which is smoother and less contrasted. In order to characterize and discriminate these two textures, instead of exploiting two entire signals inside the two circles, we can use only the local maxima and local minima (represented by the red points and black points, respectively) by exploiting their amplitudes and the relative distances among them. In the case of 2-D images, the intensity and spatial information represented by some measures of geometric distances and orientations of the local maxima and minima will be taken into account to represent and characterize different textural features. This principle leads to our keypoint-based approach for texture analysis and representation within this chapter.

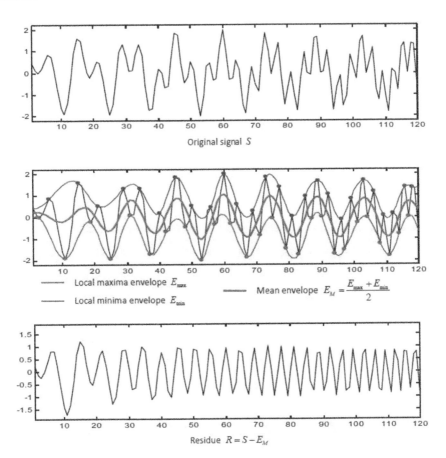

**Figure 7.1.** *Illustration of the first iteration to calculate the first IMF using the EMD method. For a color version of this figure, see www.iste.co.uk/atto/change1.zip*

We now describe the method to extract the local maximum and local minimum pixels from an image. A pixel is supposed to be a local maximum (respectively, local minimum) if it has the highest (respectively, lowest) intensity within a search window centered at it. Denote $S_\omega^{max}(I)$ (respectively, $S_\omega^{min}(I)$) the set of local maximum (respectively, local minimum) pixels extracted from an image $I$ using a search window of size $\omega \times \omega$ pixels, we define:

$$p \in S_\omega^{max}(I) \Leftrightarrow \left\{ I(p) = \max_{q \in \mathcal{N}_\omega(p)} I(q) \right\}, \qquad [7.1]$$

$$p \in S_\omega^{min}(I) \Leftrightarrow \left\{ I(p) = \min_{q \in \mathcal{N}_\omega(p)} I(q) \right\}, \qquad [7.2]$$

where $I(p)$ denotes the intensity value of pixel $p$, and $\mathcal{N}_\omega(p)$ represents a set of neighboring pixels of $p$ within the $\omega \times \omega$ search window. For implementation, the sliding window of size $\omega \times \omega$ pixels is shifted pixel by pixel on the image plane. If the centered pixel has the highest (respectively, lowest) intensity, it is detected as a local maximum (respectively, local minimum) point. In Figure 7.3, we show an example of detecting the local maxima (in red, on the left) and the local minima (in blue, on the right) from an image patch using a $3 \times 3$ search window. In the figure, each square is a pixel on the image plane and the numerical value represents the pixel intensity. By applying equations [7.1] and [7.2] with $\omega = 3$, 16 local maxima and 14 local minima are detected as observed.

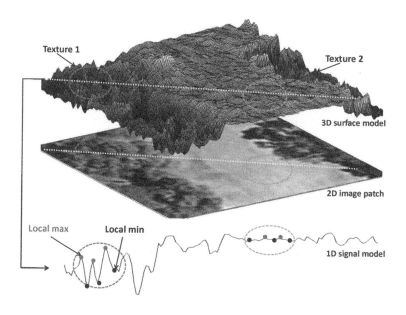

**Figure 7.2.** *Texture representation and discrimination using the local maximum and the local minimum pixels within a keypoint-based approach. For a color version of this figure, see www.iste.co.uk/atto/change1.zip*

### 7.2.2. *Local extrema keypoints within SAR images*

Our studies related to texture characterization in optical remote sensing images (Pham *et al.* 2015, 2016a, b) have proved that the local extrema keypoints are able to capture and characterize the spatial and contextual information of the image from which they are extracted. This chapter focuses on their exploitation to perform a texture tracking algorithm applied to image change detection. Within this context, we propose to exploit the local maximum pixels and note that using the local minimum pixels also provides similar performance. Depending on the nature of changes, the choice of local max or local min keypoints may result in a slightly better performance than the other. In general, image regions with higher intensity involve more information than the lower ones. In these cases, the local maxima are more relevant. However, the local minima may be more suitable in cases where we need to focus on low-intensity regions such as roads, airports, rivers, etc. To this end, we mainly exploit the local maximum keypoints to conduct the experimental study in this chapter.

| 15 | 23 | 12 | 45 | 81 | 63 | 21 | 17 | 20 | 4 |
|----|----|----|----|----|----|----|----|----|----|
| 42 | 9 | 25 | 17 | 42 | 12 | 28 | 33 | 56 | 41 |
| 12 | 26 | 91 | 33 | 24 | 18 | 8 | 30 | 12 | 17 |
| 66 | 7 | 71 | 41 | 33 | 44 | 52 | 45 | 47 | 44 |
| 8 | 22 | 32 | 22 | 81 | 33 | 45 | 12 | 31 | 29 |
| 56 | 10 | 55 | 23 | 13 | 8 | 15 | 32 | 65 | 28 |
| 5 | 44 | 57 | 52 | 61 | 17 | 56 | 56 | 23 | 33 |
| 16 | 26 | 42 | 3 | 15 | 78 | 22 | 71 | 21 | 74 |
| 81 | 20 | 19 | 32 | 41 | 46 | 45 | 51 | 49 | 23 |
| 14 | 37 | 12 | 52 | 74 | 42 | 23 | 35 | 33 | 48 |

| 15 | 23 | 12 | 45 | 81 | 63 | 21 | **17** | 20 | **4** |
|----|----|----|----|----|----|----|----|----|----|
| 42 | **9** | 25 | 17 | 42 | 12 | 28 | 33 | 56 | 41 |
| 12 | 26 | 91 | 33 | 24 | 18 | **8** | 30 | **12** | 17 |
| 66 | **7** | 71 | 41 | 33 | 44 | 52 | 45 | 47 | 44 |
| 8 | 22 | 32 | 22 | 81 | 33 | 45 | **12** | 31 | 29 |
| 56 | 10 | 55 | 23 | 13 | **8** | 15 | 32 | 65 | 28 |
| **5** | 44 | 57 | 52 | 61 | 17 | 56 | 56 | 23 | 33 |
| 16 | 26 | 42 | **3** | 15 | 78 | 22 | 71 | **21** | 74 |
| 81 | 20 | 19 | 32 | 41 | 46 | 45 | 51 | 49 | 23 |
| **14** | 37 | **12** | 52 | 74 | 42 | **23** | 35 | 33 | 48 |

**Figure 7.3.** *Detection of local maximum pixels (in red) and local minimum pixels (in blue) from an image patch with $\omega = 3$. For a color version of this figure, see www.iste.co.uk/atto/change1.zip*

In cases where the image $I$ contains a low level of noise (e.g. an optical image), the local maximum keypoints can be directly extracted using equation [7.1] as done in related works (Pham *et al.* 2015, 2016b, 2017; Pham 2018). Here, the present task has to deal with SAR images which are perturbed by speckle noise. In order to account for its presence, the local maximum keypoints will be extracted from a smoothed version of $I$, instead of the image itself. We note that this smoothing step is not a major issue so that for a fast implementation, a simple low-pass filter such as *Average*, *Median* or *Gaussian* can be used. Besides, we may wonder whether a despeckling filter is necessary for this stage; the response is that a low-pass filter should be more suitable, in our point of view. In fact, we expect a stationary filter which homogeneously smoothens the image in order to ensure a good distribution of keypoints for all image regions. Meanwhile, a despeckling filter tends to considerably suppress speckle in homogeneous zones but effectively preserve fine details such as contours, corners, salient features, etc., hence inducing a filtered image with a non-constant number of looks. Therefore, it may cause keypoints to be mostly extracted on fine structures of the image but very sparsely on homogeneous zones, which is not expected in this study. To this end, our implementation employs a Gaussian filter for image smoothing.

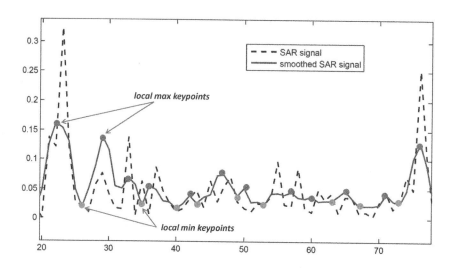

**Figure 7.4.** *Appearance of local max and min keypoints on a sample SAR signal. For a color version of this figure, see www.iste.co.uk/atto/change1.zip*

In Figure 7.4, we show an example of how the local maximum and local minimum keypoints appear within a SAR signal. Since the original signal (black dashed line) contains a lot of speckle noise, a smoothing procedure is first applied and the local extrema are detected from the smoothed signal (blue solid line). In the case of two-dimensional signals such as images, using the smoothed signal implicitly considers a pixel neighborhood (with the size of the smoothing filter), not each pixel itself, to detect local max and local min keypoints. Hence, the influence of speckle on each individual pixel is reduced.

Another question may arise concerning the possibility of using other types of feature points, such as Harris corner points, SIFT (scale-invariant feature transform), SURF (speeded up robust features), etc. (Tuytelaars and Mikolajczyk 2008), to perform our strategy. As a reminder, the main objective here is to detect land-cover changes. Hence, it is important to have keypoints covering all regions from the image so that we can ensure that all image zones will be considered for measuring changes. Such feature points like Harris corners, SIFT or SURF may not be relevant since their appearance and distribution on the image plane usually focuses on corners, edges and salient features. Hence, we may probably miss points from some homogeneous regions where changes can occur (increase MD rate). One example can be found in Figure 7.5, where we compare the appearance of 2,790 local extrema keypoints (Figure 7.5(a)) and 2790 Harris corner points (Figure 7.5(b)) detected from a SAR image. We observe that in Figure 7.5(b), there are some homogeneous regions that contain no points. Therefore, if these Harris corner points are used for change detection, we certainly miss changes from these regions. On the other hand, the local extrema points prove their capacity to cover all image zones involving any variation of intensity. They are more relevant for this application of change detection.

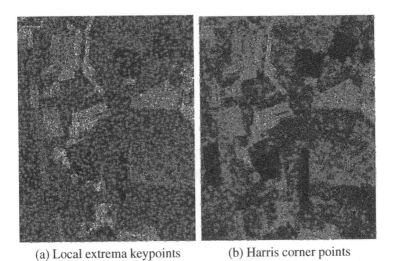

(a) Local extrema keypoints                    (b) Harris corner points

**Figure 7.5.** *Appearance of keypoints (red) extracted from a SAR image: (a) using the local extrema extractor and (b) using the Harris corner extractor. For a color version of this figure, see www.iste.co.uk/atto/change1.zip*

Finally, it should be noted that our method does not detect changes based on the evolution of keypoints between two images, like the principle of change detection based on SIFT keypoints proposed by Dellinger *et al.* (2015). In that work, the authors detect SIFT keypoints from both images and measure changes based on SIFT descriptors. Here, our local extrema keypoints are extracted from only one of the two images to construct a weighted graph. Then, change levels are derived from the irrelevance of the other image to the constructed graph structure.

## 7.3. Unsupervised change detection

### 7.3.1. *Proposed framework*

An outline of the proposed algorithm for unsupervised change detection using bitemporal SAR images is highlighted in Figure 7.6. The first stage involves the extraction of a set of characteristic points, denoted by $S_\omega$, from the first image $I_1$ to capture significant information from $I_1$. Next, a weighted graph $\mathcal{G}$ is constructed from these keypoints. In the final stage, change measures (CMs) between $I_1$ and $I_2$ at the extracted keypoints are generated with the help of the intrinsic structure of graph $\mathcal{G}$.

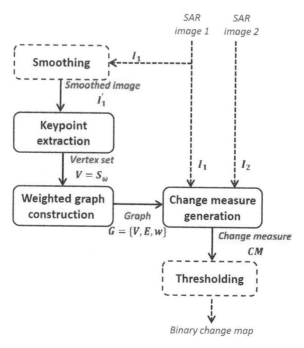

**Figure 7.6.** *Proposed framework for keypoint graph-based unsupervised change detection using bitemporal SAR images. For a color version of this figure, see www.iste.co.uk/atto/change1.zip*

It is worth noting that the choice of one image between the two inputs (i.e. $I_1$ or $I_2$) for graph construction is flexible. That means we can also generate a graph $\mathcal{G}'$ to encode the image $I_2$. Then, using a similar principle, CM can be derived from how much $I_1$ conforms and adapts to the structure of $\mathcal{G}'$. Our experimentation shows that, in both cases, we obtain similar detection performance of the proposed algorithm. Hence, without any loss of generality, the proposed strategy described in the rest of this chapter will exploit $I_1$ for the graph construction stage, as in Figure 7.6.

## 7.3.2. *Weighted graph construction from keypoints*

Signal processing on graphs has become an emerging field, with several applications in many diverse domains including social, energy, transportation, sensor and neural networks (Shuman *et al.* 2013). One of the main interests of our study is to incorporate the proposed keypoint-based image analysis approach with graph theory, in order to exploit available tools of signal processing on graphs for texture characterization. In Pham *et al.* (2014a, b, 2015), spectral analysis with graph wavelets was adopted to perform keypoint-based texture characterization in optical remote sensing images, applied to segmentation and classification tasks. In this chapter, we exploit the capacity of the graph's spatial domain (i.e. vertex domain) for texture tracking. In Figure 7.6, the role of the graph is to represent and encode the geometric structure of the first image regarding its keypoint set. Denote $\mathcal{G} = \{V, E, w\}$ the weighted graph to be constructed, we define:

– Vertex set:

$$V = S_\omega, |V| = |S_\omega| = N, \qquad\qquad [7.3]$$

– Edge set:

$$E = \{(p_n, p_k); p_n, p_k \in V, p_k \in \mathcal{N}_K(p_n) \vee p_n \in \mathcal{N}_K(p_k)\}, \qquad [7.4]$$

where $\mathcal{N}_K(p_n)$ (respectively, $\mathcal{N}_K(p_k)$) denotes the set of $K$-closest keypoints of $p_n$ (respectively, $p_k$) in terms of the spatial distance on the image plane of $I_1$.

– Weight function:

$$w(p_n, p_k) = e^{-\gamma\left[dist(p_n, p_k)\right]}, \forall (p_n, p_k) \in E, \qquad [7.5]$$

where the term $dist(p_n, p_k)$ represents a distance measure of radiometric information between two vertices $p_n$ and $p_k$, and $\gamma$ is a free parameter fixed to 1 in our implementation.

We can imagine that on the image plane of $I_1$, each keypoint $p_n \in S_\omega$ now becomes a graph vertex and is connected to its $K$ closest neighbors (i.e. in terms of spatial distance) by the graph $\mathcal{G}$. The edge weight $w(p_n, p_k)$ represents the similarity between two vertices $p_n$ and $p_k$ in terms of intensity. In general, this weight is calculated using an exponential function of an intensity-based distance measure between $p_n$ and $p_k$. However, it should be noted that in the scope of SAR image processing, a distance measure of intensity between two pixels is generally computed by taking into account the two pixel patches around them rather than themselves (due to the effect of speckle noise). For this task, several measures can be investigated such as distances based on the histogram of local patches, the ratio operator and the Kullback–Leibler divergence (KLD), etc., previously mentioned in our introduction. Here, we propose to employ the log-ratio (LR) distance of pixel patches around graph vertices. This operator has been proved to be robust to speckle in SAR imaging. Moreover, our experiments show that this measure is quite appropriate for small-sized pixel patches which are expected in this study. Let us denote by $w_p$ the patch size considered for each vertex, the log-ratio distance can be defined:

$$dist(p_n, p_k) = dist_{LR}(p_n, p_k)$$
$$= \left| \log \mu_1(p_n) - \log \mu_1(p_k) \right| = \left| \log \frac{\mu_1(p_n)}{\mu_1(p_k)} \right|, \qquad [7.6]$$

where $\mu_1(p_n)$ (respectively, $\mu_1(p_k)$) represents the mean intensity of the $w_p \times w_p$ patch around vertex $p_n$ (respectively, $p_k$) from the first image $I_1$.

As a result, the edge weight between $p_n$, $p_k$ is computed as follows:

$$w(p_n, p_k) = e^{-\gamma \left| \log \frac{\mu_1(p_n)}{\mu_1(p_k)} \right|}. \tag{7.7}$$

### 7.3.3. *Change measure (CM) generation*

Once the weighted graph $\mathcal{G}$ is constructed to connect all keypoints from $S_\omega$, signal processing on the graph vertex domain can be applied. For this stage, we propose to exploit the graph adjacency matrix $\mathcal{W}$ to perform the concentration of information at each vertex. We note that the random walk matrix $\mathcal{P}$ can also be used to take over this task. Since the graph $\mathcal{G}$ is capable of characterizing the local geometric structure of the image $I_1$ at keypoint positions, our proposition is that the change level between $I_1$ and $I_2$ can be considered the coherence and compatibility of radiometric information captured by the vertices of $\mathcal{G}$ from these two images. In other words, the local texture structure at each keypoint from $I_1$ encoded by $\mathcal{G}$ will be tracked on $I_2$ to search for the most coherent one. To perform this strategy, we define the two following signals in $\mathbb{R}^N$:

$$
\begin{aligned}
f_1 &= [\log \mu_1(p_1), \log \mu_1(p_2), \dots, \log \mu_1(p_N)]^T, \\
f_2 &= [\log \mu_2(p_1), \log \mu_2(p_2), \dots, \log \mu_2(p_N)]^T,
\end{aligned}
\tag{7.8}
$$

where $\mu_1(p_n)$ and $\mu_2(p_n)$ ($n = 1, \dots, N$) are defined as in equation [7.6]. They represent the mean intensity of the $w_p \times w_p$ patch around the vertex $p_n$ computed from the images $I_1$ and $I_2$. The logarithm operator is proposed to theoretically reduce the influence of speckle noise.

The two signals $f_1$ and $f_2$ thus encapsulate the radiometric information of $I_1$ and $I_2$, respectively, captured by the position of the graph vertices. The quantity $(\mathcal{W}f_1)(p_n)$ characterizes the radiometric information and geometric structure of $I_1$ with regard to the local topology of graph $G$ at vertex $p_n$. A similar remark can be deduced for the quantity $(\mathcal{W}f_2)(p_n)$. Therefore, let $CM(p_n)$ be the CM between two images at keypoint $p_n$ and $||.||_1$ be the $\mathcal{L}^1$ norm, the proposed method defines:

$$
\begin{aligned}
CM(p_n) &= \left\| (\mathcal{W}f_1)(p_n) - (\mathcal{W}f_2)(p_n) \right\|_1 \\
&= \left| \sum_{p_k \sim p_n} w(p_n, p_k) \log \mu_1(p_k) - \sum_{p_k \sim p_n} w(p_n, p_k) \log \mu_2(p_k) \right| \\
&= \sum_{p_k \sim p_n} w(p_n, p_k) \left| \log \frac{\mu_1(p_k)}{\mu_2(p_k)} \right|.
\end{aligned}
\tag{7.9}
$$

We observe that the generated CM at each keypoint can be considered a weighted summing of log-ratio distances derived from other keypoints thanks to the graph structure. This issue satisfies our expectation of taking advantage of a weighted graph to encode the keypoint inter-connection. It also confirms the effectiveness of the graph model when carrying out a pointwise approach. As previously mentioned, the random walk matrix $\mathcal{P}$ could also be investigated to generate CM. The calculation of $CM(p_n)$ by exploiting $\mathcal{P}$ becomes:

$$CM(p_n) = \left\| (\mathcal{P}f_1)(p_n) - (\mathcal{P}f_2)(p_n) \right\|_1$$

$$= \frac{1}{\sum\limits_{p_k \sim p_n} w(p_n, p_k)} \sum_{p_k \sim p_n} w(p_n, p_k) \left| \log \frac{\mu_1(p_k)}{\mu_2(p_k)} \right|. \qquad [7.10]$$

In this case, the weighted summing of log-ratio measures from neighboring keypoints is normalized by dividing the sum of weights. Hence, we may recognize a certain similarity between the proposed method and the non-local mean (NLM) model presented in Yousif and Ban (2013). Indeed, our approach is essentially distinct from the NLM method. More discussions will be provided to distinguish the two methods within our experimental study.

## 7.4. Experimental study

In this section, we present our experimental study conducted on two real SAR image data sets in order to evaluate performance and validate the effectiveness of the proposed method. Reference unsupervised change detectors consisting of the MRD, LRD, the Gaussian-based KLD (GKLD), the cumulant-based KLD (CKLD) and the non-local mean (NLM) model were also implemented for a comparative study. We first introduce two SAR data sets used in our experiments and some evaluation criteria. The experiment procedure is then described in detail with several qualitative and quantitative results to evaluate detection performance. As mentioned previously, a detailed comparison between the proposed method and the NLM model is addressed in section 7.4.4. Then, an analysis of the algorithm complexity is provided.

### 7.4.1. *Data description and evaluation criteria*

#### 7.4.1.1. *Data description*

The first dataset (Dataset 1) is a couple of $800 \times 400$ images acquired by the RADARSAT-1 satellite in F2 and F5 modes before and after the eruption of the Nyiragongo volcano (January 2002) in the Democratic Republic of the Congo. These images have a final spatial resolution of 10 m and cover a semi-urban area of $8 \times 4$ km, including the Goma International Airport in Goma city. Our experiments exploited the 8-bit coded version for the image intensity. The thematic change map ground truth is available for quantitative evaluation of change detection performance. For visualization, the two input images and the ground truth mask are shown in Figure 7.7(a–c).

The second dataset (Dataset 2) is a series of 10 multitemporal SAR images acquired within the same orbit by the RADARSAT-2 satellite from January to August 2010. These 12-bit coded images have a spatial resolution of 5 m and cover an intensive agriculture area near the region of Chartres, France. They are mainly exploited for extracting vegetation indexes and studying different stages of crop growth for monitoring the agricultural surfaces within the area. For our change detection experiments, we employed the two images acquired on April 25 and May 19 as they involve a strong land-cover change coming from vegetation developments. Since the entire image size is 10,310 × 8,234 pixels, a region of interest (ROI) of 1,000 × 850 pixels was extracted from each image to perform our experiment. These ROIs are shown in Figure 7.9(a) and (b). No ground truth is available for this dataset.

### 7.4.1.2. *Evaluation criteria*

For datasets whose ground truth is available, quantitative evaluation can be performed. We propose to plot the receiver operating characteristic (ROC) curve and to calculate the percentage of total errors (TE) ($P_{TE}$) as well as the percentage of overall accuracy (OA) ($P_{OA}$) for each detector. The ROC plots the GD rate in function of the FA rate when the CM is thresholded from minimum to maximum values (Inglada and Mercier 2007). In order to generate these evaluation indicators, let us remind ourselves of some quantities resulting from a detection procedure:

– true positives (TP): the number of changed points correctly detected;

– true negatives (TN): the number of unchanged points correctly detected;

– false positives (FP): the number of unchanged points incorrectly detected as changed (i.e. FAs);

– false negative (FN): the number of changed points incorrectly detected as unchanged (i.e. missed detections).

Now, let $N$ be the total number of keypoints considered for the change detection algorithm, and $N_c$ and $N_u$ be, respectively, the number of *changed* points and *unchanged* points from ground truth change map ($N_c + N_u = N$), the aforementioned indicators are calculated as follows:

– FA rate and GD rate used to plot the ROCs:

$$P_{FA} = \frac{FP}{N_u}, \quad P_{GD} = \frac{TP}{N_c},$$

– percentage of TE consisting of FAs and missed detections:

$$P_{TE} = \frac{FP + FN}{N} \times 100\%,$$

– percentage of OA:

$$P_{OA} = \frac{TP + TN}{N} \times 100\%.$$

### 7.4.2. *Change detection results*

Experiments were conducted on our two datasets following the processing workflow in Figure 7.6. For keypoint extraction, a search window of 3 × 3 pixels ($\omega = 3$) was set for both datasets to ensure a good density of keypoints for texture representation. As as result, the number of extracted keypoints (i.e. graph vertices) were, respectively, 9,545 for Dataset 1 and 31,356 for Dataset 2. As mentioned, other change detection methods including the MRD, LRD, GKLD and CKLD were also implemented for comparison. A neighborhood window of 35 × 35 pixels was set for these reference methods. For our method, the graph $\mathcal{G}$ was constructed with $K = 50$ edges for each vertex and the patch size around each keypoint was set to 15 × 15 pixels ($w_p = 15$). It should be noted that in our approach, the number $K$ implicitly represents the size of a spatial neighborhood around each understudied keypoint in which we search for its closest neighbors within the graph construction stage. In other words, $K$ shows how far, on the image plane, the centered keypoint is connected to the others. We note that when $K$ is fixed, the search neighborhood size dedicated to each keypoint is varied. Indeed, if the density of keypoints is high, the implicit search neighborhood size will be smaller and vice versa. Experiments showed that for $K = 50$, the average neighborhood size was estimated to be about 35 × 35 pixels. That is why we selected a window size of 35 × 35 pixels for the reference methods in order to ensure an equivalent comparison.

### 7.4.2.1. *Results for Dataset 1*

Figure 7.7 shows change detection results from Dataset 1 yielded by the proposed method compared against four reference methods. Compared with the ground truth mask at keypoints in Figure 7.7(e), the proposed method visually provided the highest number of GDs but it also yielded several FAs. On the contrary, the CKLD produced the least number of FAs but it ignored a lot of changed points, which certainly increases the MD rate. The three remaining methods including MRD, LRD and GKLD produced quite similar behaviors which also involved the trade-off between the number of FAs and MDs. For a better evaluation of CM performance, Figure 7.8 shows the ROC plots for all detectors. As a reminder, the ROC is used to evaluate the quality of the CM yielded by a detector by taking into account its FA rate and GD rate, regardless of the thresholding method. As observed in the figure, the proposed method (blue) considerably outperforms the other ones. This means that for any threshold value, our detection strategy is more efficient than reference methods in terms of the GD rate with respect to the FA rate. Hence, the effectiveness of the proposed method is confirmed.

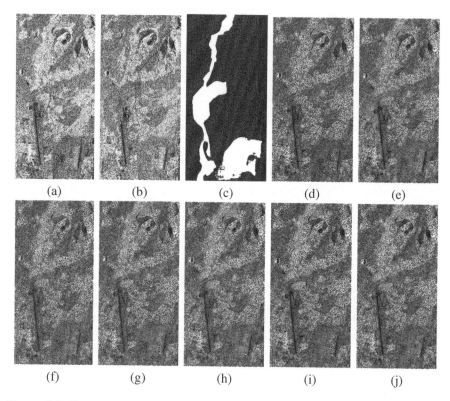

(a)                (b)                (c)                (d)                (e)

(f)                (g)                (h)                (i)                (j)

**Figure 7.7.** *Experimental study on Dataset 1. (a) Image before volcano eruption. (b) Image after volcano eruption. (c) Ground truth change mask. (d) Extracted 9545 keypoints. (e) Ground truth change mask at keypoints including $N_c = 2011$ changed points (in red) and $N_u = 7534$ unchanged points (in blue). From (f) to (j) Change detection results yielded by different detectors: (f) MRD, (g) LRD, (h) GKLD, (i) CKLD and (j) proposed method. For a color version of this figure, see www.iste.co.uk/atto/change1.zip*

For a quantitative comparison, we propose to compute the ratio $P_{GD}/P_{FA}$ and the percentages $P_{TE}$, $P_{OA}$ obtained from each detector by using the three different thresholding techniques including the K-means clustering (Hartigan and Wong 1979), the Otsu thresholding (Otsu 1975) and the Kittler–Illingworth (KI) thresholding (Kittler and Illingworth 1986). Quantitative results are shown in Table 7.1. From this table, there is always a compromise between the number of FAs and MDs. If a detector yields a small number of FAs, it may probably ignore the changed points and hence increase the number of MDs. As observed in the table, the K-means approach provided slightly better performance than the other two for most detectors. However, during our experiments, we observed that the threshold values calculated by the K-means, Ostu and KI approaches were quite close. Hence, despite slightly better efficiency from K-means, any of the three techniques could be adopted for this thresholding stage. In terms of detection accuracy, the proposed method provided the best performance (highest $P_{GD}/P_{FA}$ and $P_{OA}$, lowest $P_{TE}$) for all three thresholding techniques. This confirms not only the effectiveness of the proposed strategy but also its robustness to different thresholding approaches.

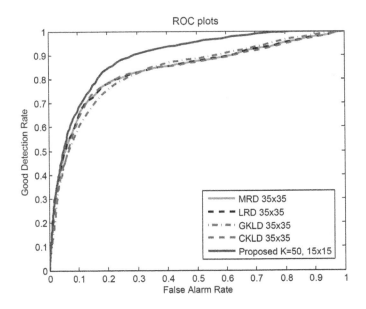

**Figure 7.8.** *ROC plots for change detection on Dataset 1. For a color version of this figure, see www.iste.co.uk/atto/change1.zip*

### 7.4.2.2. *Results for Dataset 2*

Figure 7.9 shows the two input $1000 \times 850$ ROIs extracted from Dataset 2 and change detection results generated by the proposed method compared to three reference ones, including the MRD, LRD and GKLD. Here, CM from each detector is thresholded by using the Otsu technique. We note that from our experiments, the thresholding step performed by the K-means or the KI approaches also provided a similar result to the Otsu technique. Since the ground truth change mask for this data set is not available, only visual assessment can be considered. To help readers to have some ideas about where changes may occur between two input ROIs, Figure 7.9(c) shows the grayscale change map obtained by the LRD (not the ground truth) in which change levels increase in intensity. As mentioned, these SAR data were acquired from an agricultural field with different periods of crop growth. Thematic changes between these images thus mainly come from these various stages. Therefore, our expectation is to obtain a change map in which changed portions appear quite homogeneous. Moreover, the expected change detector needs to be robust to speckle.

| Thresholding method | Detector | FA (points) | MD (points) | GD (points) | $P_{GD}/P_{FA}$ | $P_{TE}$ (%) | $P_{OA}$ (%) |
|---|---|---|---|---|---|---|---|
| K-means | MRD | 804 | 690 | 1321 | 6.1555 | 15.65 | 84.35 |
|         | LRD | 686 | 775 | 1236 | 6.7501 | 15.31 | 84.69 |
|         | GKLD | 662 | 886 | 1125 | 6.3666 | 16.22 | 83.78 |
|         | CKLD | 533 | 959 | 1052 | 7.3944 | 15.63 | 84.37 |
|         | Proposed | 549 | 795 | 1216 | **8.2980** | **14.08** | **85.92** |
| Otsu | MRD | 840 | 652 | 1359 | 6.0611 | 15.63 | 84.37 |
|      | LRD | 701 | 768 | 1243 | 6.6430 | 15.39 | 84.61 |
|      | GKLD | 733 | 835 | 1176 | 6.0106 | 16.43 | 83.57 |
|      | CKLD | 554 | 939 | 1072 | 7.2493 | 15.64 | 84.36 |
|      | Proposed | 583 | 766 | 1245 | **8.0004** | **14.13** | **85.87** |
| KI | MRD | 723 | 754 | 1257 | 6.5134 | 15.47 | 84.53 |
|    | LRD | 688 | 775 | 1236 | 6.7304 | 15.33 | 84.67 |
|    | GKLD | 534 | 979 | 1032 | 7.2402 | 15.85 | 84.15 |
|    | CKLD | 766 | 739 | 1272 | 6.2212 | 15.77 | 84.23 |
|    | Proposed | 645 | 722 | 1289 | **7.4870** | **14.32** | **85.68** |

**Table 7.1.** *Change detection performance on Dataset 1*
*($N_c = 2,011$ changed points, $N_u = 7,534$ unchanged points)*

According to Figure 7.9, the first observation is that the MRD (Figure 7.9(e)) yielded a lot of over-detected points in its change map. On the contrary, the GKLD (Figure 7.9(g)) produced a large amount of missed detections since several changed portions remain undetected. Next, the LRD and the proposed detector (Figures 7.9(f)) and 7.9(h), respectively) provided better performance (visually). However, compared to our approach, the LRD still produced more FAs. In order to clarify these remarks, let us consider and zoom in on two studied crops from the top left and the bottom right of the ROI, as shown in Figure 7.9(a). To ease our explanation, the two crops have been named *Red* and *Green*. Their results are shown in Figure 7.10. Visually, we observe that the proposed method provided the best detection performance. Let us observe the yellow circle of the *Red* crop including a small detail (marked by a yellow arrow) which should not be detected as changed in our point of view. From the results, MRD and LRD detected it as changed (Figure 7.10(e) and (f)). Although GKLD marked it as unchanged, this detector missed many other changed points (Figure 7.10(g)).

On the contrary, the proposed method was capable of recognizing that unchanged detail, as well as correctly providing the other changed portions (Figure 7.10(h)). For the *Green* crop, we again observe the best behavior from the proposed approach. The shape of the changed portion in Figure 7.10(l) is quite homogeneous and squared, which is relevant for scene interpretation from the data. Three reference detectors (Figure 7.10(i–k)) produced less interesting results with many outlier FAs. Consequently, the effectiveness of the proposed method is confirmed and validated for Dataset 2.

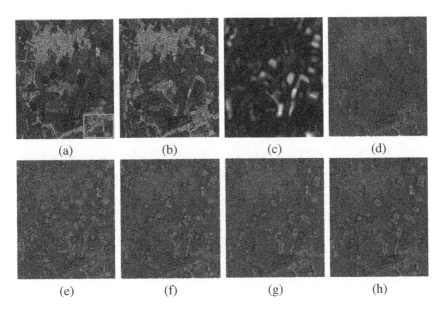

**Figure 7.9.** *Experimental study for Dataset 2. (a) ROI from the image acquired on April 25. (b) ROI from the image acquired on May 19. (c) The grayscale LRD image. (d) Extracted keypoints. From (e) to (h) Change detection results yielded by different detectors: (e) MRD, (f) LRD, (g) GKLD and (h) proposed method. The two rectangles in red and green in (a) mark the positions of the two studied crops (namely* Red *and* Green*) that will be analyzed in detail in Figure 7.10. For a color version of this figure, see www.iste.co.uk/atto/change1.zip*

### 7.4.3. *Sensitivity to parameters*

This subsection aims to analyze the sensitivity of the proposed method to its parameters: the window size ($\omega$) used for keypoint extraction, the number of closest neighbors $K$ within the graph construction stage and the patch size $w_p$ considered around each keypoint. We exploited the ROC plots performed on Dataset 1 for these experiments.

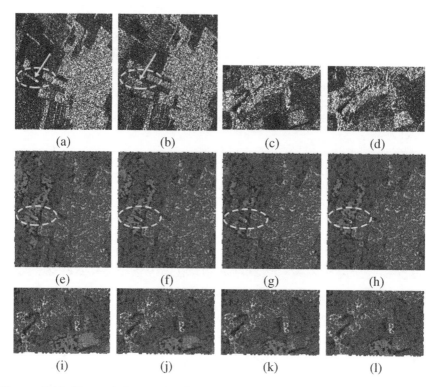

**Figure 7.10.** *Zoomed in results for the* Red *and* Green *crops of Dataset 2 (Figure 7.9(a)). (a),(b)* Red *crop from two images. (c),(d)* Green *crop from two images. From (e) to (h) Change maps yielded by four detection methods for* Red *crop: (e) MRD, (f) LRD, (g) GKLD and (h) proposed method. The yellow dashed circle highlights an interesting detail for discussion. From (i) to (l) Change maps yielded for* Green *crop. For a color version of this figure, see www.iste.co.uk/atto/change1.zip*

### 7.4.3.1. *Sensitivity to the keypoint density*

This density of keypoints concerns their capacity to represent the information provided by the image. In fact, in terms of visualization, we may observe some information loss from the image regions where there is no detected keypoint. However, thanks to their ability to capture most of the significant information of the image content (i.e. appearance within any intensity variation from the image), the local extrema can produce an excellent image representation and approximation. In Figure 7.11, ROC plots and the detection accuracy ($P_{OA}$) are used to quantitatively compare the performance of the dense approach and keypoint-based (i.e. pointwise) approach with different keypoint densities for change detection. We propose to perform the experiments employing the LRD since it can have both dense and pointwise versions. The Otsu technique was adopted for the thresholding stage. We note that the density of local max keypoints is characterized by the window size

($\omega$) used for keypoint extraction (section 7.2). As depicted in the figure, both dense and keypoint-based approaches (with $\omega$ varying from 3 to 7) provide very close performance in terms of ROC as well as $P_{OA}$. Then, in terms of complexity, the computational time of the pointwise approaches was significantly reduced compared to that of the dense one. This is because the dense approach detects changes for all pixels (image size = 800 × 400, hence 320,000 pixels), while pointwise approaches detect changes only on local max keypoints (9,545, 3,902 and 2,974 points corresponding to the 3 × 3, 5 × 5 and 7 × 7 window, respectively). Therefore, we can conclude that the sensitivity of the proposed algorithm to parameter $\omega$ is very low. Moreover, if we ensure a good density of keypoints (i.e. $\omega$ is set from 3 to 9), such a keypoint-based approach can provide a stable detection performance without any concern about information loss.

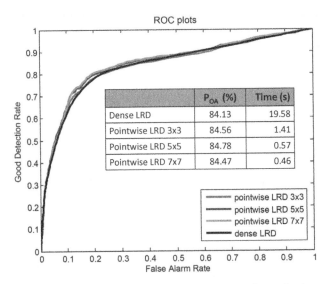

**Figure 7.11.** *Comparison of the dense and pointwise (keypoint-based) LRD methods (with different window sizes ($\omega$) for keypoint extraction) for change detection. For a color version of this figure, see www.iste.co.uk/atto/change1.zip*

### 7.4.3.2. Sensitivity to $K$ and $w_p$

The next experiment studies the parameter $K$ and the patch size $w_p$. To investigate the sensitivity to $K$, we fixed the patch size $w_p$ to 15 × 15 pixels while $K$ varies from 10 to 90. The corresponding result is shown in Figure 7.12(a). As observed, when $K$ increases, the performance is considerably enhanced at the beginning ($K$ from 10 to 50) but the enhancement slows down when $K$ is greater than 70. Then, when $K$ attains a value of 90 or higher, we observe a saturated phenomenon of ROCs. This behavior can be explained as follows. We have already mentioned that the parameter

$K$ implicitly represents the size of a neighborhood used for searching for the closest keypoints during the graph construction stage. That is, $K$ plays a similar role as a sliding neighborhood window considered for SAR image analysis and processing due to the presence of speckle. It is proved that the more the neighborhood is expanded, the better an operator can perform on SAR images, as long as the SAR signal is considered to be stationary or at least locally stationary in the neighborhood. However, the performance will be saturated when the neighborhood size is too large, which explains this analogous behavior of $K$.

Finally, the sensitivity to the patch size $w_p$ is studied in which we varied it from $11 \times 11$ pixels to $19 \times 19$ pixels. The parameter $K$ was set to 50. The related experimental result can be found in Figure 7.12(b). We can observe that $w_p$ does not create a strong impact on the algorithm's performance. Let us zoom into two stages of the ROCs as shown in the figure. It can be seen that large windows perform better within the first stage but are less efficient during the second. In addition, the variation of the five ROCs is not too high. These remarks enable us to conclude that the proposed method is not significantly influenced by the parameter $w_p$. Here again, we note that only the first-order statistic (i.e. the mean value) of the $w_p \times w_p$ patch around each keypoint is required within our algorithm. Hence, a small patch size could be enough for the estimation. To conclude this section, although the proposed strategy is significantly dependent on the parameter $K$, the influence caused by $w_p$ is quite inconsiderable.

### 7.4.4. Comparison with the NLM model

In this section, we distinguish the proposed method from the NLM model proposed in Yousif and Ban (2013). We propose this comparison as readers may expect to do so when they reach equation [7.10] which involves the generation of our CM using the graph random walk matrix $\mathcal{P}$, instead of the graph adjacency matrix $\mathcal{W}$. As a reminder, using $\mathcal{P}$ provides a CM involving a normalized weighted summing of log-ratio distances derived from neighboring keypoints via graph structure (see equation [7.10]), which has certain similarity to the NLM model.

The first important point to discriminate the two methodologies is the way each of them tackles the problem of change detection for SAR images. In fact, the NLM model involves a filtering process to reduce speckle noise (based on the NLM denoising filter (Buades *et al.* 2005)) during the change detection algorithm. Meanwhile, the proposed strategy aims to investigate the coherence of local structure and radiometric information between the two images. Our starting point is not a despeckling approach but a texture tracking approach based on a keypoint-based image representation strategy via a graph model. Let us summarize the two CMs using the NLM model proposed by Yousif and Ban (2013):

$$CM_1^{NLM}(p_n) = LR\left\{I_1^{NLM}(p_n), I_2^{NLM}(p_n)\right\}, \qquad [7.11]$$

$$CM_2^{NLM}(p_n) = \frac{1}{\sum_{p_k \in \mathcal{N}(p_n)} w_{LR}(p_n, p_k)} \sum_{p_k \in \mathcal{N}(p_n)} w_{LR}(p_n, p_k) I_{LR}(p_k)$$

[7.12]

where

– $LR$ denotes the classical log-ratio operator;

– $I_i^{NLM}$, $i = \{1, 2\}$ is the NLM filtered version of image $i$:

$$I_i^{NLM}(p_n) = \frac{1}{\sum_{p_k \in \mathcal{N}(p_n)} w_i(p_n, p_k)} \sum_{p_k \in \mathcal{N}(p_n)} w_i(p_n, p_k) I_i(p_k);$$     [7.13]

– $I_{LR}$ is the log-ratio DI derived from the two input images;

– $w_i(p_n, p_k)$, $i = \{1, 2\}$ and $w_{LR}(p_n, p_k)$ refer to the similarity weight between two pixels $p_n$, $p_k$ computed from the image $I_i$, $i = \{1, 2\}$ and from $I_{LR}$, respectively;

– $\mathcal{N}(p_n)$ represents the dense search neighborhood around pixel $p_n$ considered for the NLM model (Buades *et al.* 2005).

Let us compare the two NLM CMs generated by equations [7.11] and [7.12] to the measure yielded by our proposed method in equation [7.10]. A crucial remark is that the weighting function in the NLM approach is calculated for each image (i.e. the first model, equation [7.11]) or directly from the LR DI (i.e. the second model, equation [7.12]). On the contrary, in our strategy, the similarity weight is computed only for the first image $I_1$ within the graph construction stage.

Another significant point which makes our algorithm distinct from the NLM model is that for each point $p_n$, only a number of $K$ closest neighboring keypoints are taken into account for change measuring. Meanwhile, in the NLM model, all pixels inside the dense search neighborhood $\mathcal{N}(p_n)$ are considered. This issue leads to the main drawback of the NLM model, the computational complexity. If $W \times W$ refers to the size of $\mathcal{N}(p_n)$, we need to investigate all $W^2$ pixels for change measurement at $p_n$ using the NLM model. This amount is much higher than the number of points $K$ within our method. Thus, using the proposed approach could reduce the complexity by the factor of $K/W^2$ in comparison to the NLM model. Moreover, it should be noted that our algorithm works using keypoints that are previously selected. Thus, similarity weight functions can be directly derived from these points. On the contrary, the NLM model works using dense neighborhoods from which we need to calculate weights for every pixel inside that neighborhood and then select the most relevant ones. Furthermore, when $K$ is fixed, the proposed method implicitly considers a search neighborhood of flexible size which varies depending on the density of keypoints around each keypoint $p_n$. For the NLM model, the size of $\mathcal{N}(p_n)$ is usually fixed, which ignores the proper local structure of the image at $p_n$. We will address all of these remarks in more detail during analysis of the algorithm complexity of the proposed approach, compared to reference methods, in the next section.

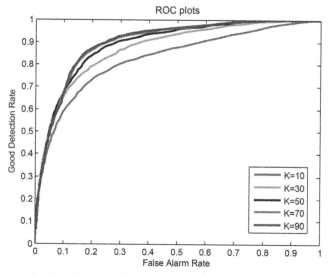

(a) Sensitivity to the number of closest neighbors $K$

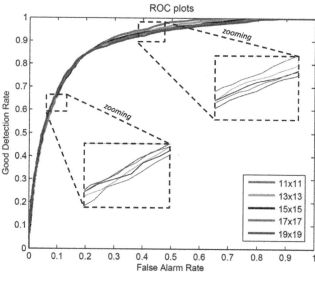

(b) Sensitivity to the patch sizes $w_p$

**Figure 7.12.** *ROC plots for the proposed method within the variation of its parameters. (a) The number of closest neighbors ($K$) for the graph construction stage. (b) The patch size $w_p$ considered for each keypoint. For a color version of this figure, see www.iste.co.uk/atto/change1.zip*

### 7.4.5. *Analysis of the algorithm complexity*

Figure 7.13 shows an outline of different types of support neighborhoods employed by different methods in order to measure the change level at each pixel. As a reminder, classical methods based on dense neighborhoods such as MRD, LRD, GKLD and CKLD use all pixels inside a fixed large-sized window (denoted by $W \times W$; see Figure 7.13(a)) around the understudied pixel (marked in red). Next, the NLM and our method perform a weighted averaging operator of small patches within the larger neighborhood around the pixel, in order to generate its CM. However, as previously mentioned, while the NLM usually considers all patches inside the fixed-size $W \times W$ neighborhood (see Figure 7.13(b)), our method only takes into account patches at pre-selected keypoints within a flexible neighborhood whose size depends on the image's local properties around that pixel (see Figure 7.13(c)). These analyses reveal some ideas of the complexity of each method. In general, the computational time increases as follows: *classical dense methods (MRD, LRD, GKLD, CKLD) < proposed method < NLM method.*

Table 7.2 provides the complexity and calculation time of different methods, together with their detection performance. Denote $w_p \times w_p$ the size of small patches within the NLM model and the proposed algorithm, the algorithm complexity can be estimated as $O(W^2)$ for classical dense methods (MRD, LRD, GKLD, CKLD), $O(W^2 w_p^2)$ for the NLM model and $O(K w_p^2)$ for our method. Then, from the third column of the table, we observe the effect of these complexity levels on their experimental computation time. Compared to the NLM model (425.74s), the proposed strategy (15.94s) reduces the complexity by approximately a factor of $K/W^2$ (i.e. $K$ is set to 50 and $W$ is set to 35 in the experiment). Here, all the implementations are effectuated using MATLAB on a Xeon 3.6GHz, 16 GB RAM.

Lastly, we may wonder about the superior performance in terms of detection accuracy of the proposed approach compared to that of the NLM model (85.87% compared to 84.79%). In fact, our strategy only considers patches at keypoint locations for the averaging procedure. When choosing the local maximum pixels as keypoints, we are likely to select *"good"* patches for each central patch since the local maxima implicitly involve the notion of similarity among their patches. On the other hand, the NLM model accumulates all patches for its weighted averaging. In our experiment, the NLM approach has been implemented following equation [7.12] without any optimization for weighting function or patch regularization because our main objective here is to study its complexity rather than to optimize its detection performance. More details about the optimization of the NLM model can be found in Yousif and Ban (2013). In conclusion, the efficiency of the proposed method consists of superior detection performance and intermediate complexity between classical dense methods and the NLM approach.

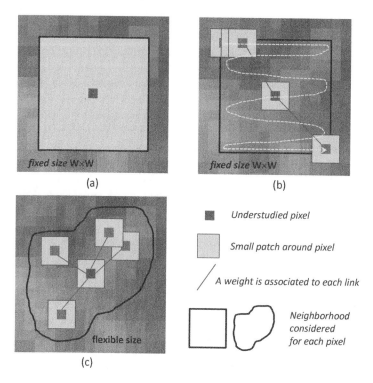

fixed size W×W        (a)          fixed size W×W        (b)

■  Understudied pixel

▢  Small patch around pixel

／  A weight is associated to each link

▢◯  Neighborhood considered for each pixel

flexible size    (c)

**Figure 7.13.** *Support neighborhood considered for measuring the change level at each pixel. (a) By MRD, LRD, GKLD and CKLD methods. (b) By NLM approach. (c) By the proposed approach. For a color version of this figure, see www.iste.co.uk/atto/change1.zip*

| Method | Complexity | Computation time (s) | $P_{GD}/P_{FA}$ | $P_{OA}$ (%) |
|---|---|---|---|---|
| MRD | $O(W^2)$ | 1.51 | 6.0611 | 84.37 |
| LRD | $O(W^2)$ | 1.54 | 6.6430 | 84.61 |
| GKLD | $O(W^2)$ | 2.08 | 6.0106 | 83.57 |
| NLM | $O(W^2 w_p^2)$ | 425.74 | 7.0186 | 84.79 |
| Proposed | $O(K w_p^2)$ | 15.94 | 8.0004 | 85.87 |

**Table 7.2.** *Comparison of computational complexity and detection performance from different methods. Experiments were conducted on Dataset 1 (Otsu thresholding)*

## 7.5. Application to glacier flow measurement

In this section, the proposed texture tracking technique is applied to the measurement of glacier flows over time using SAR images. The objective is to search for the displacement vector which shows the flow magnitude and direction of each pixel of interest located on the glacier. We continue to exploit the dissimilarity measure generated by the weighted graph structure to search for the most relevant displacement of each keypoint between two SAR images. This study is proposed to check the behavior of a graph-based texture tracking strategy to detect displacements instead of measuring changes between two images. Let us now describe the proposed method and provide some experimental results on TerraSAR-X data.

### 7.5.1. *Proposed method*

The proposed method for glacier displacement detection is highlighted in Figure 7.14. Let us consider the two SAR images, namely the Master and the Slave for this study. In general, the Master image is chronologically acquired before and the Slave is captured later. Similar to our change detection framework (Figure 7.6), a set of local max keypoints are first extracted from the Master. A weighted graph is then constructed to connect all keypoints. For each understudied keypoint from the Master, we search from the Slave the corresponding pixel which is the most adapted to the local graph structure located at the keypoint. In other words, the local texture information around each keypoint is tracked with the help of the constructed graph structure. In practice, the searching process for each keypoint is limited to a research zone, as opposed to the whole image, due to the prior knowledge of the maximum displacement occurring from the two images.

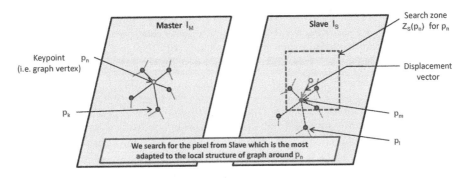

**Figure 7.14.** *Outline of the proposed graph-based texture tracking for glacier flow detection and measurement. For a color version of this figure, see www.iste.co.uk/atto/change1.zip*

Denote $p_n$ the keypoint located at position $(x_n, y_n)$ on the Master plane having the intensity $I^M(p_n)$. The displacement vector at $p_n$ is calculated:

$$\vec{v}(p_n) = p_m^* - p_n, \qquad [7.14]$$

$$p_m^* = \arg \min_{p_m \in \mathcal{Z}_S(p_n)} \mathcal{D}(p_n, p_m), \qquad\qquad [7.15]$$

where $\mathcal{Z}_S(p_n)$ denotes the search zone of $p_n$ from the plane of $I_S$. $\mathcal{D}(p_n, p_m)$ is the dissimilarity measure between $p_n$ from the Master $I_M$ and each pixel $p_m \in \mathcal{Z}_S(p_n)$ from the Slave $I_S$. It refers to the difference between the local information around $p_n$ and $p_m$, with regard to the structure of $\mathcal{G}$. This distance can be computed as follows:

$$\begin{aligned}\mathcal{D}(p_n, p_m) &= \left\|(\mathcal{W}f_M)(p_n) - (\mathcal{W}f_S)(p_m)\right\|_1 \\ &= \sum_{p_k \sim p_n} w(p_n, p_k) \left| \log \frac{\mu_M(p_k)}{\mu_S(p_l)} \right|, \qquad [7.16]\end{aligned}$$

in which $p_l = (p_m - p_n) + p_k$ (the implicit connection between $p_m$ and $p_l$ on $I_S$ corresponds to the real connection between $p_n$ and $p_k$ on $I_M$, as shown in Figure 7.14). The signal $f_M$ (respectively, $f_S$) is defined to encapsulate the radiometric information of $I_M$ (respectively, $I_S$) captured by the position of the graph vertices: $f_M(p_n) = \log \mu_M(p_n)$. Mean intensity and logarithm operator are used to reduce speckle influence with SAR images. The weight function $w(p_n, p_k)$ is computed as in [7.7].

### 7.5.2. Results

Experiments were carried out on the two SAR intensity images acquired from the Argentiere Glacier, located in the French Alps. These images were captured by the TerraSAR-X (TSX) satellite using the Stripmap descending mode with spatial resolution of 1.4 m in range and 2.5 m in azimuth. Here, we study the glacier displacement from the two images acquired on July 12, 2009 and August 14, 2009. They are shown in Figure 7.15(c) and (d) together with the studied area and a reference optical image on the top.

Figure 7.16(a) shows the glacier displacement result provided by the proposed strategy. Here, the red vectors indicate displacements in good directions and the green ones are in wrong directions. The experiment was carried out by setting a search window size of $5 \times 5$ pixels ($w = 5$) for the local max keypoint extraction. Then, the weighted graph was built by preserving $K = 200$ connections for each vertex. We note that the mean intensity (i.e. $\mu_M, \mu_S$) was computed for a small $3 \times 3$ window size to reduce the effect of speckle noise. About 94% of displacements are detected in good direction (marked in red) from Figure 7.16(a). For a better qualitative assessment, we propose to compute a reliability index (RI) (i.e. confidence index) at each point. Here, RI at point $p_n$ is calculated as the standard deviation of $\mathcal{D}(p_n, p_m), \forall p_m \in \mathcal{Z}(p_n)$. A high RI reveals an accurate estimation of flow vector and vice versa. Figure 7.16(b) shows the RI normalized in $[0, 1]$. We observe that high RI is generally obtained from rough surfaces and crevasse regions of the glacier. On the contrary, low RI is observed in most homogeneous areas.

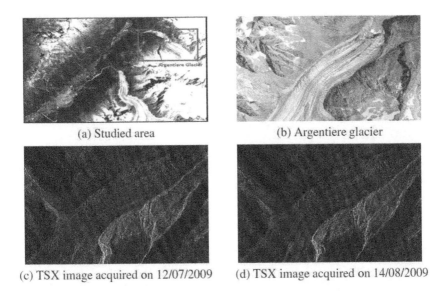

(a) Studied area                    (b) Argentiere glacier

(c) TSX image acquired on 12/07/2009    (d) TSX image acquired on 14/08/2009

**Figure 7.15.** *Studied area, a reference optical image and two input TerraSAR-X images acquired from the Argentiere Glacier, ©Airbus DS. For a color version of this figure, see www.iste.co.uk/atto/change1.zip*

Let us now analyze the result in more detail by zooming into two regions of interest marked by the two rectangles (namely *Yellow* crop and *White* crop). The *White* crop is extracted from a homogeneous (i.e. smooth) region of the glacier. The *Yellow* one is cut from a crevasse area with a rough surface and very structural texture produced by fast-moving glaciers down to the serac fall. The zoomed in results of these two crops are shown in Figure 7.16(c) and (d), respectively. The result of the *White* crop consists of several falsely detected vectors (in green). Also, red vectors diverge in different directions and magnitudes. In fact, the corresponding RI values from Figure 7.16(b) are very low which explains those unreliable estimations. Hence, the performance of the proposed algorithm is still limited for smooth regions. Meanwhile, the detection result for the *Yellow* crop in the crevasse region is quite consistent (high RI from Figure 7.16(b)). All detected vectors reveal the glacier flow direction. Then, these vector lengths tend to increase at the serac fall. The maximum vector attains 9 pixels in range and 4 pixels in azimuth which corresponds to a displacement of about 16 m in 33 days (duration between two acquisition dates). Hence, the maximum displacement at serac fall is approximately 0.48 m/day. We note that the annual measurement estimates that the displacement at this serac fall region is about 0.4 m/day (Harant *et al*. 2010). The above observations show that our strategy is able to provide good performance on crevasse areas with strong and structural texture information. However, the performance is limited for homogeneous and smooth regions. In fact, glacier flow measurement using the texture tracking approach always encounters challenges within homogeneous and flat areas. This behavior has also been found in previous studies in the literature (Harant *et al.* 2010; Fallourd *et al.* 2011).

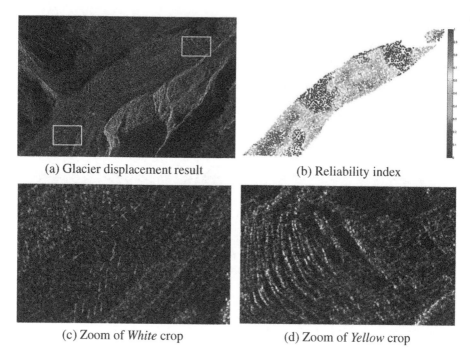

(a) Glacier displacement result

(b) Reliability index

(c) Zoom of *White* crop

(d) Zoom of *Yellow* crop

**Figure 7.16.** *Glacier displacement result yielded by the proposed algorithm. Vector flows with good direction are marked in red. For a color version of this figure, see www.iste.co.uk/atto/change1.zip*

## 7.6. Conclusion

We have presented a keypoint graph-based texture tracking method to tackle unsupervised change detection and glacier displacement measurement using bitemporal SAR images. To perform such an approach, we exploited the local extrema as keypoints for non-dense texture representation and adopted the spatial domain (vertex domain) of a weighted graph for texture characterization. CM was derived from the coherence and compatibility of radiometric information provided by the two images with the support of the constructed graph's local structure. Speckle noise was reduced by the application of the log-ratio operator. For change detection, our results have demonstrated the superior performance of the proposed algorithm compared to several reference methods, in terms of detection accuracy. Its robust behavior to different thresholding techniques was also confirmed. For the second application of detecting and measuring glacier displacements, our method was found to be relevant for rough surfaces. It can provide a fast estimation of displacements, especially for crevasse areas of the glacier. However, it is not robust enough to deal with flat or smooth areas. Future work will focus on improving the algorithm performance for homogeneous regions. Then, by taking into account the distortion offsets in range and azimuth of TSX images, a quantitative and comparative study could be performed.

## 7.7. References

Asokan, A. and Anitha, J. (2019). Change detection techniques for remote sensing applications: A survey. *Earth Science Informatics*, 12(2), 143–160.

Ban, Y. and Yousif, O. (2012). Multitemporal spaceborne SAR data for urban change detection in China. *IEEE Journal of Selected Topics in Applied Earth Observations and Remote Sensing*, 5(4), 1087–1094.

Bazi, Y., Bruzzone, L., Melgani, F. (2005). An unsupervised approach based on the generalized Gaussian model to automatic change detection in multitemporal SAR images. *IEEE Transactions on Geoscience and Remote Sensing*, 43(4), 874–887.

Bovolo, F. and Bruzzone, L. (2005). A detail-preserving scale-driven approach to change detection in multitemporal SAR images. *IEEE Transactions on Geoscience and Remote Sensing*, 43(12), 2963–2972.

Bovolo, F. and Bruzzone, L. (2007). A split-based approach to unsupervised change detection in large-size multitemporal images: Application to tsunami-damage assessment. *IEEE Transactions on Geoscience and Remote Sensing*, 45(6), 1658–1670.

Buades, A., Coll, B., Morel, J.M. (2005). A non-local algorithm for image denoising. *Computer Vision and Pattern Recognition*, 2(60), 60–65.

Del Frate, F., Pacifici, F., Solimini, D. (2008). Monitoring urban land cover in Rome, Italy, and its changes by single-polarization multitemporal SAR images. *IEEE Journal of Selected Topics in Applied Earth Observations and Remote Sensing*, 1(2), 87–97.

Dellinger, F., Delon, J., Gousseau, Y., Michel, J., Tupin, F. (2015). SAR-SIFT: A SIFT-like algorithm for SAR images. *IEEE Transactions on Geoscience and Remote Sensing*, 53(1), 453–466.

Fallourd, R., Harant, O., Trouvé, E., Nicolas, J.-M., Gay, M., Walpersdorf, A., Mugnier, J.-L., Serafini, J., Rosu, D., Bombrun, L., Vasile, G., Cotte, N., Vernier, F., Tupin, F., Moreau, L., Bolon, P. (2011). Monitoring temperate glacier displacement by multi-temporal terraSAR-X images and continuous GPS measurements. *IEEE Journal of Selected Topics in Applied Earth Observations and Remote Sensing*, 4(2), 372–386.

Flandrin, P., Rilling, G., Goncalves, P. (2004). Empirical mode decomposition as a filter bank. *IEEE Signal Processing Letters*, 11(2), 112–114.

Gong, M., Zhou, Z., Ma, J. (2012). Change detection in Synthetic Aperture Radar images based on image fusion and fuzzy clustering. *IEEE Transactions on Image Processing*, 21(4), 2141–2151.

Harant, O., Bombrun, L., Vasile, G., Ferro-Famil, L., Gay, M. (2010). Displacement estimation by maximum-likelihood texture tracking. *IEEE Journal of Selected Topics in Signal Processing*, 5(3), 398–407.

Hartigan, J.A. and Wong, M.A. (1979). Algorithm as 136: A k-means clustering algorithm. *Journal of the Royal Statistical Society. Series C (Applied Statistics)*, 28(1), 100–108.

Hou, B., Wei, Q., Zheng, Y., Wang, S. (2014). Unsupervised change detection in SAR image based on Gauss-log ratio image fusion and compressed projection. *IEEE Journal of Selected Topics in Applied Earth Observations and Remote Sensing*, 7(8), 3297–3317.

Huang, N.E., Shen, Z., Long, S.R., Wu, M.C., Shih, H.H., Zheng, Q., Yen, N.-C., Tung, C.C., Liu, H.H. (1998). The empirical mode decomposition and the Hilbert spectrum for nonlinear and non-stationary time series analysis. *Proceedings of the Royal Society of London. Series A: Mathematical, Physical and Engineering Sciences*, 454(1971), 903–995.

Inglada, J. (2003). Change detection on SAR images by using a parametric estimation of the Kullback–Leibler divergence. *Proceedings of the 2003 IEEE International Geoscience and Remote Sensing Symposium*, 6, 4104–4106, Toulouse, France.

Inglada, J. and Mercier, G. (2007). A new statistical similarity measure for change detection in multitemporal SAR images and its extension to multiscale change analysis. *IEEE Transactions on Geoscience and Remote Sensing*, 45(5), 1432–1445.

Kittler, J. and Illingworth, J. (1986). Minimum error thresholding. *Pattern Recognition*, 19(1), 41–47.

Ma, J., Gong, M., Zhou, Z. (2012). Wavelet fusion on ratio images for change detection in SAR images. *IEEE Geoscience and Remote Sensing Letters*, 9(6), 1122–1126.

Mercier, G., Derrode, S., Trouvé, E., Bombrun, L. (2010). Change detection in remote sensing observations. In *Multivariate Image Processing: Methods and Applications*, Chanussot, J., Collet, C., Chehdi, K. (eds). ISTE Ltd, London and John Wiley & Sons, New York.

Nunes, J.C., Bouaoune, Y., Delechelle, E., Niang, O., Bunel, P. (2003). Image analysis by bidimensional empirical mode decomposition. *Image and Vision Computing*, 21(12), 1019–1026.

Otsu, N. (1975). A threshold selection method from gray-level histograms. *Automatica*, 11(285–296), 23–27.

Pham, M.-T. (2018). Efficient texture retrieval using multiscale local extrema descriptors and covariance embedding. *Proceedings of the European Conference on Computer Vision (ECCV)* [Online]. Available at: https://arxiv.org/pdf/1808.01124.pdf.

Pham, M.T., Mercier, G., Michel, J. (2014a). Textural features from wavelets on graphs for very high resolution panchromatic Pléiades image classification. *Revue française de photogrammétrie et de télédétection*, (208), 131–136.

Pham, M.-T., Mercier, G., Michel, J. (2014b). Wavelets on graphs for very high resolution multispectral image texture segmentation. *2014 IEEE Geoscience and Remote Sensing Symposium*, 2273–2276, Quebec, Canada.

Pham, M.-T., Mercier, G., Michel, J. (2015). Pointwise graph-based local texture characterization for very high resolution multispectral image classification. *IEEE Journal of Selected Topics in Applied Earth Observations and Remote Sensing*, 8(5), 1962–1973.

Pham, M.-T., Mercier, G., Michel, J. (2016a). PW-COG: An effective texture descriptor for VHR satellite imagery using a pointwise approach on covariance matrix of oriented gradients. *IEEE Transactions on Geoscience and Remote Sensing*, 54(6), 3345–3359.

Pham, M.-T., Mercier, G., Regniers, O., Michel, J. (2016b). Texture retrieval from VHR optical remote sensed images using the local extrema descriptor with application to vineyard parcel detection. *Remote Sensing*, 8(5), 368.

Pham, M.-T., Mercier, G., Bombrun, L. (2017). Color texture image retrieval based on local extrema features and Riemannian distance. *Journal of Imaging*, 3(4), 43.

Radke, R.J., Andra, S., Al-Kofahi, O., Roysam, B. (2005). Image change detection algorithms: A systematic survey. *IEEE Transactions on Image Processing*, 14(3), 294–307.

Rignot, E.J.M. and van Zyl, J.J. (1993). Change detection techniques for ERS-1 SAR data. *IEEE Transactions on Geoscience and. Remote Sensing*, 31(4), 896–906.

Shuman, D.I., Narang, S.K., Frossard, P., Ortega, A., Vandergheynst, P. (2013). The emerging field of signal processing on graphs: Extending high-dimensional data analysis to networks and other irregular domains. *IEEE Signal Processing Magazine*, 30(3), 83–98.

Tuytelaars, T. and Mikolajczyk, K. (2008). Local invariant feature detectors: A survey. *Foundations and Trends® in Computer Graphics and Vision*, 3(3), 177–280.

Yousif, O. and Ban, Y. (2013). Improving urban change detection from multitemporal SAR images using PCA-NLM. *IEEE Transactions on Geoscience and Remote Sensing*, 51(4), 2032–2041.

Zheng, J. and You, H. (2013). A new model-independent method for change detection in multitemporal SAR images based on Radon transform and Jeffrey divergence. *IEEE Geoscience and Remote Sensing Letters*, 10(1), 91–95.

# 8

# Multitemporal Analysis of Sentinel-1/2 Images for Land Use Monitoring at Regional Scale

Andrea GARZELLI and Claudia ZOPPETTI

*University of Siena, Italy*

## 8.1. Introduction

Human activities such as urban and industrial development or agricultural practices can be classified as landscape disturbance and can be detected and tracked through remote sensing analysis at different temporal and spatial scales (Lambin *et al.* 2006).

Such an investigation allows us to detect new land cover types, and possibly states varying the destination of use, i.e. land use transitions. This goal can be pursued by following two distinct approaches: a classification-based change detection or a feature-/pixel-based change detection (Zhang *et al.* 2019). In the first case, the analysis first produces classification maps and then finds changes between labeled pixels or objects of the classification maps at different times: a change map will be produced by comparing available maps with the classification map of recently acquired remote sensing images. According to the second approach, processing is applied directly to remote sensing data to produce a reliable change map. This chapter presents an experimental study following a feature-based approach for building detection, time-tracking of a construction site and changed area estimation at a large, regional scale.

*Change Detection and Image Time Series Analysis 1*,
coordinated by Abdourrahmane M. ATTO, Francesca BOVOLO and Lorenzo BRUZZONE.
© ISTE Ltd 2021.

Building detection from satellite images was almost impossible a few decades ago due to the low spatio-temporal resolution of satellite images, which did not allow the identification of individual buildings in an image. Therefore, building detection could only be achieved by employing aerial images. In the last two decades, there have been significant advances in satellite sensor technology, thus making the detection of man-made structures from satellite images possible and more accurate than ever before (Aiazzi *et al.* 2013; Konstantinidis 2017) especially if a multisensor (jointly from passive and active sensors) approach is adopted (Sun *et al.* 2019).

The development and constant update of digital urban maps can be extremely helpful for municipalities and city planning services, and also to detect and map illegal building activity. Building detection can be achieved manually by human experts from optical multispectral images. However, the time needed to perform manual labeling and the landscape variability due to seasonal changes makes this process very time-consuming and almost unfeasible for large-scale monitoring.

Accurate and efficient automatic building detection can be a really challenging task, due to the variety of building appearances in satellite optical images and sensor limitations, for example, acquisition noise, which is a characteristic of active sensors, such as synthetic aperture radar (SAR). Furthermore, high-resolution images enable the development of a more accurate and robust building detection system. On the other hand, they introduce a large amount of data, whose processing can tremendously affect the efficiency of an algorithm. This is particularly relevant for the methods based on interferometric SAR data (Plank 2014; Amitrano *et al.* 2015, 2016), whose computational complexity makes an interferometric-based, automatic, large-scale operational system – through coherence exploitation and derived representations – practically unfeasible. In fact, as reported in Amitrano *et al.* (2019), basic pre-processing of a time series of six complex images (i.e. calibration, deburst, co-registration and standard despeckling) using the Sentinel Application Platform (SNAP) requires approximately 11 h on a high-end eight-core, 128-GB RAM machine and accounts for more than 120 GB of storage. Ground range detected (GRD) products are therefore preferred in an operational scenario since pre-processed images can be downloaded from the Copernicus Open Access Hub or the Google Earth Engine.

Finally, in order to compare images and identify differences, images should be properly registered. Such an alignment is not always an easy task, in particular for very high spatial resolution and/or narrow-swath data requiring accurate mosaicking. Registration errors can lead to the degradation of the performance of the whole processing system.

The use of open image collections and parallel processing tools, such as the Google Earth Engine (GEE), helps in overcoming the above-mentioned limitations. GEE consists of a huge analysis-ready data catalog with a high-performance, intrinsically parallel processing service. It is accessed and controlled through an Internet-accessible application programming interface (API) and an associated Web-based interactive development environment (IDE) that enables rapid prototyping and visualization of results (Gorelick *et al.* 2017). The data catalog includes a large repository of publicly available geospatial data that are pre-processed to a ready-to-use information-preserving form, allowing fast, easy and efficient access.

With the recent free availability of open-access satellite datasets, wide-area analysis is possible, specifically by processing high-resolution images provided by the European Union's Earth Observation Programme Copernicus. Short-revisit-time multispectral Sentinel-2 images and C-band SAR Sentinel-1 data offer great potential to improve continuous monitoring activities of the Earth's surface. Large-scale change monitoring requires a long observation period – several months to one year to characterize urban transformations – and frequent revisits to provide for adequate temporal resolution. The resulting data volume is therefore impressive and pre-processed data, i.e. calibrated, geometrically corrected, geocoded images, are necessary to make the problem affordable in a reasonable time. In this sense, the GEE ready-to-use image catalog can help to solve the problem.

Compared with optical instruments, SAR sensors can observe the Earth's surface in all weather conditions and can provide useful information on urban areas, as they are sensitive to the geometric characteristics of urban structures. SAR sensors are also less sensitive to seasonal vegetation changes with respect to optical sensors. Combining images of the same area from both ascending and descending orbits allows two lines of sight of the same structure to be exploited, hence increasing the chance of observing the characteristic double-bounce mechanism that generates high backscattering (Chini *et al.* 2018). Multitemporally filtered intensities (Quegan and Yu 2001) in the two co-polarized acquisitions, VV and HH, for each available orbit, either ascending and descending, are considered. The four input SAR features form the dataset for the first step of the processing chain, i.e. the multitemporal building detection.

The complementary characteristics of the multispectral Sentinel-2 images on the same area can eventually be exploited to estimate the extension of the urban transformation previously detected by the SAR sensors.

## 8.2. Proposed method

The goal of the proposed method is to monitor the construction of new buildings in urban and suburban scenarios at a large, regional scale.

The scheme reported in Figure 8.1 illustrates the complete processing flow for the proposed method, where both SAR and optical processing are used in a cascade line. Starting from the top of the scheme, SAR (Sentinel-1) and optical (Sentinel-2) data are required as inputs of the processing chain. In the GEE development environment, it is possible to query the database for an image collection[1] with specific requirements imposed by the end-user itself, such as area extension (zones selection) and start–end dates (observation period). Other several filters on data characteristic features (e.g. polarization) can also be set to further select the batch of images of interest. After this first selection, the data to be processed are:

– image collection of $N_1$ dates for Sentinel-1 SAR data. This is a set of images defined as:

$$\{N_1\} = \{\mathcal{I}_1, \mathcal{I}_2, \ldots, \mathcal{I}_{N_1}\}_{S1}^{[t_{start}, t_{end}]} \in \{R_{geo}\}$$

where $\mathcal{I}_k$ is an image belonging to the Sentinel-1 collection of $N_1$ elements, $[t_{start}, t_{end}]$ is the observation period and $R_{geo}$ is an arbitrary geographical region of interest;

– image collection of $N_2$ dates for Sentinel-2 multispectral data. This is a set of multiband images defined as:

$$\{N_2\} = \{\mathcal{I}_1, \mathcal{I}_2, \ldots, \mathcal{I}_{N_2}\}_{S2}^{[t_{start}, t_{end}]} \in \{R_{geo}\}$$

where $\mathcal{I}_k$ is an image belonging to the Sentinel-2 collection of $N_2$ elements, $[t_{start}, t_{end}]$ is the observation period and $R_{geo}$ is the geographical region of interest.

It is obvious that $[t_{start}, t_{end}]$ and $R_{geo}$ must be the same for both data series, while $N_1$ and $N_2$ could be different, typically $N_1 > N_2$, due to cloud cover limitations for the optical acquisitions.

In Figure 8.1, after the data selection, the processing chain evolves as:

– *SAR data processing layer*: the $\{N_1\}$ set of images of Sentinel-1 data is fed as input to the dedicated sub-module (see details in section 8.3). The goal of this sub-module is to process the whole time series to detect and then extract regions of interest (ROIs) of structural (urban/man-made, more specifically) change. These ROIs are spatial regions that are agglomerated into a single image, which serves as a logical mask, accounting for all bi-temporal change detection between the oldest, reference, $\mathcal{I}_1$ image, and the current, $\mathcal{I}_k$, acquisition. The expected output of this step is a set of *change maps*, where it is possible to recover the spatial location and, possibly, the spatial extent of the structural changes occurred in a geographical region, for a specific couple of images (temporally in a row). This makes the SAR processing block a powerful pre-screening tool to explore large geographical zones, where manual inspection is practically unfeasible;

---

1. For example, to select Sentinel-1: `ee.ImageCollection("COPERNICUS/S1_GRD")`. For Sentinel-2: `ee.ImageCollection("COPERNICUS/S2")`.

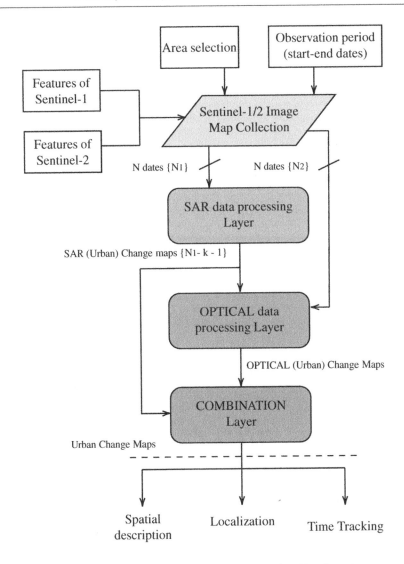

**Figure 8.1.** *Flowchart of the large-scale monitoring algorithm for urban scenarios.*
*For a color version of this figure, see www.iste.co.uk/atto/change1.zip*

– *OPTICAL data processing layer*: both the resulting change maps from the SAR processing block ($\{N_1 - k - 1\}$) and the $\{N_2\}$ set of images of Sentinel-2 data are fed into this dedicated sub-module (see details in section 8.4). The goal of this sub-module is to exploit the information of the pre-screening step obtained from the SAR processing layer through the available ROIs in each change map and to recover the geometric details and specific characteristics of the corresponding optical data.

The expected output of this sub-module is a set of *urban* optical maps along the $\{N_2\}$ series of input. This would increase the reliability of the overall change detection, but, most significantly, it refines the time tracking and characterization of the structural changes;

– *Combination layer*: the set of change maps and the set of urban optical maps are fed as input to this sub-module. The goal of this last sub-module is to deliver a final integration between SAR and optical analysis in order to produce the urban evolution information. It implements the event characterization, which leads to the detection of macroscopic events (intended as structural events) in a time series.

At the end of the processing chain, for each detected structural change, a sort of *urban evolution* is finally available: the end-user is provided with a *tagged* time series, where spatial description (e.g. extent and/or other geometrical details can be deduced), localization (the image collections from GEE are georeferenced data) and time track (topic dates) of variations are related to the urban structures. This useful and operation-oriented tagging method of time series data strongly relies on the combination of SAR and optical source.

The rationale behind this approach is to use the specificities of each type of data:

– SAR acquisitions are not very sensitive to atmospheric phenomena (e.g. cloud coverage) and free vegetation or seasonal variations of crops, while very responsive on building edges. On the other hand, unless we intend to have very high-resolution SAR images with interferometric information, they are not suitable for easily segmenting objects of interest on which to perform measurements for extracting accurate geometrical characteristics;

– optical acquisitions are very sensitive to atmospheric phenomena, but they provide spatial and geometrical details on objects together with the availability of rich spectral diversity for discrimination/classification purposes.

The key idea is therefore to use the SAR data to obtain a robust change map for the detection of built-up structures and then to recover geometrical details on the optical data.

### 8.2.1. *Test site and data*

The proposed method of analysis is designed to work on a regional scale, based on the Italian regional division, but this concept can be easily extended to other geographical entities by processing areas whose size is about 25,000 square kilometers. This extension does not make automatic, or even manual, inspection of SAR or optical image an easy task. Furthermore, when analyzing the series of optical temporal images, cloud cover can frequently occur and limit the temporal resolution of data. On the other hand, manual inspection of SAR images, which are insensitive to clouds, is intrinsically difficult to analyze because the image features, especially those associated with built-up areas, are quite easy to detect and locate, but they can hardly be characterized geometrically at the resolution of 10 m, which is typical of Sentinel-1 ground-detected data (see Figure 8.4). Even at a smaller scale – by focusing on a province, in the case of Italy – it is neither easy nor fast to identify the areas affected by structural changes. For this work, the fifth-largest Italian region was chosen, Tuscany ($\approx$23,000 km$^2$). Since it was difficult to obtain the whole regional cadastral data with high temporal resolution concerning building changes throughout the region, attention was focused on the province of Grosseto ($\approx$4,500 km$^2$). As can be seen in Figure 8.2, even the province alone appears to be a very large area, for which it is not immediately possible to identify and track the changes.

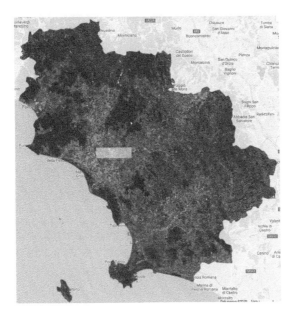

**Figure 8.2.** *Building detection test area, Grosseto province, $\approx$4,500 km$^2$. Sentinel-2 L2 true-color composite. The detail area for accurate visual inspection is highlighted in yellow ($\approx$ 51 km$^2$). For a color version of this figure, see www.iste.co.uk/atto/change1.zip*

Finally, in order to provide both visual and objective feedback and quantify the area affected by the change, a detail area has been considered, which is highlighted in yellow in Figure 8.2. A close-up view of this area, shown in Figure 8.3, was affected by the construction of a shopping center in the period from September 2015 to October 2016 (opened on October 27, 2016, construction work began in September 2015 and ended around mid-January 2016). The construction area is highlighted in red. As can be seen in Figure 8.3, in fact, in August 2015, the area had been prepared for construction, but no structure was present. By the end of December 2015, the main block had been completed, as well as four additional square-shaped commercial buildings on the east side of the main block.

**Figure 8.3.** *True-color Sentinel-2 on the detail area highlighted in Figure 8.2: August 3, 2015 (top), December 31, 2015 (bottom). The construction area is highlighted in red. For a color version of this figure, see www.iste.co.uk/atto/change1. zip*

The time series considered is that from August 2015 to January 2016. Therefore, two ee.ImageCollection have been selected on GEE, one for Sentinel-1 data and one for Sentinel-2 data with time limits 01/08/2015–31/01/2016 and approximately 51 km$^2$ of extension. The considered image patches are 407 × 1255 pixels, both for Sentinel-1 and Sentinel-2. The ee.ImageCollection related to Sentinel-1 is:

– filtered by date: 01/08/2015–31/01/2016;

– filtered by polarization: VV, HH, ascending and descending;

– filtered by geometry: the area highlighted in yellow[2] in Figure 8.2;

2. Corresponding to the polygon with geo-coordinates [11.039887, 42.762731], [11.191979, 42.762731], [11.191979, 42.796497], [11.039887, 42.796497], [11.039887, 42.762731].

and therefore composed of 29 elements at 10 m resolution. The corresponding Sentinel-2 time series is:

- filtered by date: 01/08/2015–31/01/2016;
- filtered by bands: VNIR, SWIR, at 10 or 20 m resolution;
- filtered by cloud cover, not exceeding 5% of the total acquisition extension;
- filtered by `geometry`: the area highlighted in yellow in Figure 8.2;

and composed of 15 (originally 32, reduced to 15 due to the cloud cover removal) images at 10 m resolution (VNIR, excluding the three red-edge bands at 20 m and the 60 m coastal aerosol band) and 20 m resolution (SWIR, excluding the 60 m atmospheric bands).

## 8.3. SAR processing

Sentinel-1 images are collected with several different instrument configurations and resolutions, with both ascending and descending orbits. Because of this heterogeneity, it is usually necessary to properly select the images and collect them into separate homogeneous subsets before starting processing.

Imagery in the Earth Engine "COPERNICUS/S1_GRD" Sentinel-1 collection consists of Level-1 Ground Range Detected (GRD) scenes processed to backscatter coefficient $\sigma°$ represented in the dB scale. The backscatter coefficient represents the target backscattering area (radar cross-section) per unit ground area. It measures whether the radiated terrain scatters the incident microwave radiation preferentially away from the SAR sensor (negative dB values) or towards the SAR sensor (positive dB values). This scattering behavior depends on the physical characteristics of the terrain, primarily the geometry of the terrain elements and their electromagnetic characteristics. The Google Earth Engine uses the following pre-processing steps (as implemented by the European Space Agency Sentinel-1 Toolbox) to derive the backscatter coefficient at each pixel:

- apply orbit file: updates orbit metadata with a provided orbit file;
- GRD border noise removal: removes low-intensity noise and invalid data on scene edges;
- thermal noise removal: removes additive noise in sub-swaths to help reduce discontinuities between sub-swaths for scenes in multi-swath acquisition modes (this operation cannot be applied to images produced before July 2015);
- radiometric calibration: computes backscatter intensity using sensor calibration parameters in the GRD metadata;
- terrain correction (orthorectification): converts data from ground-range geometry, which does not take terrain into account, to $\sigma°$ using the SRTM 30 meter DEM or the ASTER DEM for high latitudes (greater than 60°or less than -60°).

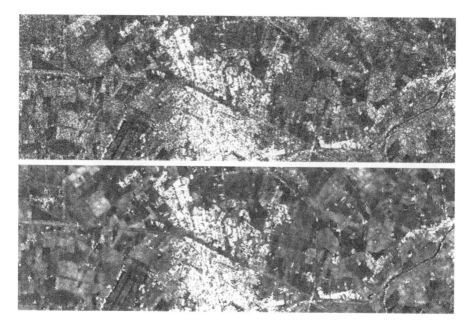

**Figure 8.4.** *Close-ups of original (top) and multitemporally filtered (bottom) Sentinel-1A SAR backscattering. VV-pol image acquired on August 2, 2015. Despeckling obtained from $N_1 = 29$ ascending-orbit acquisitions from August to January 2016 (Quegan and Yu 2001)*

In Figure 8.5, the main steps of the SAR processing chain are reported. The SAR processing layer requires us to apply a multitemporal filtering (Quegan and Yu 2001): an example of the effect of this filter is shown in Figure 8.4.

Under the assumptions, which are reasonably verified for Sentinel-1 data, that the speckle is temporally uncorrelated (or at least weakly correlated) and the number of looks $L$ is the same in each channel, i.e. for all dates (nominal value $L = 3.9$), the multitemporal filter reduces to the following form:

$$J_k = \frac{\sigma_k}{N_1} \sum_{i=1}^{N_1} \frac{\mathcal{I}_i}{\sigma_i} \qquad k = 1, 2, \dots, N_1. \tag{8.1}$$

The original version (Quegan and Yu 2001) estimates the local mean backscattering coefficient $\sigma_i$ at each date $i = 1, 2, \dots, N_1$ by averaging the intensity values $\mathcal{I}_i$ in a local window around each pixel. Differently from the original multitemporal filter, and also from the algorithm proposed by Wegmüller *et al.* (2013), adopting a structural spatial filtering (Lee *et al.* 1999) for $\sigma_i$ estimation, here we apply a Gamma-MAP filter (Lopes *et al.* 1990) for the preliminary single-date despeckling step.

The integration of the Gamma-MAP filter within the multitemporal filtering procedure presents an advantage for the application goal of this work. A high-texture mask is made available by the Gamma-MAP filter, which is obtained by comparing the local, pixel-based variation coefficient $c_u$ to the constant $c_{max} = \sqrt{2/\text{ENL}}$. An example of this mask ($c_u > c_{max}$) is reported in Figure 8.7. For each acquisition date, this mask can be used to focus on potential changes occurring from unbuilt areas, in the reference image, to built-up areas in the current image.

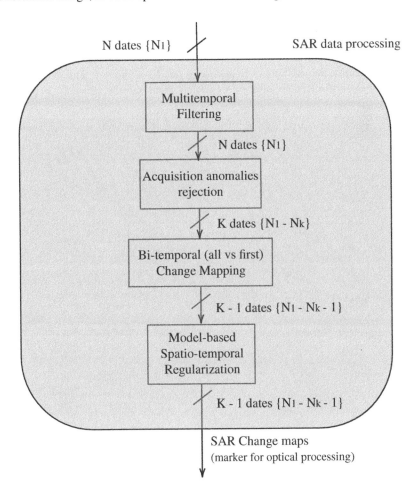

Figure 8.5. *Flowchart of the SAR processing block*

After this step, $N_1$ images are available for testing the global Kullback–Leibler divergence (KLD) [8.3] with respect to the reference (oldest) image. Anomalous acquisitions, as the one shown in red in Figure 8.8, are automatically discarded for their abnormal KLD value, due to exceptional meteorological conditions or flawed pre-processing results. These images, if considered in the next step of bi-temporal computation of change maps based on *local* KLD, would have a harmful effect on the multitemporal analysis to be carried out. These $N_K$ outliers are finally detected within the series and removed from the collection. The remaining $N_1 - N_K$ dates are fed into a procedure to compute bi-temporal changes. The key idea is to use all the changes occurring between a single image $\mathcal{I}_k$ with respect to the first of the time series $\mathcal{I}_1$, thus generating $N_1 - N_k - 1$ change features, $\mathcal{C}_{k,1}$, with $k > 2$, and the corresponding change maps $\mathcal{M}_{k,1}$, $k > 2$, obtained through thresholding. This allows us to retain the information strictly related to structural changes, instead of analyzing the overall time series that can lead to different results. Due to the computation with respect to the first image of the series, the remaining change maps are $N_1 - N_k - 1$. This is obtained by thresholding the local KLD computed on a $7 \times 7$ local window (70 m $\times$ 70 m).

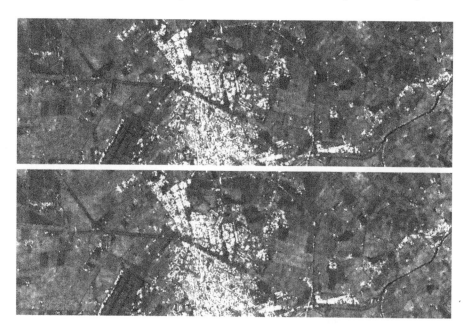

**Figure 8.6.** *Multitemporally filtered Sentinel-1 SAR images: December 12 (top); December 30 (bottom)*

The Kullback–Leibler (KL) divergence between two probability density functions (PDF) $f_X$ and $f_y$ of the random variables $X$ and $Y$ is given by

$$K(Y|X) = \int \log \frac{f_X(x)}{f_Y(x)} f_X(x) dx. \tag{8.2}$$

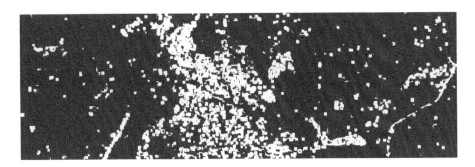

**Figure 8.7.** *Detail of the high-texture mask (in white) of the Sentinel-1 SAR backscattering (VV-pol, December 30, 2015) from the preliminary Gamma-MAP single-date despeckling*

This is a measure of the PDF divergence from $Y$ to $X$. $K(Y|X)$ is not symmetric, but a symmetric version may be defined as

$$D(X, Y) = D(Y, X) = K(Y|X) + K(X|Y),$$    [8.3]

which is called the KL distance[3]. By assuming that the statistics of SAR images can be modeled by the family of probability distributions known as the Pearson system and adopting a cumulant-based approximation through the Edgeworth series expansion (KL$_E$), a change feature, denoted as $c_{CKLD}$, has finally been proposed (Inglada and Mercier 2007):

$$c_{CKLD} = KL_E(X, Y) + KL_E(Y, X).$$    [8.4]

Since moments up to the fourth order have to be computed, $c_{CKLD}$ provides accurate local PDF distance estimation between two SAR images, using a sliding window with excellent false-alarm rate capabilities but reduced geometrical accuracy of the changed regions detected. This is not a limitation for the proposed method, since SAR processing is adopted as a preliminary change detection step here. Therefore, no geometrically accurate – and more computationally demanding – approaches (Garzelli and Zoppetti 2019) have been considered here.

Application-oriented rules are then applied: changes are retained only if: (a) they are not generated by high-backscattering pixels on the first reference image; (b) they are generated by high-backscattering pixels on the current image; (c) their location corresponds to high-texture pixels on the current image (from Gamma-MAP) and (d) they form a sufficiently large region, by considering medium-size buildings as a reference.

---

3. The term *distance* is used at large, in contrast to a standard *metric distance* that requires the *triangle inequality* property.

In the last step, a model-based temporal regularization is applied. The regularization step is intended to refine and isolate the zones of structural changes on each change map: a change region is retained if $\mathcal{M}_{k,1}$ has persistent changes in the following acquisition dates (except possible outliers, no more than $n_{out}$, with $n_{out}$ equal to 1 or 2, typically). The goal is to reject false alarms and produce refined change maps $\mathcal{M}_{k,1}^*$, with $k > 2$, and to accumulate the changes along the time series, making them "grow" towards the end of the timeline considered, just as happens during the construction of urban structures.

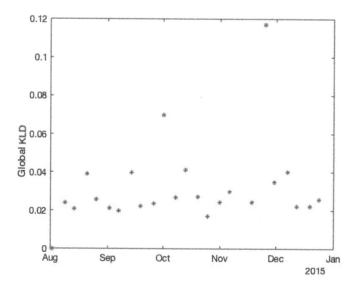

**Figure 8.8.** *Kullback–Leibler divergence of each SAR acquisition with respect to the first one. The value is computed over the whole image. The abnormal value on November 25 (highlighted in red), due to heavy rain in the previous days, is automatically discarded. For a color version of this figure, see www.iste.co.uk/atto/change1.zip*

By accumulating the regularized change maps to $\mathcal{H} = \sum_k \mathcal{M}_{k,1}^*$, we obtain a description of the time evolution of the construction sites. An example of $\mathcal{H}$ is reported in Figure 8.9. Brighter colors correspond to the oldest changes within the timescale of the observation, which is, in this case, from September to December 2015, for a total of 24 Sentinel-1 acquisitions. The commercial building in 1, shown in white, was constructed starting in September 2015. The hospital renovation was started in November 2015 and different buildings of the mall in 3 from September to December 2015.

The SAR processing layer produces the set $\mathcal{M}^*_{k,1}$ of robust change maps, which is used in the optical layer as a *marker* to detect geometrically accurate change regions from the $N_2$ multispectral images.

**Figure 8.9.** *Time evolution of the construction changes. The color bar indicates the time when the building change first appears, from the oldest change (white) to the newest change (dark red): (1) commercial building; (2) hospital renovation; (3) mall. For a color version of this figure, see www.iste.co.uk/atto/change1.zip*

## 8.4. Optical processing

A schematic description of the second layer is shown in Figure 8.10. The $\{N_2\}$ set of optical images is processed to perform a change detection step on every image belonging to the time series ($\forall Image \in \{N_2\}$): the analysis is first performed on the whole scene and then focused on specific areas (ROIs) that come from SAR processed data. The pre-screening ROIs obtained through SAR processing are selected on the change maps that are available for a specific date and then transmitted to the optical change detection module.

Optical change detection is obtained by considering six bands of the Sentinel-2 data (2-3-4-8-11-12). The 2nd–3rd–4th bands are 10 m blue–red–green acquisitions; the 8th band provides a 10 m image in the NIR wavelengths, while bands 11 and 12 are SWIR bands at 20 m spatial resolution.

Optical change detection is based on the spectral angle only, which is more robust in rejecting false changes with respect to the MS pixel intensity. This is relevant when changes related to buildings are considered. Therefore, given the two spectral vectors, $\mathbf{v}$ and $\mathbf{v_k}$, both with $N$ components, in which $\mathbf{v_1}$ is the reference spectral pixel vector (at date $k = 1$) and $\mathbf{v_k}$ is the test spectral pixel vector (at date $k$), the spectral angle SA is computed as:

$$\mathrm{SA}(\mathbf{v_1}, \mathbf{v_k}) = \arccos\left(\frac{\langle \mathbf{v_1}, \mathbf{v_k}\rangle}{||\mathbf{v_1}||_2 \cdot ||\mathbf{v_k}||_2}\right).$$

[8.5]

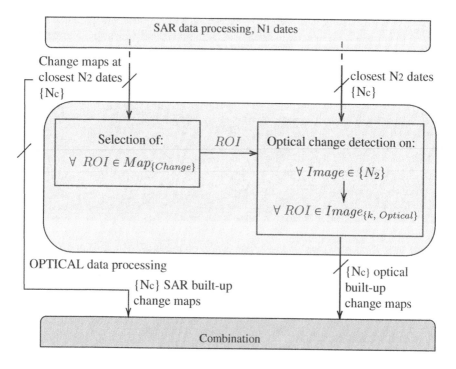

**Figure 8.10.** *Flowchart of the OPTICAL processing block. For a color version of this figure, see www.iste.co.uk/atto/change1.zip*

SA is usually expressed in degrees and is equal to zero if and only if the two vectors are *spectrally* identical, i.e. they are parallel and may differ only by their moduli. The spectral angle is clustered into two classes, changed and unchanged, by applying the K-means algorithm.

The normalized difference vegetation/water indexes (NDVI/NDWI) are then computed. NDWI is computed from bands 8 and 11 (NIR and SWIR) to exclude water areas (e.g. rivers and/or lakes), which are not related to structural changes, from the image. NDVI is computed from bands 4 and 8 to exclude vegetation areas from the image under investigation (but not from the reference image). Both indexes are then thresholded to obtain a logical mask filtering out undesired changes, specifically seasonal changes in vegetated areas.

Figure 8.11 reports the Sentinel-2 change map of the last image in the collection, acquired on December 30, 2015, with respect to the first one, acquired on August 3, 2015. The resulting map does not contain seasonal changes, but several structures with different spectral signatures with respect to the reference image are detected. Among them, the main block and the smaller four buildings of the commercial center are highlighted in yellow. The final combination layer will reduce false alarms by retaining built-up structures while preserving the geometrical accuracy at the same time.

The optical data sets made available on the GEE platform obviously do not temporally match other datasets of different data sources. Persistent cloud coverage may aggravate the problem. Therefore, it may happen that an SAR image, from which a change map has been obtained, as reported in Figure 8.5, does not have a corresponding image among the optical images. For this reason, the temporally closest optical and SAR images will be selected to apply the combination layer and perform the final change detection. From the optical change detection module driven by the pre-screened SAR ROIs, $\{N_c\}$ optical urban change maps (on the right-hand side of the scheme in Figure 8.10) are finally obtained. The urban optical change maps, together with the SAR change maps ($\{N_c\}$), are propagated to the combination layer.

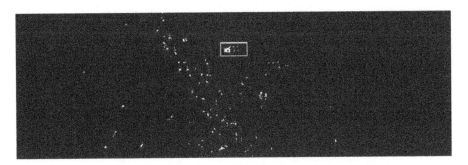

**Figure 8.11.** *December 30 Sentinel-2 change map with respect to the first date. The test construction site is highlighted in yellow. For a color version of this figure, see www.iste.co.uk/atto/change1.zip*

## 8.5. Combination layer

The combination layer is where the information coming from SAR and multispectral images is merged (Figure 8.12). In particular, there are change maps coming from Sentinel-1 SAR processing, acting as a marker and providing the temporal information of changes, as reported in section 8.3. At the same time, we have the change maps obtained from Sentinel-2 multispectral data, as explained in section 8.4. These two types of binary maps are chronologically ordered and possibly matched when the time lag between two Sentinel-1/2 acquisitions is sufficiently low. This operation is useful in confirming structural changes due to new built-up areas and rejecting undesired changes.

The final map receives the geometrical information from optical images, while the temporal resolution of changed areas is derived from SAR. Spatial description and localization in Figure 8.12 refer to morphological reconstruction of the detected ROIs from MS data using the logical AND of the corresponding SAR and optical change areas as markers. The final combined map allows us to quantify the extension of the built-up area as shown in Table 8.1.

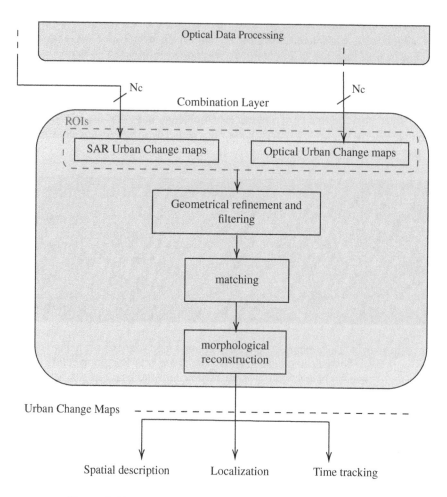

**Figure 8.12.** *Flowchart of the combination layer. For a color version of this figure, see www.iste.co.uk/atto/change1.zip*

It is possible to keep track of the temporal variations (time tracking) and their corresponding spatial variation (spatial description) along the time series. In general, the procedure allows us to identify, within large areas, variations due to the construction of urban structures (localization, in Figure 8.12).

## 8.6. Results

Figure 8.13 shows the combined Sentinel-1/2 change map on the last acquisition date (December 30, 2015, from Sentinel-2) with respect to the first date (August 3, 2015, from Sentinel-2). The highlighted construction site map correctly identifies five buildings, the main block of the commercial center and four smaller buildings at its side. Other detected changes correspond to a commercial building (see the comments on Figure 8.9) and the renovation of the city hospital (bottom-right in Figure 8.13). It is worth noting that the map describes the urban changes automatically detected in a test 51 km$^2$ region. The close-ups in Figure 8.14 give evidence of the detection capabilities of the proposed method, including for isolated buildings.

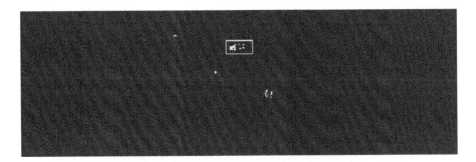

**Figure 8.13.** *Combined Sentinel-1/2 change map with respect to the first date. The test construction site is highlighted in yellow. For a color version of this figure, see www.iste.co.uk/atto/change1.zip*

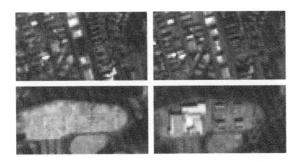

**Figure 8.14.** *Sentinel-2 close-ups of the commercial building (top) and the mall area (bottom, in the yellow box of Figure 8.13) on August 3 (left) and December 30 (right). For a color version of this figure, see www.iste.co.uk/atto/change1.zip*

Even if processing is possible at a large scale (on regions extended over 25,000 km$^2$ or more), good localization and quite accurate size estimation can be obtained also on isolated medium-size buildings. Table 8.1 reports the estimated size of different buildings detected from Sentinel-1/2 images on the region under investigation. The true extension is also reported, which has been provided by cadastral data of the local administration or by manual measurement from very-high-resolution optical imagery at sub-meter spatial resolution. The size of the commercial building, which has a 20 m × 60 m footprint, has been very accurately estimated. The sizes of the main block of the commercial center and the hospital changed areas were slightly underestimated, while the poorer results have been obtained from blocks 1–3 due to the limited Sentinel-1/2 spatial resolution, together with particular conditions. In fact, the spectral characteristics of part of the roof covering of these buildings have determined partial misdetection of change and the final underestimation of the building footprints. However, the estimation capability of the proposed method is generally very promising.

| Building | est. size (m$^2$) | size (m$^2$) |
|---|---|---|
| Mall – main block | 29,700 | 32,300 |
| Mall – block 1 | 1,400 | 1,900 |
| Mall – block 2 | 1,000 | 1,900 |
| Mall – block 3 | 1,400 | 1,900 |
| Mall – block 4 | 2,000 | 1,900 |
| Commercial building | 1,300 | 1,200 |
| Hospital – South block | 12,100 | 13,000 |
| Hospital parking | 5,900 | 6,468 |

**Table 8.1.** *Final building size estimation on detailed area*

## 8.7. Conclusion

Large-scale built-up area monitoring is possible by exploiting the complementary characteristics of SAR and optical multispectral acquisitions provided by the Sentinel-1/2 missions.

The proposed method can be applied to long observation periods and has the ability to cope with a short revisit time. This is possible, despite the huge data volume, by applying simple yet robust algorithms implemented on the high-performance parallel architecture of the Google Earth Engine. Thanks to the availability of pre-processed, radiometrically and geometrically corrected georeferenced images, the final change maps and the spatial estimation of changes over a 25,000 km$^2$ region can be obtained in a few minutes.

It has been proved that the method is able to accurately estimate the extension of the urban transformation which is continuously monitored by the SAR Sentinel-1 sensor and is geometrically characterized by the Sentinel-2 spectral scanner.

## 8.8. References

Aiazzi, B., Alparone, L., Baronti, S., Garzelli, A., Zoppetti, C. (2013). Nonparametric change detection in multitemporal SAR images based on mean-shift clustering. *IEEE Transactions on Geoscience and Remote Sensing*, 51(4), 2022–2031.

Amitrano, D., Di Martino, G., Iodice, A., Riccio, D., Ruello, G. (2015). A new framework for SAR multitemporal data RGB representation: Rationale and products. *IEEE Transactions on Geoscience and Remote Sensing*, 53(1), 117–133.

Amitrano, D., Belfiore, V., Cecinati, F., Di Martino, G., Iodice, A., Mathieu, P.-P., Medagli, S., Poreh, D., Riccio, D., Ruello, G. (2016). Urban areas enhancement in multitemporal SAR RGB images using adaptive coherence window and texture information. *IEEE Journal of Selected Topics in Applied Earth Observations and Remote Sensing*, 9(8), 3740–3752.

Amitrano, D., Guida, R., Ruello, G. (2019). Multitemporal SAR RGB processing for Sentinel-1 GRD products: Methodology and applications. *IEEE Journal of Selected Topics in Applied Earth Observations and Remote Sensing*, 12(5), 1497–1507.

Chini, M., Pelich, R., Hostache, R., Matgen, P., Lopez-Martinez, C. (2018). Towards a 20 m global building map from Sentinel-1 SAR data. *Remote Sensing*, 10(11), 1833.

ESA (2014–2020a). Copernicus Open Access Hub. ESA [Online]. Available at: https://scihub.copernicus.eu.

ESA (2014–2020b). Sentinel Application Platform (SNAP). ESA Science Toolbox Platform. [Online]. Available at: https://step.esa.int/main/toolboxes/snap/.

Garzelli, A. and Zoppetti, C. (2019). Geometrically accurate change mapping from VHR SAR images. *IGARSS 2019 – 2019 IEEE International Geoscience and Remote Sensing Symposium*, 25–28, Yokohama, Japan, 28 July–2 August.

Gorelick, N., Hancher, M., Dixon, M., Ilyushchenko, S., Thau, D., Moore, R. (2017). Google Earth Engine: Planetary-scale geospatial analysis for everyone. *Remote Sensing of Environment*, 202, 18–27.

Inglada, J. and Mercier, G. (2007). A new statistical similarity measure for change detection in multitemporal SAR images and its extension to multiscale change analysis. *IEEE Transactions on Geoscience and Remote Sensing*, 45(5), 1432–1445.

Konstantinidis, D. (2017). Building detection for monitoring of urban changes. PhD Thesis, Department of Electrical and Electronic Engineering, Imperial College London.

Lambin, E.F., Geist, H., Rindfuss, R.R. (2006). *Land-Use and Land-Cover Change: Local Processes and Global Impacts*. Springer-Verlag, Berlin Heidelberg.

Lee, J.-S., Grunes, M.R., de Grandi, G. (1999). Polarimetric SAR speckle filtering and its implication for classification. *IEEE Transactions on Geoscience and Remote Sensing*, 37(5), 2363–2373.

Lopes, A., Touzi, R., Nezry, E. (1990). Adaptive speckle filters and scene heterogeneity. *IEEE Transactions on Geoscience and Remote Sensing*, 28(6), 992–1000.

Plank, S. (2014). Rapid damage assessment by means of multi-temporal SAR – A comprehensive review and outlook to Sentinel-1. *Remote Sensing*, 6(6), 4870–4906.

Quegan, S. and Yu, J.J. (2001). Filtering of multichannel SAR images. *IEEE Transactions on Geoscience and Remote Sensing*, 39(11), 2373–2379.

Sun, Z., Xu, R., Du, W., Wang, L., Lu, D. (2019). High-resolution urban land mapping in China from Sentinel 1A/2 imagery based on Google Earth Engine. *Remote Sensing*, 11(7), 752.

Wegmüller, U., Santoro, M., Werner, C. (2013). Multi-temporal SAR data filtering for land applications. *Proceedings of the SA Living Planet Symposium*, 5, Edinburgh, UK, 9–13 September.

Zhang, C., Wei, S., Ji, S., Lu, M. (2019). Detecting large-scale urban land cover changes from very high resolution remote sensing images using CNN-based classification. *ISPRS International Journal of Geo-Information*, 8(4), 189.

# 9

# Statistical Difference Models for Change Detection in Multispectral Images

**Massimo ZANETTI[1], Francesca BOVOLO[1]
and Lorenzo BRUZZONE[2]**

*[1] Fondazione Bruno Kessler, Trento, Italy*
*[2] University of Trento, Italy*

## 9.1. Introduction

For decades, the large number of launched Earth Observation (EO) satellites have provided a unique way to observe our living planet from space. Thanks to the revisiting properties of EO satellites, a large number of multitemporal images are now available in archives. The increasing demand coming from the different application domains has promoted new advances in technology and processing capability to guarantee operational continuity and provide observations for the next generation of operational products, such as land-cover maps, land-use change detection maps and geophysical variables. This allows for an accurate monitoring of the land surface changes in wide geographical areas according to both long-term (e.g. yearly) and short-term (e.g. daily) observations. The detection and understanding of the changes that occur at the ground level is essential for studying global change, environmental evolution and anthropic phenomena. For this reason, the development of change-detection techniques for the analysis of multitemporal remotely sensed images is still one of the most important research topics in remote sensing.

*Change Detection and Image Time Series Analysis 1,*
coordinated by Abdourrahmane M. ATTO, Francesca BOVOLO and Lorenzo BRUZZONE.
© ISTE Ltd 2021.

(a)                                        (b)

**Figure 9.1.** *A fire occurred in Sardinia Island (Italy) between August 7 and 9, 2013 (the total extension of the event is approximately 2,400 hectares): (a) environmental image of the event, the village on the left is Laconi; (b) Landsat 8 image of the scene, spatial resolution is 30* $m$. *For a color version of this figure, see www.iste.co.uk/atto/ change1.zip*

Change detection (CD) is the process of identifying changes that occurred in the same geographical area between different observation times. From the application viewpoint, there are different approaches of analysis and related methodological procedures. The analysis of changes occurring at the ground level is widely exploited in different fields, especially for the monitoring of natural disasters. The new generation of satellite sensors has increased the availability of MS images and now provides data with a significantly short revisiting time, allowing for almost real-time estimations of the area involved in disrupting events such as fires, earthquakes or tsunami (see, for example, Figure 9.1).

Such estimations can greatly help the authorities in planning first aid and related maneuvers. In response to this, the development of effective methods for change detection is needed and the accuracy of the final results must be improved in order to guarantee a well-balanced dislocation of resources. The current spatial/spectral level of details available in MS images enables the identification of the spectral signature of certain change classes and their characterization and detection. Given its well-recognized importance in terms of applications, CD is a widely covered topic in the literature. A plethora of models and methods have been proposed to solve many different problems. However, in most of the cases, the methodological development of CD procedures is driven by the problem, and the literature, lacks in general models. This fact limits the possibility of passing and adapting the knowledge learned from certain problems to even slightly different applicative contexts and makes the general understanding of the underlying physical mechanism more difficult. Another limitation of current state-of-the-art methods is that many empirical models that have worked well for the first generation of MS imagery are inefficient when addressing the new challenges introduced with the last-generation products.

To address these issues, the aim of this chapter is to present a general mathematical framework for the representation and analysis of multispectral images. In the applicative context of CD, this framework provides both (1) a mathematical explanation of already existing methodologies and (2) a framework to extend them to more general cases for addressing problems of increasing complexity. We will focus, in particular, on the description of the statistical properties of the images. It is a matter of fact that the full information content present in an image can only be completely modeled in ideal cases. Rather, simplified models of the images are always (explicitly or implicitly) used as a basis for the rationale of most of the image processing techniques. Unfortunately, when these ideal models are not clear to the practitioner, it is difficult to interpret the results obtained after processing in a meaningful and reasonable way. Often, RS images are modeled as realizations of a set of random variables following a specific statistical distribution. However, in some cases, the statistical models are not flexible enough to allow for a precise description of the associated images. As a result, some methodologies that rely on too simple statistical models may give inaccurate results.

In this chapter, we introduce two statistical models for the description of the distribution of spectral difference-vectors, and we derive from them change detection methods based on image difference. Section 9.2 presents an overview of the change detection problem in multispectral imagery and the methods proposed in the literature to address it, with emphasis on the statistical models associated with the difference image and their challenges. Section 9.3 introduces the standard two-class unchange/change model for binary CD, as derived from the hypothesis of the Gaussian distribution of natural classes in the difference image. When coordinates are changed to magnitude, the two-class model can be described by a Rayleigh–Rice mixture. Parameter estimation of this mixture is a non-trivial task as this model is non-conventional. Therefore, a version of the expectation–maximization (EM) algorithm, which is specifically tailored for the Rayleigh–Rice mixture, is presented. Section 9.4 provides a generalization of the two-class unchange/change model to the multiclass case. The typical two-class approach is sometimes not flexible enough to model the spectral behavior of the difference image well. This is evident in last-generation multispectral images, where the radiometric resolution is sensibly improved and more classes can be represented via their spectral characteristics. Therefore, we weaken the constraints of imposing *a priori* assumptions on the difference image and we derive a multiclass model from scratch, solely starting from very general assumptions on the single time images. Section 9.5 presents an extended experimental analysis of the models involved in terms of both statistical fitting and change detection performance. Section 9.6 draws the conclusions of this chapter.

## 9.2. Overview of the change detection problem

The modern society organization strongly relies on the cyclic monitoring-planning paradigm for the efficient control and management of natural resources and human infrastructure development. The remote sensing community assists this fundamental process by steadily providing up-to-date technologies to collect data from around the globe and the know-how to extract the useful information from it. A comprehensive and systematic understanding of global change is possible thanks to one of the leading remote sensing applications: the change detection (Coppin *et al.* 2004), which substantially embodies the main principles of this paradigm. Indeed, CD is gaining increasingly more attention due to its strong impact in our daily life and many efforts and resources have been, and are going to be, developed with the purpose of providing accurate, up-to-date and reliable operational products, such as land-cover maps, land-use change detection maps and geophysical variables variations (Lu *et al.* 2004).

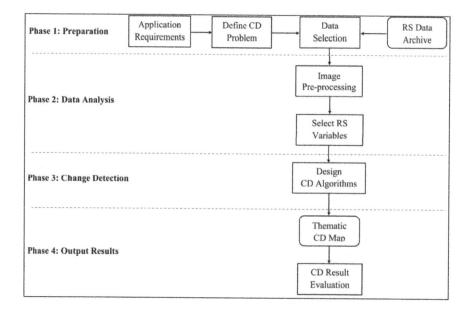

**Figure 9.2.** *High-level scheme for the design and implementation of a change detection procedure*

Technically, CD is the process that identifies the changes that occurred between two (or more) dates in a specific geographical location, by analysis of RS images acquired over the investigated area (Bruzzone and Bovolo 2013). It is worth noting that change detection is a comprehensive procedure that requires a set of analysis and processing phases (Lu *et al.* 2014) (see Figure 9.2). Given the intrinsic non-objective nature of the *change* meaning (Rensink 2002; Spotorno and Faure 2011), the CD procedure often starts with a problem understanding phase that includes the change definition. This first stage always includes a selection step where suitable RS data types are chosen with the aim of emphasizing the change characteristics by increasing their discriminability. The design of the CD algorithm is generally driven by the application. Typically, the practitioner aims at finding, and exploiting, a strong correlation between the variation of image properties (e.g. pixel radiance value, texture and shape) and the land-cover material changes on the ground. However, other changes may also be detected, caused by factors such as variation in atmospheric conditions, sensor conditions, illumination differences and seasonal effects. The detection of these specific kinds of changes, which are often considered sources of noise, strictly depends on the real application requirements and goals.

### 9.2.1. *Change detection methods for multispectral images*

In the literature, many approaches have been developed to detect changes in multitemporal images. Extensive overviews are available from both the image processing (Radke *et al.* 2005) and remote sensing (Coppin *et al.* 2004; Ban and Yousif 2016) viewpoints.

A common way to group the majority of the CD methods proposed in the literature is based upon the availability of reference information (labeled data) for the considered scene. According to this principle, there are supervised and unsupervised approaches to change detection. The former group includes methods that are based on the use of supervised classifiers; see, for instance (Bruzzone and Serpico 1997; Bruzzone *et al.* 2004; Volpi *et al.* 2013). Supervised methods require ground reference information for the training phase. Such information may be required for all available acquisitions, or for only one of them (e.g. when semisupervised and domain adaptation methods are considered (Bruzzone and Cossu 2002; Demir *et al.* 2012)) and is typically obtained from highly expensive *in situ* campaigns or by dedicated photo-interpretation procedures. In light of the unprecedented huge amount of data now available in archives and the given rate at which data are collected nowadays, the cost of obtaining ground truth information cannot be afforded. By means of automatic techniques, we can gradually reduce the need for conventional field investigations with a drastic reduction of the operational cost. As a result, the most attractive CD techniques are the ones that automatically detect the changes. This is the case for the unsupervised methods (Bruzzone and Prieto 2000a, 2000b, 2000c; Bovolo and Bruzzone 2007; Dalla Mura *et al.* 2008; Bovolo *et al.* 2010b; Celik 2010).

#### 9.2.1.1. *Mid-/high-spatial-resolution images*

Generally speaking, unsupervised methods to CD are mainly able to detect the presence/absence of changes (Aach and Kaup 1995; Bruzzone and Prieto 2000b; Celik 2010). In some cases, they can distinguish among different changes (Bovolo *et al.* 2012), but given the unavailability of reference data, they usually cannot associate semantic information (e.g. a specific land-cover transition) to them. Many unsupervised methods are based on pixel-wise comparison (Bruzzone and Prieto

2000c; Chen *et al.* 2011; Bruzzone and Bovolo 2013). The comparison phase, which usually consists of applying a mathematical operation to each pixel value, returns a change index. The most common change index is the spectral difference of a bitemporal image pair. Inference about the presence or absence of changes based on the change index is typically done via threshold or clustering approaches.

Threshold-based methods differ among each other based on how the threshold value is assigned. In some cases, the threshold is empirical and can be obtained by application of well-known image processing algorithms, such as the Kittler–Illingworth algorithm (Kittler and Illingworth 1986), the Otsu algorithm (Otsu 1975) or the maximum entropy algorithm (Sahoo *et al.* 1988). In some other cases, a more change-detection-oriented formulation of the problem is given and some theoretical models have been proposed for the definition of the threshold. A prominent approach in this direction is based on the maximum *a posteriori* (MAP) assignment, which follows from a statistical modeling of the unchange and change classes (Bruzzone and Prieto 2000b, 2000c; Bovolo and Bruzzone 2007). What is typically observed after image differencing is that unchanged pixels have pixel intensity, which is approximately null. On the contrary, changed pixels intensity is likely non-null. In Bruzzone and Prieto (2000b), two Gaussian distributions are associated with the unchange and change classes, respectively. The threshold value that separates between unchanged and changed pixels is then defined in an MAP Bayesian framework to produce the minimum overall error of decision. In the case we want to assign different weights to commission and omission errors, a minimum cost approach also applies (Bruzzone and Prieto 2000c). The statistical study of the binary detection of changes can be further refined by analyzing the magnitude of the spectral difference. In Bovolo and Bruzzone (2007), a theoretical model based on the Rayleigh–Rice mixture has been proposed to represent the typical bi-modal shape of the magnitude of the difference image. An adaptive multiple-threshold approach is used in Aach and Kaup (1995), where the CD problem is seen as a hypothesis test. Here, the unchange/change state of each pixel is decided adaptively on the basis of a significance test.

Differently to threshold-based approaches, clustering algorithms try to separate between unchanged and changed pixels according to some homogeneity principle characterizing these two classes. In the literature we can find methodological approaches based on k-means and kernel k-means clustering (Volpi *et al.* 2012), fuzzy c-means and Gustafson–Kessel clustering (Ghosh *et al.* 2011), nonlinear support vector clustering (De Morsier *et al.* 2012), fuzzy clustering (Gong *et al.* 2014) and many others.

The detection of changes can be carried on in the original spectral domain (this is the case for all of the methods mentioned above) or in a transformed domain. In the latter case, the transformation is meant to enhance the change representation, and in many cases, it is driven by the data. Well-known transformation techniques successfully applied to change detection are canonical correlation (Nielsen 2002), principal component analysis (PCA) (Celik 2009b; Baisantry *et al.* 2012) and independent component analysis (ICA) (Marchesi and Bruzzone 2009). In Gong (1993), PCA is applied to the difference image and changes are recognized as the first few principal components. In Collins and Woodcock (1994), an orthogonal representation of the changes based on the Gram–Schmidt procedure was used. In Rogan *et al.* (2002), the tasseled cap transformation was applied to detect the vegetation change from Landsat images. It is also worth mentioning the multivariate alteration detection (MAD) technique (Nielsen *et al.* 1998), which is based on the canonical correlation analysis (Nielsen 2002). An improved version named iterative reweighted MAD (IR-MAD) was proposed in Nielsen (2007) to provide more reliable output components, thus emphasizing changes.

The main disadvantage of the above-mentioned transformation-based CD approaches is that they require a strong interaction with the end-users to select the most informative components emphasizing the specific changes of interest, which is usually time-consuming. On the other hand, the transformation-based methods do not provide a clear number of changes. The number of detected changes highly depends on the selected number of components and the change information represented in those components. Some changes might still be mixed and unidentified in a given component. Therefore, the transformation-based approaches are good at extracting features for enhancing the detection of specific kinds of changes in CD, but in general, they are not suitable for detecting all of the possible change classes. Among pixel-based approaches to change detection, we also find methods based on fuzzy set theory (Gong 1993; Robin *et al.* 2010) and similarity measures (Bovolo *et al.* 2008). All of the aforementioned methods demonstrated their effectiveness on moderate- and high-geometrical-resolution images (from tens to hundreds of meters of spatial resolution) and in several applications.

### 9.2.1.2. *Very high-spatial-resolution images*

A major drawback of pixel-based methods to CD is that they only consider the change/unchange information within a single pixel, even if its neighbors contain significant information. Implicitly, these methods consider the pixels to be spatially independent. Although this is an acceptable assumption for moderate-/high-spatial-resolution images, it is not for images that exhibit very high spatial resolution (VHR). Indeed, when the geometrical resolution of images increases up to less than 1 meter, spatial correlation among pixels becomes non-negligible and the straightforward application of the above-mentioned methods may easily fail to give acceptable results. To account for geometrical additional information, many change detection methods have been adapted to a spatial-contextual framework.

Spatial-context information can be modeled by applying fixed-shape neighborhood systems for texture information extraction (Healey and Slater 1997; Smits and Annoni 1999; Li and Leung 2002), Markov random fields (Bruzzone and Prieto 2000b; Moser *et al.* 2011) and morphological filters (Dalla Mura *et al.* 2008, 2010). More advanced methods perform a context-sensitive analysis by considering adaptive neighborhoods modeled by multitemporal parcels (Bruzzone and Prieto 2000a, 2002; Bovolo 2009) and object properties (Hazel 2001; Carlotto 2005; Molinier *et al.* 2007; Huo *et al.* 2010; Lu *et al.* 2011). They better capture the spatial correlation information present in the scene and become particularly promising for VHR images showing complex objects (e.g. buildings and other man-made structures). In order to effectively model objects in the images at different scales, some of the concepts employed in the previously mentioned papers, such as morphological filters, multitemporal parcels and even Markov random fields can be adapted and used in multiscale/multilevel analysis (Dalla Mura *et al.* 2008; Bovolo 2009; Bovolo and Bruzzone 2009; Moser *et al.* 2011), together with specific multiscale/multilevel representation tools such as a wavelet transform (Celik 2009a; Celik and Ma 2010, 2011).

When dealing with unsupervised change detection, the pre-processing of multitemporal images becomes highly important because most of the approaches suffer from differences in image radiometry and/or geometry. In the literature, studies exist on the effects of residual misregistration on the change detection results (Dai and Khorram 1998; Roy 2000; Bovolo *et al.* 2009), and techniques devoted to mitigating these effects (and thus change detection errors associated with them) have been proposed (Aldrighi and Dell'Acqua 2009; Ding *et al.* 2010; Marchesi *et al.* 2010). Other papers are devoted to the analysis of the effects of pan-sharpening algorithms (Bovolo *et al.* 2010a) and radiometric differences (Yang and Lo 2000; Inamdar *et al.* 2008) on the change detection performance.

### 9.2.2. *Challenges addressed in this chapter*

Many studies of the change detection problem based on the analysis of the spectral vector difference can be grouped as specializations derived from a general framework well-known as change vector analysis (CVA) (Singh and Talwar 2013). CVA was introduced in Malila (1980), and it gives a theoretical foundation for the representation of change vectors both in Cartesian (Johnson and Kasischke 1998) and polar coordinates (Bovolo and Bruzzone 2007). In the remote sensing application, depending on which representation system is used, the specific properties of the change vectors are put in relationship with the change class on the ground, and methodologies are developed to identify and extract difference vectors belonging to the same class. The application of CVA to binary change detection is very typical, and has been applied in both the Cartesian (Bruzzone and Prieto 2000b) and polar (Bovolo and Bruzzone 2007) coordinate systems. In particular, in the latter case, the magnitude representation of the change vectors allows us to implement a simple, intuitive yet effective concept: change vectors with a small magnitude most likely represent unchanged pixels, whereas those with high magnitude values can be considered as changed pixels. From a statistical point of view, we can assume that the unchange and change classes follow specific distributions, estimate distribution parameters from data and then make decisions according to a Bayes decision rule. In Bruzzone and Prieto (2000b), the bi-modal distribution of the magnitude is empirically approximated by a mixture of Gaussians. In Bovolo and Bruzzone (2007), by assuming that the unchange and change classes are Gaussian distributed in the difference image, a theoretical model based on the Rayleigh–Rice mixture has been conjectured to better fit the real distribution of the magnitude, but actual results could not be given due to the highly non-conventionality of the model involved. This is the starting point for the research presented in this chapter, where (1) the assumptions made in Bovolo and Bruzzone (2007) are generalized to further enhance the statistical description of MS images and (2) numerical algorithms are derived to actually implement solutions for investigating the conjecture.

## 9.3. The Rayleigh–Rice mixture model for the magnitude of the difference image

This section introduces the standard two-class unchange/change model for binary CD, as derived from the hypothesis of the Gaussian distribution of natural classes in the difference image. When coordinates are changed to magnitude, the two-class model can be described by a Rayleigh–Rice mixture. Parameter estimation of this mixture is a non-trivial task as this model is non-conventional. The complexity related to the derivation of a parameter estimation method involving the Rayleigh and Rician distributions is addressed by means of the EM algorithm (Zanetti *et al.* 2015). An EM-like numerical method is derived, which is computationally convenient as it does not require any complex optimization routine being only based on an iterative updating of the parameters. Through estimated parameters, it is then shown how to implement a binary classifier for inferring the unchanged and changed classes.

### 9.3.1. *Magnitude image statistical mixture model*

Let us consider two multispectral images $\mathbf{y}^1, \mathbf{y}^2$ acquired by passive remote sensing sensors at different times $t_1, t_2$, respectively, and representing the same geographical area. Let us assume that the two images are co-registered and radiometrically corrected and that there has been (only) one relevant change in the scene between the two dates. Therefore, the pixels can only be divided into two classes: $\omega_n$ (unchanged pixels) and $\omega_c$ (changed pixels). The aim is to discriminate between changed and unchanged pixels in an unsupervised way. The detection of the changes that occurred between $t_1$ and $t_2$ is based on the study of the so-called difference image

$$\mathbf{d} := \mathbf{y}^2 - \mathbf{y}^1. \tag{9.1}$$

When images acquired by passive sensors are considered, the statistical distribution of natural classes within each spectral band can be reasonably modeled by Gaussian densities (Chen 2007). From now on, our analysis will be restricted to considering two bands among all of the available ones[1]. The following theoretical analysis holds for any multi-band image where classes can be modeled as Gaussian densities, both in the case where they are independent or jointly distributed as Gaussian. In these cases, we assume that the classes $\omega_n, \omega_c$ in the difference image are Gaussian distributed; thus, let us assume they are modeled by $\mathcal{N}(\mu_{b,n}, \sigma_{b,n})$ and $\mathcal{N}(\mu_{b,c}, \sigma_{b,c})$, for each band $b = 1, 2$.

In polar coordinates, the magnitude of pixels can be exploited for discriminating between unchanged and changed pixels, so we are interested in describing how this model can be represented when the difference image is transformed. Since we are considering two-band images, we assume that every pixel $\mathbf{d}(i, j)$ is a two-dimensional vector. Hence, it is uniquely determined by its magnitude $\rho(i, j)$ and direction $\boldsymbol{\theta}(i, j)$ with respect to a fixed reference direction. Given the pixel in spatial position $(i, j)$, if no change has occurred on the ground between the two dates $t_1$ and $t_2$, then the magnitude $\rho(i, j)$ is expected to be close to zero. Conversely, whenever a change has occurred, the magnitude is expected to be significantly different from zero.

We are now interested in modeling the theoretical distribution of the magnitude. To this aim, let us denote the random variable that describes this feature by $\rho$. Because of the above-mentioned assumption of normality of classes within bands, the distribution of $\rho$ is theoretically given by the distribution of the magnitude of a two-dimensional point, whose coordinates are Gaussian distributed random variables. The obtained model is quite complex, but with some additional reasonable assumption, it can be greatly simplified (Rice 1944). A first crucial assumption is the spatial independence of pixels. From the application viewpoint, this assumption is reasonable and widely supported in the literature if optical images at medium-spatial resolution (e.g. 30 m) are considered (Bruzzone and Prieto 2000b; Bruzzone and Bovolo 2013). Then, since the two images are co-registered and radiometrically corrected, we can assume that in those areas where pixels are not changed, the distributions are not significantly different, therefore

$$\mu_{1,n} = \mu_{2,n} = 0$$
$$\sigma_{1,n} = \sigma_{2,n} =: \sigma_n \qquad [9.2]$$

and we assume that the magnitude of unchanged pixels is modeled by a Rayleigh distribution

$$p\left(\rho | \omega_n\right) = \frac{\rho}{b_n^2} \exp\left(-\frac{\rho^2}{2b_n^2}\right) \qquad \rho \geq 0, \qquad [9.3]$$

---

1. This is to simplify the notation and the exposition and it is not a technical restriction. The generalization of this theory to the case where an arbitrary number of bands $n$ are considered can be found in Zanetti (2017, Appendix 6.A.5).

where the parameter $b_n = \sigma_n$. In the case of changed pixels, we still assume that the distributions have the same variance, but they can have different non-zero means. Hence,

$$\mu_{1,c} \neq \mu_{2,c} \qquad \mu_{1,c}, \mu_{2,c} \neq 0$$

$$\sigma_{1,c} = \sigma_{2,c} =: \sigma_c.$$
[9.4]

and the magnitude of changed pixels follows the more general Rician distribution, (Rice 1944)

$$p\left(\rho|\omega_c\right) = \frac{\rho}{\sigma_c^2} \exp\left(-\frac{\rho^2 + \nu_c^2}{2\sigma_c^2}\right) I_0\left(\frac{\rho\nu_c}{\sigma_c^2}\right) \qquad \rho \geqslant 0.$$
[9.5]

Here, $\nu_c = \sqrt{\mu_{1,c}^2 + \mu_{2,c}^2}$ is the so called non-centrality parameter and $I_0(.)$ is the zeroth-order modified Bessel function of the first kind (Watson 1966). In conclusion, the theoretical mixture density that models the distribution of the magnitude of pixels is given by

$$p\left(\rho\right) = p\left(\omega_n\right) p\left(\rho|\omega_n\right) + p\left(\omega_c\right) p\left(\rho|\omega_c\right)$$
[9.6]

where $p\left(\omega_h\right)$, $h = n, c$, are the prior probabilities of classes. According to the given assumptions, the magnitude image $\rho := \{\rho(i, j) : i, j\}$ can be considered as a set of i.i.d. samples drawn from the theoretical distribution (9.6). For images where the i.i.d. assumption is not reasonable, further modelization of the spatial-contextual dependence of pixels is required. For example, this can be done using Markov random fields (MRFs) (Bruzzone and Prieto 2000b, 2002).

## 9.3.2. Bayesian decision

The theoretical formulation of the distribution of the pixel magnitude as a mixture model allows for a formal characterization of a threshold that separates pixels into two classes according to their magnitude, by means of the Bayesian decision theory. The two probability models involved in the mixture model, the Rayleigh and the Rician distributions, share the same domain (the non-negative portion of the real axis); therefore, there exist non-null probabilities $e_n$ and $e_c$ of mis-classifying unchanged and changed pixels, respectively. It is well known that the overall error $e_n + e_c$ can be minimized by selecting the separating threshold as the solution $\rho = T$ (solving for $\rho$) of the equation

$$\frac{p\left(\omega_c\right)}{p\left(\omega_n\right)} = \frac{p\left(\rho|\omega_n\right)}{p\left(\rho|\omega_c\right)} \qquad \rho \geqslant 0$$
[9.7]

that corresponds to the intersection of the two curves $\mathrm{p}(\omega_n)\,\mathrm{p}(\rho|\omega_n)$ and $\mathrm{p}(\omega_c)\,\mathrm{p}(\rho|\omega_c)$, which lies between the two modes (it is worth noting that this equation generally has more than one solution). This equation can be equivalently written as

$$\left(\frac{1}{2b_n^2} - \frac{1}{2\sigma_c^2}\right)\rho^2 + \log \mathrm{I}_0\left(\frac{\rho\nu_c}{\sigma_c^2}\right) = \frac{\nu_c}{2b_n^2} + \log\frac{\sigma_c^2\,\mathrm{p}(\omega_n)}{b_n^2\,\mathrm{p}(\omega_c)}. \qquad [9.8]$$

The classification that corresponds to the minimum overall error is given by

$$
\begin{aligned}
W_n &= \{(i,j) : \rho(i,j) \leqslant T\}\\
W_c &= \{(i,j) : \rho(i,j) > T\},
\end{aligned}
\qquad [9.9]
$$

where $W_n, W_c$ are the sets of predicted unchanged and changed pixels, respectively. In section 9.3.3, we provide an EM-type algorithm for finding an accurate estimation of the parameters $b_n, \nu_c, \sigma_c$ and the prior probabilities $\mathrm{p}(\omega_n)$, $\mathrm{p}(\omega_c)$, in such a way that the change detection can be performed by thresholding the magnitude of the difference image at $T$, which is obtained by solving [9.8].

### 9.3.3. *Numerical approach to parameter estimation*

Problems involving the Rician distribution are often seen in engineering applications, particularly in remote sensing (Bovolo and Bruzzone 2007) and magnetic resonance imaging (MRI) (Benedict and Soong 1967; Sijbers *et al.* 1998a, 1998b; Karlsen *et al.* 1999; Hennemuth *et al.* 2008). Rician distribution parameter estimation has drawn strong attentions as it is crucial for studies involving the magnitude of Gaussian densities (Rice 1944). Important results have been achieved by using the method of moments (MOM) (Talukdar and Lawing 1991; Sijbers *et al.* 1998a) and maximum-likelihood (ML) approaches (Sijbers and den Dekker 2004; Talukdar and Lawing 1991). Unfortunately, the MOM is shown to be inefficient at low signal-to-noise ratios (SNRs) (Benedict and Soong 1967; Sijbers *et al.* 1998b), while ML equations do not have, in general, a unique solution (Carobbi and Cati 2008). Because of the latter property, the solution of the ML problem becomes an optimization problem. Some papers propose adaptive techniques for selecting the initial starting values (Benedict and Soong 1967; Sijbers *et al.* 1998b), while in other cases, slightly different Bayesian estimators are proposed in order to stabilize the problem (Lauwers *et al.* 2009).

When mixtures of Rician components are considered, the estimation problem increases its complexity. When the non-centrality of the signal is high, the Rician density is often approximated with a Gaussian one (Hennemuth *et al.* 2008). Other papers directly address the approximation of the parameters of a mixture model involving one (optional) Rayleigh and $J$ Rician distributions, with all of them having a common scale parameter $\sigma$. In Maitra and Faden (2009), a fitting procedure is followed by an approximated EM-like estimation of $\sigma$. In Maitra (2013), an additional parameter is included in the model as missing information, leading to a substantial simplification in the maximization step. In practice, in the two above-mentioned works, the parameter $\sigma$ describes a common characteristic of the noise, which is supposed to appear with different non-centralities and same-scale parameters. Therefore, the estimation of $\sigma$ from $J$ Rician components makes the model robust. Other methods are based on local noise estimation (Rajan *et al.* 2010) and wavelet-based noise estimation (Nowak 1999). In many application problems, forcing the components of the Rayleigh–Rice mixture to have the same-scale parameters is a strong assumption. In particular, in CD on remote sensing real images, such similarity is rarely observed, and it does not have theoretical justification. Therefore, an empirical use of the algorithms in Maitra and Faden (2009) and (Maitra 2013) to fit the distribution of the magnitude of the difference image, and therefore solve the binary CD problem, is expected to present limitations.

To overcome these limitations, an EM-type method for the estimation of all shape and mixture parameters of a Rayleigh–Rice mixture density has been derived in Zanetti *et al.* (2015). This work, by providing a variational interpretation of the EM algorithm as a problem related to a fixed point equation, both:

(1) derives explicit formulas for an iterative method based on subsequent updates of the parameters enjoying good asymptotic properties;

(2) establishes a lower bound on the speed of convergence of the iterations for reaching a maximum of the expectation. The algorithm does not need any optimization routine; thus, many issues related to the choice of optimal maximization strategies and their impact on the solution are avoided. In the following, these results are presented. For details on the convergence analysis, the reader is referred to Zanetti *et al.* (2015).

### 9.3.3.1. *EM algorithm*

Let us consider the family of density functions depending on the set of parameters $\Psi = (\alpha, \Theta)$, where $\Theta = (\theta_1, \theta_2)$ with $\theta_1 = b$ and $\theta_2 = (\nu, \sigma)$, given by

$$\mathrm{p}\,(\rho|\Psi) = \alpha_1\,\mathrm{p}\,(\rho|\omega_1, \theta_1) + \alpha_2\,\mathrm{p}\,(\rho|\omega_2, \theta_2), \qquad [9.10]$$

where $\alpha_1 = \alpha$, $\alpha_2 = 1 - \alpha$ with $0 < \alpha < 1$, and

$$\mathrm{p}\,(\rho|\omega_1, \theta_1) = \frac{\rho}{b^2}\exp\left(-\frac{\rho^2}{2b^2}\right) \qquad [9.11]$$

$$\mathrm{p}\,(\rho|\omega_2, \theta_2) = \frac{\rho}{\sigma^2}\exp\left(-\frac{\rho^2 + \nu^2}{2\sigma^2}\right)\mathrm{I}_0\left(\frac{\rho\nu}{\sigma^2}\right). \qquad [9.12]$$

Let $\mathbf{x}$ be a set of $N$ i.i.d. samples drawn from the distribution [9.10] determined by the set of parameters $\bar{\Psi}$, i.e. $\mathrm{p}\,(\rho|\bar{\Psi})$. The aim of the EM algorithm is to estimate the real values $\bar{\Psi}$ using the samples $\mathbf{x}$. In particular, here, we consider the case where each sample $x \in \mathbf{x}$ is unlabeled; thus, the sampling is incomplete. We recall that a complete sample would be of the form $y = (x, \omega)$, where $\omega \in \{\omega_1, \omega_2\}$ is the *label* of the sample $x$ (i.e. the index representing the population from which the observed value $x$ comes from). The EM algorithm gives, under certain hypotheses, an estimation of $\bar{\Psi}$ as a local maximum $\hat{\Psi}$ of the so-called log-likelihood of the samples $\mathbf{x}$

$$L(\Psi) = \sum_{x \in \mathbf{x}} \log \mathrm{p}\,(x|\Psi). \qquad [9.13]$$

The key point of the EM algorithm is Dempster *et al.* (1977): given $\Psi'$, then $L(\Psi) \geqslant L(\Psi')$ if $\Psi$ maximizes the *conditional log-expectation*

$$Q(\Psi|\Psi') = \sum_{x \in \mathbf{x}} \sum_{h=1,2} \mathrm{p}\,(\omega_h|x, \Psi') \log\left(\alpha_h\,\mathrm{p}\,(x|\omega_h, \theta_h)\right), \qquad [9.14]$$

where for $h = 1, 2$ and for each $x \in \mathbf{x}$, the weight

$$\mathrm{p}\,(\omega_h|x, \Psi') := \frac{\alpha'_h\,\mathrm{p}\,(x|\omega_h, \theta'_h)}{\mathrm{p}\,(x|\Psi')} \qquad [9.15]$$

is the posterior probability that $x$ originated in the $h$-th component of the population, given $\Psi'$ (see Figure 9.3).

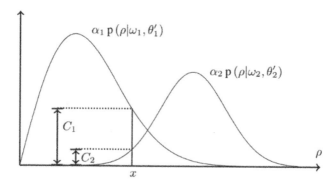

**Figure 9.3.** *Geometrical interpretation of the posterior probability that $x$ originated in the $h$-th component given $\Psi'$, as $\mathrm{p}\,(\omega_h|x, \Psi') = C_h/(C_1 + C_2)$ for $h = 1, 2$*

In its more general fashion, the EM algorithm is implemented as follows: first, an approximation $\Psi^0$ is chosen, then for $k = 0, 1, \ldots$ the conditional log-expectation $Q(\Psi|\Psi^k)$ is evaluated (E-step) and the next iterate is found (M-step) as $\Psi^{k+1} := \arg\max_\Psi Q(\Psi|\Psi^k)$. A recursive formula for updating the mixing proportions can be formally derived and the M-step can also be formulated as:

$$\alpha^{k+1} := N^{-1} \sum_{x \in \mathbf{x}} \mathrm{p}\,(\omega_1|x, \Psi^k)$$

$$\Theta^{k+1} := \arg\max_\Theta Q((\alpha^k, \Theta)|\Psi^k). \qquad [9.16]$$

Exploiting information theory, the EM algorithm to the parameter estimation of [9.10] can be further simplified. In the considered statistical model, all parameters $b, \nu, \sigma$ are mutually independent (see Zanetti *et al.* (2015, Appendices A–C)). Thus, following Redner and Walker (1984), the EM algorithm can be split into separated maximization steps

$$\alpha^{k+1} := N^{-1} \sum_{x \in \mathbf{x}} \mathrm{p}\left(\omega_1 | x, \Psi^k\right)$$

$$b^{k+1} := \arg\max_{b} Q((\alpha^k, b, \nu^k, \sigma^k) | \Psi^k)$$

$$\nu^{k+1} := \arg\max_{\nu} Q((\alpha^k, b^k, \nu, \sigma^k) | \Psi^k)$$

$$\sigma^{k+1} := \arg\max_{\sigma} Q((\alpha^k, b^k, \nu^k, \sigma) | \Psi^k).$$

[9.17]

Note that the difference between [9.16] and [9.17] is substantial. Without the parameter independence assumption, the iterative search of maximums cannot be separated and the implementation must rely on *ad hoc* optimization techniques. For example, this is the case in Maitra and Faden (2009) with $J = 2$, where $\theta_1 = (\nu_1, \sigma)$ and $\theta_2 = (\nu_2, \sigma)$, the parameters of two Rician distributions, are obviously not independent. In the sequel, we take the advantage of [9.17] and show that each partial maximization step can be performed by updating the corresponding variable according to an iterative rule.

### 9.3.3.2. *Iterative equations*

By defining $\ell(\Psi) := Q(\Psi | \Psi)$, the iterative procedure [9.17] can be instantiated by an iterative method attempting to solve

$$\nabla \ell(\Psi) = 0.$$

[9.18]

By writing gradient equations and performing math (see Zanetti *et al.* (2015, Appendices A and B)), we get:

$$\frac{\partial \ell}{\partial \alpha} = \sum_{x \in \mathbf{x}} \frac{1}{\alpha} \mathrm{p}\left(\omega_1 | x, \Psi\right) - \frac{1}{1 - \alpha} \mathrm{p}\left(\omega_2 | x, \Psi\right)$$

$$\frac{\partial \ell}{\partial b} = \sum_{x \in \mathbf{x}} \mathrm{p}\left(\omega_1 | x, \Psi\right) \left[ \frac{x^2}{b^3} - \frac{2}{b} \right]$$

$$\frac{\partial \ell}{\partial \nu} = \sum_{x \in \mathbf{x}} \mathrm{p}\left(\omega_2 | x, \Psi\right) \left[ \frac{x}{\sigma^2} \frac{\mathrm{I}_1\left(\frac{x\nu}{\sigma^2}\right)}{\mathrm{I}_0\left(\frac{x\nu}{\sigma^2}\right)} - \frac{\nu}{\sigma^2} \right]$$

$$\frac{\partial \ell}{\partial \sigma} = \sum_{x \in \mathbf{x}} \mathrm{p}\left(\omega_2 | x, \Psi\right) \left[ \frac{x^2 + \nu^2}{\sigma^3} - \frac{2}{\sigma} - \frac{2x\nu}{\sigma^3} \frac{\mathrm{I}_1\left(\frac{x\nu}{\sigma^2}\right)}{\mathrm{I}_0\left(\frac{x\nu}{\sigma^2}\right)} \right]$$

[9.19]

where $I_1(.)$ is the first-order modified Bessel function of the first kind (Watson 1966). As we can see, gradient equations are highly nonlinear. Formally, we derive a set of iterative equations for approximating the solution of [9.18] according to the method of subsequent approximations (see Zanetti *et al.* (2015, Appendices A–D)). After some analytical manipulations, we get the following iterative rules:

$$\alpha^{k+1} = N^{-1} \sum_{x \in \mathbf{x}} \mathrm{p}\left(\omega_1 | x, \Psi^k\right)$$

$$(b^2)^{k+1} = \frac{\sum_{x \in \mathbf{x}} \mathrm{p}\left(\omega_1 | x, \Psi^k\right) x^2}{2 \sum_{x \in \mathbf{x}} \mathrm{p}\left(\omega_1 | x, \Psi^k\right)}$$

$$\nu^{k+1} = \frac{\sum_{x \in \mathbf{x}} \mathrm{p}\left(\omega_2 | x, \Psi^k\right) \frac{I_1\left(\frac{x\nu^k}{(\sigma^k)^2}\right)}{I_0\left(\frac{x\nu^k}{(\sigma^k)^2}\right)} x}{\sum_{x \in \mathbf{x}} \mathrm{p}\left(\omega_2 | x, \Psi^k\right)} \qquad [9.20]$$

$$(\sigma^2)^{k+1} = \frac{\sum_{x \in \mathbf{x}} \mathrm{p}\left(\omega_2 | x, \Psi^k\right) \left[x^2 + (\nu^k)^2 - 2x\nu^k \frac{I_1\left(\frac{x\nu^k}{(\sigma^k)^2}\right)}{I_0\left(\frac{x\nu^k}{(\sigma^k)^2}\right)}\right]}{2 \sum_{x \in \mathbf{x}} \mathrm{p}\left(\omega_2 | x, \Psi^k\right)}.$$

The above formulas fully determine our algorithm. In general, the method of subsequent approximations converges with linear speed at least, provided that the spectral radius of the Jacobian matrix of the iterative function, computed at the exact solution, is strictly less than one. Of course, the convergence properties of the algorithm strongly depend on the choice of the first iterate.

### 9.3.3.3. *Initialization*

In order to increase the probability to converge to an optimal stationary point of the objective energy $\ell(\Psi)$, an adequate initial approximation $\Psi^0$ must be found. A standard approach to this aim is based on a first raw classification of the data followed by maximum likelihood (ML) estimates of the parameters. Let us assume that the samples drawn from the mixture are divided into two approximate classes $W_n^0$ and $W_c^0$ in such a way that $\mathbf{x} = W_n^0 \cup W_c^0$. The ML estimates of shape parameters (hereafter denoted by the ML superscript) are derived as the solutions of the so-called log-likelihood equations. Samples in $W_n^0$ are used to approximate $b$, whereas samples in $W_c^0$ are used to approximate $\nu, \sigma$. For an explicit computation of their values, we refer the reader to the existing literature (Benedict and Soong 1967; Talukdar and Lawing 1991; Sijbers *et al.* 1998b; Lauwers *et al.* 2009). Once the ML estimates $b^{ML}, \nu^{ML}, \sigma^{ML}$ are computed, we use their values as the initial set of parameters $\Theta^0$ for triggering the EM algorithm:

$$\Theta^0 = (b^{ML}, (\nu^{ML}, \sigma^{ML})). \qquad [9.21]$$

As the initial value for the mixing proportion, we use the ratio ($\#$ denotes the number of samples)

$$\alpha^0 = \frac{\#W_n^0}{\#X}.$$   [9.22]

According to the method that is used to populate the approximate classes $W_n^0, W_c^0$, we have different initializations of the EM algorithm. The more these classes are good representatives of the true classes $\omega_1, \omega_2$, the more the ML parameter estimates of the two distributions $p(\rho|\omega_h, \theta_h)$, $h = 1, 2$ will be close to the real values. A simple yet effective way to populate such approximate classes is given by thresholding the values of the samples x (in Bruzzone and Prieto (2000b), a similar approach is used in the case of a mixture of Gaussian densities). Let us define, for any fixed value $T \geqslant 0$, the approximate classes as follows:

$$W_n^0 := \{x \in X : x \leqslant T\},$$
$$W_c^0 := \{x \in X : x > T\}.$$   [9.23]

In terms of Bayes decision theory, the choice of the threshold $T$ can be interpreted as an attempt of approximating a solution of [9.7]. In this context, the problem of defining the approximate classes $W_n^0, W_c^0$ is turned into the problem of choosing the separating threshold $T$. At this stage, proper knowledge on the specific dataset should be used in order to simplify the task of computing $T$. On the one hand, such $T$ should be able to give at least a coarse discrimination of the data, for example, by properly exploiting the bi-modal behavior of the histogram. On the other hand, the computational complexity of this step, being a preliminary step itself, should be kept low. A choice often encountered in applications that meets the two above-mentioned important requirements (Bruzzone and Prieto 2000b) is that of using

$$T = T_{mid} := \frac{\max X - \min X}{2}.$$   [9.24]

Whenever the two modes of the mixture described by equation [9.10] are well separated by $T_{mid}$, we expect to have sufficiently accurate preliminary ML estimates of the mixture parameters for triggering the EM algorithm. Of course, other strategies can be used.

## 9.4. A compound multiclass statistical model of the difference image

To improve the fitting capabilities of the statistical representation of the unchanged and changed pixels and the change detection performance, in this section, a compound multiclass model to the statistical representation of the difference image is presented (Zanetti and Bruzzone 2017), that generalizes the statistical description given in section 9.3. To provide a meaningful context for multiple classes in the difference image, imposing *a priori* assumptions on the difference image, as done in section 9.3, is a limitation. In this section, it is shown how by starting solely from a well-known joint distribution model, which has strong connections with the compound-classification approach to CD (Bruzzone and Serpico 1997; Demir *et al.* 2013a) that is suitable for the representation of single time images, it is possible to derive an appropriate multiclass statistical distribution of the difference image. Based on this, a general definition of the change detection problem is given in the framework of CVA, where both the unchange and change classes are multiple. Indeed, these two are seen as macro classes, including subclasses that in turn represent different statistical behaviors for both unchanged and changed pixels. Building on this, the statistical multiclass mixture that describes the magnitude of the difference image is derived and an EM-like algorithm is presented to estimate the mixture parameters and infer whether the binary classification is unchanged/changed.

## 9.4.1. *Difference image statistical mixture model*

We provide a theoretical derivation of the statistical distribution of the difference image, starting from the hypothesis of the Gaussian distribution of natural classes in the single time images. Based on this model, we give a formal definition of the multiple unchange and change classes.

### 9.4.1.1. *Mathematical formulation*

Let $\mathbf{y}^t$, with $t = 1, 2$, be two multispectral images acquired over the same area at two different times. Each image has $B$ bands; therefore, each pixel value at location $(i, j)$ is a $B$-dimensional vector $\mathbf{y}^t(i, j) \in \mathbb{R}^B$, where $t = 1, 2$. In a general statistical interpretation, the multispectral image formation is modeled as a joint realization of certain $B$-dimensional random variables. To each pixel location $(i, j)$, a random variable $(y^t, \Phi^t)$ is assigned, where $y^t \in \mathbb{R}^B$ is associated with the observed spectral values of the pixel at time $t$, and $\Phi^t \in \{\phi_1, \dots, \phi_C\}$ is associated with its class label at time $t$. Hereafter, we will assume that these random variables are i.i.d.; thus, the statistical distribution of the images can be fully described by defining one random variable $(y^t, \Phi^t)$ for each single time $t$. Two remarks about the notation are used hereafter. First, probability density functions are denoted by $\mathrm{p}(.)$ for convenience. Second, given $t = 1, 2$ and $h = 1, \dots, C$, the probabilistic event $\Phi^t = \phi_h$ is written in a more compact way as $\phi_h^t$.

A typical and commonly used (Bruzzone and Serpico 1997; Demir *et al.* 2012, 2013a, 2013b) joint probabilistic model for $y^1, y^2$ assumes that the couple $(y^1, y^2)$ depends on $(\Phi^1, \Phi^2)$. By marginalizing with respect to the class variables, this leads to the following distribution:

$$\mathrm{p}(y^1, y^2) = \sum_{h,k=1}^{C} \mathrm{p}(\phi_h^1, \phi_k^2)\, \mathrm{p}(y^1, y^2 | \phi_h^1, \phi_k^2). \qquad [9.25]$$

With the assumption that the realization of the variable $y^t$ only depends on its associated class label $\Phi^t$, for each $t = 1, 2$, we slightly simplify our joint model by assuming the following conditional independence[2] (Demir *et al.* 2013a):

$$y^1 \perp y^2 \mid (\Phi^1, \Phi^2)$$

$$y^1 \perp \Phi^2 \mid \Phi^1 \qquad\qquad [9.26]$$

$$y^2 \perp \Phi^1 \mid \Phi^2$$

With these assumptions, we can split the joint conditional distribution appearing in equation [9.25] to obtain

$$\mathrm{p}\,(y^1, y^2) = \sum_{h,k=1}^{C} \mathrm{p}\,(\phi_h^1, \phi_k^2)\,\mathrm{p}\,(y^1 | \phi_h^1)\,\mathrm{p}\,(y^2 | \phi_k^2). \qquad [9.27]$$

In the most general case, the two images might not present the same set of observable classes: we assume that $\{\phi_1, \ldots, \phi_C\}$ is the joint set of class labels, which are observable in both images, where $C \geqslant 1$ is the total number of classes. The fact that some classes might not be observed in one of the single time images is formalized by setting the corresponding class prior probabilities to zero. For instance, if class $\phi_h$ is not observable at time $t = 1$, then $\mathrm{p}\,(\phi_h^1, \phi_k^2) = 0$ for all $k = 1, \ldots, C$. A similar argument works for a class that is not observable at time $t = 2$. Therefore, we let $0 \leqslant \mathrm{p}\,(\phi_h^1, \phi_k^2) \leqslant 1$ and

$$\sum_{h,k=1}^{C} \mathrm{p}\,(\phi_h^1, \phi_k^2) = 1 \qquad\qquad [9.28]$$

in order for equation [9.27] to be consistent as a probability model. Now, let us assume that natural classes are distributed as multidimensional Gaussians in the two images. This is a common and reasonable assumption in the literature when multispectral images are considered (Chen 2007). A natural class that is observed at both times may be described by different statistical parameters in the two images due to seasonal effects, different radiometric conditions, co-registration errors, etc. Therefore, we model them as

$$y^t | \phi_h^t \sim \mathcal{N}(y^t; \mu_h^t, \Sigma_h^t) \qquad\qquad [9.29]$$

where $\mu_h^t, \Sigma_h^t$ are the mean vectors and the covariance matrices of the class $\phi_h$ observed at time $t = 1, 2$.

Under the hypothesis of a joint model, as in equations [9.27]–[9.29], the distribution of the difference $d := y^1 - y^2$ can be written as a mixture of (at most) $C^2$

---

2. Following a standard notation, for $A \perp B \mid C$, we say that $A$ and $B$ are conditionally independent, given $C$. In other words, the knowledge of $C$ makes $A$ and $B$ independent.

Gaussian components (see Zanetti and Bruzzone (2017, Appendix B)). The density function of the difference turns out to be

$$p(d) = \sum_{h,k=1}^{C} p(\phi_h^1, \phi_k^2) \mathcal{N}(d; \mu_h^1 - \mu_k^2, \Sigma_h^1 + \Sigma_k^2) \tag{9.30}$$

where the mixture terms are the class prior probabilities $p(\phi_h^1, \phi_k^2)$.

### 9.4.1.2. *Physical interpretation*

The distribution equation [9.30] formalizes the intuitive concept that the difference image is populated by a set of classes, each one representing a possible class-by-class matching among the classes that populate the single time images. As mentioned above, we allow the same class $\phi_h$ to have different parameters $\mu_h^t$ and $\Sigma_h^t$ in correspondence of the two acquisitions at times $t = 1, 2$. Every pixel that can be considered as drawn from the distribution $\mathcal{N}(\mu_h^1, \Sigma_h^1)$ in $\mathbf{y}^1$ and from the distribution $\mathcal{N}(\mu_h^2, \Sigma_h^2)$ in $\mathbf{y}^2$ is an unchanged pixel, as it belongs to the same natural class $\phi_h$. It follows that each class $\phi_h$ has its own *unchange* behavior if and only if the class is observed in both images. Conversely, a pixel that can be considered as drawn from the distribution $\mathcal{N}(\mu_h^1, \Sigma_h^1)$ in $\mathbf{y}^1$ and from the distribution $\mathcal{N}(\mu_k^2, \Sigma_k^2)$ in $\mathbf{y}^2$, with $h \neq k$, is a changed pixel that changed its class from $\phi_h$ to $\phi_k$. As a result, each class may have at most $C - 1$ different *change* behaviors.

In order to better understand which classes are changed and which ones are unchanged, we can reason about priors. Each mixing term $p(\phi_h^1, \phi_k^2)$ is exactly the joint probability that class $\phi_h$ is observed at time $t = 1$ and class $\phi_k$ is observed at time $t = 2$. These probabilities can be arranged in a useful way into a square matrix

$$\mathbf{Q} = \begin{pmatrix} p(\phi_1^1, \phi_1^2) & p(\phi_1^1, \phi_2^2) & \cdots & p(\phi_1^1, \phi_C^2) \\ p(\phi_2^1, \phi_1^2) & p(\phi_2^1, \phi_2^2) & \cdots & p(\phi_2^1, \phi_C^2) \\ \vdots & \vdots & \ddots & \vdots \\ p(\phi_C^1, \phi_1^2) & p(\phi_C^1, \phi_2^2) & \cdots & p(\phi_C^1, \phi_C^2) \end{pmatrix}. \tag{9.31}$$

If all of the entries of the matrix $\mathbf{Q}$ are non-null, the distribution function $p(d)$ has exactly $C^2$ mixture class components. If class $\phi_h$ is not observable at time $t = 1$, then the $h$-th row of the matrix is null. Similarly, if class $\phi_k$ is not observable at time $t = 2$, then the $k$-th column of matrix $\mathbf{Q}$ is null. Other simplifications of matrix $\mathbf{Q}$ can be done (i.e. setting to zero some of its entries) if prior knowledge about the studied scene is available. As an example, if we know that in the considered image pair it is impossible to find a change from class $\phi_h$ to class $\phi_k$, then its corresponding prior probability can be set to zero, i.e. $p(\phi_h^1, \phi_k^2) = 0$. All of the non-null entries of the matrix $\mathbf{Q}$ define the prior probabilities of the mixture components that populate the difference image. Each of these mixture components describe the statistical distribution of the pixels that belong to class $\phi_h$ at time $t = 1$ and to class $\phi_k$ at time $t = 2$. It follows that, if $h = k$, then these pixels are not changed, whereas if $h \neq k$, then the pixels have changed their class from $\phi_h$ to $\phi_k$. In both cases, their distributions are given explicitly. This interpretation allows us to give a formal definition of the unchange and change classes, in the difference image, as multiple classes.

DEFINITION 9.1 (Unchange class).– *Each pixel that belongs to class $\phi_h$, both at times $t = 1$ and $t = 2$, is said to belong to the* unchange class $\omega_h$, *where $h \in \{1, \ldots, C\}$. The distribution of the unchange class $\omega_h$ in the difference image is Gaussian with parameters*

$$d|\omega_h \sim \mathcal{N}(d; \mu_h^1 - \mu_h^2, \Sigma_h^1 + \Sigma_h^2).$$

*The set of all unchange classes is denoted by $\Omega_n$, and it contains all classes that are associated with the non-null diagonal entries of the matrix $\mathbf{Q}$:*

$$\Omega_n := \{\omega_h : p(\phi_h^1, \phi_h^2) \neq 0\}.$$

DEFINITION 9.2 (Change class).– *Each pixel that belongs to class $\phi_h$ at time $t = 1$ and to class $\phi_k$ at time $t = 2$ is said to belong to the* change class $\omega_{hk}$, *where $h, k \in \{1, \ldots, C\}$ and $h \neq k$. The distribution of the change class $\omega_{hk}$ in the difference image is Gaussian with parameters*

$$d|\omega_{hk} \sim \mathcal{N}(d; \mu_h^1 - \mu_k^2, \Sigma_h^1 + \Sigma_k^2).$$

*The set of all change classes is denoted by $\Omega_c$, and it contains all classes that are associated with the non-null off-diagonal entries of the matrix $\mathbf{Q}$:*

$$\Omega_c := \{\omega_{hk} : p(\phi_h^1, \phi_k^2) \neq 0, h \neq k\}.$$

As a simple consequence of the two definitions above, the distribution of the difference image can be split into two parts, as

$$p(d) = p(d|\Omega_n) + p(d|\Omega_c), \tag{9.32}$$

where the first term describes the statistical distribution of the multiple unchange class:

$$p(d|\Omega_n) := \sum_{h=1}^{C} p(\phi_h^1, \phi_h^2) \mathcal{N}(d; \mu_h^1 - \mu_h^2, \Sigma_h^1 + \Sigma_h^2), \tag{9.33}$$

and the second term describes the statistical distribution of the multiple change class:

$$p(d|\Omega_c) := \sum_{\substack{h,k=1 \\ h \neq k}}^{C} p(\phi_h^1, \phi_k^2) \mathcal{N}(d; \mu_h^1 - \mu_k^2, \Sigma_h^1 + \Sigma_k^2). \tag{9.34}$$

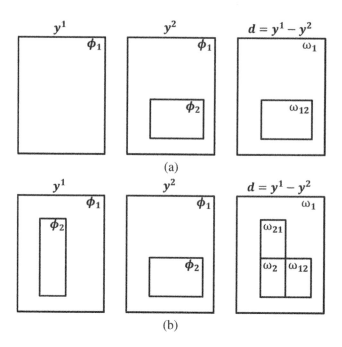

**Figure 9.4.** *Example of statistical dependency of the difference image with respect to the input pair, when the number of natural classes is $C = 2$. (a) The natural class $\phi_2$ is only observable in image $\mathbf{y}^2$, thus the resulting difference image only has one unchange behavior $\omega_1$ and one change behavior $\omega_{12}$ (from class $\phi_1$ to $\phi_2$). (b) Both natural classes $\phi_1, \phi_2$ are observable in the two images. Therefore, they have their own unchange statistical behaviors $\omega_1, \omega_2$, and mutual change behaviors $\omega_{12}$ (from class $\phi_1$ to $\phi_2$) and $\omega_{21}$ (from class $\phi_2$ to $\phi_1$)*

Some important remarks are needed here. It is common practice in the literature to model the change class as a mixture of different components (Liu *et al.* 2015). However, the underlying assumption is always that the principal changes (the more statistically evident) are a small subset of all of the ones that can be formulated theoretically. In particular, this also affects the model of the unchange class, which is commonly reduced to a single class. The increased radiometric resolution of last-generation multispectral sensors typically results in more natural classes than the ones typically observed in older images. Thus, the mentioned approaches may not be appropriate anymore (a simple example about this distinction when $C = 2$, i.e. when images can be represented by two natural classes, is depicted in Figure 9.4). The statistical model in equation [9.30] can be considered a general model that takes into account some of the complexities arising, by considering that both the unchange and change classes are multiple classes. Also note that some of the typical approaches to change detection already given in the literature can be derived as specializations of this model. In the remainder of this section, it is shown how this model generalizes the arguments given in section 9.3.

### 9.4.2. *Magnitude image statistical mixture model*

The framework presented in section 9.4.1 is general and flexible enough to fit many possible real scenarios of change detection. On the counterpart, the model has several free parameters to be estimated from data; thus, the development of unsupervised methods exploiting this model (e.g. multivariate Gaussian fitting) could present critical issues (e.g. initialization criteria, convergence of parameter estimation methods, decision rules, limited robustness, etc.) and may result in being too numerically expensive to apply in reasonable time. Nevertheless, when a problem such as binary CD is considered, the number of parameters can be significantly reduced. The theoretical setting given in the previous section allows us to derive precise relationships between the parameters of the model in the original feature space and those modeling the reduced space. Here, we aim at defining an unsupervised method for binary decision based on a multiclass model for the magnitude distribution. In order to do this, some simplifying assumptions on the general model presented in section 9.4.1 are made. First, we assume similar radiometric conditions and no seasonal differences in the two images $y^1, y^2$. Therefore, we expect the parameters of the same class to not vary between the two acquisitions, in such a way that

$$\mu_h^1 = \mu_h^2 =: \mu_h$$
$$\Sigma_h^1 = \Sigma_h^2 =: \Sigma_h$$

[9.35]

for all $h = 1, \ldots, C$. Second, since our purpose is to exploit the magnitude information in the decision process, some regularity assumptions on the structure of the covariance matrices $\Sigma_h$ are needed in order to derive the theoretical distribution of the magnitude as a Rice-like mixture type (Rice 1944). In practice, we assume that covariances are scalar matrices of the type

$$\Sigma_h = \sigma_h^2 I_B$$

[9.36]

where $I_B$ is the identity matrix of size $B \times B$ and $\sigma_h$ are positive scalars representing the standard deviation of each class. It is common practice in change detection to select a few bands (the most representatives of the changes of interest) that correspond to distant frequencies in the spectrum. With them being highly uncorrelated, we see that the assumption of diagonality of the matrices $\Sigma_h$ is not very strict. For simplicity, in the sequel, only two bands are considered (i.e. $B = 2$) in order to get the well-known Rician distributions associated with the magnitude variable. However, all of the arguments presented can be generalized to any finite dimension by taking into account that Rician distributions have more complex analytical expressions when $B > 2$. This technical extension is considered in Zanetti (2017, Appendix 6.A.5).

Finally, we recall again (following on from the discussion in section 9.4.1) that the spatial independence of pixels is assumed here. Therefore, each pixel value of the difference image is considered to be drawn from the distribution equation [9.30], independent of the others.

By taking into account equation [9.35], the difference image distribution $p(d)$ can be written in the simpler form

$$p(d) = \sum_{h,k=1}^{C} q_{hk} \mathcal{N}(d; \mu_h - \mu_k, \Sigma_h + \Sigma_k) \qquad [9.37]$$

where the mixture terms $q_{hk}$ are the entries of matrix $Q$ given in equation [9.31], i.e. $q_{hk} := p(\phi_h^1, \phi_k^2)$. Note that each class component of the multiple unchange class is 0-mean and its covariance matrix is proportional (by factor 2) to the covariance matrix of the associated (unchanged) natural class

$$p(d|\Omega_n) = \sum_{h=1}^{C} q_{hh} \mathcal{N}(d; 0, 2\Sigma_h). \qquad [9.38]$$

Regarding the class components of the multiple change class, they are mutually symmetric with respect to the origin

$$p(d|\Omega_c) = \sum_{\substack{h,k=1 \\ h \neq k}}^{C} q_{hk} \mathcal{N}(d; \mu_h - \mu_k, \Sigma_h + \Sigma_k). \qquad [9.39]$$

Indeed, we have $\mu_h - \mu_k = -(\mu_k - \mu_h)$ and, obviously, $\Sigma_h + \Sigma_k = \Sigma_k + \Sigma_h$.

These considerations enable us to describe the distribution $p(d)$ when coordinates are changed to magnitude. Indeed, given the previous assumptions, the theoretical derivation of the distribution of the random variable $\rho := |d| = |y^1 - y^2|$ is possible (the operator $|.|$ denotes the Euclidean norm). It follows that the magnitude image $\rho := \{|d(i,j)| : (i,j)\}$ can be considered as a sample drawn from this distribution. Let us recall the general form of the Rician distribution that is given by

$$\mathcal{R}(\rho; \nu, \delta) = \frac{\rho}{\delta^2} \exp\left(-\frac{\rho^2 + \nu^2}{2\delta^2}\right) I_0\left(\frac{\rho \nu}{\delta^2}\right) \qquad \rho \geqslant 0 \qquad [9.40]$$

where $I_0(.)$ is the 0-th order modified Bessel function of the first kind (Watson 1966). By defining the magnitude variable as $\rho := |d|$, the distribution of $\rho$ follows:

$$p(\rho) = \sum_{h,k=1}^{C} q_{hk} \mathcal{R}(\rho; \nu_{hk}, \delta_{hk}) \qquad [9.41]$$

where $\nu_{hk} = |\mu_h - \mu_k|$ and $\delta_{hk} = \sqrt{\sigma_h^2 + \sigma_k^2}$. Let us point out some important remarks here. Since $\nu_{hh} = 0$ for every $h = 1, \ldots, C$, we easily assume that any component related to the unchange class is actually Rayleigh. Moreover, the scale parameters of these Rayleigh distributions only depend on the variances of the associated unchanged classes. More specifically, $\delta_{hh} = \sigma_h\sqrt{2}$ for each $h$. The unchange class in the magnitude space is therefore described by

$$p\left(\rho|\Omega_n\right) = \sum_{h=1}^{C} q_{hh}\, \mathcal{R}(\rho; 0, \sigma_h\sqrt{2}). \qquad [9.42]$$

All of the other cross terms in equation [9.41] are mutually equal as $\nu_{hk} = \nu_{kh}$ and $\delta_{hk} = \delta_{kh}$ for each couple $(h, k)$ such that $h \neq k$. Moreover, each non-centrality term is, in general, $\nu_{hk} \neq 0$; thus, all components related to the change class are Rician. It follows that all of the components of the multiple change class group together two-by-two and their mixture parameters are summed up:

$$p\left(\rho|\Omega_c\right) = \sum_{\substack{h,k=1 \\ h<k}}^{C} \left(q_{hk} + q_{kh}\right) \mathcal{R}(\rho; \nu_{hk}, \delta_{hk}). \qquad [9.43]$$

This means that, in the magnitude space, the change from class $\phi_h$ to $\phi_k$ (class $\omega_{hk}$) and the opposite change (class $\omega_{kh}$) are statistically equivalent. Therefore, the number (and the meaning) of change classes in the magnitude space is different from that in the difference space. In light of this, we change the notation for the unchange and change classes in the magnitude space by adding a superscript $\rho$, namely $\Omega_n^\rho$ and $\Omega_c^\rho$.

Once the structure of the matrix $\mathbf{Q}$ is known, i.e. when the indices of its non-null entries (and not necessarily their values) are known, the number of unchange and change class members in equation [9.41] can be easily obtained. Let us denote $C' := \#(\Omega_n^\rho)$ as the number of members of the unchange class and $C'' := \#(\Omega_c^\rho)$ as the number of members of the change class. On the one hand, only classes that are observable in both images can have their unchange behavior; therefore, we have, in general

$$0 \leqslant C' \leqslant C. \qquad [9.44]$$

On the other hand, each natural class can have at most $C - 1$ different change behaviors. Thus, in view of the above-mentioned statistical equivalence of change classes $\omega_{hk}$ and $\omega_{kh}$, we have

$$0 \leqslant C'' \leqslant \frac{C(C - 1)}{2}. \qquad [9.45]$$

For ease of notation, in the following, the mixture indices are re-ordered and the mixture and shape parameters are re-named accordingly. We now write the distribution of the magnitude as

$$p\left(\rho\right) = \sum_{h=1}^{H} \alpha_h \, \mathcal{R}(\rho; \nu_h, \delta_h) \qquad [9.46]$$

where $H = C' + C''$ and, of course, $\sum_{h=1}^{H} \alpha_h = 1$. In the same manner, we denote class labels as $\omega_h \in \Omega_n^\rho$ for $h = 1, \ldots, C'$, and $\omega_h \in \Omega_c^\rho$ for $h = C' + 1, \ldots, H$.

### 9.4.3. Bayesian decision

The theoretical model [9.46] describes the distribution of the magnitude of the difference image in the multiclass case and enables us to define a Bayesian framework for binary decision based on the maximum *a posteriori* (MAP) principle and the thresholding of the magnitude variable. By following the MAP approach, for any given value of the target variable, we select as the most likely originating class, the one that maximizes the posterior probability of observing that value among all classes. It is well known that this procedure minimizes the overall probability of committing classification errors. Therefore, given the mixture model equation [9.46], we define the MAP classification function

$$W[\rho] := \arg\max_{\omega_h \in \Omega^\rho} \alpha_h \, p\left(\rho | \omega_h\right) \qquad [9.47]$$

where $\Omega^\rho := \Omega_n^\rho \cup \Omega_c^\rho = \{\omega_1, \ldots, \omega_H\}$ is the set of all classes. It is worth noting that, with each competing class being either $\omega_h \in \Omega_n^\rho$ or $\omega_h \in \Omega_c^\rho$, this approach has an intrinsic binary interpretation. Indeed, each value $W[\rho]$ identifies (and associates to $\rho$) one member of the two multiple unchange or change classes. Thus, the binary classification based on the thresholding of the magnitude of the difference image can be defined by

$$W_n = \{(i,j) : W[\rho(i,j)] \in \Omega_n^\rho\}$$
$$W_c = \{(i,j) : W[\rho(i,j)] \in \Omega_c^\rho\}, \qquad [9.48]$$

where $W_n, W_c$ are the sets of predicted unchanged and changed pixels, respectively.

The Bayes decision method presented here generalizes the two-class approach for binary change detection presented in Zanetti *et al.* (2015), as this last one can be derived from equations [9.47] and [9.48] when two natural classes are considered (i.e. $C = 2$), with the additional assumption that one class is observable in only one of the two input images (i.e. $C' = C'' = 1$). An example of this situation is illustrated in

Figure 9.4(a), whereas in Figure 9.4b, a more general case involving all possible class unchange and change behaviors is illustrated.

### 9.4.4. *Numerical approach to parameter estimation*

With some simplifying assumptions, the theoretical distribution of the magnitude of the difference image is derived from the density [9.30]. Then, a framework for binary change detection is developed by following a multiclass maximum *a posteriori* (MAP) approach. Finally, a numerical method based on the EM algorithm (Redner and Walker 1984) for parameter estimation of the derived mixture density is presented. Parameter estimates are finally used to compute the optimal value that separates magnitude values in the unchanged and change predicted classes.

#### 9.4.4.1. *Model assumptions*

The binary change detection problem is usually addressed in the literature by assuming the unchange class to be a single class (Bruzzone and Prieto 2000b, 2002; Bovolo and Bruzzone 2007; Yetgin 2012; Zanetti *et al.* 2015). Sometimes, such an assumption is also extended to the change class (Bovolo and Bruzzone 2007; Zanetti *et al.* 2015), while in other cases, the change class is modeled as multiple (Bovolo *et al.* 2012). By a careful analysis of the matrix $\mathbf{Q}$ and its relationship with the mixture components in equation [9.46], we see that:

– A model that assumes both the unchange and change classes to be single is represented (in the simplest case) by a matrix of size $2 \times 2$. More specifically, the possible cases are:

$$\mathbf{Q} = \begin{pmatrix} q_{11} & q_{12} \\ 0 & 0 \end{pmatrix}, \begin{pmatrix} q_{11} & 0 \\ q_{21} & 0 \end{pmatrix}, \begin{pmatrix} q_{11} & q_{12} \\ q_{21} & 0 \end{pmatrix},$$

where we recall that the changes $\omega_{12}$ and $\omega_{21}$ are statistically equivalent in the magnitude space; thus, the last case relates to a single change.

– The assumption of having more than one change in the magnitude space puts a constraint on the number of natural classes in the model, which must be $C \geqslant 3$. The description of all possible cases becomes increasingly more complex when $C$ increases.

As we can see, the model of the problem can be arbitrarily complex if we do not have any prior knowledge about the classes involved. Some information about the structure of the matrix $\mathbf{Q}$ can be recovered in a supervised or semi-supervised way, by separately analyzing the single time images $\mathbf{y}^1, \mathbf{y}^2$ and their difference $\mathbf{d}$. However, this kind of approach may result in being too articulated for the specific purpose of binary change detection, whereas it seems more appropriate to be developed in the context of multiple change detection. On the contrary, a model can also be fixed *a priori*, and a change detection method can be derived accordingly. In formulating the *a priori* assumptions for the development of our method, we mainly consider that:

1) simple models proved to be effective for addressing the specific binary change detection problem; 2) typically, the solution of the EM algorithm is sub-optimal (local max); thus, the introduction of several additional parameters will decrease the significance of the solution itself. In view of these points, let us consider the case where only one relevant change can be identified in the image pair, so that we can focus the attention on the multiple unchange class. Therefore, the matrix $\mathbf{Q}$ can be assumed to be of the form

$$\mathbf{Q} = \begin{pmatrix} q_{11} & & & & & \\ & \ddots & & q_{hk} & & \\ & & \ddots & & & \\ & q_{kh} & & \ddots & & \\ & & & & & q_{CC} \end{pmatrix}, \qquad [9.49]$$

where $h, k \in \{1, \ldots, C\}$ are fixed. We stress the fact that for the derivation of the statistical model in equation [9.46], some regularity assumptions on the natural classes are made; see equations [9.35] and [9.36]. In addition to allowing the derivation of a precise model for the magnitude distribution, such assumptions have the remarkably positive effect of collapsing many subtle natural classes into a few dominant ones. Indeed, according to [9.38], *all* natural classes that are described by the same covariance matrix can be grouped into one single unchange class in the difference space as their distributions coincide. More specifically, let us assume that for a fixed $p \in \{1, \ldots, C\}$, there is a set of classes $\mathcal{B}_p \subset \{1, \ldots, C\}$ such that $\Sigma_h = \Sigma_p$, for all $h \in \mathcal{B}_p$. Then,

$$\sum_{h \in \mathcal{B}_p} q_{hh} \, \mathcal{N}(d; 0, 2\Sigma_h) = \mathcal{N}(d; 0, 2\Sigma_p) \sum_{h \in \mathcal{B}_p} q_{hh}. \qquad [9.50]$$

This simple mathematical fact proves that the complexity of the unchange class (in terms of number of distinguishable class members) does not depend on the real number of natural classes, but only on those that have different covariance matrices. Note in particular that, under the considered assumptions, the mean vector of each class (i.e. the feature vector that mainly characterizes the spectral signature of each class) does not play any role in the definition of the unchange class members.

Accordingly, we devise a distribution model that is able to represent the unchange multiple class in terms of dominant classes, while it does not increase the overall complexity of the associated estimation problem too much. Without putting a constraint on the *actual* number $C$ of natural classes that populate the images, we just assume that two main groups $\mathcal{B}_p$ and $\mathcal{B}_q$, with $p, q \in \{1, \ldots, C\}$, can be formed out of all classes, which are homogeneous in terms of covariance matrices. Thus, we can write

$$p\left(d|\Omega_n\right) = \mathcal{N}(d; 0, 2\Sigma_p) \sum_{h \in \mathcal{B}_p} q_{hh} + \mathcal{N}(d; 0, 2\Sigma_q) \sum_{h \in \mathcal{B}_q} q_{hh}. \qquad [9.51]$$

In principle, this simplification could be extended to any number of groups. Nonetheless, in the experimental part we will show how the simple choice of assuming two dominant classes proved to be sufficiently general to provide a change detection performance, which is nearly optimal.

### 9.4.4.2. *EM algorithm*

The magnitude of the difference image $\rho$ is considered to be a set of samples independently drawn from distribution [9.46]. In order to apply the MAP approach for decision, the parameters of this distribution must be numerically estimated. In the theoretical model presented in section 9.4.2, the parameters are constrained by their dependency on the natural class parametrization. In order to partially recover some of the flexibility that we lost in imposing conditions, such as in equations [9.35] and [9.36], we implement a version of the EM algorithm without parameter constraints. In addition to greater flexibility, this also gives the advantage of implementing an unconstrained optimization. Given this, from the *a priori* model equation [9.49] coupled with equation [9.51] and applied to the distribution equation [9.46], we can write the probability distribution of the magnitude of the difference image as

$$p\left(\rho\right) = \alpha_1 \, \mathcal{R}(\rho; 0, \delta_1) + \alpha_2 \, \mathcal{R}(\rho; 0, \delta_2) + \alpha_3 \, \mathcal{R}(\rho; \nu, \delta) \qquad [9.52]$$

where $\alpha_3 = 1 - \alpha_1 - \alpha_2$. For notation simplicity, we omitted the subscripts of the parameters of the Rician component (the third term in the summation). Let $\Psi = (\alpha_1, \alpha_2, \delta_1, \delta_2, \nu, \delta)$ be the vector of shape and mixture parameters involved in equation [9.52], then the dependency of this probability distribution with respect to the parameters can be expressed by writing $p\left(\rho|\Psi\right)$. For any $r \in \rho$, we define

$$p\left(\omega_h|r, \Psi'\right) := \frac{\alpha_h' \, p\left(r|\omega_h, \Psi'\right)}{p\left(r|\Psi'\right)} \qquad [9.53]$$

to be the posterior probability that the sample $r$ originated in the $h$-th component of the population, given $\Psi'$.

### 9.4.4.3. *Iterative equations*

By using the same arguments developed in Zanetti *et al.* (2015), it is possible to define an iterative version of the EM algorithm for the estimation of the parameters of [9.52] as follows

$$\alpha_i^{k+1} = N^{-1} \sum_{r \in \boldsymbol{\rho}} \mathrm{p}\left(\omega_i | r, \Psi^k\right)$$

$$(\delta_i^2)^{k+1} = \frac{\displaystyle\sum_{r \in \boldsymbol{\rho}} \mathrm{p}\left(\omega_i | r, \Psi^k\right) r^2}{2 \displaystyle\sum_{r \in \boldsymbol{\rho}} \mathrm{p}\left(\omega_i | r, \Psi^k\right)}$$

$$\nu^{k+1} = \frac{\displaystyle\sum_{r \in \boldsymbol{\rho}} \mathrm{p}\left(\omega_3 | r, \Psi^k\right) \frac{\mathrm{I}_1\left(\frac{r\nu^k}{(\delta^k)^2}\right)}{\mathrm{I}_0\left(\frac{r\nu^k}{(\delta^k)^2}\right)} r}{\displaystyle\sum_{r \in \boldsymbol{\rho}} \mathrm{p}\left(\omega_3 | r, \Psi^k\right)} \qquad\qquad [9.54]$$

$$(\delta^2)^{k+1} = \frac{\displaystyle\sum_{r \in \boldsymbol{\rho}} \mathrm{p}\left(\omega_3 | r, \Psi^k\right)\left[r^2 + (\nu^k)^2 - 2r\nu^k \frac{\mathrm{I}_1\left(\frac{r\nu^k}{(\delta^k)^2}\right)}{\mathrm{I}_0\left(\frac{r\nu^k}{(\delta^k)^2}\right)}\right]}{2 \displaystyle\sum_{r \in \boldsymbol{\rho}} \mathrm{p}\left(\omega_3 | r, \Psi^k\right)}.$$

for $i = 1, 2$, where $\mathrm{I}_1(.)$ is the first-order modified Bessel function of the first kind (Watson 1966).

### 9.4.4.4. *Initialization*

The iterative versions of the EM algorithm are known to be typically slow (Redner and Walker 1984). Moreover, the algorithm iteratively updates the parameters of three different mixture components, for a total of two mixture and four shape parameters. This makes the initialization of the algorithm a very crucial point, as a bad strategy may easily result in a stagnation of the parameters updates. In particular, after many numerical experiments (both on synthetic and real data), we observed that the typical approach of median thresholding (Bruzzone and Prieto 2000b; Zanetti *et al.* 2015) cannot be used for the preliminary maximum likelihood (ML) estimate of the parameters.

For a correct initialization, we found that the typical local minimum that separates the two main modes of the histogram of the magnitude must be precisely identified in order to have a first separation of the samples into two approximate classes: $W_n^0$ (unchanged samples) and $W_c^0$ (changed samples). Under the hypothesis that this local minimum is the stationary point of the underlying pdf with less curvature, it can be found as the point of lower variation of the corresponding cdf. A more stable numerical computation can be done by calculating the maximum point of the derivative of the quantile function. More specifically, let $Q : [0, 1] \rightarrow [0, 1]$ be the quantile function of the magnitude histogram and let $t^0 := \arg\max_{t \in [0,1]} Q'(t)$. Then, the two approximate classes are defined as

$$W_n^0 = \{(i,j) : \rho(i,j) \leqslant t^0\}$$
$$W_c^0 = \{(i,j) : \rho(i,j) > t^0\},$$

[9.55]

Since in the target mixture the components that represent unchanged pixels are two, the samples in $W_n^0$ are further divided into two sets $W_{n,1}^0$, $W_{n,2}^0$ by median thresholding. Finally, the shape and mixture parameters of the mixture are estimated via the ML approach (refer to Talukdar and Lawing (1991)) using the samples in the approximate classes. The shape parameters $\delta_i$ are estimated using the samples in $W_{n,i}^0$, with $i = 1, 2$ and $\nu, \delta$ are estimated using the samples in $W_c^0$. The mixture parameters $\alpha_i$ are approximated by their corresponding proportions $\#(W_{n,i}^0)/\#(\rho)$, for $i = 1, 2$.

## 9.5. Experimental results

In this section, we present an extensive experimental analysis aimed at assessing the theoretical models presented in sections 9.3 and 9.4. The purpose of this experimental section is twofold. First, experiments are conducted to demonstrate that the Rayleigh–Rice mixture model described in section 9.3 improves the statistical fitting of real data (magnitude of the difference image) if compared to state-of-the-art methods, and the observed improved fitting always corresponds to enhanced CD performance. Second, the multiclass Rician mixture derived from the compound multiclass statistical model presented in section 9.4 is tested against the two-class Rayleigh–Rice mixture, showing that the fitting performance can be further enhanced and binary CD can be pushed close to optimal performance. After presenting all of the image data used in the experiments, a detailed explanation of the experimental setup is given. Then, the results are presented and analyzed in detail.

### 9.5.1. *Dataset description*

The datasets considered in the experiments consist of bitemporal image pairs from different space-borne multispectral sensors. All images are co-registered and radiometrically corrected, and they are accompanied by reference maps of the changes, i.e. binary maps representing the classes $\omega_n, \omega_c$. Note that minor changes (i.e. mapped changes that do not belong to the main change class of interest) are depicted in the reference maps in red; see Figure 9.5.

### *Dataset A*

Two multispectral images acquired by the Thematic Mapper (TM) multispectral sensor of the Landsat 5 satellite. The scene represents an area including Lake Mulargia (Sardinia Island, Italy), at a resolution of 30 m. The images consist of $300 \times 412$

pixels. The dates of acquisition are September 1995 ($t_1$) and July 1996 ($t_2$). Between the two dates, one relevant change, which is related to the extension of the lake surface, occurred in the observed area. The scene presents $116, 120$ unchanged and $7, 480$ changed pixels (where 214 of them belong to a minor change related to an open quarry). The prior probabilities of class are given by

$$p\left(\omega_n\right) = \frac{116, 120}{123, 600} = 0.94, \qquad p\left(\omega_c\right) = \frac{7, 480}{123, 600} = 0.06.$$

The two bands that better represent the change of interest are TM4 and TM7 (channels 4 and 7), the near infrared (NIR) and the middle infrared (MIR) (Bovolo and Bruzzone 2007), respectively.

*Dataset B*

Two multispectral images acquired by the Enhanced Thematic Mapper Plus (ETM+) multispectral sensor of the Landsat 7 satellite. The scene represents the same subject of Dataset A (Lake Mulargia, Sardinia). Spatial resolution is 30 m. The images consist of $310 \times 449$ pixels. The dates of acquisition are May 2001 ($t_1$) and May 2003 ($t_2$). The scene presents $133, 453$ unchanged and $5, 737$ changed pixels (222 of which belong to minor changes related to small clouds and variations of the lake surface). The class prior probabilities are given by

$$p\left(\omega_n\right) = \frac{133, 453}{139, 190} = 0.96, \qquad p\left(\omega_c\right) = \frac{5, 737}{139, 190} = 0.04.$$

Bands ETM+4 (NIR) and ETM+7 (MIR) are selected as most representative of the change (lake enlargement) (Zanetti and Bruzzone 2017).

*Dataset C*

Two multispectral images acquired by the Operational Land Imager (OLI) multispectral sensor of the Landsat 8 satellite. The investigated area includes Lake Omodeo and a portion of Tirso River (Sardinia Island, Italy). The images consist of $700 \times 650$ pixels at a resolution of 30 m. The dates of acquisition are July 25, 2013 ($t_1$) and August 10, 2013 ($t_2$). The main change is a fire that occurred between August 7 and 9 in the south of Ghilarza village. The area affected by the fire is mostly agricultural, with an extension of approximately 100 ha. The scene presents 420227 unchanged and 34773 changed pixels (where 1636 of them belong to minor changes related to small clouds and variations of the lake surface). The class prior probabilities are given by

$$p\left(\omega_n\right) = \frac{420227}{455000} = 0.92, \qquad p\left(\omega_c\right) = \frac{34773}{455000} = 0.08.$$

The two bands selected as most representative of the changes are bands 5 and 6, the near infrared (NIR) and the first short-wavelength infrared (SWIR1) (Zanetti *et al.* 2015), respectively.

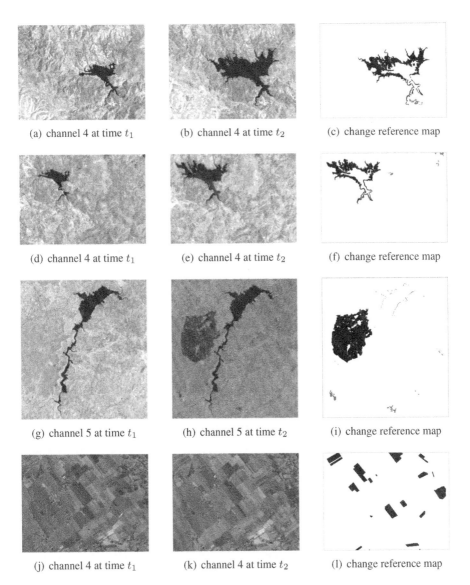

(a) channel 4 at time $t_1$        (b) channel 4 at time $t_2$        (c) change reference map

(d) channel 4 at time $t_1$        (e) channel 4 at time $t_2$        (f) change reference map

(g) channel 5 at time $t_1$        (h) channel 5 at time $t_2$        (i) change reference map

(j) channel 4 at time $t_1$        (k) channel 4 at time $t_2$        (l) change reference map

**Figure 9.5.** *Illustration of the datasets analyzed in the experiments. The pictures show pre and post images in one band and a reference map of the changes (red pixels are minor changes with respect to the main changes that are represented by black pixels) for (a,b,c) dataset A, (d,e,f) dataset B, (g,h,i) dataset C and (j,k,l) dataset D. For a color version of this figure, see www.iste.co.uk/atto/change1.zip*

*Dataset D*

Two multispectral images acquired by the Multispectral Instrument (MSI) of the Sentinel 2a satellite. The images consist of $300 \times 400$ pixels at a resolution of 10 m. The dates of acquisition are December 31, 2015 ($t_1$) and January 20, 2016 ($t_2$). The investigated area includes the surrounding of Tesis village (Pordenone, Italy). The main changes are all related to variations in soil conditions due to human activities on crops. The class prior probabilities are given by

$$p\left(\omega_n\right) = \frac{112868}{120000} = 0.94, \qquad p\left(\omega_c\right) = \frac{7132}{120000} = 0.06.$$

The two bands selected as most representative of the changes are bands 3 and 4, the red and NIR channels (Zanetti and Bruzzone 2017), respectively.

## 9.5.2. *Experimental setup*

Both the two-class and multiclass statistical models for the magnitude of the difference image (as presented in sections 9.3 and 9.4) are tested using the same rationale. Nonetheless, the experimental results are split into two separate test sessions, namely sections 9.5.3 and 9.5.4. For each of the two models, first, a detailed explanation of the models involved in the computations is given, then a report and analysis of the outcome are provided. The quality of the output and the performance are evaluated in terms of (1) EM parameter estimates and the statistical fitting and (2) change detection accuracy.

Each experimental session consists of the following main steps:

1) initialization of the EM algorithm;

2) run EM algorithm for parameter estimation of the models;

3) evaluate and assess fitting properties of the estimated mixture densities. Fitting is measured in terms of the $\chi_P^2$ ($\chi^2$–Pearson) divergence and the Kolmogorov–Smirnov (KS) distance between the data and the estimated densities;

4) compute threshold values according to the Bayes decision criterion and optimal choice via reference map trial-and-error evaluations;

5) populate the change detection classes $W_n, W_c$;

6) assess change detection performance (FA, MA, OE) by comparing the estimated classes $W_n, W_c$ with the reference classes $\omega_n, \omega_c$.

## 9.5.3. *Test 1: Two-class Rayleigh–Rice mixture model*

### 9.5.3.1. *Test description*

The fitting and change detection performance of the two-class Rayleigh–Rice mixture model presented in section 9.3 is tested against two reference models for parameter estimation already present in the literature: the first one based on Gaussian mixture, (Bruzzone and Prieto 2000c) and the second one based on a mixture of Rician distributions with a common scale parameter (Maitra and Faden 2009). Parameter notations used in this experimental session:

## Rayleigh–Rice mixture (rR)

$$p(\rho|\omega_n) = \mathrm{Rayl}(b), \quad p(\rho|\omega_c) = \mathrm{Rice}(\nu, \sigma).$$

## Gaussian mixture (GG)

$$p(\rho|\omega_n) = \mathcal{N}(\mu_1, \sigma_1), \quad p(\rho|\omega_c) = \mathcal{N}(\mu_2, \sigma_2).$$

## Rician mixture with common scale parameter (MF)

$$p(\rho|\omega_n) = \mathrm{Rice}(\nu_1, \beta), \quad p(\rho|\omega_c) = \mathrm{Rice}(\nu_2, \beta).$$

Iterative formulas for implementing parameter estimation in the **GG** model can be found in Bovolo *et al.* (2012). Implementation for parameter estimation in the **MF** case is presented in Maitra and Faden (2009). Initialization of **rR** follows the principles outlined in section 9.3.3.3.

### 9.5.3.2. *EM algorithm and fitting performance*

The numerical values of the estimated parameters and fitting performance in terms of statistical measures are shown in Table 9.1. For a qualitative understanding of the fitting of the estimated models, a plot of the histograms of the magnitude images with superimposed estimated densities is given in Figure 9.6.

In general, the real prior probability of the unchange class $p(\omega_n)$ is always well approximated by $\alpha$, as no significant differences are observed among the trials. The **rR** model results in the best fitting for all datasets A, B and C, confirming that this model is more suitable for representing the real distribution of the magnitude. The **GG** model is flexible enough to follow the bimodal behavior of the histogram, but it is never as precise as the **rR**. The limitations in using the **MF** model are evident. This model assumes the same scale parameter for both the mixture components; however, from the EM estimates of the **rR** model, we can see that the scale parameters of the mixture components are significantly different in all datasets. Data fitting measurements for the **MF** model show that the common scale parameter is a too strong assumption, which gives very poor approximations of the real distributions (this can be seen very clearly from Figure 9.6). Thus, the model is inadequate to address the change detection problem. Also note that the non-centrality parameter $\nu_1$ converged approximately to 0 in all cases, confirming that the first component of the mixture (related to the distribution of unchanged pixels) is Rayleigh in real data.

| Mix | Estimated parameters | | | | | $\chi_P^2$ | KS |
|---|---|---|---|---|---|---|---|
| | Dataset A | | | | | | |
| rR | $\alpha$ 0.92 | $b$ 9.36 | $\nu$ 60.24 | $\sigma$ 17.37 | | 0.0136 | 0.0362 |
| GG | $\alpha$ 0.90 | $\mu_1$ 11.10 | $\sigma_1$ 5.97 | $\mu_2$ 52.73 | $\sigma_2$ 22.57 | 0.0420 | 0.0836 |
| MF | $\alpha$ 0.93 | $\nu_1$ 0.06 | $\nu_2$ 66.91 | $\beta$ 9.78 | | 0.0239 | 0.0590 |
| | Dataset B | | | | | | |
| rR | $\alpha$ 0.91 | $b$ 4.59 | $\nu$ 8.93 | $\sigma$ 26.65 | | 0.0487 | 0.0740 |
| GG | $\alpha$ 0.89 | $\mu_1$ 5.44 | $\sigma_1$ 3.20 | $\mu_2$ 29.72 | $\sigma_2$ 20.57 | 0.0981 | 0.1257 |
| MF | $\alpha$ 0.96 | $\nu_1$ 0.02 | $\nu_2$ 55.20 | $\beta$ 5.70 | | 0.1256 | 0.1767 |
| | Dataset C | | | | | | |
| rR | $\alpha$ 0.90 | $b$ 2.67 | $\nu$ 23.84 | $\sigma$ 14.90 | | 0.0215 | 0.0400 |
| GG | $\alpha$ 0.89 | $\mu_1$ 3.25 | $\sigma_1$ 1.70 | $\mu_2$ 26.35 | $\sigma_2$ 14.13 | 0.0500 | 0.0778 |
| MF | $\alpha$ 0.93 | $\nu_1$ $\approx 0$ | $\nu_2$ 34.82 | $\beta$ 3.41 | | 0.1414 | 0.1880 |

**Table 9.1.** *Session 1: EM algorithm parameter estimation and data fitting evaluation for mixture densities* **rR**, **GG** *and* **MF**

### 9.5.3.3. *Change detection results*

The outcome of the experiments is detailed in Table 9.2, where the CD performance is evaluated in terms of false and missed alarms and overall errors, and in Figure 9.7, which shows the corresponding CD maps.

It follows from the analysis in section 9.5.3.2 that the mixture component representing $\omega_n$ is better approximated by a Rayleigh density. The high non-symmetry of the Rayleigh component forces its Gaussian approximation to be slightly overestimated on the right side; thus, its right descending slope is steeper than the Rayleigh version. It follows that, in general, the decision threshold in the **GG** case is smaller than in the **rR** case. As a result, the overall error of **rR** is always smaller than the error of **GG**. Moreover, the change detection by using the **GG** mixture presents less missed alarms, but many more false alarms with respect to the **rR** case.

Note that, though in some cases the Bayes thresholds are not very close to the optimal values, the **rR** model always returned a better approximation of the optimal threshold with respect to the standard **GG** model. For dataset A, the **opt** threshold corresponds to 770 overall errors, whereas the **rR** and the **GG** models returned 1,820 and 3,982 overall errors, respectively. Similar results are obtained in the case of datasets B and C, where again the **rR** model performed better and the overall error is more than halved in general.

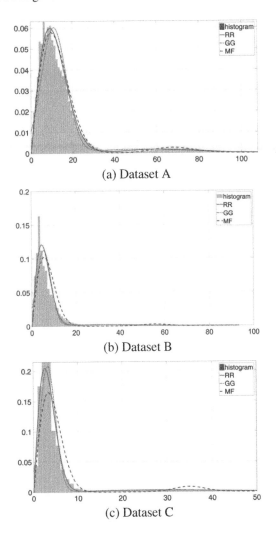

(a) Dataset A

(b) Dataset B

(c) Dataset C

**Figure 9.6.** *Session 1: Histograms of the magnitude of the difference image and plot of the estimated densities. For a color version of this figure, see www.iste.co.uk/atto/change1.zip*

Figure 9.7 shows the change detection maps obtained by thresholding the magnitude of the difference image in the three datasets. Note that, in general, the smaller number of missed alarms given by **rR** results in a much less noisy change map compared to the one given by **GG**. In the optimal case, the change maps are very clean. Since in these cases the number of missed alarms is the highest, some details of the changes are lost (e.g. the thin boundaries of the lake and a portion of the fire). A possible improvement of the change detection maps could be obtained by using the distributions of the classes obtained by this technique within a context-sensitive approach (e.g. based on MRFs (Bruzzone and Prieto 2000b)).

| mix | $T$ | MA (%) | FA (%) | OE (%) |
|---|---|---|---|---|
| | | Dataset A | | |
| **rR** | 33.95 | 36 (0.48%) | 1,784 (1.54%) | 1,820 (1.47%) |
| **GG** | 28.02 | 9 (0.12%) | 3,973 (3.42%) | 3,982 (3.22%) |
| **opt** | 47.11 | 356 (4.76%) | 414 (0.36%) | 770 (0.62%) |
| | | Dataset B | | |
| **rR** | 15.93 | 335 (5.84%) | 5,654 (4.24%) | 5,989 (4.30%) |
| **GG** | 14.76 | 285 (4.97%) | 7,232 (5.42%) | 7,517 (5.40%) |
| **opt** | 30.90 | 1,082 (18.86%) | 478 (0.36%) | 1,560 (1.12%) |
| | | Dataset C | | |
| **rR** | 9.92 | 956 (2.75%) | 7,805 (1.86%) | 8,761 (1.93%) |
| **GG** | 8.63 | 727 (2.09%) | 12,856 (3.06%) | 13,583 (2.99%) |
| **opt** | 15.23 | 1,964 (5.65%) | 2,657 (0.63%) | 4,621 (1.02%) |

**Table 9.2.** *Session 1: Performance of change detection based on the rR and GG models, compared with opt results*

### 9.5.4. *Test 2: Multiclass Rician mixture model*

#### 9.5.4.1. *Test description*

The fitting and change detection performance of the multiclass Rician mixture model presented in section 9.4 is tested against[3] the two-class model from section 9.3. Parameter notations used in this experimental session:

Rayleigh-Rice mixture (rR)

$$p(\rho|\omega_n) = \mathrm{Rayl}(b), \quad p(\rho|\omega_c) = \mathrm{Rice}(\nu, \sigma).$$

Multiclass Rician mixture (rrR)

$$p(\rho|\omega_{n,i}) = \mathrm{Rayl}(\delta_i), i = 1, 2, \quad p(\rho|\omega_c) = \mathrm{Rice}(\nu, \delta).$$

---

3. Note that, different from section 9.5.3, image values are normalized to [0,1] in this session. This has an impact on some results that cannot be compared in absolute/quantitative terms among the two sessions. However, the relationship between the two sessions is still clear and results are comparable in relative/qualitative terms.

The initialization of the EM algorithm in these two cases follows the principles outlined in sections 9.3.3.3 and 9.4.4.4, respectively.

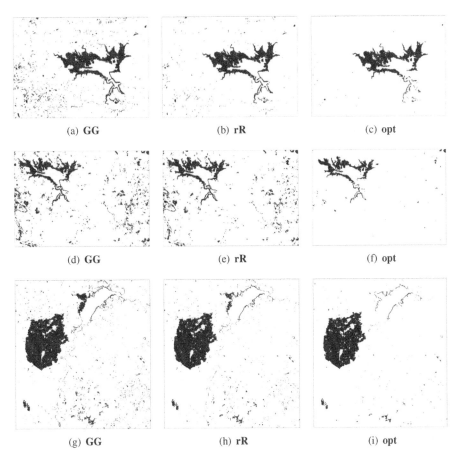

(a) GG            (b) rR            (c) opt

(d) GG             (e) rR            (f) opt

(g) GG             (h) rR            (i) opt

**Figure 9.7.** *Session 1: Change detection maps corresponding to:* **GG** *model (a,d,g),* **rR** *model (b,e,h) and* **opt** *choice (c,f,i). The estimated changed pixels $W_c$ are in black, and the estimated unchanged pixels $W_n$ are in white*

### 9.5.4.2. *EM algorithm and fitting performance*

The numerical values of the estimated parameters and EM iteration details are shown in Table 9.3. The plots in Figure 9.8 both give a qualitative understanding of the fitting of the estimated models, by superimposing the estimated densities to the histograms and also report fitting performance results in terms of statistical measures.

| MIX | $k$ | Estimated parameters | | | | | | Secs |
|---|---|---|---|---|---|---|---|---|
| | | **Dataset A** | | | | | | |
| | | $\alpha$ | - | b | - | $\nu$ | $\sigma$ | |
| **rR** | 0 | 0.93 | - | 0.04 | - | 0.25 | 0.06 | 4.0 |
| | 60 | 0.92 | - | 0.04 | - | 0.23 | 0.07 | |
| | | $\alpha_1$ | $\alpha_2$ | $\delta_1$ | $\delta_2$ | $\nu$ | $\delta$ | |
| **rrR** | 0 | 0.79 | 0.14 | 0.03 | 0.07 | 0.25 | 0.06 | 73.2 |
| | 1258 | 0.71 | 0.23 | 0.03 | 0.05 | 0.26 | 0.05 | |
| | | **Dataset B** | | | | | | |
| | | $\alpha$ | - | b | - | $\nu$ | $\sigma$ | |
| **rR** | 0 | 0.96 | - | 0.02 | - | 0.20 | 0.06 | 3.5 |
| | 66 | 0.91 | - | 0.02 | - | 0.03 | 0.10 | |
| | | $\alpha_1$ | $\alpha_2$ | $\delta_1$ | $\delta_2$ | $\nu$ | $\delta$ | |
| **rrR** | 0 | 0.90 | 0.06 | 0.02 | 0.05 | 0.20 | 0.06 | 13.9 |
| | 270 | 0.62 | 0.34 | 0.01 | 0.03 | 0.18 | 0.07 | |
| | | **Dataset C** | | | | | | |
| | | $\alpha$ | - | b | - | $\nu$ | $\sigma$ | |
| **rR** | 0 | 0.92 | - | 0.01 | - | 0.12 | 0.04 | 10.6 |
| | 57 | 0.90 | - | 0.01 | - | 0.09 | 0.06 | |
| | | $\alpha_1$ | $\alpha_2$ | $\delta_1$ | $\delta_2$ | $\nu$ | $\delta$ | |
| **rrR** | 0 | 0.87 | 0.06 | 0.01 | 0.02 | 0.12 | 0.04 | 65.4 |
| | 400 | 0.79 | 0.13 | 0.01 | 0.02 | 0.12 | 0.04 | |
| | | **Dataset D** | | | | | | |
| | | $\alpha$ | - | b | - | $\nu$ | $\sigma$ | |
| **rR** | 0 | 0.98 | - | 0.002 | - | 0.013 | 0.004 | 2.15 |
| | 51 | 0.75 | - | 0.001 | - | 0.001 | 0.004 | |
| | | $\alpha_1$ | $\alpha_2$ | $\delta_1$ | $\delta_2$ | $\nu$ | $\delta$ | |
| **rrR** | 0 | 0.90 | 0.08 | 0.002 | 0.005 | 0.013 | 0.004 | 6.01 |
| | 400 | 0.55 | 0.38 | 0.001 | 0.002 | 0.002 | 0.007 | |

**Table 9.3.** *Session 2: EM algorithm parameter estimation and iteration details for the mixture densities rR and rrR*

In the run of the iterative algorithm for parameter estimation of the **rR** mixture, the classical median thresholding technique for the initialization worked well. However, it resulted in never-ending iterations (the relative variation of the objective energy has never reached values below tolerance) in the **rrR** case, for all three datasets. Therefore, the more appropriate initialization strategy based on the quantile function (described in section 9.4.4.4) has been used. The initial approximate threshold values obtained in the calculations are $t^0 = 0.1477, 0.1091, 0.0559, 0.0100$ for datasets A, B, C and D, respectively. These values are placed in the central portion of the histograms (see histograms in Figure 9.8) between the two principal modes. Note that this does not hold true in the case of the median thresholding; indeed, the corresponding values obtained in the computations are $t^{mid} = 0.2105, 0.1833, 0.2511, 0.0216$. As we can see, such values are significantly shifted to the right in the corresponding histograms.

This proved to be a limitation for the initial estimation of the two Rayleigh components in the **rrR** mixture, as the unchange class is sensibly overestimated.

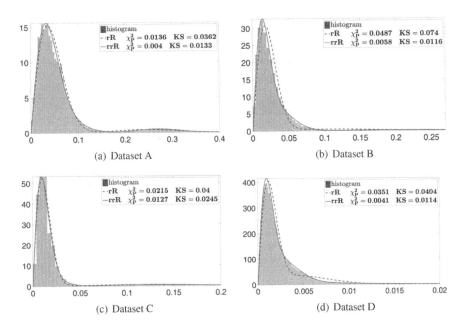

(a) Dataset A

(b) Dataset B

(c) Dataset C

(d) Dataset D

**Figure 9.8.** *Session 2: Histograms of the magnitude of the difference image and plot of the estimated densities. In the legends, the distance metrics between the estimated densities and the histograms are also given. For a color version of this figure, see www.iste.co.uk/atto/change1.zip*

From the iteration details and the initial and final values of the estimated parameters shown in Table 9.3, we see that, as expected, the number of iterations and the time of computation increase in the case of **rrR**, as there are two additional parameters to be estimated in the model. Note that, between the first and last iterations, the parameters that are more significantly changed are the prior probabilities of classes, i.e. $\alpha$ in the **rR** case and $\alpha_1, \alpha_2$ in the **rrR** case.

A qualitative analysis of the fitting performance can be done by looking at the plots of the estimated densities **rR** and **rrR**, which are superimposed to the histogram of the magnitude in Figure 9.8. The figure also provides quantitative evaluation of the fitting in terms of the $\chi^2$-Pearson divergence and Kolmogorov–Smirnov (KS) distance between data and estimated densities. From the results, we can see that the **rrR** model fits the data in a satisfying way, and much better than **rR**.

| mix | $T$ | MA (%) | FA (%) | OE (%) |
|---|---|---|---|---|
| | | **Dataset A** | | |
| rR | 0.1332 | 139 (1.81) | 1,672 (1.44) | 1,811 (1.47) |
| rrR | 0.1741 | 402 (5.22) | 498 (0.43) | 900 (0.73) |
| opt | 0.1825 | 491 (6.38) | 392 (0.34) | 883 (0.71) |
| | | **Dataset B** | | |
| rR | 0.0624 | 451 (7.57) | 5,421 (4.07) | 5,872 (4.22) |
| rrR | 0.1028 | 975 (16.36) | 801 (0.60) | 1,776 (1.28) |
| opt | 0.1119 | 1,115 (18.71) | 567 (0.43) | 1,682 (1.21) |
| | | **Dataset C** | | |
| rR | 0.0390 | 1,104 (3.03) | 6,309 (1.51) | 7,413 (1.63) |
| rrR | 0.0548 | 2,029 (5.57) | 1,789 (0.43) | 3,818 (0.84) |
| opt | 0.0570 | 2,140 (5.88) | 1,617 (0.39) | 3,757 (0.83) |
| | | **Dataset D** | | |
| rR | 0.0033 | 841 (11.79) | 18,963 (16.80) | 19,804 (16.50) |
| rrR | 0.0071 | 2,563 (35.94) | 1,074 (0.95) | 3,637 (3.03) |
| opt | 0.0072 | 2,626 (36.82) | 1,002 (0.89) | 3,628 (3.02) |

**Table 9.4.** *Session 2: Performance of change detection based on the **rR** and **rrR** models, compared with **opt** results*

### 9.5.4.3. *Change detection results*

The theoretical framework presented in section 9.4 has been developed with the aim of better representing the typical distributions that characterize the multispectral data acquired by new-generation sensors. Following the expected (and confirmed) increased fitting performance of the resulting model, an improvement in the change detection performance was also expected due to the increased capability of the model of representing the specific unchange and change multiple classes. Indeed, this has been confirmed in the binary change detection phase of our tests. Table 9.4 reports the computed threshold value $T$ and the change detection performance in terms of missed/false alarms and overall errors for each dataset and each considered mixture model. The results can be compared with optimal performance based on a usual trial-and-error procedure applied to the reference maps of the changes.

As we can see, the **rrR** mixture model for binary change detection proved to be sufficiently flexible in modeling the unchange and change classes in the datasets well, as it is able to return the same thresholds (with precision at the second decimal digit) that are obtained in the optimal case. A qualitative understanding of the performance is possible by looking at the change detection maps illustrated in Figure 9.9. With respect to the **rR** case, the **rrR** model presents much less false alarms at the expense of very few additional missed alarms. Note that the change maps obtained in the optimal case are not illustrated in the picture as their differences with respect to the maps obtained with the **rrR** model cannot just be seen visually.

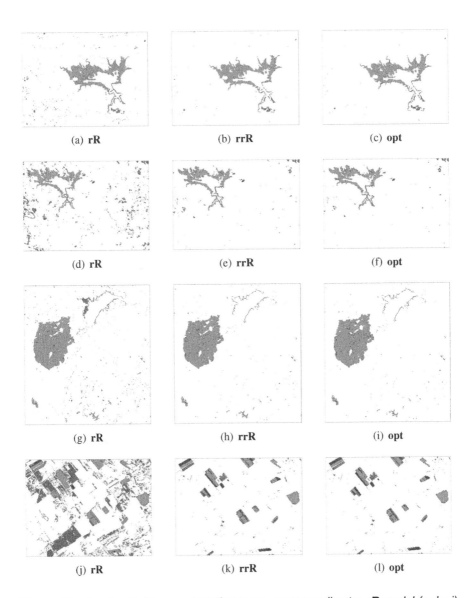

**Figure 9.9.** *Session 2: Change detection maps corresponding to: **rR** model (a,d,g,j), **rrR** model (b,e,h,k) and **opt** choice (c,f,i,l). Blue pixels are MA, red ones are FA and green ones are correctly detected changes. For a color version of this figure, see www.iste.co.uk/atto/change1.zip*

## 9.6. Conclusion

The new generation of multispectral sensors mounted on satellite missions such as Landsat 8 and Sentinel 2 offers a unique opportunity of studying and monitoring the Earth's surface, by providing images at a very short revisit time and with ever-increasing radiometric resolutions. A consequence of the enhanced spectral detail is the augmented statistical variability of multispectral data, which poses a serious challenge in the field of change detection. Indeed, many change detection methods based on the statistical modeling of multispectral images that worked well on data acquired by older satellite missions are no longer able to address the new challenges arising in this important field of remote sensing.

In this chapter, a theoretical study of the change detection problem is given, which addresses the above-mentioned issues. Specifically, a general framework is presented for the statistical modeling of the difference image in two different scenarios.

In the first case, the standard two-class Gaussian mixture is proven to be sub-optimal as a model for the magnitude of the difference image. Indeed, starting from common assumptions for multispectral images, it is shown that the magnitude likely follows a Rayleigh–Rice mixture. However, this kind of statistical distribution is highly unconventional and it deserves dedicated study for applications in remote sensing. An EM-like method is therefore presented for the parameter estimation of the Rayleigh–Rice distribution, together with an approach for binary change detection, for which results are outperforming many of the theoretical and empirical models given in the literature.

In the second case, the two-class model is generalized to multiclass. The aim of the proposed study is in fact defining a model with sufficient degrees of freedom to represent the intrinsic multiclass nature of multispectral imagery well. No *a priori* assumptions are made on the difference image. Instead, by solely starting from a joint distribution widely used as a model for single time images, a multiclass distribution is derived for the difference image. Building on this, a general definition of the change detection problem is given in the framework of CVA, where both unchange and change classes are multiple. This is further developed when coordinates are changed to magnitude, leading to a Rician mixture with different components. A more general EM-like algorithm is therefore presented for the estimation of mixture parameters. Leveraging on this, an implementation of a MAP approach for the inference of unchange and change classes is given. Experiments on different image pairs from different sensors confirmed that the improved fitting of the magnitude histogram corresponds to a nearly optimal change detection accuracy.

## 9.7. References

Aach, T. and Kaup, A. (1995). Bayesian algorithms for adaptive change detection in image sequences using Markov random fields. *Signal Processing: Image Communication*, 7(2), 147–160.

Aldrighi, M. and Dell'Acqua, F. (2009). Mode-based method for matching of pre and postevent remotely sensed images. *IEEE Geoscience and Remote Sensing Letters*, 6(2), 317–321.

Baisantry, M., Negi, D.S., Manocha, O.P. (2012). Change vector analysis using enhanced PCA and inverse triangular function-based thresholding. *Defence Science Journal*, 62(4), 236–242.

Ban, Y. and Yousif, O. (2016). Change detection techniques: A review. In *Multitemporal Remote Sensing: Methods and Applications*, Ban, Y. (ed.). Springer, New York.

Benedict, T. and Soong, T. (1967). The joint estimation of signal and noise from the sum envelope. *IEEE Transactions on Information Theory*, 13(3), 447–454.

Bovolo, F. (2009). A multilevel parcel-based approach to change detection in very high resolution multitemporal images. *IEEE Geoscience and Remote Sensing Letters*, 6(1), 33–37.

Bovolo, F. and Bruzzone, L. (2007). A theoretical framework for unsupervised change detection based on change vector analysis in the polar domain. *IEEE Transactions on Geoscience and Remote Sensing*, 45(1), 218–236.

Bovolo, F. and Bruzzone, L. (2009). An adaptive multiscale random field technique for unsupervised change detection in VHR multitemporal images. *IEEE International Geoscience and Remote Sensing Symposium*, vol. 4, IV–777.

Bovolo, F., Bruzzone, L., Marconcini, M. (2008). A novel approach to unsupervised change detection based on a semisupervised SVM and a similarity measure. *IEEE Transactions on Geoscience and Remote Sensing*, 46(7), 2070–2082.

Bovolo, F., Bruzzone, L., Marchesi, S. (2009). Analysis and adaptive estimation of the registration noise distribution in multitemporal VHR images. *IEEE Transactions on Geoscience and Remote Sensing*, 47(8), 2658–2671.

Bovolo, F., Bruzzone, L., Capobianco, L., Garzelli, A., Marchesi, S., Nencini, F. (2010a). Analysis of the effects of pansharpening in change detection on VHR images. *IEEE Geoscience and Remote Sensing Letters*, 7(1), 53–57.

Bovolo, F., Camps-Valls, G., Bruzzone, L. (2010b). A support vector domain method for change detection in multitemporal images. *Pattern Recognition Letters*, 31(10), 1148–1154.

Bovolo, F., Marchesi, S., Bruzzone, L. (2012). A framework for automatic and unsupervised detection of multiple changes in multitemporal images. *IEEE Transactions on Geoscience and Remote Sensing*, 50(6), 2196–2212.

Bruzzone, L. and Bovolo, F. (2013). A novel framework for the design of change-detection systems for very-high-resolution remote sensing images. *Proceedings of the IEEE*, 101(3), 609–630.

Bruzzone, L. and Cossu, R. (2002). A multiple-cascade-classifier system for a robust and partially unsupervised updating of land-cover maps. *IEEE Transactions on Geoscience and Remote Sensing*, 40(9), 1984–1996.

Bruzzone, L. and Prieto, D.F. (2000a). An adaptive parcel-based technique for unsupervised change detection. *International Journal of Remote Sensing*, 21(4), 817–822.

Bruzzone, L. and Prieto, D.F. (2000b). Automatic analysis of the difference image for unsupervised change detection. *IEEE Transactions on Geoscience and Remote Sensing*, 38(3), 1171–1182.

Bruzzone, L. and Prieto, D.F. (2000c). A minimum-cost thresholding technique for unsupervised change detection. *International Journal of Remote Sensing*, 21(18), 3539–3544.

Bruzzone, L. and Prieto, D.F. (2002). An adaptive semiparametric and context-based approach to unsupervised change detection in multitemporal remote-sensing images. *IEEE Transactions on Image Processing*, 11(4), 452–466.

Bruzzone, L. and Serpico, S.B. (1997). An iterative technique for the detection of land-cover transitions in multitemporal remote-sensing images. *IEEE Transactions on Geoscience and Remote Sensing*, 35(4), 858–867.

Bruzzone, L., Cossu, R., Vernazza, G. (2004). Detection of land-cover transitions by combining multidate classifiers. *Pattern Recognition Letters*, 25(13), 1491–1500.

Carlotto, M.J. (2005). A cluster-based approach for detecting man-made objects and changes in imagery. *IEEE Transactions on Geoscience and Remote Sensing*, 43(2), 374–387.

Carobbi, C.F. and Cati, M. (2008). The absolute maximum of the likelihood function of the Rice distribution: Existence and uniqueness. *IEEE Transactions on Instrumentation and Measurement*, 57(4), 682–689.

Celik, T. (2009a). Multiscale change detection in multitemporal satellite images. *IEEE Geoscience and Remote Sensing Letters*, 6(4), 820–824.

Celik, T. (2009b). Unsupervised change detection in satellite images using principal component analysis and k-means clustering. *IEEE Geoscience and Remote Sensing Letters*, 6(4), 772–776.

Celik, T. (2010). Method for unsupervised change detection in satellite images. *Electronics Letters*, 46(9), 624–626.

Celik, T. and Ma, K.-K. (2010). Unsupervised change detection for satellite images using dual-tree complex wavelet transform. *IEEE Transactions on Geoscience and Remote Sensing*, 48(3), 1199–1210.

Celik, T. and Ma, K.-K. (2011). Multitemporal image change detection using undecimated discrete wavelet transform and active contours. *IEEE Transactions on Geoscience and Remote Sensing*, 49(2), 706–716.

Chen, C.H. (2007). *Image Processing for Remote Sensing*, 1st edition. CRC Press, Boca Raton, FL.

Chen, J., Chen, X., Cui, X., Chen, J. (2011). Change vector analysis in posterior probability space: A new method for land cover change detection. *IEEE Geoscience and Remote Sensing Letters*, 8(2), 317–321.

Collins, J.B. and Woodcock, C.E. (1994). Change detection using the Gramm–Schmidt transformation applied to mapping forest mortality. *Remote Sensing of Environment*, 50(3), 267–279.

Coppin, P., Jonckheere, I., Nackaerts, K., Muys, B., Lambin, E. (2004). Digital change detection methods in ecosystem monitoring: A review. *International Journal of Remote Sensing*, 25(9), 1565–1596.

Dai, X. and Khorram, S. (1998). The effects of image misregistration on the accuracy of remotely sensed change detection. *IEEE Transactions on Geoscience and Remote Sensing*, 36(5), 1566–1577.

Dalla Mura, M., Benediktsson, J.A., Bovolo, F., Bruzzone, L. (2008). An unsupervised technique based on morphological filters for change detection in very high resolution images. *IEEE Geoscience and Remote Sensing Letters*, 5(3), 433–437.

Dalla Mura, M., Benediktsson, J.A., Waske, B., Bruzzone, L. (2010). Morphological attribute profiles for the analysis of very high resolution images. *IEEE Transactions on Geoscience and Remote Sensing*, 48(10), 3747–3762.

De Morsier, F., Tuia, D., Gass, V., Thiran, J.-P., Borgeaud, M. (2012). Unsupervised change detection via hierarchical support vector clustering. *IAPR Workshop on Pattern Recognition in Remote Sensing (PRRS)*, IEEE, 1–4.

Demir, B., Bovolo, F., Bruzzone, L. (2012). Detection of land-cover transitions in multitemporal remote sensing images with active-learning-based compound classification. *IEEE Transactions on Geoscience and Remote Sensing*, 50(5), 1930–1941.

Demir, B., Bovolo, F., Bruzzone, L. (2013a). Classification of time series of multispectral images with limited training data. *IEEE Transactions on Image Processing*, 22(8), 3219–3233.

Demir, B., Bovolo, F., Bruzzone, L. (2013b). Updating land-cover maps by classification of image time series: A novel change-detection-driven transfer learning approach. *IEEE Transactions on Geoscience and Remote Sensing*, 51(1), 300–312.

Dempster, A.P., Laird, N.M., Rubin, D.B. (1977). Maximum likelihood from incomplete data via the EM algorithm. *Journal of the Royal Statistical Society*, 39(1), 1–38.

Ding, M., Tian, Z., Jin, Z., Xu, M., Cao, C. (2010). Registration using robust kernel principal component for object-based change detection. *IEEE Geoscience and Remote Sensing Letters*, 7(4), 761–765.

Ghosh, A., Mishra, N.S., Ghosh, S. (2011). Fuzzy clustering algorithms for unsupervised change detection in remote sensing images. *Information Sciences*, 181(4), 699–715.

Gong, P. (1993). Change detection using principal component analysis and fuzzy set theory. *Canadian Journal of Remote Sensing*, 19(1), 22–29.

Gong, M., Su, L., Jia, M., Chen, W. (2014). Fuzzy clustering with a modified MRF energy function for change detection in synthetic aperture radar images. *IEEE Transactions on Fuzzy Systems*, 22(1), 98–109.

Hazel, G.G. (2001). Object-level change detection in spectral imagery. *IEEE Transactions on Geoscience and Remote Sensing*, 39(3), 553–561.

Healey, G. and Slater, D. (1997). Computing illumination-invariant descriptors of spatially filtered color image regions. *IEEE Transactions on Image Processing*, 6(7), 1002–1013.

Hennemuth, A., Seeger, A., Friman, O., Miller, S., Klumpp, B., Peitgen, S.O.H.O. (2008). A comprehensive approach to the analysis of contrast enhanced cardiac MR images. *IEEE Transactions on Medical Imaging*, 27(11), 1592–1610.

Huo, C., Zhou, Z., Lu, H., Pan, C., Chen, K. (2010). Fast object-level change detection for VHR images. *IEEE Geoscience and Remote Sensing Letters*, 7(1), 118–122.

Inamdar, S., Bovolo, F., Bruzzone, L., Chaudhuri, S. (2008). Multidimensional probability density function matching for preprocessing of multitemporal remote sensing images. *IEEE Transactions on Geoscience and Remote Sensing*, 46(4), 1243–1252.

Johnson, R.D. and Kasischke, E.S. (1998). Change vector analysis: A technique for the multispectral monitoring of land cover and condition. *International Journal of Remote Sensing*, 19(3), 411–426.

Karlsen, O.T., Verhagen, R., Bovee, W.M. (1999). Parameter estimation from Rician-distributed data sets using a maximum likelihood estimator: Application to T1 and perfusion measurements. *Magnetic Resonance in Medicine*, 41(3), 614–623.

Kittler, J. and Illingworth, J. (1986). Minimum error thresholding. *Pattern Recognition*, 19(1), 41–47.

Lauwers, L., Barbé, K., Moer, W.V., Pintelon, R. (2009). Estimating the parameters of a Rice distribution: A Bayesian approach. *IEEE Instrumentation and Measurement Technology Conference (I2MTC'09)*, 114–117.

Li, L. and Leung, M.K. (2002). Integrating intensity and texture differences for robust change detection. *IEEE Transactions on Image Processing*, 11(2), 105–112.

Liu, S., Bruzzone, L., Bovolo, F., Zanetti, M., Du, P. (2015). Sequential spectral change vector analysis for iteratively discovering and detecting multiple changes in hyperspectral images. *IEEE Transactions on Geoscience and Remote Sensing*, 53(8), 4363–4378.

Lu, D., Mausel, P., Brondizio, E., Moran, E. (2004). Change detection techniques. *International Journal of Remote Sensing*, 25(12), 2365–2401.

Lu, P., Stumpf, A., Kerle, N., Casagli, N. (2011). Object-oriented change detection for landslide rapid mapping. *IEEE Geoscience and Remote Sensing Letters*, 8(4), 701–705.

Lu, D., Li, G., Moran, E. (2014). Current situation and needs of change detection techniques. *International Journal of Image and Data Fusion*, 5(1), 13–38.

Maitra, R. (2013). On the expectation–maximization algorithm for Rice–Rayleigh mixtures with application to noise parameter estimation in magnitude MR datasets. *Sankhya B*, 75(2), 293–318.

Maitra, R. and Faden, D. (2009). Noise estimation in magnitude MR datasets. *IEEE Transactions on Medical Imaging*, 28(10), 1615–1622.

Malila, W.A. (1980). Change vector analysis: An approach for detecting forest changes with Landsat. *LARS Symposia*, 385.

Marchesi, S. and Bruzzone, L. (2009). ICA and kernel ICA for change detection in multispectral remote sensing images. *IGARSS*, 2, 980–983.

Marchesi, S., Bovolo, F., Bruzzone, L. (2010). A context-sensitive technique robust to registration noise for change detection in VHR multispectral images. *IEEE Transactions on Image Processing*, 19(7), 1877–1889.

Molinier, M., Laaksonen, J., Hame, T. (2007). Detecting man-made structures and changes in satellite imagery with a content-based information retrieval system built on self-organizing maps. *IEEE Transactions on Geoscience and Remote Sensing*, 45(4), 861–874.

Moser, G., Angiati, E., Serpico, S.B. (2011). Multiscale unsupervised change detection on optical images by Markov random fields and wavelets. *IEEE Geoscience and Remote Sensing Letters*, 8(4), 725–729.

Nielsen, A.A. (2002). Multiset canonical correlations analysis and multispectral, truly multitemporal remote sensing data. *IEEE Transactions on Image Processing*, 11(3), 293–305.

Nielsen, A.A. (2007). The regularized iteratively reweighted MAD method for change detection in multi-and hyperspectral data. *IEEE Transactions on Image Processing*, 16(2), 463–478.

Nielsen, A.A., Conradsen, K., Simpson, J.J. (1998). Multivariate alteration detection (MAD) and MAF postprocessing in multispectral, bitemporal image data: New approaches to change detection studies. *Remote Sensing of Environment*, 64(1), 1–19.

Nowak, R.D. (1999). Wavelet-based Rician noise removal for magnetic resonance imaging. *IEEE Transactions on Image Processing*, 8(10), 1408–1419.

Otsu, N. (1975). A threshold selection method from gray-level histograms. *Automatica*, 11(285–296), 23–27.

Radke, R.J., Andra, S., Al-Kofani, O., Roysam, B. (2005). Image change detection algorithms: A systematic survey. *IEEE Transactions on Image Processing*, 14(3), 294–307.

Rajan, J., Poot, D., Juntu, J., Sijbers, J. (2010). Noise measurement from magnitude MRI using local estimates of variance and skewness. *Physics in Medicine and Biology*, 55(16), N441.

Redner, R.A. and Walker, H.F. (1984). Mixture densities, maximum likelihood and the EM algorithm. *SIAM Review*, 26(2), 195–239.

Rensink, R.A. (2002). Change detection. *Annual Review of Psychology*, 53(1), 245–277.

Rice, S.O. (1944). Mathematical analysis of random noise. *Bell System Technical Journal*, 23(3), 282–332.

Robin, A., Moisan, L., Le Hegarat-Mascle, S. (2010). An a-contrario approach for subpixel change detection in satellite imagery. *IEEE Transactions on Pattern Analysis and Machine Intelligence*, 32(11), 1977–1993.

Rogan, J., Franklin, J., Roberts, D.A. (2002). A comparison of methods for monitoring multitemporal vegetation change using Thematic Mapper imagery. *Remote Sensing of Environment*, 80(1), 143–156.

Roy, D.P. (2000). The impact of misregistration upon composited wide field of view satellite data and implications for change detection. *IEEE Transactions on Geoscience and Remote Sensing*, 38(4), 2017–2032.

Sahoo, P.K., Soltani, S., Wong, A.K. (1988). A survey of thresholding techniques. *Computer Vision, Graphics, and Image Processing*, 41(2), 233–260.

Sijbers, J. and den Dekker, A.J. (2004). Maximum likelihood estimation of signal amplitude and noise variance from MR data. *Magnetic Resonance in Medicine*, 51(3), 586–594.

Sijbers, J., den Dekker, A.J., Scheunders, P., Dyck, D.V. (1998a). Maximum-likelihood estimation of Rician distribution parameters. *IEEE Transactions on Medical Imaging*, 17(3), 357–361.

Sijbers, J., den Dekker, A.J., Audekerke, J.V., Verhoye, M., Dyck, D.V. (1998b). Estimation of the noise in magnitude MR images. *Magnetic Resonance Imaging*, 16(1), 87–90.

Singh, S. and Talwar, R. (2013). Review on different change vector analysis algorithms based change detection techniques. *IEEE Second International Conference on Image Information Processing (ICIIP)*, 136–141.

Smits, P.C. and Annoni, A. (1999). Updating land-cover maps by using texture information from very high-resolution space-borne imagery. *IEEE Transactions on Geoscience and Remote Sensing*, 37(3), 1244–1254.

Spotorno, S. and Faure, S. (2011). Change detection in complex scenes: Hemispheric contribution and the role of perceptual and semantic factors. *Perception*, 40(1), 5–22.

Talukdar, K.K. and Lawing, W.D. (1991). Estimation of the parameters of the Rice distribution. *The Journal of the Acoustical Society of America*, 89(3), 1193–1197.

Volpi, M., Tuia, D., Camps-Valls, G., Kanevski, M. (2012). Unsupervised change detection with kernels. *IEEE Geoscience and Remote Sensing Letters*, 9(6), 1026–1030.

Volpi, M., Tuia, D., Bovolo, F., Kanevski, M., Bruzzone, L. (2013). Supervised change detection in VHR images using contextual information and support vector machines. *International Journal of Applied Earth Observation and Geoinformation*, 20, 77–85.

Watson, G.N. (1966). *A Treatise on the Theory of Bessel Functions*. 2nd edition. Cambridge University Press, Cambridge.

Yang, X. and Lo, C. (2000). Relative radiometric normalization performance for change detection from multi-date satellite images. *Photogrammetric Engineering and Remote Sensing*, 66(8), 967–980.

Yetgin, Z. (2012). Unsupervised change detection of satellite images using local gradual descent. *IEEE Transactions on Geoscience and Remote Sensing*, 50(5), 1919–1929.

Zanetti, M. (2017). Advanced methods for the analysis of multispectral and multitemporal remote sensing images. PhD Thesis, University of Trento.

Zanetti, M. and Bruzzone, L. (2017). A theoretical framework for change detection based on a compound multiclass statistical model of the difference image. *IEEE Transactions on Geoscience and Remote Sensing*, 56(2), 1129–1143.

Zanetti, M., Bovolo, F., Bruzzone, L. (2015). Rayleigh–Rice mixture parameter estimation via EM algorithm for change detection in multispectral images. *IEEE Transactions on Image Processing*, 24(12), 5004–5016.

# List of Authors

Abdourrahmane M. ATTO
University Savoie Mont Blanc
Annecy
France

Lionel BOMBRUN
University of Bordeaux
France

Francesca BOVOLO
Fondazione Bruno Kessler
Trento
Italy

Arnaud BRELOY
Paris Nanterre University
France

Lorenzo BRUZZONE
University of Trento
Italy

Morton J. CANTY
Formerly Jülich Research Center
Germany

Knut CONRADSEN
Technical University of Denmark
Kongens Lyngby
Denmark

Qian DU
Mississippi State University
Starkville
USA

Philippe DURAND
CNES
Toulouse
France

Andrea GARZELLI
University of Siena
Italy

Sophie GIFFARD-ROISIN
Université Grenoble Alpes
France

Guillaume GINOLHAC
University Savoie Mont Blanc
Annecy
France

Guillaume JAMES
Inria Grenoble – Rhône-Alpes
Research Center
and
CNES
Toulouse
France

Fatima KARBOU
Université Grenoble Alpes
University of Toulouse
CNRM
CNRS
Centre d'Études de la Neige at
Météo-France
Grenoble
France

Sicong LIU
Tongji University
Shanghai
China

Grégoire MERCIER
eXo maKina
Digital Technologies
Paris
France

Ammar MIAN
CentraleSupélec
Paris-Saclay University
Gif-sur-Yvette
and
University Savoie Mont Blanc
Annecy
France

Pedro MORETTIN
University of São Paulo
Brazil

Allan A. NIELSEN
Technical University of Denmark
Kongens Lyngby
Denmark

Jean-Philippe OVARLEZ
ONERA
Palaiseau
France

Frédéric PASCAL
CentraleSupélec
Paris-Saclay University
Gif-sur-Yvette
France

Minh-Tan PHAM
IRISA Laboratory
Université Bretagne Sud
Lorient
France

Aluísio PINHEIRO
University of Campinas
Brazil

Henning SKRIVER
Technical University of Denmark
Kongens Lyngby
Denmark

Xiaohua TONG
Tongji University
Shanghai
China

Massimo ZANETTI
Fondazione Bruno Kessler
Trento
Italy

Claudia ZOPPETTI
University of Siena
Italy

# Index

# Summary of Volume 2

Printed and bound by CPI Group (UK) Ltd, Croydon, CR0 4YY